# VIEWING LIBRARY METRICS
# FROM DIFFERENT PERSPECTIVES

# VIEWING LIBRARY METRICS FROM DIFFERENT PERSPECTIVES

## Inputs, Outputs, and Outcomes

ROBERT E. DUGAN, PETER HERNON,
AND DANUTA A. NITECKI

**LIBRARIES UNLIMITED**
*An Imprint of ABC-CLIO*

A B C CLIO

Santa Barbara, California • Denver, Colorado • Oxford, England

**Library of Congress Cataloging-in-Publication Data**

Dugan, Robert E., 1952-
   Viewing library metrics from different perspectives : inputs, outputs, and outcomes / Robert E. Dugan, Peter Hernon, and Danuta A. Nitecki.
      p. cm.
   Includes bibliographical references and index.
   ISBN 978-1-59158-665-4 (acid-free paper)  1. Academic libraries—United States—Statistics.  2. Library statistics—United States.  3. Academic libraries—United States—Evaluation.  4. Libraries—United States—Evaluation.  5. Libraries and colleges.  6. Libraries and institutions.  I. Hernon, Peter.  II. Nitecki, Danuta A. III. Title.
   Z669.8.D84   2009
   025.5'877—dc22        2009016899

13   12   11   10   09        1   2   3   4   5

This book is also available on the World Wide Web as an eBook.
Visit www.abc-clio.com for details.

ABC-CLIO, LLC
130 Cremona Drive, P.O. Box 1911
Santa Barbara, California 93116-1911

This book is printed on acid-free paper ∞
Manufactured in the United States of America

# CONTENTS

# ILLUSTRATIONS

## FIGURES

## TABLES

# PREFACE

In 2002, *The Journal of Academic Librarianship* published a paper in which Robert E. Dugan and I attempted to broaden the discussion of relevant metrics for academic and other types of libraries. We noted that

Libraries tend to view data collection from one of three distinct perspectives: the user in the life of the library, the user and the library in the life of the institution, and the library and institution in the life of the user. Each perspective has its proponents and provides useful information to enhance institutional effectiveness. Clearly, inputs and outputs do not reflect all three perspectives, and the profession needs to develop knowledge, measures, and data-collection techniques that cut across perspectives. The result is a more complete view of a "jigsaw" puzzle entitled "the library as a partner and contributor to advancement of the institutional mission."[1]

That article serves as a foundation for this book, *Viewing Library Metrics from Different Perspectives*, which looks at those three perspectives while adding a fourth: the library and the institution in the life of stakeholders (e.g., parents of students, the executive and legislative branches of government, accreditation organizations, and donors and others contributing funds to support libraries). As libraries collaborate with a wide assortment of campus partners, be they teaching faculty or units that operate complementary services (e.g., those associated with a campus learning commons), there are increased opportunities to expand the range of metrics—input, process, output, and outcome—that might be compiled, reported, and used for purposes of accountability and improvement in the educational experience and the quality of services provided to the community. Those metrics might involve quantitative or qualitative data collection, and they indicate the extent to which the library and its institution meet their mission and demonstrate their effectiveness and efficiency. As the range of metrics covered in this book illustrates, academic librarianship is embarking on a new journey, one that stands to place more libraries at the cross-roads of their institution.[2]

Various higher education stakeholders (prospective students and their parents, enrolled students and their parents, government officials and agencies, taxpayers, community members, employers, alumnae, and accrediting organizations) increasingly expect accountability in a transparent manner from institutional administrators concerning the quality of education, and the costs and benefits of that education. In turn, institutions expect all of their organizational units to demonstrate how they contribute to their educational mission and their operations. Academic libraries are not immune from being accountable about day-to-day operations and contributing to the accomplishment of the institutional mission.

Individuals bring a differing perspective depending on what stakeholder they comprise. Parents of prospective students have a different perspective of the institution, and of the academic library, than would parents of enrolled students or institutional administrators. Each stakeholder perspective has differing information needs. Academic libraries must be cognizant of the expectations and values of each stakeholder perspective and must address the information needs for each perspective in an available communications mode and by using understandable language and terms.

Libraries demonstrate their contribution and value to stakeholders, in part, by measuring their efforts and reporting their impact on customers. A metric is a verifiable qualitative or quantitative measure. Libraries want to learn about services and usage, the attributes of their infrastructure (their facilities, technologies, staff, and collections), funds received and costs, and student learning. They do so by collecting, organizing, reviewing, and analyzing the following:

- input metrics—the resources received and assets available to be used
- outputs metrics—the products and services produced using the available resources and assets
- process metrics—the transformation of inputs into outputs
- usage metrics—the level of activity concerning inputs, processes, and outputs
- outcome metrics—the consequences of the individual's contact with the library

In addition, libraries and institutions collect data about the characteristics and demographics of the users in aggregate.

Libraries use metrics to:

- learn what they have done or accomplished in such terms as how much (many), or how much it cost
- establish baseline desired benchmarks and determine the amount of progress made toward meeting these benchmarks
- identify gaps in services and collections and to use that analysis to improve
- engage in peer comparisons

This book identifies numerous but not all metrics that an academic library might use to address the information needs of the various stakeholders as well as provide guidance as to compiling, managing, interpreting, synthesizing, and presenting these suggested metrics to the intended stakeholders.

Any relevant metrics meaningful for today and tomorrow should address more than the perspective known as the user in the life of the library. They should demonstrate the library's contribution in helping the institution to achieve its mission and vision. The contribution should be evident to key groups: college and university presidents, provosts, and deans; users or customers; and other stakeholders.

Clearly, it is time to recognize and address all four perspectives. Furthermore, as Jeannette Woodward so aptly argues, it may be time to replace the word *user* with *customer*; the word *customer* "reminds us of . . . [the] new emphasis on running higher education as a business enterprise." She continues,

Many of us find this idea repugnant. However, to survive and prosper in the twenty-first century, librarians will probably have to put aside any affection they may feel for the ivory tower library of the past. We know that customers make demands, but we rarely think of patrons demanding anything. Instead, the term brings to mind individuals who give rather than receive. You might think of patrons of the arts, for example. Their role is to support the arts, not make demands of them. Customers on the other hand, demand high-quality facilities, resources, and services. They want a library that is focused on their needs, and they have no intention of going out of their way to meet the library's needs or expectations.[3]

As a consequence, the perspective of customers, or whatever name you associate with library users, likely differs from that of the library. For example, customers do not care about how many people the library serves on a daily, weekly, monthly, or annual basis; they care about the services they use and the extent to which their needs and expectations are met. Customers might be internal to the library or members of an external community. They might also come from stakeholder groups and, for instance, comprise the children of parents who graduated from the institution. Thus, there may be some synergy between and among the four perspectives.

The desire for greater accountability and being engaged in continuous quality improvement should lead libraries and their parent institutions or organizations to adopt greater openness and transparency. As discussed in chapter 7, openness and transparency lead to greater trust on the part of stakeholders because they receive the information they need and want for making decisions in a clear and easy-to-understand format. They might receive that information in publicly available reports and Web sites that perhaps contain graphical dashboards that visually present information in the form of charts and gauges similar to ones found in automobiles (see chapter 11).

Various stakeholders are pressuring accreditation organizations to disclose the results of their periodic reviews and to show that the institutions being accredited are working to improve the quality of the educational experience. Institutions could release data beyond those that show above-average performance. Consequently, transparency, which serves to achieve accountability, should exist at the program level, or even lower or higher. Transparency applies to activities to which libraries could participate and ensures that best practices and benchmarking draw on good and relevant evidence and lead to meaningful and valid comparisons.

Undoubtedly, new metrics will arise in the future and continue to challenge libraries and their institutions to reflect on what they do and how to demonstrate their impact on those they serve and to report how well they accomplish their stated mission. The numerous metrics presented in chapters 4 through 9, as well as the appendices, do not apply exclusively to academic libraries. They might, for instance, also appeal to public libraries and their social and service roles. Social roles refer to the "societal purposes for which libraries exist and which communities, individuals, and governments expect as the public library's contributions to society, whereas service roles are specific attempts by libraries to respond to social roles and meet these expectations through traditional and Internet-enabled services."[4]

Those roles and expectations will lead to additional metrics, ones highlighted in this book.

The first three chapters of *Viewing Library Metrics from Different Perspectives* introduce key concepts and the relevant literature as well as differentiate between assessment and evaluation. Chapter 1 sets the stage by introducing stakeholders and their perspectives. It indicates what stakeholders value and the need to communicate with stakeholders on their own terms. Chapters 4 through 9 examine the four perspectives and assorted metrics culled from a diverse literature and past experience. Libraries can select whichever metrics are relevant to them. Since the book itself does not explain how to collect the data for insertion into a metric, we ask readers to consult sources listed in Table 2.1 and the accompanying Wiki (see http://library-metrics.pbwiki.com/). Many of the metrics presented in the appendices have been used by the Mildred F. Sawyer Library at Suffolk University, and the Wiki enables readers to make their comments and to help us to maintain an ongoing dialogue about the four perspectives and relevant metrics.

Chapter 10 discusses a management information system that might contain assorted metrics, and chapter 11 aids readers in presenting, interpreting, and displaying metrics. Both chapters discuss the balanced scorecard and how to report the content to different audiences. The final chapter (12) revisits the key themes discussed in the previous chapters. The adoption of a selective list of metrics that addresses both accountability and improved customer services, while meeting the needs and expectations of different stakeholders, requires an administrative commitment to the provision of high-quality service and fulfilling an important educational role. Accountability involves a demonstration of managerial leadership and a commitment to maintain an effective and efficient operation that involves collaboration around the campus and beyond.

To challenge our thinking and make the book even more relevant to the profession, we asked Danuta A. Nitecki of Yale University Library to join us as an equal partner. Anyone browsing the table of contents or the opening section of a chapter will notice that we have not listed any one of us as the sole or principal author. Each of us drafted four chapters and the other two authors made critical comments. Before the book was finalized, all of us agreed on a chapter's content; thereby we became joint authors of each chapter.

Various stakeholders will continue to increase their monitoring of higher education and their calls for greater accountability. There will likely be even more questioning about the affordability of higher education in the future and what are appropriate metrics. For outcomes at the institutional level, there seems to be a greater emphasis on surveys such as the Collegiate Learning Assessment to portray student engagement. Furthermore, the major national associations of public universities have created a Voluntary System of Accountability whereby numerous institutions report concrete student results (see chapter 7).[5] Clearly, the landscape of assessment is becoming broader and new metrics will emerge. In any discussion of that landscape that focuses on institutional accountability, openness and transparency, and self-improvement, it is important that the role of libraries is neither lost nor forgotten.

We have tried to include a representative selection of writings from different parts of the world; to make connections to literatures outside library and information science (LIS), when appropriate; and to illustrate outcomes or the impact of library services on those communities served and to whom libraries and their institutions report. Such a broad perspective was especially important for conceiving chapters 1 and 3 (assessment and evaluation), 7 (stakeholders), and 8 (benchmarking and best practices).

*Viewing Library Metrics from Different Perspectives* should be of interest to anyone working in an academic or public library in a managerial leadership capacity, students in graduate schools of LIS taking a broad spectrum of courses on management and evaluation, the stakeholders that libraries serve and deal with (e.g., planners, fiscal managers, and other administrators), librarians working in collaborative roles and consortial endeavors, librarians trying to develop mutually beneficial metrics for purposes of accountability and improvement, vendors supplying use data to libraries and consortia, and leaders within professional associations in the United States and elsewhere who focus on issues of accountability and continuous quality improvement. Librarians around the world will undoubtedly see some differences between what goes on in the United States and elsewhere. Outcomes assessment is a good example of a difference. Still, as the vast literature included in this book illustrates, we must all continue to learn from each other. It is our sincere hope that *Viewing Library Metrics from Different Perspectives* represents a new chapter in the discussion of metrics, one that looks at all four perspectives.

*Peter Hernon*

## NOTES

1. Robert E. Dugan and Peter Hernon, "Outcomes Assessment: Not Synonymous with Inputs and Outputs," *The Journal of Academic Librarianship* 28, no. 6 (November 2002), 380.

2. Ibid.

3. Jeannette Woodward, *Creating the Customer-driven Academic Library* (Chicago: American Library Association, 2009), 178.

4. Charles R. McClure and Paul T. Jaeger, *Public Libraries and Internet Service Roles: Measuring and Maximizing Internet Services* (Chicago: American Library Association, 2009), 2.

5. See Tamar Lewin, "Higher Education May Soon Be Unaffordable for Most Americans, Report Says," *New York Times* (December 3, 2008): A17; Kevin Carey, "'Measuring up': The Right Report at the Right Time," *The Chronicle of Higher Education* (December 5, 2008), A88.

# ACKNOWLEDGMENTS

We wish to thank ALA Editions for letting us quote from Jeannette Woodward, *Creating the Customer-driven Academic Library* (Chicago: American Library Association—ALA Editions, 2009), 178 (in the preface); and for allowing us to adapt Table 5.1 from Peter Hernon and Ellen Altman, *Assessing Service Quality: Satisfying the Expectations of Library Customers* (Chicago: American Library Association—ALA Editions, 1998), 39–41.

We also thank the Association of College and Research Libraries for letting us quote from Steven Bell, "What's Our Contribution to Retention," ACRLog [Association of College & Research Libraries], available at http://acrlblog.org/2006/10/02/whats-our-contribution-to-retention/ (in chapter 6); David W. Lewis, "A Strategy for Academic Libraries in the First Quarter of the 21st Century," *College & Research Libraries* 68, no. 5 (September 2007): 418–34 (in chapter 8); and Kathlin L. Ray, "The Postmodern Library in an Age of Assessment," ACRL Tenth National Conference, March 15–18 (Denver, CO: Association of College and Research Libraries, 2002), 250–54, available at http://www.ala.org/ala/mgrps/divs/acrl/events/pdf/kray.pdf (in chapter 4).

We also thank the EDUCAUSE Center for Applied Research (ECAR), for its permission to include Elazar C. Harel and Toby D. Sitko, "Digital Dashboards: Driving Higher Education Decisions," EDUCAUSE *Research Bulletin* 19 (2003).

# 1

---

# INTRODUCTION

Today, stakeholders increasingly want to learn about what a higher education institution, or any enterprise or organization for that matter, is accomplishing. These stakeholders neither represent a monolithic perspective nor do they blindly accept the institution's self-proclaimed, historical legacy of educating students and serving the larger community. Further, they are challenging institutions to demonstrate the extent to which they meet their missions and respond to critical information requests that go beyond self-proclaimed declarations about how productive the faculty and institution are.

For the purposes of this book, stakeholders in higher education include the following groups:

- prospective students and their parents/guardians
- those directly and currently affiliated with the institution, such as trustees involved with governance and policy, administrators, faculty, staff, students, and parents
- those involved in funding and governmental regulation and oversight, including the executive and legislative branches of local, regional, state, and federal government
- taxpayers who may not be involved in direct funding or the policy decisions of government, but who contribute indirectly through their tax dollars
- federally recognized, institutional accreditation organizations, whether they focus on regional and program accreditation or federally recognized accreditation organizations (institutional or program)
- alumni of the institution
- donors and foundations providing funding to the institution
- prospective and current employers of an institution's graduates or those individuals who were enrolled in a program but did not graduate
- the *larger community* of stakeholders that is not directly affiliated with the institution, but that has indirect relationships through contacts with the institution's employees, services, cultural events, internships, and so on

The perspectives of stakeholder are based on, and change, depending on the current interests and knowledge of stakeholders. An alumnus, for instance, may view the institution differently than a governor. However, complicating matters, a governor may also be an alumnus, and a parent of a prospective student may also be an alumnus and an employer or prospective employer of institutional attendees and graduates.

## INFORMATION NEEDS

Accountability is concerned with the institution informing those with a direct or indirect interest in what is occurring or has happened, either proactively or reactively. Accountability in higher education involves issues that affect the institution, including ones related to accessibility and affordability of a college education; internal assessment and evaluation; quality assurance and quality control; efficiency and effectiveness; and the willingness and capability to improve when the data gathered indicate the need.

The information needs surrounding accountability and higher education institutions of any size or type in the 21st century are numerous and complex. Nonetheless, these needs

- reflect the decision-making process
- demonstrate and provide a foundation to improve institutional effectiveness and efficiency
- present a case about institutional impacts and influences within a specified environment

An awareness of stakeholders and their different perspectives suggests what the information needs are. Prospective students and their families, for example, seek information to decide which institution to attend. Addressing this consumer-oriented perspective requires information about access and quality, and consideration of the following questions:

- Can we afford to send our son or daughter here?
- How much financial aid is provided to students?
- What is the source of this aid (grants or loans), and for how long would my son or daughter receive it?

Stakeholders also want assurances about the quality and value of the education received for the money they spend, measured in terms of the reputation of the institution and the extent to which its graduates gain employment and lead successful lives. In this context, key questions become:

- Is the education worth the investment in tuition?
- How many students graduate from that program?
- How many years does it take to graduate?
- What are the employment opportunities at the time of graduation, and what types of positions do graduates obtain? Do they find employment in their chosen field?
- Are graduates being admitted to advanced professional or graduate programs?

The information needs of some stakeholders relate to an understanding about how the institution functions (see Figure 1.1). Those proposing, and those approving government-based funding, as well as those providing fiscal and financial oversight,

Consumers (prospective students and their parents, alumni, employers)

| | |
|---|---|
| information supports: | decision making |
| general information needs: | accessibility of college education<br>institutional quality and reputation<br>affordability<br>value for the investment |
| broad indicators: | acceptance rates<br>costs to attend, including tuition, fees,<br>    and net price<br>retention rates<br>average number of students per course<br>average time to graduation<br>graduation rates<br>postgraduate employment opportunities<br>postgraduate acceptance rate into graduate<br>    and other programs |

Oversight (institutional trustees, government, taxpayers, and accrediting organizations)

| | |
|---|---|
| information supports: | ensuring institutional integrity and<br>    quality |
| general information needs: | planning undertaken<br>governance structure<br>administrative oversight<br>financial management and oversight<br>education and learning<br>assessment and evaluation systems in<br>    place and used<br>evidence of continuous improvement |
| broad indicators: | indicators supporting consumers<br>efficiency metrics<br>effectiveness metrics<br>self studies<br>outcomes<br>learning outcomes |

Community (a defined geopolitical area for which the institution serves)

| | |
|---|---|
| information supports: | institutional contribution |
| general information needs: | contribution of social, educational, and<br>    economic well being to the defined<br>    geopolitical area<br>support received by the institution for its<br>    operations from the defined geopolitical<br>    area |
| broad indicators: | measured impact on social, educational,<br>    and economic well-being<br>perception of the institution held by the<br>    community |

Figure 1.1   Institutional Accountability and the Information Needs of Stakeholders

want assurance that funds are applied as intended and that they are not internally diverted. Interested stakeholders also want assurances that funds are not being wasted through duplication of effort or mismanagement, or are not being consumed by inefficient bureaucratic layers. Accreditation organizations to which the federal government looks for a review and evaluation of an institution, and to inform the public of their findings, want to know about an institution's efficiencies in operations and effectiveness in administration and educating students. They want answers to questions such as:

- Does the institution conduct meaningful and substantive self studies and evaluations, and are those findings applied internally to improve and make changes?
- How do institutions know and document what students learn? Does what students learn match what the institution has identified as part of its educational mission?
- Are institutions applying the findings from self studies and evaluations to make internal adjustments to improve both efficiencies and educational effectiveness in teaching and learning?

Internally, the culture of accountability of an institution's governance, administration, and faculty directly affect the process for measuring learning and for applying any data gathered for making improvements.

Increasingly, the community at large wants to know how the institution contributes to its social, educational, and economic well-being. That community in part consists of the immediate geopolitical area in which an institution is located, and stakeholders in that area directly and indirectly influence the institution. Local government, for example, subsidizes the institution's tax-exempt land and property holdings and provides assistance for campus safety and with health services. Taxpayers within that area underwrite the commitment that local government makes.

Stakeholders may be skeptical about whether they receive the information that truly answers their questions. Prospective students and their parents are frustrated by the information provided by institutions concerning costs and financial aid when their requests for data concerning student retention and graduation rates go unanswered. Institutions provide little information about their endowments and the relationship between endowments and financial aid, thus creating an affordability concern for some and for others a concern about what the institution does with their donations. "Why is tuition so high?" may be answered by offering a comparison to another institution's tuition, but such information may seem irrelevant to the requestor. Those asking the question may not discover the extent to which the institution adds value to what students learn, how learning objectives are identified and measured, or how the institution ensures that students learn something meaningful.

State and federal governments are poised to expand their role in consumer protection and to force answers to questions of accountability. They will do this by influencing the funding support provided to an institution, increasing oversight through required reporting, or doing both. Elected officials are constantly asked about the rationale for costs and are told by their constituents that high costs hinder their children from receiving a college education. The legislative and executive branches of government are critical of higher education's self-regulating system of accreditation in which the public can learn from the accreditor if an institution or a program is accredited, but they cannot discover how well the institution or program performs unless the institution or its program directly provides that information.

To learn more about an institution before paying the ever-increasing tuition, as well as the cost of room and board, prospective students and their families want to know if the institution or program is likely to meet their education and career expectations. The institution may not have the answer, or it may be unwilling to provide the information because, from its perspective, the question is the wrong one: the answer will not help the requestor to make a decision. In the worse case, the answer casts the institution in an unflattering light. Accreditation organizations cannot respond to education consumers in any detail. As a result of this information gap, commercial enterprises have begun to provide information about institutions to paying requestors. The information is culled from institutional reports and view books, from publicly available Internal Revenue Service and other federal reporting forms, and from surveys. In turn, institutions complain that the information provided by these third parties is oftentimes incorrect and misrepresents what they do. As a result, prospective students might draw the wrong conclusion.[1]

Governments and other stakeholders have increased their oversight, or threatened to do so, by holding institutions accountable for the investment of government funds and family based resources, and by forcing institutions to be more open in providing information to them. Most, if not all, stakeholders want institutions to become more transparent—providing and explaining the information that stakeholders believe is critical for comparing and evaluating institutions so that individuals make an informed decision about which one to attend—in their external reporting and communications.

## TRANSPARENCY

It is difficult to determine if the concerns of the various stakeholders about higher education are a result of the lack of information or the high cost of receiving an education. It is in fact likely both. Stakeholders would welcome institutional transparency to resolve, in part, accountability issues. Information could be broadly available, while simultaneously focused on the needs of specific stakeholders. Many stakeholders want to know about how an institution spends the money it receives. Prospective students and their parents could incorporate the answer into their decision-making process about the choice of institution and program into which to invest their money. Aggregate information and success stories about students could be communicated not only for recruitment purposes, but also to help alumni to appreciate better the value of their degrees and employers to learn about student skills, abilities, and competitive and critical-thinking capabilities. The larger community could learn about the direct and indirect benefits that the institution provides to enrich the lives of students and area residents. Additionally, greater transparency may slow the efforts to increase intervention from the federal and state government, and accreditation organizations, thus enabling institutions to retain greater autonomy.

### Information Content

Information needs focus on costs and student academic performance and success, the requirements of compliance with formal reports, and the expectations for internal assessment and improvement. Unfortunately, conflict among these three areas may arise. Institutions need to inform the stakeholders better by being more open about costs (revenue and expenditures) and how costs have an impact on the value of dollars received. Institutions also need to explain better what comprises student success and to identify the key metrics that demonstrate such success.

Institutions maintain that they are unique by pointing to their mission statement, which the internal environment (e.g., academic program, facilities, culture, and organization structure) and external environment (e.g., physical location, demographics, and governance) influences. Yet, stakeholders may not fully understand the importance of those mission statements in conveying the uniqueness of an institution.

These statements, which are essentially a formal advertisement of what an institution offers, set the context for the uniqueness of the institution and its programs. In some context, institutions need to explain how well they meet their mission statement, and how they add value to the education experience. Typically, in their reports to stakeholders, institutions provide the average number of students per course. They may not, however, explain the trend over the past decade: has the number increased, and what is the cause of any change in average class size? Additionally, institutions relate data on acceptance and retention rates per entering cohort for a number of years. Stakeholders, as previously mentioned, are also interested in learning about the academic performance and success of students as well as

- What is the graduation rate?
- For that graduation rate, what is the percentage by gender, race, and so forth?
- Are the graduates finding jobs in their chosen field?
- What are the success rates on professional examinations and licensing tests?
- What percentages of students attend graduate or postgraduate programs?

Much of what the institution makes available can be categorized as inputs and outputs. These are important metrics; additional information, however, should be shared with stakeholders. Institutions could improve the information provided concerning student costs. For instance, readily available information includes tuition, fees, and room and board. Past trends in these costs (e.g., the average annual percentage and average dollar increases over a decade), however, are not often available. Average net price (tuition and fees, less applied financial aid) is also difficult to learn.

Information about the sources and level of funding would be useful, for instance, to parents of prospective students and government officials. Both groups may want to know:

- To what extent does government funding highly subsidize tuition?
- How much of the endowment in percentage and dollar amounts is applied to scholarships?

Institutions could be more forthcoming about their internal operations. Support costs (e.g., building construction and subsequent management/maintenance; managing the endowments; managing debt; public relations, including alumni magazines; and the costs for student recruitment) are often unidentified. As an example, parents of prospective students may characterize costs for dormitories as high. However, the costs for a 21st-century dormitory with its expected amenities are much higher than for those built in the past century. The ratio of personnel to nonpersonnel operations costs is an efficiency measure: How does the institution spend the money it receives? How do its expenditures add value?

Some would probably argue that providing this information during the initial campus visit with neatly arranged tables of numbers or a fact sheet would bore everyone taking a campus tour. Compelling narratives could help illustrate the numeric and text-based facts presented. An example includes recognizing the role and influence that the institution exercises on the locality and the region.

## Communicating Information

If transparency is an important aspect of institutional accountability, effective communications supports transparency. The information presented must be simple and clear as institutions of higher education and their subunits explain what they do and why they do it. The purpose is to ensure that various stakeholders understand the information they receive and, it is hoped, use it.

Some stakeholders need, or want to use, information for the purpose of comparing decision-making processes across institutions. Oftentimes, that information is compiled and presented by a third party, usually as a paid subscription. For instance, there is high interest in the rankings listed in the U.S. News and World Report. Other stakeholders want information to support accountability that demonstrates value and institutional effectiveness and efficiency. Naturally, there are differences in how the information is presented in order to address value, effectiveness, and efficiency. For example, the tone and the content of a report differ depending on the expected audience. Depending on the perspective of the stakeholder, the data presented may not be wanted or comparable, and the data that are not comparable hinder any legitimate ranking. Figure 1.2 illustrates an institutional process to communicate metrics to stakeholders.

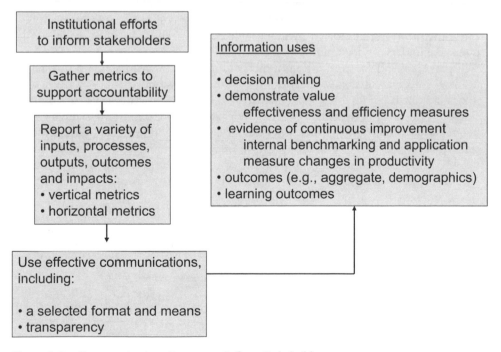

Figure 1.2 Communications Process to Inform Stakeholders

Additionally, there is an ongoing call for higher education institutions to apply business models to their operations in order to gather and report useful information, similar to how businesses issue a report to their shareholders. However, there are important differences between for-profit businesses and most institutions of higher education. Businesses look at the costs to produce, market, and sell a product, and they adjust the number of products produced in an effort to generate a profit. Those costs, the subsequent revenue generated from the product, and the arithmetic difference is measurable and can be reported. Nonetheless, many in higher education deny that the product created—an educated individual—can be similarly measured and as easily reported.

There is a threat that if institutions do not become more transparent in what information they report and how they report it, state and federal governments will mandate the content and means of such communications.[2] For example, the Higher Education Opportunity Act (P.L. 110–315), which was signed into law in August 2008, requires the secretary of education to post publicly a list of the five percent of all higher education institutions that participate in programs under Title IV (student assistance) that have the highest tuition and fees, as well as the five percent of institutions that have the highest net price for the most recent academic year for which data are available (see sections132[c][1][A-F]). The institution must identify and explain the areas with the greatest budget increases; if the institution makes this list in two consecutive years, it must file a report with the secretary concerning its progress toward addressing the increases (sections 132[e][1][A-E]).

## APPLYING METRICS

Institutions can improve their accountability efforts through a transparent communication of stakeholder-requested information in a multiplicity of formats and means. Metrics play an important role as part of the communicated message because the numbers, supported by graphs, charts, and explanatory language, facilitate stakeholders' understanding of the institution within the intended context.

To comprehend the application of metrics, one must first understand the stakeholders' information needs. Metrics must address those needs; if they do not, a metric merely becomes a statistic. Stakeholders want information for making decisions and choosing between alternatives. Relevant information might include costs, net costs, acceptance rates, retention rates, and graduation rates, as well as indicators of student success as evidenced by learning and career outcomes. Stakeholders want to know how an institution of higher education can determine if its students are successful, as defined by a set of metrics, and how the institution uses the metrics to improve the quality of the educational experience.

Metrics are also used internally to quantify and evaluate inputs, processes, outputs, and outcomes. Once identified and analyzed, those metrics are compiled to indicate past trends and patterns. Any set of metrics must be viewed in the context of the planning process and the creation of measurable objectives useful for making future estimates and projections. Such metrics could include a workload indicator (process 50,000 applications in 12 months), a performance indicator (file those applications with less than a 1% error rate), or a success indicator (80% of the students taking the Graduate Record Examination [GRE] will score in the 95th percentile). Metrics might also be used for oversight of daily operations. Such metrics, known as process indicators, reflect how much was spent or the number of specific activities completed that lead to an output. That output, which identifies problems when they occur, indicates if the applied solution worked. Process indicators also capture activities for review and analysis, and they enable comparisons to a measurable objective, for the purpose of learning if the result was achieved. This internal systematic process of planning, compiling, and analyzing inputs, processes, and outputs applies to efficiency metrics (workload indicators) and to effectiveness metrics (aggregate student outcomes and student learning outcomes).

The information captured from the internal process described above enables a better understanding of the institutional status quo. It may also be used to determine where processes need revision in order to institute changes that lead to improvements in efficiency and effectiveness. The objectives that guide this process can be revised and restated as internal benchmarks, and assorted activities can then be measured, compiled, analyzed, and reviewed to gauge change and whether improvement occurs.

Metrics address varying questions that stakeholders raise. Accountability as defined in terms of efficiency can be met through internal efficiency metrics that involve workload input and output indicators. Demonstrating how institutions add value to student learning can be met through effectiveness indicators that include aggregate student outcomes and the more elusive student learning outcomes. Long-term studies illustrate the differences in the lifelong earnings of an institution's graduates versus nongraduates. Those stakeholders wanting to implement business models might be satisfied with indicators that address return on investment (ROI) and that prove that the use of internal continuous assessment improves institutional efficiencies and effectiveness brought about by internal changes. Metrics from economic impact studies of the geographical area may document institutional relevancy to the larger community.

Metrics are influenced by the environment and culture in which they are designed, measured, compiled, analyzed, and reported. An external environment metric that is outside the institution's influence might have an impact on an internal metric. For example, a demographic metric (e.g., an increase in the mean age of those applying for admittance to the institution) might affect an internal metric (e.g., the percentage of students requiring on-campus housing and the percentage of commuters requiring parking spaces).

Metrics must be reliable and valid. Accuracy and the lack of bias influence both reliability and validity. Metrics for higher education must also be timely because outdated data do not help stakeholders in carrying out their obligations. The time span during which data are gathered also affects the validity of metrics, as for example, student study behavior (e.g., the number of hours spent per day reading), which when measured (as an average) over years or months is likely to give a more accurate picture than when measured over days or weeks when seasonal fluctuations influence the results. Further, institutions of higher education need to consider whether the proposed metric can actually be measured. The key question here is, "Can the institution afford the costs for a comprehensive suite of metrics, or will a few metrics that contribute to closing the information gap for stakeholders be sufficient?" Institutions need not all answer this question in the same way, but they should be aware of the information in Figure 1.3, which identifies the categories and several of the metrics compiled by institutions.

Broad categories of metrics compiled by institutions
- Efficiency
- Availability
- Accessibility
- Affordability
- Use and usage
- Process
- Effectiveness
- Student learning
- Faculty teaching
- Institutional and community service
- Research
- Productivity

Specific metrics often compiled by institutions
- Acceptance rates
- Costs
  - tuition and fees
  - average net price to student
  - federal subsidies
  - endowment used for scholarships
    + percentage of endowment
    + average scholarship per student
  - internal operations, including but not limited to:
    + personnel
    + facilities
    + operating
    + debt service
- Retention rates
- Average number of students per course
- Graduation rates
- Employment placement in graduate's chosen field of study
- Postgraduate acceptance rate into graduate, professional, and posteducation programs
- Impact on geopolitical area
  - economic impact studies, including area businesses
  - social and education impacts
- Satisfaction with the institution by
  - students
  - employers with graduates
  - community at large with institution's presence
- National instruments
  - Collegiate Learning Assessment (CLA)
  - National Survey of Student Engagement (NSSE)

Figure 1.3   Institutional Metrics


## Comparative Data

Some stakeholders, such as prospective students and their families, are looking for comparative information as well as institutional information. Furthermore, these stakeholders want the comparative information to be presented in such a way that they can rank institutions. The difficulty is in comparing institutions when their demographics and mission statements uniquely identify them. Some institutions have large student bodies in the tens of thousands, while many others have fewer students. Another demographic variable concerns the number and type of degree awarded, from baccalaureate to doctorate. Some institutions may emphasize teaching, while others also incorporate a research focus. There are likely to be differences between institutions located in urban areas and those in rural settings. Furthermore, it is difficult to comparatively define success when the educational standards and objectives are based on different institutional mission statements.

Complicating matters, institutions closely control the type of information they release to the public. Institutional and program accreditors do not release information to the public other than to identify those institutions that achieved accreditation, never mind comparing institutions. Education associations that compile comparative indicators may only provide them to the public if the participating institution agrees to their release.

There are differences in types of metrics and their application for creating comparative rankings of institutions, for conducting internal accountability, and for improving the educational experience. While parents and prospective students want comparative information for determining which college to attend, institutions also want comparative information, but they are likely to use different metrics to review internal progress. The internal benchmarks indicate the extent to which objectives derived from the mission statement and their supportive internal planning documents may have comparative value for institutions that are similar in terms of missions, programs, demographics, and educational objectives.

Comparative information is useful when it is applied internally. When applied to internal benchmarking, an institution decides how closely the assessed quantitative and effectiveness metrics compare with the objectives and standards that it has established. The institution therefore determines whether internal expectations, as stated in the mission statement and supported by the objectives, are realistic. Gaps between expectations for the information compiled and what the metrics actually report should be addressed and any necessary internal adjustments made.

Stakeholders use comparative information for choosing the institutions with which they want to invest their education dollars. The information gathered, however, might not be comparative. In such an instance, the information misinforms readers and creates faulty rankings. To invest in comparative metrics, an institution must first gather data internally. Comparative metrics require the use of common and accepted definitions, and collection processes, that produce data that are applicable elsewhere. After all, institutional differences may be explained by the institutional mission, aspirations, and other characteristics of compared institutions. In some instances, some of the differences might also be explained by the lack of standardized metrics, the definition of the components of a metric, what data are gathered, when they are gathered, and how they are compiled and presented in narratives, reports, and charts as well as institutional differences concerning demographics and mission.

Many stakeholders want to include comparative information (e.g., costs and student academic performance and success) as components of their decision-making process. Metrics applied at the institutional level can be difficult to define, gather, understand, and convey in a way that is meaningful to stakeholders. The following metrics are often suggested as examples for making comparisons among institutions:

- Wealth. Is it measured by the value of its assets or by the lack of its debt?
- Prestige. Is institutional prestige, which is a subjective measure, based on a historical legacy or the last decade; the graduates or the faculty; the contribution to global scholarship or employers hiring graduates?
- Student diversity. Can diversity be accurately measured if the responses are generated by the responder to diversity questions on a survey form?
- Scholarships and financial aid (gifts vs. loans). What is the financial burden of the graduate? Does the burden for those not graduating matter?
- Faculty compensation. Is it defined in terms of salary, release time for conducting research, sabbaticals, or productivity (scholarship and grants received)?
- Teaching loads. Are they determined by the number of courses taught; the presence or absence of teaching assistants; whether the courses taught are undergraduate or graduate, or discipline-based or survey courses; and so on?
- Nonacademic facilities. Athletics fits here, but the emphasis and thereby the resources placed on athletic programs differ from institution to institution. Are overhead costs included as a nonacademic facility? Overhead costs could have a considerable impact when comparisons between two or more institutions are made.

It may be best to set institutional benchmarks for success and not to depend on the use of comparative metrics. An institution could identify and measure student skills and values upon entering college, and then measure them again when students graduate. The extent of difference between both sets of data collection indicates both how well educational objectives (framed within the content of the institutional mission) are met and areas in which to make improvement. However, to conclude that these measured differences are the sole result of the institution's influence is an example of the difficulty in measuring outcomes—other factors in the students' lives also contribute to their evolving life skills and development of values.

Institutional data useful for comparative review might appear as follows:

- Reports or fact sheets prepared for stakeholders. Stakeholders, in turn, might recompile the data to reflect a broad range of institutions, and they might conduct a "kitchen table top" review of the data for their decision making. The data, however, may or may not be comparable based on the local definitions applied.
- Publications or a Web site available at a cost to those wishing to use the data. A third party compiles and offers selective institutional data. Any comparison involves the use of charts and tables to identify institutions in rows and institutional data in columns. Oftentimes, the third party ranks this type of data and presentation. The U.S. News and World Report, for example, produces *America's Best Colleges.*
- Visuals and tables that compare selected data by state. A third party compiles and provides the data. *Measuring Up,* a Web-based biennial report card first available in 2000, evaluates, compares, and provides letter grades on the performance of higher education in all 50 states, but not by institution. The performance areas, with accompanying metrics (framed from the questions listed below), include the following:
  - preparation for college (are high school graduates ready for college-level work?)
  - participation (do people in the state have access to education and training beyond high school?)
  - completion (do students complete certificate and degree programs?)
  - affordability (how difficult is it to pay for college when considering family income, the cost to attend college, and financial assistance?)

- benefits (how do workforce-trained and college-educated residents contribute to the economic and civic well-being of the state?)
- learning (how do college-educated residents perform on a variety of measures of knowledge and skills?).[3]

- Reports and charts provide data about the institution and institutional comparative data. When compiled by a third party, subscription-based data are oftentimes only provided to the institution and are not released publicly unless done so by the institution or by the third party with institutional permission. An example is the National Survey of Student Engagement (NSSE), which is an annual survey about "student participation in programs and activities that institutions provide for their learning and personal development. The results provide an estimate of how undergraduates spend their time and what they gain from attending college."[4] The survey provides institutions with five comparative benchmarks: level of academic challenge, active and collaborative learning, student-faculty interaction, enriching educational experiences, and supportive campus environment.[5] Another example is the Collegiate Learning Assessment (CLA), which assesses an institution's contribution to student learning. The institution receives the results of the testing, together with comparative measures, for participating institutions to use for internal purposes.[6]

- Data that a third party complies and presents to the institution. While these data are intended only for the institution, the third party uses a template so that reports from other participating institutions are structured identically, thereby making the data more easily comparable. An example is the Voluntary System of Accountability (VSA), which compiles and reports data on the undergraduate student experience through a common Web-reporting template, known as the College Portrait. Developed through a partnership between the American Association of State Colleges and Universities (AASCU) and the National Association of State Universities and Land-Grant Colleges (NASULGC), the VSA is a voluntary initiative for four-year public colleges and universities. It is designed to help institutions demonstrate accountability and stewardship to the public, measure educational outcomes for the purpose of identifying effective educational practices, and assemble data that are accessible, understandable, and comparable.[7]

  - The institution creates the College Portrait by entering data into the Web-based template, which converts them into text, tables, and charts, and the institution receives a Web-mountable report. The report is available through the VSA Web site (http://www.voluntarysystem.org/index.cfm?page=templates), the institution's Web site, or both. The institutionally common data available in the College Portrait include the characteristics of the institution and its students, cost per student for attending the institution for a year (e.g., tuition, room and board, required fees, books, transportation), student engagement with the learning process, and core educational outcomes. The data are intended for use by students, families, policymakers, campus faculty and staff, the general public, and other higher education stakeholders.[8] Only those institutions participating in the VSA have a College Portrait, and the reports do not exclude comparative data from other institutions. Stakeholders wanting to compare two or more institutions need to examine other institutional reports.

- Institutional data compiled and made available to the public. An example is the Minnesota State Colleges and Universities system, which produces the Board of Trustees Accountability Dashboard.[9] The dashboard, which is discussed in chapter 11, covers variables such as net tuition and fees as percent of median income, student persistence and completion, related employment of graduates, licensure exam pass rates, percent change in enrollment, and the condition of facilities.

- Reports comparing selective institutional data. A stakeholder complies and enables other stakeholders to create reports. An example is the College Navigator, an interactive Web-based tool intended to help those seeking to "find the right college."[10] provided by the

National Center for Education Statistics (NCES), within the Institute of Education Sciences of the U.S. Department of Education. Site users can search the College Navigator by the name of an institution, by state, or by a group of states. Other search criteria include program majors, degree awarded, and institutional type (e.g., public or private). Reports can be generated and printed about one institution, or users may create a report with side-by-side columns of institutionally reported data for two or more institutions. The data come from the institution's filing of the Integrated Postsecondary Education Data System (IPEDS) required for institutions receiving federal student aid, and from other institutions voluntarily filing with IPEDS.[11]

## ACADEMIC LIBRARIES

Academic libraries are not insulated from demonstrating their accountability. To be accountable, they must strategically plan on how to stay relevant and how to add value to the institution.[12] To support and enrich the institutional mission, a library considers the following:

- How does its infrastructure contribute to the overall mission?
- How successful is the library in contributing to the overall mission?
- What does the library do with information gathered?
- How does the library inform stakeholders about its successes?

As part of the institution, the library seeks a visible role in addressing accountability. The library may accomplish this by becoming an institutional leader in developing and deploying metrics that support broad-based accountability. Library accountability is demonstrated through the measured accomplishment of short-term goals and expected educational results that are linked to the institution's stated purpose as declared in the mission statement. Ultimately, this means that the mission and goals of the library and those of the institution are aligned. The library explains this alignment in its planning document, identifying the objectives that indicate what the library will do and the strategies it will follow to accomplish those objectives. The library also states how progress will be measured and evaluated. The library might document its part in student recruitment and retention as well as in student performance and success throughout a program of study and at the time of graduation.

While library stakeholders may be the same as those of the institution, stakeholder roles differ. Those shared with the institution have differing perspectives and want different accountability information. For example, university administrators have accountability needs placed on them from external stakeholders. In turn, the same administrators are library stakeholders and have accountability needs that include metrics that demonstrate how the library adds value to the institution's educational goals and objectives and contributes to economic efficiency. Such metrics might not be presented externally.

In meeting the needs of stakeholders, academic libraries often exercise transparency in their reporting and communications. Many of them offer transparency through content provided on their Web sites, in their reports, and by participating in voluntary surveys. They indeed may serve as an example of transparency for other parts of the institution.

## Metrics

Institutional accountability is demonstrated, in part, by the development, compilation, review, and analysis of effectiveness and efficiency metrics. These metrics are continuously applied to quantify and qualify the library's progress toward meeting its stated mission and purpose. Additionally, metrics affect, and are affected by, internal and external environments. These environmental influences cannot be ignored; library managers use metrics to measure processes, form opinions, make judgments, and reach decisions. Such information can be applied internally to improve processes, and to manage the academic library in an ongoing effort to improve functions, operations, and services. Both the internal and external environments influence the relationship between managerial actions and the resulting outputs.

For years, academic libraries have applied metrics to demonstrate accountability by reporting on different services. Most often they report quantitative indicators of inputs and outputs. As will be discussed in later chapters:

- Inputs are the resources used to support the library's infrastructure: collections, staffing, the physical facility, and installed information technologies.
- Activities and processes refer to what each program does with the inputs to fulfill its mission (e.g., shelves books and teach classes).
- Outputs are the direct products of program activities. Outputs identify how much work is performed and/or how many units of service are provided (e.g., the number of books circulated or the number of reference questions answered).

Inputs and outputs are invaluable metrics for making administrative and operational decisions about the provision of library services.

Increasingly, academic libraries report aggregate outcomes and learning outcomes. Outcomes emphasize results-oriented goals directly related to education, research, and service processes. Student outcomes refer to aggregate statistics on groups of students (e.g., graduation, retention, and transfer rates). College and university administrators are also interested in understanding how organizational units support student retention and learning, and overall student satisfaction. Student learning outcomes document the change in students' knowledge, abilities, ways of knowing, skill, habits of mind, attitudes, and values over the duration of a program of study. Such outcomes answer:

- What do students know that they did not know before?
- What can they do that they could not do before?

Outcomes focus on results (the impact of programs of study on students and other constituents) and the quality of services provided. Learning outcomes, in part, measure changes on students as a result of their contact with an academic library's programs, resources, and services. Complicating matters, there are differences between (and among) outcomes for administrative and student support services, and outcomes for academic programs. The library's goals and objectives focus on both support services and academic programs by providing library resources and services and by participating in instruction to improve students' research, information, and visual literacy skills. Student learning outcomes and assessment plans identify the relevant educational objectives.

Metrics of academic library performance and success should be gauged in the context of internal and institutional objectives and standards. For example, if the library has identified an increase in the circulation of reserve materials as a measure of success, and a measured increase occurs, the library may claim success for this organizational objective. However, is the success a result of the library promoting the availability of reserve items, or the library's inclusion of more reserve items on course syllabi that can be borrowed from the library? As this example indicates, metrics may invite interpretation and may not always withstand scientific rigor. It should be noted, however, that an academic library can be *successful* without adding value to the institutional mission if it only uses internal metrics and standards and does not relate those, or institutionally established metrics, to the institutional mission.

## Types of Accountability Metrics Involving Outcomes

Eleven types of quantitative and qualitative metrics covering outcomes apply to accountability:

1.  Efficiency metrics, defined in terms of economic efficiency. They relate the amount of work performed or service provided in terms of the amount of resources consumed.

2.  Availability metrics, defined as the availability of resources. Two examples are the amount of time necessary to reshelve returned resources and the number of hours open. Another metric is the number of hours that professional staff make information and technical assistance available to users.

3.  Accessibility metrics, defined as the asynchronous equity of access regardless of location or time. One example is the extent and ease of access to library catalogs, collections, and databases for on- and off-campus constituents. Interlibrary loan encompasses a number of accessibility metrics. A metric gaining popularity is the gate count, the number of users entering the library.

4.  Affordability metrics, which are increasingly important to stakeholders. Sample metrics include the percentage of required course materials available through library reserves, thereby reducing the cost to students in acquiring texts. Another metric to reduce those costs includes the amount of technology equipment available for student loan or the availability of passes to area museums. A popular metric is the number of pages that students print without per-page fees.

5.  Use metrics, which are the most common set of outputs compiled by libraries. Besides the usual counts concerning collections and service, these metrics include the number of on- and off-campus logins to the online public access catalog (OPAC); the number of page visits to library-maintained Web pages; and user willingness to recommend others to use the library (satisfaction). Use, therefore, is linked to service quality and satisfaction. Additionally, academic libraries can overlay use metrics on changes in their infrastructure and the use and condition of collections, facilities, and technologies. For example, libraries might measure the amount of circulation before and after relocating to a new or renovated library facility. In constructing such metrics it is important to remember that the before phase cannot be measured after the fact and that some type of experimental research design may be required to offer a meaningful interpretation.

6.  Process metrics, which indicate the conversion of measurable inputs into measurable outputs. An example is the amount of time required to reshelve books.

7. Effectiveness metrics, which deal with the results or performance related to teaching-learning, scholarly activity (research), and community service. Such metrics focus on the library's dual roles of assisting academic programs and providing administrative support. Generally, effectiveness centers on human-based knowledge or skills.

8. Learning and teaching metrics, which are related to library-conducted information literacy or research instruction, and the library's support for faculty teaching efforts in the same area. Metrics also focus on student attitudes and values. Learning outcomes examine the impact of library services, resources, and instruction on the development of students' ability to search, retrieve, and evaluate information and information resources effectively; foster community and individual values about the ethical uses of information; and recognize a need for lifelong learning. Metrics include the extent and effect on integrating the use of library resources within academic programs and across the curriculum. Metrics might also address student perceptions of the effects of electronic databases on becoming information literate and improving academic performance. Another metric compares, on an annual basis, student self-rating about their level of confidence in performing specific information fluency skills. Metrics might include perceptions of recent graduates about how their information fluency skills contribute to their success in graduate or professional programs and on the job.

9. Service metrics, defined in terms of the library staff serving on institutional and school or program committees. A simple metric focus on the number of library staff who are members of nonlibrary committees that contribute to campus programs and services.

10. Research metrics, defined as the availability and provision of library services and resources that have an influence on faculty research and publication, or as enabling undergraduate and graduate students to understand the various components of the inquiry process associated with the conduct of research. Metrics include faculty perceptions and experiences about the impact of information services and resources on their research and scholarship, or the ability of students to prepare proper literature reviews across disciplines as they develop a research proposal. Additionally, metrics might include library staff participation or attendance at a professional development forum that supports library services, and librarian participation in faculty research grants.

11. Productivity metrics, which combine efficiency and effectiveness into a single indicator. Metrics are used to ensure that there is an authentication process for legal access to leased subscription databases from off-campus users via a proxy server. Another metric is the extent to which the library participates in cooperative resource-sharing agreements and the number and type of resource contracts with external information and document providers. These contracts have cost advantages; economies of scale result in the addition of more databases than could be offered to the academic community if the library was not a consortia participant.[13]

In summary, much of the information that libraries provide to stakeholders is related to efficiency and process metrics (*how much*), output metrics (*how many*), and some effectiveness metrics (*how well*) that accompany expenditure data. Given this situation, it is useful to ask:

- Are libraries providing the information that their stakeholders want?
- Does what they measure support the institutional mission?
- Is the information provided indeed useful to the stakeholders?

The authors of this book suspect that, in actuality, much of the information that academic libraries provide is more useful to other libraries for benchmarking and making comparisons than it is directly to stakeholders.

## Comparative Metrics

Metrics resulting from the application of instruments such as the NSSE, CLA, and IPEDS do not generally indicate how libraries demonstrate their accountability in support of the institutional mission. In other words, generic instruments do not address local circumstances and do not enable institutions to make the necessary refinements. In the case of student learning outcomes, the instruments examine the whole picture, do not focus on scoring rubrics, and measure student progress very narrowly. As a consequence, academic libraries need (and, in some instances, have developed) metrics that address value and effectiveness. Nonetheless, any set of metrics may fail to address student progress as measured in terms of a progression, outlined in rubrics, that faculty and libraries jointly develop.

Regarding inputs and outputs, the academic library community has many metrics that demonstrate efficiency and oftentimes effectiveness. In some cases, the metrics are compiled and organized for comparative organizational purposes. They might appear in annual reports that a library submits to the institution, and they might cover usage counts and efficiency ratios concerning staff, collections, technology, the facility, and student and faculty demographics. Furthermore, most academic libraries contribute to the Academic Library Survey (ALS) administered biennially by the NCES.[14] The government agency provides a Web-based interactive tool of the submitted and confirmed individual library data so that it is possible to "compare academic libraries."[15] While this tool is available to everyone, those most interested parties would be academic librarians and researchers.

Many libraries contribute statistical information to local or regional library consortia, which in turn compile the data and provide them back to member libraries in the form of a report, usually with charts and tables that are useful for making comparisons. Most of the data collected and reported mirrors the ALS. Consortium reports tend to be released in a timelier manner than is the ALS. An example of a consortium's statistical compilation and reporting efforts is the statistical and measurement program of the Association of Research Libraries, which has an annual publication.[16] Additionally, more than 1,000 libraries contribute to the American Library Association's (ALA) Association of College and Research Libraries' (ACRL) annual *Academic Library Trends and Statistics Report*.[17] The data are compiled and made available through printed volumes and an online subscription. The online subscription enables and facilitates selecting, compiling, and reporting of comparative metrics.

State library agencies also compile statistics and make them available in print reports and/or through the Web. An example is the Texas Academic Library Statistics Web site administrated by the Texas State Library and Archives Commission. This site collects academic library data based upon the ALS, but in the years opposite to those in which the ALS is administered. The data are presented for each institution; through an interactive search, the site enables a comparison of academic library statistics for a multiplicity of libraries.[18]

Libraries use surveys or various methods that indicate the extent to which various services are effective;[19] effectiveness is a type of accountability (see chapter 7).

Academic libraries might create, or contribute to the creation of, metrics and tools intended to demonstrate the library's contribution to information literacy as aligned with coverage in the ACRL's *Information Literacy Competency Standards for Higher Education*.[20] Additionally, libraries have developed internal quizzes, activities, and other measurement tools, or they have applied tools created elsewhere (e.g., Project SAILS).[21] Other examples include George Mason University Libraries' Go for the Gold[22] and iSkills of the Educational Testing Service.[23] The challenge is to ensure alignment between any instrument used and scoring rubrics that define and document student progress over time.

### Libraries and a Business Model

There have been suggestions that libraries adopt a business model for their operations. Except in a few instances, however, libraries do not receive significant income to maintain self-sufficiency. They are more concerned with availability, accessibility, affordability, use, and the goodwill that their infrastructure generates. Additionally, libraries emphasize nontangible returns (e.g., advocacy support, referral, and satisfaction of influential stakeholders), and they offer what for-profit companies consider to be a good return on investment with some of their services. The OPAC is a good example. If the OPAC is used for less than 10 percent of the processing cycles available from the integrated library system, or by less than 10 percent of the library's users, a business model would likely consider the costs for implementing and maintaining an OPAC as a bad investment. This example shows that libraries' return on investment includes nontangibles, providing a needed public service in lieu of proving their positive economic benefits.[24]

## CONCLUSION

Transparency is one way in which institutions communicate with stakeholders. Reports are a basis for transparency, and different metrics (whether quantifiable or qualitative) help to explain and demonstrate an institution's effectiveness and efficiency. Academic libraries as an organizational unit of the institution are not immune from the pressures of accountability. They have traditionally been more transparent than the parent institution and have inserted quantifiable metrics in their reports, and they have participated in numerous surveys. They assume a visible and direct role in supporting the institution's mission statement and in demonstrating how they collaborate with other units on campus. Metrics again play a critical role in showing how libraries advance the mission of the institution and how they cooperate with other units to achieve a common end. Metrics, in sum, play a role in strategic and other types of planning.

The authors of this text see the value in having various metrics that indicate what is occurring and that have relevance to making the transition to a new future. In effect, metrics provide information for managing change; to help improve the quality of the programs and services offered, including the learning experience; and for making more effective linkages to different stakeholders. As a result, metrics and accountability rely on institutional and organizational missions, and the institutional and organizational culture. When they are broadly based, metrics offer data to address the influences that arise from the internal and external environments.

## NOTES

1. Scott Jaschik, "Refusing to Rank Inside Higher Ed," *Inside Higher Education* (August 17, 2007). Available at http://www.insidehighered.com/news/2007/08/17/usnews (accessed June 28, 2008).

2. Howard P. (Buck) McKeon, "Real Progress (Finally) on College Affordability," *Inside Higher Education* (February 7, 2008). Available at http://www.insidehighered.com/views/2008/02/07/mckeon (accessed on June 28, 2008).

3. The National Center for Public Policy and Higher Education, *Measuring Up 2008: The National Report Card on Higher Education* (San Jose, CA: The National Center for Public Policy and Higher Education, 2008). Available at http://measuringup2008.highereducation.org/print/NCPPHEMUNationalRpt.pdf (accessed December 15, 2008).

4. National Survey of Student Engagement, "About NSEE." Available at http://nsse.iub.edu/html/quick_facts.cfm (accessed on July 13, 2008).

5. National Survey of Student Engagement, "Benchmarks of Effective Educational Practice." Available at http://nsse.iub.edu/pdf/nsse_benchmarks.pdf (accessed July 6, 2008).

6. Collegiate Learning Assessment. Available at http://www.cae.org/conent/pro_collegiate.htm (accessed July 8, 2008).

7. Voluntary System of Accountability, "Welcome to the VSA Online!" Available at http://www.voluntarysystem.org/index.cfm?page=homepage (accessed July 8, 2008).

8. Voluntary System of Accountability, "About VSA." Available at http://www.voluntarysystem.org/index.cfm?page=about_vsa (accessed July 6, 2008).

9. Minnesota State University, Mankato, "News: Minnesota State Colleges, Universities System Launched an Online Accountability Dashboard to Track Performance." Available at http://www.mnsu.edu/news/read/?id=1213796988&paper=topstories (accessed on July 6, 2008).

10. U.S. Department of Education, "College Navigator." Available at http://nces.ed.gov/collegenavigator/ (accessed July 8, 2008).

11. U.S. Department of Education, National Center for Education Statistics, "About IPEDS." Available at http://nces.ed.gov/IPEDS/about/ (accessed July 8, 2008).

12. American Library Association, Association of College and Research Libraries, Research Committee, "Environmental Scan 2007" (Chicago: Association of College and Research Libraries, 2007), 17. Available at http://www.ala.org/ala/acrl/acrlpubs/whitepapers/Environmental_Scan_2.pdf (accessed July 10, 2008).

13. Ideas for several of the metrics in this section of the chapter were derived from Bonnie Gratch Lindauer, "Defining and Measuring the Library's Impact on Campuswide Outcomes," *College & Research Libraries* 59, no. 6 (November 1998): 546–70.

14. U.S. Department of Education, National Center for Education Statistics, "Library Statistics Program: Academic Libraries" (Washington, DC: National Center for Education Statistics). Available at http://nces.ed.gov/surveys/libraries/Academic.asp (accessed July 8, 2008).

15. U.S. Department of Education, National Center for Education Statistics, "Library Statistics Program: Compare Academic Libraries" (Washington, DC: National Center for Education). Available at http://nces.ed.gov/surveys/libraries/compare/index.asp?LibraryType=Academic (accessed July 8, 2008).

16. Association of Research Libraries, "Statistics & Measurement" (Washington, DC: Association of Research Libraries). Available at http://www.arl.org/stats/annualsurveys/arlstats/index.shtml (accessed July 8, 2008).

17. American Library Association, Association of College and Research Libraries, "Academic Library Statistics" (Chicago: Association of College and Research Libraries). Available at http://www.ala.org/ala/acrl/acrlpubs/acadlibrarystats/academiclibrary.cfm (accessed July 8, 2008).

18. Texas State Library and Archives Commission, Texas Academic Library Statistics, "2005 Academic Library Statistics" (Austin: Texas State Library and Archives Commission).

Available at http://www.tsl.state.tx.us/ld/pubs/als/2005/find.html (accessed July 8, 2008).

19. LibQUAL+™ addresses service improvements but, in some instances, has mistakenly been used to demonstrate accountability. For a better understanding of the role of this instrument, see Association of Research Libraries, "Welcome to LibQUAL+™" (Washington, DC: Association of Research Libraries). Available at http://www.libqual.org/ (accessed July 8, 2008).

20. American Library Association, Association of College and Research Libraries, *Information Literacy Competency Standards for Higher Education* (Chicago: American Library Association, 2000). Available at http://www.ala.org/ala/acrl/acrlstandards/information literacycompetency.cfm (accessed July 8, 2008).

21. Project SAILS, "About Project SAILS" (Kent, OH: Kent State University). Available at https://www.projectsails.org/sails/aboutSAILS.php (accessed July 8, 2008).

22. George Mason University Libraries, "Go for the Gold" (Fairfax, VA: George Mason University Libraries). Available at https://www.lib.jmu.edu/gold/secure.aspx (accessed July 8, 2008).

23. Educational Testing Service, "ETS iSkills Assessment: Overview" (Washington, DC: Educational Testing Service). Available at http://www.ets.org/iskills/ (accessed July 8, 2008).

24. One example of such a study is Paula Kaufman and Scott Walter, *The Library as Strategic Investment: Results of the University of Illinois "Return on Investment" Study*. Available at http://hdl.handle.net/2142/8768 (accessed August 9, 2008).

# 2

———◆———

# RELATED LITERATURE

Searching two topics, *performance measures libraries* and *outcome measures libraries*, in Google™ produces more than 1.5 million hits. The word *library*, however, might merely refer to a collection of resources and not an organization that serves academic institutions, cities and counties, and so on. The writings on performance measures, for instance, include bibliographies, tables, and charts showing what libraries are reporting, overviews of the concept, books, and articles, and these writings address inputs and outputs, perhaps ones relevant to a digital environment. Inputs "are the easiest to quantify and gather and have been used by librarians a long time. Typically input measures are grouped into five broad categories: budget, staff, collections, facilities, and technology. Input measures are usually counts or a numerical value."[1] Outputs, on the other hand,

are used to indicate the degree to which the library and its services are being utilized. More often than not, output measures are simply counts to indicate volumes of activity. Historically, use of output measures has been regarded as a measure of goodness—after all, the library's collection (physical and electronic) and its services were being used, often intensively so! Therefore, the library was doing "good." A multiplicity of measures exist to demonstrate use of services, use of the collections (physical and electronic), use of facilities (gate count, program attendance), visits to the library's Web site, and so forth.[2]

The writings on outcomes measures included in Google™ and various databases might define outcomes as the effect of exposure to services on the library's constituency or effectiveness of library programs and services, or as:

a systematic method of assessing the extent to which a program has achieved its intended result. It attempts to answer the questions, "What difference did the program make?" and, "How did the participant benefit?" Referred to by various names, including Outcome Based Evaluation (OBE) and outcomes assessment, it is useful as both a planning tool and an evaluation tool. Outcomes are beneficial changes for program participants that include changes in their skills, knowledge, behavior, attitude, status, or life condition.[3]

Other writings might explain the value of engaging in outcomes assessment and how to do so, confuse outcomes with outputs, suggest how a library might achieve a culture of assessment, and so on. Finally, the identification of different metrics should not be concluded without a brief mention of process metrics, which are associated with management information systems and the throughput phase of the open systems model. This phrase, which sees the transformation from inputs to outputs, focuses on:

- total costs per activity
- amount of time per activity

This chapter highlights selected writings, including ones within and outside library and information science (LIS); indicates a preference for the use of the word *metric* over *measures;* identifies guides, manuals, and other key sources on the topic of library planning and different types of metrics; and identifies key scholarly writings, some of which provide historical coverage.

## USE OF THE WORD *METRIC*

There is no general consensus regarding the preference for the word *measure* or *metric*. The U.S. Government Accountability Office, formerly known as the General Accounting Office, has produced reports on financial management, information security, contact centers, and aspects of accountability (e.g., the effectiveness of e-government) that use *metrics,* perhaps as a means to compare performance among agencies. For instance, that comparison might apply to contact centers that handle inquiries via multiple channels such as telephone, Web page, e-mail, and postal mail to provide the public with accurate information and to ensure that proper oversight exists.[4]

The word *metric* might refer to something that is quantifiable and perhaps reported with a decimal; however, some metrics could involve the collection and reporting of qualitative data. Metrics, which are useful for program or service oversight and improvement, might relate to inputs, outputs, or outcomes that individual government agencies use to determine their effectiveness and efficiency. Metrics for making the content of Web sites readily accessible to the public might identify *targets* and the extent to which they have been achieved. For example, one output metric reports the "number of clicks to access relevant loan information," and one input metric covers the "median time for processing archival electronic records."[5] For these metrics, no target was specified. For the "number of electronic comments submitted through Regulations.gov,"[6] the target is 200,000 and the "reported status" is 509.

The authors of this book see a metric as a new way to grasp the complex relationship between libraries and other stakeholders and the array of input, output, and outcome measures presented in this book. LIS, in our opinion, has relied too long largely on metrics that reflect the library perspective and its focus on inputs and outputs, be they for a digital or print environment. As noted by one report of the National Partnership for Reinventing Government, produced by the Clinton administration to redefine how government manages its information resources, as well as its relationship with the public, in an effective and efficient manner,[7] it is important to balance different perspectives (e.g., the roles of customer, stakeholder, and employee in an organization's daily operations). Whatever metrics are used might go beyond inputs and be results oriented. Our purpose is not to recommend any particular perspective or set of metrics; rather, this book adopts multiple perspectives and identifies choices among which readers can select. In so doing, it sets itself apart from the other writings discussed in subsequent sections of this chapter.

## HISTORICAL CONTEXT

In a selective historical review of performance measurement in libraries, Deborah L. Goodall traces the concept back to Philip M. Morse's *Library Effectiveness: A Systems Approach,* a pioneering book on library effectiveness published by MIT Press in 1968. Extending her coverage through the mid-1980s, she concludes that "one cannot help feeling that the research has been of a circular nature and that although plenty has been written on the subject there is a surprising lack of originality in the writings." She then encourages subsequent work to concentrate on outputs.[8] As the writings covered in Table 2.1 illustrate, subsequent writings do just that; however, with the late 1990s and the 21st century, an interest in the digital environment, as well as outcomes, emerged.

**Table 2.1**
**Selected Guides, Manuals, Textbooks, and Other Works Covering**
**Library Planning and Metrics**

Abbott, Christine. *Performance Measurement in Library and Information Services.* London: Aslib, 1994.

Association of Research Libraries. *Measures for Electronic Resources (E-Metrics)*, five parts. Washington, DC: Association of Research Libraries, 2002.

Bertot, John C., and Denise Davis. *Planning and Evaluating Library Networked Services and Resources.* Westport, CT: Libraries Unlimited, 2004.

Bertot, John C., Charles R. McClure, and Joe C. Ryan. *Statistics and Performance Measures for Public Library Networked Services.* Chicago: American Library Association, 2000.

Brophy, Peter. *Measuring Library Performance: Principles and Techniques.* New York: Neal-Schuman (distr.), 2006.

Childers, Thomas A., and Nancy A. Van House. *What's Good? Describing Your Public Library's Effectiveness.* Chicago: American Library Association, 1993.

Covey, Denise Troll. *Usage and Usability Assessment: Library Practices and Concerns.* Washington, DC: Digital Library Federation and Council on Library and Information Resources, 2002.

Cronin, Mary J. *Performance Measurement for Public Services in Academic and Research Libraries.* Washington, DC: Association of Research Libraries, Office of Management Studies, 1985.

DeProspo, Ernest R., Ellen Altman, and Kenneth E. Beasley. *Performance Measures for Public Libraries.* Chicago: American Library Association, 1973.

Durrance, Joan, and Karen E. Fisher, with Marian B. Hinton. *How Libraries and Librarians Help: A Guide to Identifying User-Centered Outcomes.* Chicago: American Library Association, 2005.

(*Continued*)

**Table 2.1**
**Selected Guides, Manuals, Textbooks, and Other Works Covering**
**Library Planning and Metrics (*Continued*)**

Kantor, Paul B. *Objective Performance Measures for Academic and Research Libraries*. Washington, DC: Association of Research Libraries, 1984.

King Research Ltd. *Keys to Success: Performance Indicators for Public Libraries*. London: HMSO, 1990.

Mayo, Diane. *Technology for Results: Developing Service-based Plans*. Chicago: American Library Association, 2005.

Mayo, Diane, and Sandra Nelson. *Wired for the Future: Developing Your Library Technology Plan*. Chicago: American Library Association, 1999.

McClure, Charles R. *Performance Measures for Oklahoma Public Libraries*. Oklahoma City, OK: Oklahoma Department of Libraries, 1982.

McClure, Charles R., and Cynthia Lopata. *Performance Measures for the Academic Networked Environment* (ED 405867). Available at http://www.eric.ed.gov/ERICDocs/data/ericdocs2sql/content_storage_01/0000019b/80/16/69/f8.pdf (accessed February 1, 2008); see also http://www.cni.org/projects/assessing/ (accessed February 1, 2008).

McClure, Charles R., Amy Owen, Douglas L. Zweizig, Mary J. Lynch, and Nancy A. Van House. *Planning & Role Setting for Public Libraries: A Manual of Options and Procedures*. Chicago: American Library Association, 1987.

Nelson, Sandra S. *Implementing for Results: Your Strategic Plan in Action*. Chicago: American Library Association, 2009.

Nelson, Sandra S. *The New Planning for Results: A Streamlined Approach*. Chicago: American Library Association, 2001.

Nelson, Sandra S., Ellen Altman, and Diane Mayo. *Managing for Results: Effective Resource Allocation for Public Libraries*. Chicago: American Library Association, 2000.

Noble, Pamela. *Performance Measures and Criteria for Libraries: A Survey and Bibliography*. Brighton, England: Public Libraries Research Group (distributed by C. Batt, 1976).

Palmour, Vernon E., Marcia A. Bellassai, and Nancy V. DeWath. *A Planning Process* for Public Libraries. Chicago: American Library Association, 1980.

Poll, Roswitha, and Peter te Boekhorst. *Measuring Quality: International Guidelines for Performance Measurement in Academic Libraries*, 2nd ed. (IFLA Publications; 127). Munich, Germany: K.G. Saur, 2007.

Poll, Roswitha, Peter te Boekhorst, and Ramon Abad Hiraldo. *Measuring Quality: International Guidelines for Performance Measurement in Academic Libraries*. Munich, Germany: K.G. Saur, 1996.

Rubin, Rhea J. *Demonstrating Results: Using Outcome Measurement in Your Library*. Chicago: American Library Association, 1990.

Van House, Nancy A., and Thomas A. Childers. *The Public Library Effectiveness Study: The Complete Report*. Chicago: American Library Association, 1993.

Van House, Nancy A., Mary J. Lynch, Charles R. McClure, Douglas L. Zweizig, and Eleanor J. Rodger. *Output Measures for Public Libraries: A Manual of Standardized Procedures*. Chicago: American Library Association, 1987.

(*Continued*)

**Table 2.1**
**Selected Guides, Manuals, Textbooks, and Other Works Covering**
**Library Planning and Metrics (*Continued*)**

Van House, Nancy, Beth Weil, and Charles R. McClure. *Measuring Academic Library Performance: A Practical Approach*. Chicago: American Library Association, 1990.

Ward, Patricia L. *Performance Measures: A Bibliography*. Loughborough, England: Centre for Library and Information Management and Public Libraries Research Group, 1982.

White, Andrew C., and Eric D. Kamal. *E-metrics for Library and Information Professionals: How to Use Data for Managing and Evaluating Electronic Resource Collections*. New York: Neal-Schuman, 2005.

Zweizig, Douglas L., and Eleanor J. Rodger. *Output Measures for Public Libraries: A Manual of Standardized Procedures*. Chicago: American Library Association, 1982.

Published in the same year as the Goodall article, Ronald R. Powell reviews the literature of the 1970s and 1980s, some of which appears in Table 2.1. He links performance measurement with user studies and notes that "the performance of a library measured in terms of how well it is meeting the needs of its users (and non-users) is one of the most meaningful ways of judging the quality and effectiveness of a library's services."[9] Maintaining that the best indicators of library performance are based on data gathered from users, he identifies 17 complex user variables related to library performance (e.g., user needs and patron's expectations) and 24 ways to collect relevant and valid data.

Martha Kyrillidou provides another introduction, one that discusses accountability and quality assessment in higher education. She highlights the use of performance indicators in academic libraries, international standards, and factors affecting the reliability and validity of data (e.g., consistency, ease vs. utility, and values).[10]

## RELEVANT GUIDES, MANUALS, AND OTHER MAJOR WORKS

Table 2.1, which traces the literature back to the early 1970s, shows that a number of writings relate to public libraries and their effectiveness. It also indicates that the American Library Association is the major publisher, the names of some authors reoccur, and there is a shift from a traditional view of the library as a physical place to a digital and networked environment—use of databases and library Web sites.[11] As the table indicates, *Performance Measures for Public Libraries* is the first work to approach planning and measurement at the macro-level. In essence, it provides a foundation on which the other works listed build, and it established Rutgers University at the forefront of work on performance measurement and library effectiveness in the United States for the 1970s.

Denise Troll Covey, it merits mention, conducted interviews at 24 member institutions of the Digital Library Federation (DFL) about their assessment practices—more specifically about the use and usability of their online collections and services. She reviews different methods of data collection including, for instance, surveys, focus group interviews, and translation log analyses. Transactional log analysis, which involves transaction monitoring (e.g., the use of Web sites), is concerned with either aggregate use data and patterns or the dynamics of individual search patterns. She highlights the challenges of assessment and settling on appropriate metrics and data collection. Appendix D of her work covers input, output, and outcome measures, and it offers examples relevant to DFL members. There is even coverage of cost-effectiveness.[12]

A good source on performance measurement in libraries is *Performance Measurement and Metrics,* published by MCB University Press and included in the database Emerald Journals. Coverage is international, and any given issue contains an editorial, articles, and reviews of relevant books. Additionally information is available from the International Organization of Standards (ISO; see http://www.iso.org/iso/home.htm).

*The Chronicle of Higher Education* and *Inside Higher Education* (http://www.insidehighered.com/), as well as other specialized newspapers and newsletters, contain numerous stories that address metrics, especially input ones, and create opportunities to envision new metrics. For instance, *The Chronicle of Higher Education* reports that Boeing is dissatisfied with much of its professional workforce and envisions concentrating its hiring on those institutions of higher education and programs from which it draws its best (most productive) workers.[13] In effect, Boeing is proposing a new impact or outcome metric, one associated with higher education accountability.

Jossey-Bass publishes the quarterly *New Directions for Institutional Research.* Each issue contains a set of papers that examine an aspect of the issue theme. Coverage complements our coverage of the institutional perspective (especially chapter 6) and often advances input and output metrics. Each year, there is an *Assessment Supplement,* which ensures that issues related to assessment are not ignored and which covers developments in higher education in other countries.

## OTHER LISTS OF METRICS

The LIS literature covers the use of performance measures and learning outcomes internationally. Those writings, however, are not always current, and any conclusions about their use today must be tentatively drawn. Still, many libraries are exploring new measures that shift the focus from traditional library inputs and outputs to matters of interest to stakeholders (e.g., the financial status of libraries, library use, and staff efficiency).[14] With the evolving forms of digital services that libraries offer (and will offer), there is a need to examine and demonstrate their ability to engage in a multifaceted assessment of networked-based information services and resources,[15] as well as to focus on those services, resources, and settings related to the library as an inviting physical place.

Examples of important international initiatives in the standardization and use of input and output metrics for libraries include EQUINOX (Europe) and SCONUL (United Kingdom). EQUINOX, a library performance measurement and quality management system supported by the European Commission, offers metrics centered around an international standard quality management framework (ISO 9002) for libraries. Those metrics enhance and complement the indicators for traditional library services presented in ISO 11620, "Library Performance Indicators," and group 29 indicators into user satisfaction; public services, covering the delivery of services; and technical services, addressing the acquisition, processing, and cataloging of materials.[16] The International Federation of Library Associations (IFLA) has developed complementary, international guidelines for performance measures in academic and public libraries.[17] The National Information Standards Organization (NISO) has a dictionary of definitions, which includes e-metrics (see http://www.niseo.org/emetrics). Furthermore, standard Z39.7-2004, "Information Services and Use," includes e-metrics for libraries (see data dictionary at http://www.niso.org/emetrics/current/toc.html). Metrics in the standard also cover types of holdings, workstations, operating and other expenditures, user orientation and training, and loans and document delivery.

The Standing Conference of National and University Libraries (SCONUL), which represents all 135 university libraries and national research libraries in the United Kingdom, has collected and published comparative library statistics on member library's inputs, throughputs, and outputs; many of these resources are easily found from using an online search engine.

The Council of Australian University Librarians (CAUL) has developed a set of performance indicators that include, for instance, customer satisfaction, materials availability, and document delivery. Some of the available data cover 1995 to 2003 and enable users to make comparisons among the libraries.[18] In New Zealand, Philip Calvert and Rowena Cullen investigated suitable performance metrics for academic and public libraries.[19] Their studies, however, focus on the predigital age.

In the United States, the American Library Association's Association of College and Research Libraries (ACRL) has developed a set of competences and outcomes related to information literacy.[20] Different libraries have taken ACRL's set of outcomes and measured the extent to which students meet the stated expectations. The problem is that the teaching faculty may not have accepted the set or might favor some parts more than others. Furthermore, the outcomes do not deal with problem solving in terms of research as a formal inquiry process of data collection (with a reflective inquiry and other components). Any data gathered from the use of outcomes need to be applied continually to improve the overall learning experience, and teaching faculty should be at the forefront of setting program-wide learning goals.

Aimed at public libraries, Sara Laughlin and Ray W. Wilson discuss how to improve mission-critical processes. Data collection, as they lay out, revolves around input and output metrics, which they group into categories such as:

- accounting (e.g., cost of customer complaints, by type)
- acquisitions (e.g., average processing time, by type)
- human resources (e.g., number of benefit complaints)
- maintenance (e.g., percentage of jobs completed on schedule)
- office support (e.g., number of items misfiled/missing)
- scheduling (e.g., hours of overtime)
- timeliness (e.g., percentage of downtime, by machine).[21]

## SCHOLARLY WRITINGS

### Overview

Cullen offers a conceptual framework for evaluation and understanding different perspectives. She introduces different evaluation concepts and relevant literature and views performance measures as an essential management tool.[22] Neal Kaske, who discusses evaluation measures, identifies the general points at which measures are taken. He presents tools for evaluating libraries, and those tools range in coverage from inputs to evaluation of a program's impacts.[23]

Outcomes assessment is a central, if not *the* central, focus of accountability-driven assessment. Within this context, some authors use the terms *impact* and *outcomes* synonymously, and others see them as different concepts.[24] Complicating matters, some suggest a logical continuum ranging from inputs, activities, and processes, to outputs, outcomes, and long-term impacts, whereas others see the type of outcomes recommended by accreditation organizations for higher education in the United States as not necessarily so orderly; assessment might bypass outputs and proceed directly from inputs to outcomes.

John Carol Bertot and Charles R. McClure hypothesize six types of outcomes:

1.  Economic: outcomes that relate to the financial status of library users
2.  Learning: outcomes reflecting learning skills and abilities, and the acquisition of knowledge
3.  Research: outcomes that include, for example, the impacts of library services and resources on the research process of faculty and students
4.  Information exchange: outcomes that include the ability of users to exchange information with organizations and other individuals
5.  Cultural: the impact of library resources and services on the ability of library users to benefit from cultural activities
6.  Community: outcomes that affect a local community and in turn affect the quality of life for members of the community[25]

Peter Hernon and Robert E. Dugan, with their contributors, focus exclusively on Bertot and McClure's second type and offer the perspectives of different stakeholder, indicating that, for program and regional accreditation organizations, student satisfaction and service quality may not count as indirect methods. They also view outcomes from an institutional and program perspective.[26]

Joseph R. Matthews identifies six categories of outcomes or benefits for public libraries. These are as follows:

1.  Cognitive results: refreshed memory, new knowledge, and changed ideas
2.  Affective results: sense of accomplishment or sense of confidence
3.  Meeting expectations: getting what the public needed, getting too much, seeking substitute sources
4.  Accomplishments: ability to make more informed decisions and achieving a higher level of performance
5.  Time aspects: saved or wasted time, or had to wait for service
6.  Money aspects: the dollar value of results obtained, the amount of money saved, or the cost of using the service[27]

McClure and Paul Jaeger maintain that the Internet is changing the roles and expectations of public libraries. They note that it "has produced a major expansion of the social and service roles public libraries play in the lives of patrons, in the activities of communities, and in service to governments."[28] Using some excellent illustrative matter, they lay out the key social roles and selected Internet-enables service roles and responses. Figure 1 (p. 4 of their book), for instance, lays out basic concepts and relationships, and identifies how societal needs and expectations lead to a focus on impacts and benefits and on learning and assessment. Clearly, their figures and tables suggest areas in which meaningful metrics might be developed.

In a discussion of developments in the United Kingdom and Europe, Stephen Town finds "a perceived need for academic libraries to demonstrate the impact or outcome (particularly in relation to learning and research) of their activities."[29]

## Dissertations

John B. Harer conducted a Delphi study, which involves the use of a forecasting methodology that draws on a panel of experts to identify critical processes and performances measures that can provide a framework for academic libraries engaged in continuous quality improvement. He defines quality in terms of the Malcolm Baldrige National Quality Award, and his findings underscore the importance of viewing quality in terms of students, faculty, and other stakeholders.[30] His dissertation serves as a reminder that metrics should not be limited to quantitative ones; qualitative data collection has its place and provides a rich context to understand better where service improvements are necessary.

Enid R. Causey examined the annual reports of South Carolina academic libraries and self-study documents of the Southern Association of Colleges and Schools (SACS), as well as surveyed the library directors at 52 colleges and universities in the state. Data were collected on the types of performance measures reported. Traditional quantitative measures, Causey finds, are much more frequently mentioned than are more qualitative measures. In addition, the annual reports and recent SACS self-study documents place more emphasis on mission statements, planning, and measurement of outcomes, indicating that the so-called assessment movement has had an impact on academic libraries in the state.[31]

John E. Evans conducted a cost analysis of public services in one academic library, defined as those services offered by the departments of reference, circulation, government documents, interlibrary loan, and computer database search services. The portion of the investigation examining the use of performance measures reveals wide variation. This finding indicates a diversity of departmental functions; there was no attempt to develop a common set of metrics.[32]

Turning to public libraries, Susan E. Higgins believes that user satisfaction forms the basis for a performance metric that enables librarians to infer the effectiveness of public library service to young adults.[33] Patricia A. Lund, under the supervision of Douglas L. Zweizig, examines the use of performance standards and output measurement in public libraries. Applying the Locke Goal Setting Theory to public library performance, she concluded that the use of performance standards and output measure scores in planning is associated with improved public library performance.[34]

## Some Other Studies

Revisiting the topic of his dissertation, Harer, together with Bryan R. Cole, notes that many different organizations in the public and private sector use performance measures, ones that demonstrate quality, excellence, and effectiveness. "The movement toward performance measurement in libraries," they observe, "has been strong in Europe, especially with the nations of the Commonwealth of Great Britain, where performance measurement is mandated by law."[35] The Northumbria International Conference on Performance Measurement in Libraries and Information Services, as they note, is a forum for discussions and papers on the topic.[36] Harer and Cole also highlight some of the critics of performance measurement who question the internal validity of many metrics—whether the measurement does what it is designed to do. They conclude with a discussion of critical processes and performance metrics that measure the quality of library programs, services, and functions.

In reviewing various library performance indicators, Roswitha Poll finds that a number of them apply to national libraries. Mostly these indicators are inputs and outputs; one metric focuses on the percentage of the collection in stable condition, and another explains the correct answer fill rate, which applies to reference service as offered in a virtual or physical environment. There is some attention to cost related metrics (e.g., the cost per download per electronic resource).[37]

Although dated, Nancy A. Van House provides an excellent introduction into output measures,[38] and Curtis L. Kendrick applies performance measurement to the accuracy of a shelving operation and links his findings to performance standards for shelving.[39] Joan Stein reviews the literature of performance evaluation of interlibrary loan (ILL) and document supply operations published between1987 and 1997 in English-speaking countries. The primary criteria for evaluation focus on fill rate, turnaround time, cost, and user satisfaction. Despite the increased emphasis on quantifying the performance of ILL and document supply, there is a lack of standardization of measurement devices and definitions of terms.[40]

Writing in 2004, Steve Hiller notes a decline in the use of the physical library, at a time when academic libraries are making a substantial investment in digital resources and facing stagnant budgets. This decline, he maintains, "has led to a reappraisal of the role of the physical library in academic institutions."[41] He focuses then on the viability of academic branch libraries and advances a series of 20 metrics (inputs and outputs) grouped into use, primary user population, library dependency of primary user community, and facility quality.

Peter T. Shepherd and Denise M. Davis focus on the ISO standard on library statistics and the impact that e-metrics have on publishers, libraries, and information aggregators.[42] Writing in the United Kingdom, Angela Conyers views "user statistics as the foundation of any study of the impact of electronic services," and she defines impact in terms of inputs and outputs related to types of resources (serials, databases, e-books, and digital documents), virtual visits, and electronic inquiries. She also discusses cost measures, including value for money.[43]

It is increasingly common for authors to treat LibQUAL+™ findings as complementary to performance metrics because those findings add meaningful insights into the customer perspective. Such writings present findings as outputs or outcomes, whereas regional and program accreditation organizations do not recognize the resulting metrics (e.g., customer satisfaction) as a student learning outcome. Andrew Booth links performance measurement to evidence-based library and information practice. He maintains that the evidence gathered need not be "research-derived evidence." It can be based on user self-reports (e.g., through LibQUAL+™) or librarian observations.[44] Wanda V. Dole, Anne Liebst, and Jitka M. Hurych add that the evidence can be quantitative or qualitative.[45]

Donald W. King, Peter B. Boyce, Carol H. Montgomery, and Carol Tenopir provide a cross-section of library economic metrics for journal collections that should appeal to different stakeholders. They cast input, output, usage, outcome, and domain metrics within different perspectives: the library, user, organization, community served, and society. They conclude with an extensive bibliography of works that complement Table 2.1.[46]

Echoing King et al., Robert E. Dugan and Peter Hernon, call for metrics that have utility to the library, customers, broader organization or institution, and various stakeholders. Libraries need to present themselves in terms meaningful to each group of stakeholders and to assist the broader organization or institution in achieving its mission. This requires moving beyond performance measures to outcomes assessment.[47] Their article serves as a foundation for this book.

Andrew Breidenbaugh notes that before the Tampa-Hillsborough County Public Library initiates new services, it establishes performance measures to document the success of a service in relation to the public money invested. For the virtual reference service, they monitor *sessions* (the number of sessions per day, the number of sessions by hour of the day, session duration, time spent by the customer in the queue, customer's browser and operating system, and customer affiliation [based on entry point]) and *questions* (number received per day, number answered per day, number by status, questions transferred from chat to e-mail, and response times). Efficiency and workload goals relate to the percentage:

- increase in the number of customers (sessions) annually
- increase in the users per capital (awareness of the service)
- decrease in the wait time for customers to receive assistance
- increase in the number of questions answered (completed) at time of original transaction

In addition, the library collects customer feedback on transactions and views effectiveness and quality performance in terms of the percentage:

- increase in the use of subscription databases in virtual reference transaction
- of customers expressing satisfaction with service
- of repeat customers for the service
- increase in the number of genealogy-related questions (target awareness)
- of questions answered correctly
- of customers who found the service easy/intuitive to use.[48]

The library also developed targets such as a 5 percent increase in sessions annually and 85 percent customer satisfaction with the service.

Looking at the changing digital environment, Poll advocates the establishment of standardized definitions and methods for the assessment of input, output, and impact metrics that will enable libraries to demonstrate value for money. She relies on the framework set by the ISO.[49] The suggested impact measures, however, comprise outputs and do not actually cover changes in knowledge, skills, attitudes, behavior, or abilities resulting from access to libraries and their resources. Quality assurance is therefore often associated with outputs and not with what students (or others for that matter) learn and can apply.

Among others, Kyrillidou and Sarah Giersch discuss the Association of Research Libraries E-metrics project, whose purpose is to present new measures (inputs and outputs) that describe networked electronic resources and their value.

The appendix of their article identifies various metrics. They encourage the development of new methodologies that rely on mixed methods, which apply both quantitative and qualitative data collection.[50]

Despite the abundance of literature covering academic and public libraries, some writings extend the discussion to other settings. For instance, Steve Thornton examines the use of performance measurement in special libraries,[51] and Debbie Schachter applies performance metrics to information centers,[52] as did Betty Reifsnyder and McClure more than a decade earlier. Reifsnyder and McClure suggest that the following performance metrics developed for use in public libraries be applied to corporate information centers: awareness of library services (corporate), clients as percentage of jurisdiction population, reference transactions per capita, reference fill rate, and timeliness of information delivery.[53]

*Corporate Library Benchmarks* (2009 edition), an ongoing survey of 52 corporate and other business-oriented libraries, presents a broad range of data, including input and output metrics, on expenditures and collections. The libraries spent a mean of 117.2 hours reviewing contract terms from vendors of content licenses, although the median amount of time spent on this activity is 30 hours. The libraries expect to renew in the upcoming year 90.5 percent of their current licensing contracts for content. Furthermore, spending on e-books averaged $15,345 or about 45.5 percent as much as they spent on traditional books.[54]

Eileen G. Abels, Keith W. Cogdill, and Lisl Zach offer a taxonomy of services for hospitals and academic health science centers that focuses on mission concepts, organizational goals, and LIS contributions. They introduce, in general terms, different types of metrics (output measures, performance measures, outcome measures, and impact measures) and discuss how to collect relevant data.[55]

Coverage of performance metrics in the literature of school media centers has not been ignored. Still, much of that literature dates back more than 20 years. Evelyn H. Daniel, writing in the 1970s, notes the types of external and internal pressure that prompt performance measurement and evaluation.[56] In the early 1980s, Esther Dyer and Daniel O'Connor outline the history of program evaluation for school library media centers, and they present different models.[57] In the late 1990s, Frances B. Bradburn highlights a series of output metrics for school media centers.[58]

Finally, it merits mention that the Government Printing Office has advanced a series of metrics, predominately input metrics, to characterize its contribution to the federal depository library program. Those metrics have some value to member libraries—more to the depository collection than the library as a whole. In general, they do not reflect the contribution of the depository collection in meeting the mission and vision of the larger organization.[59]

## The Balanced Scorecard

The balanced scorecard is a management technique, associated with Robert S. Kaplan and David P. Norton,[60] that views an organization from four perspectives:

1. Customers and their satisfaction: poor performance from this perspective is thus a leading indicator of future decline, even though the current financial picture may look good.

2. Critical internal (business) processes in which the organization must excel: managers need to know how well the business is functioning and whether its products and services conform to customer requirements (the mission).

3. Financial: Kaplan and Norton do not ignore or downplay this perspective. As they explain, timely and accurate funding data will always be a priority, and managers will do whatever necessary to provide it. The point is that the current emphasis on financials leads to the *unbalanced* situation in regard to other perspectives.

4. Execution: This perspective contributes to bottom-line improvement, innovation, growth, and learning. It refers to the infrastructure (people, systems, and organizational procedures) that the organization must develop to create long-term growth and improvement.

Performance measurement is a key component of each perspective, as George Valiris and Panagiotis Chytas discuss. They issue an important reminder:

Measurement alone is not good enough. We must drive behavioural changes within the organization if we expect to execute strategy. This requires establishing a target for each measurement within the . . . balanced scorecard. Targets are designed to stretch and push the organization in meeting its strategic objectives. Targets need to be realistic so that people feel comfortable about trying to execute the target.[61]

The University of Virginia Library (as discussed in chapter 11) links metrics to each of the four perspectives. A metric contains two targets, one indicating complete success in achieving the metric. and the other partial success;[62] for a complete listing of the metrics, see http://www.lib.virginia.edu/bsc/metrics/all0607.html and http://www.lib.virginia.edu/bsc/metrics.html.

Matthews shows how public libraries can apply the balanced score to focus on resources, assess the strategic impact of collections and services, and better serve their communities. The purpose is to assist libraries in planning.[63]

Poll writes about an interesting project sponsored by the German Research Council that uses the balanced scorecard as a concept for an integrated quality management system. Performance indicators from each perspective are combined to evaluate the University and Regional Library Munster with the Bavarian State Library Munich and the State and University Library Bremen.[64] Town, who critiques the development of e-metrics for use in academic library services, proposes a framework for e-measures based on the balanced scorecard approach. He encourages future use of metrics to address scholarly communication, information literacy, developments in measuring library and e-service quality, and the critical success factors of serials staff.[65]

Increasingly, usage reports based on statistics generated from Project COUNTER (Counting Online Usage of Networked Electronic Resources) have suggested that the data reflect the extent of e-use of library collections.[66] Project metrics are often accepted as an international standard for statistical reporting of journal databases. Deborah D. Blecic, Joan B. Fiscella, and Stephen E. Wiberley, Jr., compare the effects of transitioning from non-COUNTER to COUNTER-complaint statistics within the same databases. Drawing on those statistics, they also examine the potential effects of federated searching and alert services.[67]

## Efficiency Assessment

Such an assessment addresses the relationship between the costs of a program or service and its effectiveness. This type of assessment might comprise a cost-benefit or a cost-effectiveness analysis. Paul B. Kantor's *Objective Performance Measures for Academic and Research Libraries* (see Table 2.1) provides an excellent introduction, and an application of efficiency assessment includes Coopers & Lybrand's *Valuing the Economic Costs and Benefits of Libraries,* which offers "a framework for analyzing library benefits so they reflect appropriate economic signals about resource allocation and use to library operators, funders and the users of library services."[68] Jennifer Ellis-Newman identifies cost drivers, "the events that cause changes in the behavior of costs in the activity cost pool," and offers an approach for viewing assorted costs to a library and thereby demonstrating fiscal accountability.[69]

Writing in 2001, Stephen R. Lawrence, Lynn S. Connaway, and Keith H. Brigham, who discuss the life-cycle costs of acquiring and maintaining an academic research library, develop a methodology for determining those costs. Using data collected by the Association of Research Libraries, they indicate that the cost structure of a member library is largely driven by its monograph collection.[70]

Wonsik Shim introduces Data Envelopment Analysis (DEA) to calculate the relative technical efficiency of a set of libraries, in this case, libraries with membership in the Association of Research Libraries. He shows how library inputs and outputs can be used to reveal best practices and to generate a technical efficiency score for a library.[71]

Elizabeth M. Mezick focuses on student retention at academic institutions that are highly dependent on tuition dollars to cover their operating expenses. She calculates institutional expenditures per student for several categories of library expenditures, equalizing those expenditures on a per student basis to minimize the effect of institutional size. She correlates expenditure data per student and retention rates. Mezick finds that library expenditures and professional staff correlate positively and significantly with student retention within certain categories of the Carnegie classification of institutions of higher education. Specifically, there are significant relationships between total library expenditures, total library materials expenditures, and serial expenditures at baccalaureate institutions. There is also a significant relationship between professional library staff and persistence at doctoral-granting institutions.[72]

## SOME RELEVANT WEB SITES AND SOFTWARE

*Hennen's American Public Library Ratings* (HAPLR; http://www.haplr-index. com/) ranks public libraries serving populations of more than 500,000 on fifteen input (expenditures per capita, percent budget to materials, materials expended per capita, FTE staff per 1,000 population, periodicals per 1,000 residents, and volumes per capita) and output metrics (cost per circulation, visits per capita, collection turnover, circulation per FTE staff hours, circulation per capita, reference per capita, circulation per hour, visits per hour, and circulation per visit). Additional Web pages at this site suggest other inputs, including direct spending per electronic use and direct spending per print use.

The European Commission is developing "a continuously updated database of statistics about library activities and associated costs in the context of their national economies. This project does not develop an index similar to the HAPLR-Index, however" (see http://www.cordis.lu/libraries/en/publib.html). Germany has the *BIX—The Library Index,* which is a partnership between Bertelsmann Publishing and the German library association: "The main difference between BIX and HAPLR . . . is that BIX was designed to provide comparisons of one library to another as well as over time. HAPLR compares all libraries to one another only during a given year" (see http://www.bertelsmann-stiftung.de/documents/Projekt_Info_Englisch_010112.pdf).

The Web site of the Texas State Library and Archives Commission, which covers outcomes, has links for:

- "Resources: Annotated links to online tools, publications, and websites, and bibliographies of print publications
- Contributed Examples: Outcomes measurement materials developed and contributed by library staff, identified by sample type (phase), by topic, and by library type. [View Examples] [Contribute Examples]
- Forum: Threaded discussion with your peers on topics related to outcome measurement in libraries. [View Postings] [Register to Post]
- FAQ: Frequently asked questions (and their answers)."[73]

The E-Metrics Discussion Project, funded by the Institute of Museum and Library Services, is intended to address the following goals: "provide education and training to the development, use, and implementation of selected e-metrics; provide tools that can be utilized in reporting selected e-metrics; conduct demonstrations on ways of reporting selected e-metrics and utilizing the results of e-metrics; share information regarding recent developments and activities related to selected e-metrics; and field test selected e-metrics as to their feasibility and applications in various library settings." Among its offerings is a downloadable e-metric annual report where libraries can insert data to show the value of their electronic resources and services, and selected e-metrics resources of interest and use.[74]

The Association of Research Libraries, as discussed in chapter 7, calculates an Expenditures-Focused Index (now called the ARL Library Investment Index) which comprises the five quantitative data elements among which member university libraries most resemble each other. The index, however, does not measure a library's services, quality of collections, or success in meeting the needs of users.[75]

There are efforts to develop online tools for collecting and reporting quantitative and qualitative data and to make comparisons among libraries. LibStats, developed by the University of Queensland Library, is one such tool that is available as open source software. It allows for customized implementation in other Australian university libraries and perhaps elsewhere.[76]

Finally, although dated, there was a D-Lib Working Group on Digital Library Metrics, which produced a series of interesting background papers (see http://www.dlib.org/metrics/public/metrics-documents.html). One of these authored by Ronald L. Larson, in 2002, mentions that "the range of potential metrics relating to digital libraries is immense." He goes on to discuss evaluation metrics for distributed digital libraries.[77]

## CONCLUSION

The LIS literature identifies and recommends different metrics for libraries to use and indicates how to collect relevant data. It also documents differences of opinion about the appropriate metrics to use. Some works illustrate how libraries can report results (in text, tables, or figures), and it is evident that libraries commonly use input and output metrics that reflect what they do. As Matthews indicates, "the use of performance measures [or other ones for that matter] is not an end in itself but rather a means to improve operations and services and for reporting to various stakeholders how much the library is used and how efficiently the library is operating."[78]

Peter Brophy recommends that qualitative approaches should not be forgotten when conducting evaluation or assessment research, and in selecting and applying relevant metrics. He focuses on two questions:

1.  How good is this library and its services?
2.  How much good does this library do?[79]

We would add a third question, "How well does the library support the institutional mission and serve as an effective partner and collaborator?" Qualitative approaches, such as those that Brophy describe, offer robust methods that complement quantitative data collection.

Regardless of the type of metrics collected and reported, it is important for librarians to explain how they use the results to improve the quality of service provided and to demonstrate accountability from the perspective of what matters to a stakeholder, be it resource allocation, library and resource use, or the impact or effect of using resources and services.

Felicity McGregor notes that evaluation and assessment occur in a political context and that librarians need "to demonstrate, more assertively than in the past, the value and relevance of the services they provide. Sustainability in the future may depend, not solely on the capacity to deliver relevant services, but on the capacity to demonstrate that libraries are of strategic importance in achieving the educational goals of universities" and other institutions and organizations.[80]

Finally, libraries engage in assessment to help their parent institutions demonstrate their accountability and improve their programs and services. In the case of higher education, the goal is to improve the learning process. As Victor M. H. Borden and Gary R. Pike note,

The accountability movement . . . has the potential of reducing collaboration among colleges and universities rather than increasing it. . . . [S]ome institutions are using the results of standardized accountability measures for marketing and public relations purposes, In effect, these institutions are saying that high value-added test scores imply that students who attend their institutions learn more than students who attend other institutions. To the extent that institutions use accountability measures in a win-lose rankings game, it is likely that they will decrease opportunities for collaboration and cooperation among institutions.[81]

An interesting question therefore becomes, "What metrics that a library might gather will assist an institution in its claim of competitive advantage over its peers?" Perhaps this question might be amended: Other than input data reflecting library holdings and expenditures,[82] what metrics that a library collects contribute to the reputation and competitive advantage of the institution as well as demonstrate the quality of the educational experience that students receive?

## NOTES

1. Joseph R. Matthews, *The Evaluation and Measurement of Library Services* (Westport, CT: Libraries Unlimited, 2007), 20. See also Joseph R. Matthews, *Measuring for Results: The Dimensions of Public Library Effectiveness* (Westport, CT: Libraries Unlimited, 2004).

2. Matthews, *The Evaluation and Measurement of Library Services,* 20. See also Matthews, *Measuring for Results.*

3. Texas State Library and Archives Commission, "Outcomes Measures." Available at http://www.tsl.state.tx.us/outcomes/ (accessed October 3, 2007).

4. U.S. Government Accountability Office, *Federal Contract Centers: Mechanism for Sharing Metrics and Oversight Practices,* GAO-06-270 (Washington, DC: Government Accountability Office, 2006). Available at http://www.gao.gov (accessed October 3, 2007).

5. U.S. Government Accountability Office, *Electronic Government: Initiatives Sponsored by the Office of Management and Budget Have Made Mixed Progress,* GAO-04-561T (Washington, DC: Government Accountability Office, 2004). Available at http://www.gao.gov (accessed October 3, 2007).

6. "Regulations.gov, the public face of the U.S. government's eRulemaking initiative, facilitates public participation in the federal regulatory process by improving the public's ability to find, view, and comment on federal regulatory actions. The initiative launched the first generation of *Regulations.gov* in January 2003 to provide the public with one-stop Web access to all proposed federal regulations and to give the public the ability to submit comments on all federal agencies' rulemakings." See http://www.regulations.gov/fdmspublic/component/main (accessed October 3, 2007).

7. U.S. National Partnership for Reinventing Government, *Balancing Measures: Best Practices in Performance Management* (Washington, DC: National Partnership for Reinventing Government, 1999). Available at http://govinfo.library.unt.edu/npr/library/papers/bkgrd/balmeasure.html (accessed October 7, 2007).

8. Deborah L. Goodall, "Performance Measurement: A Historical Perspective," *Journal of Librarianship* 20, no. 2 (April 1988), 140.

9. Ronald R. Powell, "The Relationship of Library User Studies to Performance Measures: A Review of the Literature," *Occasional Papers* No. 181 (Urbana-Champaign: University of Illinois, Graduate School of Library and Information Science, 1988), 3.

10. Martha Kyrillidou, "An Overview of Performance Measures in Higher Education and Libraries," *Journal of Library Administration* 35, no. 4 (2001): 7–18.

11. Some authors have documented this transformation to a digital and networked environment; see, for instance, Peter R. Young, "Electronic Services and Library Performance Measurement: A Definitional Challenge," a keynote presentation at the Fourth Northumbria International Conference on Performance Measurement in Libraries and Information Services: "Meaningful Measures for Emerging Realities," Pittsburgh, PA, August 13, 2001. Available at http://www.niso.org/committees/ay/Young_Northumbria_presentation_2001.pdf (accessed October 5, 2007).

12. Denise Troll Covey, *Usage and Usability Assessment: Library Practices and Concerns* (Washington, DC: Digital Library Federation and Council on Library and Information Resources, 2002).

13. Paul Basken, "Boeing to Rank Colleges by Measuring Graduates' Job Success," *The Chronicle of Higher Education* LV, no. 4 (September 19, 2008): A1, A16.

14. See, for instance, Jennifer Burell, "Performance Measures: Some New South Wales Experience," *APLIS* 3, no. 2 (June 1990): 81–91.

15. For background information, see John Carlo Bertot, "Libraries and Networked Information Services: Issues and Consideration in Measurement," *Performance Measurement and Metrics* 5, no. 1 (2004): 11–19.

16. EQUINOX, "Library Performance Measurement and Quality Management System: Performance Indicators for Electronic Library Services" (2000). Available at http://equinox.dcu.ie/reports/pilist.html (accessed October 3, 2007).

17. See International Federation of Library Associations. [Google™ search of Web site.] Available at http://www.google.com/custom?q=performance+measures+guidelines&safe=strict&sa=Google+Search&cof=GALT%3A%23CC0000%3BS%3Ahttp%3A%2F%2Fwww.ifla.org%3BVLC%3A%23366663%3BAH%3Aleft%3BBGC%3AWhite%3BLH%3A106%3BLC

%3A%23990000%3BL%3Ahttp%3A%2F%2Fwww.ifla.org%2Fimages%2Fiflas.gif%3BALC%3
A%23666699%3BLW%3A96%3BT%3A%23007B00%3BGIMP%3ARed%3BAWFID%3A4e
7b40884c7332ee%3B&domains=ifla.org&sitesearch=ifla.org (accessed October 6, 2007).

18. Council of Australian University Librarians, "Performance Indicators" (Canberra, ACT: Council of Australian University Librarians, 2007). Available at http://www.caul.edu.au/best-practice/PerfInd.html (accessed October 5, 2007).

19. See Philip Calvert and Rowena Cullen, "Performance Measurement in New Zealand Public Libraries: A Research Project," *APLIS* 5, no. 1 (March 1992): 3–13; Philip Calvert and Rowena Cullen, "The New Zealand Public Libraries Effectiveness Study and the New Zealand University Libraries Effectiveness Study," *Australian Academic & Research Libraries* 26 (June 1995): 97–106; Rowena Cullen and Philip Calvert, "New Zealand University Libraries Effectiveness Project: Dimensions and Concepts of Organizational Effectiveness," *Library & Information Science Research* 18 (Spring 1996): 99–119; Philip Calvert and Rowena Cullen, "Further Dimensions of Public Library Effectiveness II: The Second Stage of the New Zealand Study," *Library & Information Science Research* 16 (Spring 1994): 87–104.

20. American Library Association, Association of College and Research Libraries, *Information Literacy Competency Standards for Higher Education* (Chicago: American Library Association, 2000), available at http://www.ala.org/ala/acrl/acrlstandards/informationliteracycompetency.cfm (accessed October 14, 2007); American Library Association, Association of College and Research Libraries, *Objectives for Information Literacy Instruction: A Model Statement for Academic Librarians* (Chicago: American Library Association, 2001), available at http://www.ala.org/ala/acrl/acrlstandards/objectivesinformation.cfm (accessed October 14, 2007); American Library Association, Association of College and Research Libraries, *Information Literacy Standards for Science and Engineering/Technology* (Chicago: American Library Association, 2006), available at http://www.ala.org/ala/acrl/acrlstandards/infolitscitech.cfm (accessed October 14, 2007); American Library Association, Association of College and Research Libraries, *Information Literacy Standards for Anthropology and Sociology Students* (Chicago: American Library Association, 2008), available at http://www.ala.org/ala/acrl/acrlstandards/anthro_soc_standards.cfm (accessed April 4, 2008); American Library Association, Association of College and Research Libraries, *Political Science Research Competency Guidelines Students* (Chicago: American Library Association, 2008), available at http://www.ala.org/ala/mgrps/divs/acrl/standards/PoliSciGuide.pdf (accessed January 21, 2009).

21. Sara Laughlin and Ray W. Wilson, *The Quality Library: A Guide to Staff-driven Improvement, Better Efficiency, and Happier Customers* (Chicago: American Library Association, 2008).

22. Rowena Cullen, "Measure for Measure: A Post Modern Critique of Performance Measurement in Libraries and Information Services," ERIC ED 434 664 (ERIC Full Text, http://www.eric.ed.gov/ERICWebPortal/custom/portlets/recordDetails/detailmini.jsp?_nfpb=true&_&ERICExtSearch_SearchValue_0=ED434664&ERICExtSearch_SearchType_0=eric_accno&accno=ED434664) (accessed October 5, 2007).

23. Neal Kaske, "Choosing the Best Tools for Evaluating Your Library," Library Assessment Conference (2006). Available at http://www.nclis.gov/statsurv/presentations/ChoosingtheBestToolsforYourEvaluation8-28-6.pdf (accessed January 31, 2008).

24. See, for instance, Martha Kyrillidou, "From Input and Output Measures to Quality and Outcome Measures, or, from the User in the Life of the Library to the Library in the Life of the User." Available at http://www.arl.org/bm~doc/jal01.pdf (accessed January 31, 2008). She discusses different evaluation models and shows that the terms are still evolving.

25. John Carlo Bertot and Charles R. McClure, "Outcomes Assessment in the Networked Environment: Research Questions, Issues, Considerations, and Moving Forward," *Library Trends* 51, no. 4 (Spring 2003), 599–600.

26. See Peter Hernon and Robert E. Dugan, *An Action Plan for Outcomes Assessment in Your Library* (Chicago: American Library Association, 2002); Peter Hernon and Robert E.

Dugan, *Outcomes Assessment in Higher Education* (Westport, CT: Libraries Unlimited, 2004); Peter Hernon, Robert E. Dugan, and Candy Schwartz, *Revisiting Outcomes Assessment in Higher Education* (Westport, CT: Libraries Unlimited, 2006).

27. Matthews, *Measuring for Results,* 109–10.

28. Charles R. McClure and Paul T. Jaeger, *Public Libraries and Internet Service Roles: Measuring and Maximizing Internet Services* (Chicago: American Library Association, 2009), 90.

29. Stephen Town, "Academic Library Performance, Quality and Evaluation in the UK and Europe." Available at http://www.libqual.org/documents/admin/StephenGreecePaper.doc (accessed October 12, 2007).

30. John B. Harer, *Performance Measures of Quality for Academic Libraries Implementing Continuous Quality Improvement Programs: A Delphi Study,* Ph.D. diss. (College Station, TX: Texas A&M University, 2001), AAT 30117718. Available from *Dissertations & Theses: Full Text* (accessed February 23, 2008). For a discussion of the Baldrige award, see *The Baldrige National Quality Program: Education Criteria for Performance Excellence* (Gaithersburg, MD: National Institute of Standards and Technology, 2007).

31. Enid R. Causey, *Impact of Assessment of Institutional Effectiveness on Academic Libraries in South Carolina,* Ph.D. diss. (Columbia, SC: University of South Carolina, 1992), AAT 9239025. Available from *Dissertations & Theses: Full Text* (accessed February 2, 2008).

32. John E. Evans, *Cost Analysis of Public Services in Academic Libraries,* Ed.D. (Memphis, TN: Memphis State University, 1989), AAT 9004345. Available from *Dissertations & Theses: Full Text* (accessed February 2, 2008).

33. Susan E. Higgins, *A Study of the Effectiveness of Public Library Service to Young Adults,* Ph.D. diss. (Tallahassee, FL: The Florida State University, 1992), AAT 9306058. Available from *Dissertations & Theses: Full Text* (accessed February 2, 2008).

34. Patricia A. Lund, *An Investigation of the Use of Performance Measures in Public Libraries: An Application of the Locke Goal Setting Theory,* Ph.D. diss. (Madison, WI: The University of Wisconsin, 1990), AAT 9030802. Available from *Dissertations & Theses: Full Text* (accessed February 2, 2008).

35. John B. Harer and Bryan R. Cole, "The Importance of the Stakeholder in Performance Measurement: Critical Processes and Performance Measures for Assessing and Improving Academic Library Services and Programs," *College & Research Libraries* 66, no. 2 (March 2005), 150.

36. See Association of Research Libraries, http://www.arl.org/search/searchresults.shtml?cx=010838847903982444204%3Ah0iuju_wvse&q=northumbria&cof=FORID%3A11&sa.x=5&sa.y=7#1097 (accessed October 5, 2007); Association of Research Libraries, "Issues in Research Libraries Measurement," *ARL: A Bimonthly Report,* no. 197 (Washington, DC: Association of Research Libraries, 1998). Available at http://www.arl.org/resources/pubs/br/br197.shtml.

37. Roswitha Poll, "The Cat's Py[a]jamas? Performance Indicators for National Libraries," *Performance Measurement and Metrics* 9, no. 2 (2008): 110–17.

38. Nancy A. Van House, "Output Measures in Libraries," *Library Trends* 38, no. 2 (Fall 1989): 269–79.

39. Curtis L. Kendrick, "Performance Measures of Shelving Accuracy," *The Journal of Academic Librarianship* 17, no. 1 (1991): 16–18.

40. Joan Stein, "Measuring the Performance of ILL and Document Supply, 1986 to 1998," *Performance Measurement and Metrics* 2, no. 1 (2001): 11–72.

41. Steve Hiller, "Measure by Measure: Assessing the Viability of the Physical Library," *The Bottom Line* 17, no. 4 (2004), 126.

42. Peter T. Shepherd and Denise M. Davis," Electronic Metrics, Performance Measures, and Statistics for Publishers and Libraries: Building Common Ground and Standards," *portal: Libraries and the Academy* 2, no. 4 (October 2002): 659–63.

43. Angela Conyers, "Building on Sand? Using Statistical Measures to Assess the Impact of Electronic Services," *Performance Measurement and Metrics* 7, no. 1 (2006): 37.

44. Andrew Booth, "Counting What Counts: Performance Measurement and Evidence-based Practice," *Performance Measurement and Metrics* 7, no. 2 (2006): 63–74.

45. Wanda V. Dole, Anne Liebst, and Jitka M. Hurych, "Using Performance Measurement for Decision Making in Mid-sized Academic Libraries," *Performance Measurement and Metrics* 7, no. 3 (2006): 173–84.

46. Donald W. King, Peter B. Boyce, Carol H. Montgomery, and Carol Tenopir, "Library Economic Metrics: Examples of the Comparison of Electronic and Print Journal Collections and Collection Services (Academic Libraries)," *Library Trends* 51, no. 3 (Winter 2003): 376–405.

47. Robert E. Dugan and Peter Hernon, "Outcomes Assessment: Not Synonymous with Inputs and Outputs," *Journal of Academic Librarianship* 28, no. 6 (November 2002): 376–80.

48. Andrew Breidenbaugh, "Budget Planning and Performance Measures for Virtual Reference Services," *The Reference Librarian* 46, no. 95 (2006): 113–24.

49. Roswitha Poll, "Standardized Measures in the Changing Information Environment," *Performance Measurement and Metrics* 7, no. 3 (2006): 127–41.

50. Martha Kyrillidou and Sarah Giersch, "Qualitative Analysis of Association of Research Libraries' E-metrics Participant Feedback about the Evolution of Measures for Networked Electronic Resources," *The Library Quarterly* 74, no. 4 (2004): 423–40.

51. Steve Thornton, "Two Years of Impact Assessment," *Performance Measurement and Metrics* 1, no. 3 (2000): 147–56.

52. Debbie Schachter, "Performance Measures for Information Centers," *Information Outlook* 9, no. 8 (August 2005): 8–9.

53. Betty Reifsnyder and Charles R. McClure, "Performance Measures for Corporate Information Centers," *Special Libraries* 75, no. 3 (1984): 193–204.

54. *Corporate Library Benchmarks* (2009 Edition) (New York: Primary Research Group, 2009). This same publisher also produces a survey of academic and special libraries; there is a 2006–2007 edition.

55. Eileen G. Abels, Keith W. Cogdill, and Lisl Zach, "Identifying and Communicating the Contributions of Library and Information Services in Hospitals and Academic Health Science Centers," *JMA* [*Journal of the Medical Library Association*] 92, no. 1 (January 2004). Available at http://www.pubmedcentral.nih.gov/articlerender.fcgi?artid=314102 (accessed February 1, 2008).

56. Evelyn H. Daniel, "Performance Measures for School Librarians: Complexities and Potential," in *Advances in Librarianship* 6, edited by M. J. Voigt and M. H. Harris (New York: Academic Press, 1976), 1–51.

57. Esther Dyer and Daniel O'Connor, "The Library Quotient: Evaluating School Media Centres," *Information and Library Manager* 2, no. 3 (December 1982): 82–88.

58. Frances B. Bradburn, *Output Measures for School Media Center Programs* (Englewood, CO: Libraries Unlimited, 1999).

59. U.S. Government Printing Office, "Library Services and Content Management Performance Metrics." Available at http://www.access.gpo.gov/su_docs/fdlp/metrics/index.html (accessed February 1, 2008).

60. See Robert S. Kaplan and David P. Norton, *The Balanced Scorecard* (Boston: Harvard Business School Press, 1996).

61. George Valiris and Panagiotis Chytas, "Making Decisions Using the Balanced Scorecard and the Simple Multi-attribute Rating Technique," *Performance Measurement and Metrics* 6, no. 3 (2006), 165.

62. For a discussion of the library's use of the balanced scorecard, see, for instance, James Self, "Metrics and Management: Applying the Results of the Balanced Scorecard," *Performance Measurement and Metrics* 5, no. 3 (2004): 101–05; James Self, "From Values to Metrics: Implementation of the Balanced Scorecard at a University Library," *Performance Measurement and Metrics* 4, no. 2 (2003): 57–63; University of Virginia Library, "Balanced

Scorecard at UVa Library" (Charlottesville VA: University of Virginia Library, 2007), available at http://www.lib.virginia.edu/bsc/ (accessed October 11, 2007).

63. Joseph R. Matthews, *Scorecard for Results: A Guide for Developing a Library Balanced Scorecard* (Westport, CT: Libraries Unlimited, 2008).

64. Roswitha Poll, "Performance, Processes and Costs: Managing Service Quality with the Balanced Scorecard," *Library Trends* 49, no. 4 (Spring 2001): 709–17.

It merits mention that the balanced scorecard has also been used in other countries. See, for instance, Nicholas Davis, *Applying Theoretical Perspectives to the Balanced Scorecard* (Wagga Wagga, NSW: Faculty of Commerce, Charles Sturt University, 2006).

65. Stephen Town, "E-measures: A Comprehensive Waste of Time?" *VINE* 34, no. 4 (2004): 190–95. It merits mention that in other writings he recounts various activities in which SCONUL is engaged.

66. See, for instance, Peter T. Shepherd, "COUNTER: Usage Statistics for Performance Measurement," *Performance Measurement and Metrics* 7, no. 3 (2006): 142–52. For additional information, see the COUNTER Web site, http://www.projectcounter.org/; U.S. Library of Congress, "The ARL E-Metrics Projects: Counting and Evaluating the Use of Electronic Resources" (Washington, DC: Library of Congress, 2004), available at http://www.loc.gov/acq/conser/emetrics.html (accessed October 14, 2007).

67. Deborah D. Blecic, Joan B. Fiscella, and Stephen E. Wiberley, Jr., "Measurement of Use of Electronic Resources: Advances in Use of Statistics and Innovations in Resource Functionality," *College & Research Libraries* 68, no.1 (January 2007): 26–44.

68. Coopers & Lybrand, *Valuing the Economic Costs and Benefits of Libraries* (Wellington, New Zealand: New Zealand Library & Information Association, 1996), 3. See also Judy Luther, "University Investment in the Library: What's the Return? A Case Study at the University of Illinois at Urbana-Champaign," *LibraryConnect* (San Diego, CA: Elsevier, 2008), available at http://libraryconnect.elsevier.com/whitepapers/0108/lcwp (accessed May 14, 2008). This work contains a selected bibliography of other writings on the topic of return on investment. See *LibraryConnect Newsletter,* 6, no. 1 (January 2008), which covers "Information Valuation," available at http://libraryconnect.elsevier.com/lcn/0601/lcn0601.pdf (accessed May 14, 2008).

69. Jennifer Ellis-Newman, "Activity-based Costing in User Services of an Academic Library," *Library Trends* 51, no. 3 (Winter 2003): 335. For a discussion, albeit a dated one, of Internet costs and cost models for public libraries, see Charles R. McClure, John Carlo Bertot, and John C. Beachboard, *Internet Costs and Cost Models for Public Libraries: Final Report* (Washington, DC: National Commission on Libraries and Information Science; GPO, 1995).

70. Stephen R. Lawrence, Lynn S. Connaway, and Keith H. Brigham, "Life Cycle Costs of Library Collections: Creation of Effective Performance and Cost Metrics for Library Resources," *College & Research Libraries* 62, no. 6 (November 2001): 541–53.

71. Wonsik Shim, "Applying DEA Technique to Library Evaluation in Academic Research Libraries (Academic Libraries) (Data Envelopment Analysis)," *Library Trends* 51, no. 3 (Winter 2003): 312–33.

72. Elizabeth M. Mezick, "Return on Investment: Libraries and Student Retention," *The Journal of Academic Librarianship* 33, no. 5 (2007): 561–66.

73. Texas State Library and Archives Commission, "Outcomes Measures." See also North Carolina State University, University Planning & Analysis, *Internet Resources for Higher Education Outcomes Assessment* (Raleigh, NC: North Carolina State University, 2007). Available at http://www2.acs.ncsu.edu/UPA/assmt/resource.htm (accessed October 6, 2007).

74. E-metrics Instructional System, http://www.ii.fsu.edu/emis/index.cfm (accessed January 6, 2009).

75. Association of Research Libraries, "ARL Index" (Washington, DC: Association of Research Libraries, 2007). Available at http://www.arl.org/stats/index/ (accessed October 15, 2007).

76. Elizabeth Jordan, "LibStats: An Open Source Online Tool for Collecting and Reporting Statistics in an Academic Library," *Performance Measurement and Metrics* 9, no. 1 (2008): 18–25.

77. See Ronald L. Larson, "The DLib Test Suite and Metrics Working Group: Harvesting the Experience from the Digital Library Initiative." Available at http://www.dlib.org/metrics/public/papers/The_Dlib_Test_Suite_and_Metrics.pdf (accessed December 15, 2008).

78. Matthews, *The Evaluation and Measurement of Library Services,* 332.

79. Peter Brophy, "Telling the Story: Qualitative Approaches to Measuring the Performance of Emerging Library Services," *Performance Measurement and Metrics* 9, no. 1 (2008): 7–17.

80. Felicity McGregor, "Performance Measures, Benchmarking, and Value." Available at http://conferences.alia.org.au/alia2000/proceedings/felicity.mcgregor.html; http://ro.uow.edu.au/cgi/viewcontent.cgi?article=1028&context=asdpapers (accessed October 4, 2007).

81. Victor M. H. Borden and Gary R. Pike, "Sharing Responsibility for Student Learning," in *Assessing and Accounting for Student Learning: Beyond the Spellings Commission,* edited by Victor M. H. Borden and Gary R. Pike, New Directions for Institutional Research [Series]; Assessment Supplement (San Francisco, CA: Jossey-Bass, 2007), 87.

82. See John C. Hayek, "A Student-centered Approach for Identifying High-performing Colleges and Universities" Ph.D. diss. (Bloomington, IN: Indiana University, 2001), AAT 3024295, available from *Dissertations & Theses: Full Text* (accessed February 2, 2008); Sharon Weiner, "Library Quality and Impact: Is There a Relationship between New Measures and Traditional Measures?" *The Journal of Academic Librarianship* 31, no. 5 (2005): 432–37; Sharon Weiner, "The Contribution of the Library to the Reputation of a University," *The Journal of Academic Librarianship* 35, no. 1 (2009): 3–13.

# 3

ASSESSMENT AND EVALUATION

Institutions of higher education have assessed and evaluated their operations, programs, and services for years. They have selectively reported qualitative and quantitative information, based on the use of metrics, to internal and external stakeholders. A multiplicity of those stakeholders demand that institutions be more accountable and transparent about their income and costs, endowments, and effectiveness concerning if, and what, students learn so that they can succeed in a global-influenced environment, one facing challenges associated with social, cultural, and economic issues.

There is much debate about the values of the metrics that institutions use as evidence for assessment and evaluation: demonstrating accountability and showing the extent of success in meeting their missions. Such evidence is often anecdotal and does not provide reliable and valid insights of effectiveness.[1] Charles Miller, chairman of the Department of Education's Commission on the Future of Higher Education (also known as the Spellings Commission), publicly stated that most institutions of higher education "are not using data-driven assessments to improve their teaching, and their accreditors are not forcing them to do so."[2] Arguing for institutional autonomy and having to collect and report standardized metrics, Judith S. Eaton, president of the Council for Higher Education Accreditation, an association of degree-granting colleges and universities that recognizes sixty institutional and programmatic accrediting organizations, prefers that "judgments about how effective an institution is, or the success of students, need to be driven by the institution based upon criteria the institution deems appropriate."[3]

As a past practice, institutions of higher education and their academic libraries have compiled and provided data concerning inputs and outputs, and have engaged more in evaluation than in assessment (this chapter clarifies the difference between both terms). Both institutions and their libraries have emphasized processes and inputs as means for determining outcomes and quality. They assumed the education that students received is of high quality if the faculty know their subject area or if the library keeps adding volumes to its collection.

Institutions of higher education, in fact, might apply assessment and evaluation processes and practices to issues of efficiency, effectiveness, and performance, with the purpose of:

- learning about their current status and that of their suborganizations
- measuring progress toward meeting a stated standard, benchmark, or objective
- compiling, reviewing, analyzing, and reporting the findings from an evaluation and assessment project
- guiding changes that improve their operations, programs, and services

To stakeholders wanting greater accountability, assessment and evaluation measure how the institution, college or school, program, or course adds value to the education and experience that students receive and prepares them for future careers.

This chapter, which amplifies on the background outlined here, discusses assessment and evaluation for the institution and its academic library. Although the results from collecting evidence might inform external stakeholders, this chapter focuses on institutional and organizational processes to meet internal needs and use.

## THE INSTITUTION

Various stakeholders emphasize the need for a college educated workforce to appreciate lifelong learning and to benefit the organizations for which they work. Although increasing tuition costs limit access to higher education for some, other issues (e.g., anecdotal evidence suggesting that graduates are unprepared for the challenges of the workplace in a global setting) persist. As a consequence, some stakeholders question the value of gaining a college education. For instance, parents of prospective students, the students themselves, state and federal government officials, taxpayers without a direct involvement, and employers are asking institutions of higher education for more information, especially comparative data, concerning costs and the results promised in the institutional mission and other documentation they receive. Institutions can meet the rising expectations of stakeholders by providing more information about how they accommodate information requests, demonstrate transparency, and respond to calls for increased accountability.

Institutional characteristics remain important to parents of prospective students. Those characteristics include the size and diversity of the student body, academic reputation (as documented in rankings found in commercial reports such as those sold by U.S. News and World Report), the faculty's academic credentials, and the size of library collections and of institutional endowments. When institutions of higher education report these characteristics they normally do so in the form of inputs and outputs. Two basic inputs are simple indicators of quantity, namely the number of students admitted and reflections on academic performance: average performance on the SAT Reasoning Test (formerly the Scholastic Aptitude Test and Scholastic Assessment Test) and the ACT, average high school grade point average (GPA), the number of National Merit Scholars, the number of high school students who have advanced standing (e.g., coursework completed at the college level or have taken advanced placement courses, or are academically ready to accelerate study at the college level), and institutional admissions yield rate (percentage of students accepted who actually enroll). Two basic types of outputs indicate quantity (e.g., the number of degrees awarded) or quality (e.g., average student performance on graduate and professional school admissions tests such as the Graduate Record Examination (GRE), Graduate Management Admission Test® (GMAT®), or the Law School Admission Test (LSAT); performance on licensure examinations; and the percentage of students who have jobs after graduation).[4]

Quality output metrics are not representative of the entire student population. Only students planning to enter graduate school or seek a professional degree (e.g., business or law) take one of the above-mentioned tests. An example of student quality as an output was raised in a 2006 report from the Educational Testing Service (ETS). That report points out that two graduating students from two institutions majored in economics and received baccalaureate degrees. The question arises, "What do they know?" More specifically,

- Do they have the same knowledge of economics?
- Are they both ready to enter the workforce?
- What type of engagement did they have with their college experience?
- What types of soft skills (e.g., the ability to work in teams) do they have?[5]

Complementary to metrics that might accompany these questions are the inputs and outputs that institutions and third parties collect and make available. These data relate to:

- tuition and fees
- total number of students enrolled
- acceptance rate for those making formal application
- student to faculty ratio
- average number of students in a class
- number of library books

Additionally, data that stakeholders appreciate but that are not all readily available include:

- financial aid provided
- average debt related to educational expenses when a student graduates
- graduation rate
- retention rate

The data derived from inputs and outputs of institutional counts and student performance provide contextual data for stakeholders, but they do not give them an adequate basis for accountability. For instance, the data reveal little, if anything, about what students learn. Institutions of higher education also need to demonstrate cost-effectiveness, improvements in institutional performance and productively, educational effectiveness through the use of student learning outcomes, and what the stakeholders receive for the education dollars expended.[6]

## The Differences between Assessment and Evaluation

The terms *assessment* and *evaluation* are often used interchangeably in a multiplicity of measurement contexts: in different programs and disciplines and in their respective literatures; and in practice. These terms do not represent identical processes. Assessment is a process-oriented, cyclical activity involving the collection of information and appraisal data to measure or otherwise gauge progress toward an identified standard or other benchmark. Assessment, which precedes evaluation, can be formal and deploy standardized and normed tests, or can be informal and ongoing. Assessment uses the data and information gathered to provide feedback in order to identify and make needed changes and improvements.

Evaluation is the product-oriented process of interpreting the information and data that were collected and analyzed during assessment; estimating the overall value or worth of a policy, project, program, or service; and/or determining if established standards or benchmarks have been met. Evaluation involves the interpretation of the evidence gathered against some framework, and it involves making judgment calls and applying those decisions operationally and to planning. There are three types of evaluation: diagnostic (locate or otherwise identify problems), formative (improve ongoing programs), and summative (review a completed program).

## Institutional Assessment Process

Assessment is a process of measuring efficiency, effectiveness, and performance to learn if an institution achieves its stated mission and goals. The institutional mission serves as the starting place for an institution's organizations to formulate goals and outcomes. Relevant information is gathered, and the interpretation and analysis of evidence provide insights into the congruence between the institution's stated mission, purposes, and objectives, and the actual outcomes expounded by institutional programs and activities. Assessment findings inform decision making and guide strategic planning at the organizational and institutional levels. As an ongoing process, assessment activities are applied to measure progress, guarantee that progress is sustained, and ensure that the changes and improvements implemented are effective. Findings are conveyed to the various stakeholders in a multiplicity of formats and channels and in an understandable manner.

Stakeholders want to be assured that the institution, college or school, program, or course adds value to a student's education and experience. To support accountability and to meet the information requirements of stakeholders, student learning, its measurement and improvement, is the primary focus of assessment in higher education.[7] Other outcomes may help institutions to become more efficient and effective or improve their operations.

## The Institutional Mission Statement

Assessment and evaluation are based foremost at the institutional level, and they begin with the institution's mission statement. Those statements inform various stakeholders (e.g., students and their parents, institutional staff, governmental officials, accreditation organizations, alumni, and employers) about the institution's goals, and how those goals will be achieved. Consequently, the institutional mission statement provides the educational emphasis and strategic direction for the institution, thus enabling stakeholders to differentiate one institution from another.[8]

Many stakeholders view the mission statement as the stated identity and educational focus of the institution; the mission, in very general terms, indicates what the institution will teach and students will learn. The statement, which is publicized and visible, identifies goals and outcomes for student learning, nonlearning goals and impacts (e.g., being a good community member), and a means for institutional improvement. The common components of mission statements are: purpose, values, and the description of skills. The overall purpose captures the identity or personality of the institution and differentiates an institution from its competitors. Institutional values, beliefs, or intent are generated, in part, from institutional characteristics (e.g., public or private, large or small, urban or rural, and secular or faith-based). The mission informs others that the institution values teaching over research (or vice versa, or both equally) and about moral beliefs.

Mission statements are often created through collaborative participation that involves external and internal stakeholders, and they are periodically reviewed to reflect the institution as it moves forward. These reviews may occur as the institution prepares its self-study for accreditation or as a starting place for the revision of a long-term strategic plan. A mission statement exists for years; its purpose and values reflect the rationale for the institution's origin and continued existence. The statement should outlive a succession of administrations. Expected student learning outcomes, and how they will be accomplished, however, might be revised periodically as the educational context changes and content evolves, and as pedagogy undergoes transformation as a result of a deeper understanding of how students learn. Figure 3.1 illustrates how the institutional mission statement and those of academic and organizational units inform stakeholders about the uniqueness of the institution as well as its educational goals.

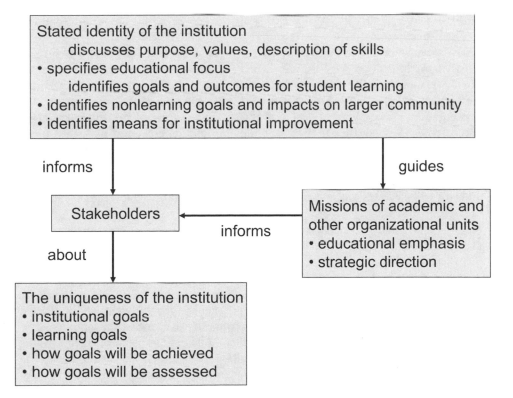

Figure 3.1 Institutional Mission Statement Informs Stakeholders

## Institutional General Education Goals

The broad educational and learning goals stated in the institutional mission statement can be restated as general education goals. These goals identify student learning outcomes and are statements of values, and the knowledge and skills that students are expected to learn, achieve, or experience. Those goals are accompanied by measurable objectives and an identification of assessment tools; such details are not usually found in an institutional mission statement. Because a multiplicity of programs within a degree level (e.g., bachelor's, master's, or professional) share general education goals, these goals are often developed by committees comprising faculty from a variety of programs and disciplines, institutional administrators, as well as other internal and external institutional stakeholders. Common general educational goals and outcomes are concerned with written, oral, and electronic communication; ethics and ethical behavior; critical thinking and analysis; problem solving; information competence; social responsibility; cultural legacies; and morals and pluralism.

## College, Program, and Course Objectives

Learning occurs at any time in any place. Within the environment of higher education, however, the classroom and course content comprise one of the most important learning areas. The classroom can be the traditional on-campus brick and mortar; it can be a conference room in a hotel, or it can be the one-to-one classroom of a student in front of a networked computer workstation. In any physical or electronic environment, the course syllabus, the framework which also serves as the basis for differentiating one course from another, drives course content and topic presentation.

The specific learning outcomes at the course level are derived from program and departmental missions, which support the institutional mission. The departmental mission statement is the starting place for faculty creating as well as assessing course education goals and objectives. Developed primarily by departmental faculty, the departmental mission is an extension of the college statement of purpose, the goals identified in the institutional mission statement, and general education curriculum goals. These goals specify the purpose of the major or program within the overall college context and clarify the contribution of the major or program to the institution. They state the ongoing educational outcomes of the major or program and identify knowledge, skills, attitudes, behaviors, values, and achievements expected of students in the program or department. Program outcomes, which are more focused, support the institutional education goals as well as those from program and professional accrediting bodies (e.g., American Psychological Association, American Chemical Society, and AACSB International [business]).

Supporting the departmental mission statement and its goals, course objectives are measurable, attainable, and outcome or result oriented rather than comprising statements of process. Objectives or outcomes are framed as "what will be the result" rather than "what will happen in the course." These objectives, prepared by the faculty member, should be stated on the course syllabus. Figure 3.2 illustrates how the institutional mission statement influences general education goals; the college, program, and departmental mission statements; and program and course objectives.

INSTITUTIONAL MISSION STATEMENT ESTABLISHES:

- Broad Education and Learning Goals
- Research and Service Goals

↓

GENERAL EDUCATION GOALS

- Student Learning Goals and Objectives
  - values, knowledge, and skills
    + written, oral, and electronic communications
    + ethics
    + critical thinking; analysis, and problem solving
    + information competence
    + social responsibility
    + cultural legacies
    + morals and pluralism
  - measurable learning objectives
  - identifies assessment tools to be applied

↓

COLLEGE, PROGRAM, AND DEPARTMENTAL MISSION STATEMENTS

- Create educational goals and objectives supporting General Education goals
- Provides purpose of major or program
- Identifies desired knowledge, skills, attitudes, behavior, values, and achievements

↓

PROGRAM AND COURSE OBJECTIVES

- Place of delivery of educational content (e.g., in a classroom, virtually)
- Syllabus identifies specific learning objectives to be achieved
- Tools are applied to assess learning

Figure 3.2   Institutional Mission Statement and Educational Goals

## Conducting Institutional Assessment

Assessment is a process that helps to determine whether or not the institution meets its goals as stated in the mission statement. Institutional assessment includes measures of aggregate outcomes as well as learning outcomes, the performance and impact of institutional and organizational programs and services, and nonlearning goals (e.g., contributing positively to the local economy or being a good community member).

Assessment is cyclical whereas evaluation is not. For example, assessment processes can be applied to student learning. As such, the goal of assessment is not to determine the success or failure of an individual student or faculty member in a specific course. Rather, it provides insights into whether general education and program-based curricula produce student success as identified in the mission statements—those of the institution, department, or program. Assessment identifies successes upon which to build and deficiencies to overcome. The assessment of student learning provides the tools and opportunity to help the institution achieve its education goals. Evaluation applies to a system and examines whether the assessment process measures the objectives as intended: yes or no, or successfully or unsuccessfully.

Efficiency, a measure of workload, may determine the level to which inputs (e.g., time and money) produce outputs (e.g., the number of applications for student financial aid reviewed). Effectiveness measures the extent to which a desired result, impact, benefit, or outcome is achieved. Efficiency and effectiveness are important evaluation concepts for institutions and their suborganizations. As previously stated, however, higher education has successfully measured efficiency for years, and, while effectiveness metrics have also been compiled for a long time, many stakeholders want to know about student learning as an outcome, and they view it as a key part of institutional effectiveness. Additionally, while efficiency is measured most often by counts, institutional effectiveness is measured, in part, through tangible evidence such as audited budget statements, the existence and content of institutional handbooks, and enrollment data; records and reports of activities and compliance with local, state, and federal requirements as well as those from accreditation organizations; and surveys of satisfaction, usage, perceptions and attitudes, and confidence. Furthermore, institutional effectiveness requires a clear articulation of purpose and objectives, ongoing measurement of learning and nonlearning objectives, and continuous efforts to gather evidence that leads to improved programs and services.[9]

Assessment at the institutional level might focus on:

- nonstudent outcomes and the characterization of effectiveness in terms of reputation for innovation or for institutional good will as viewed by geo-political community members
- efficiency in internal processes as reflected, for instance, in responding to alumni requests for transcripts in a stated number of hours or days
- aggregate student outcomes (e.g., persistence and retention rates as well as graduation rates and employment within a student's chosen field)
- students who apply and enroll and their characterization, for instance, by average SAT scores and local information (e.g., town/city, and state)
- learning environments including general education and discipline education curricula as reflected in department- or major-based programmatic and curriculum outcomes; ongoing use of rating forms and surveys (at the time vs. long term); student learning outcomes using formulative and summative assessments; and learning how the institution, college or school, program, course adds value to a student's college education and experience.[10]

Institutional evaluation, on the other hand, reviews and judges assessment as a system, asking if assessment processes do what they intend to do. Evaluation addresses such questions as:

- Is the assessment process aligned with the institutional mission? Does it contain clearly articulated institutional and organizational goals that encompass all programs, services, and initiatives? Are the goals and programs appropriately integrated with each other?
- Do statements at the institutional, program, and course level clearly state expected student learning outcomes?

- Are educational goals at the program level appropriately integrated with the broader goals that address institutional learning outcomes? Are the goals consonant with the institution's mission and with the standards of the relevant disciplines?

- To what extent does the institution employ a well-documented, organized, systematic, and sustained assessment process to review and improve student learning?

- Do the multiple qualitative and quantitative metrics used clearly relate to program or institutional goals? Does the assessment of student learning include direct evidence of student learning?

- Are the assessment metrics of sufficient quality (reliable and valid) that the results truly inform decisions?

- Are departmental assessment plans based on departmental missions and goals? Do those missions and goals align with the overall institutional mission and goals?[11]

Stakeholders want institutions of higher education to provide information concerning their operations and the value added to the students' educational experiences, and they want that information stated and arranged so that it is comparable with other educational institutions. Often-used comparative metrics include tuition and fees; financial aid distributed; the number of students who applied, were admitted, and actually enrolled (yield rate); graduation rates; and success rates of students finding employment in their desired fields.

Three metrics relate to the value added by the institution and its suborganizations to the experience that students gain in college: the measured competencies they possess before college and after college, and the measure of change between these competencies.[12]

*Assessment Tools.* Institutions often turn to large-scale assessment tools when they engage in institutional assessment. While some of these tools are institutionally developed, national assessment tools are also applied. Based upon information from The Voluntary System of Accountability, the national assessment tools used as part of their College Portrait program rely on student experiences and perceptions to provide a snapshot of the student body attending a particular college or university.[13] The premise is that the characteristics associated with student engagement serve as a proxy for quality. For example, the level of challenge and time that students spend on a task are positively correlated to persistence and subsequent success in college. Another conclusion of the body of research is that the degree to which students are engaged in their studies impacts directly on the quality of learning and the overall educational experience.[14]

Student engagement surveys include the College Student Experiences Questionnaire (CSEQ, http://cseq.iub.edu/cseq_generalinfo.cfm), the College Senior Survey (CSS, http://www.gseis.ucla.edu/heri/cssoverview.php), the National Survey of Student Engagement (NSSE, http://nsse.iub.edu/index.cfm), and the University of California Undergraduate Student Experience Survey (UCUES, http://www.universityofcalifornia.edu/studentsurvey/about/history.html).

Student learning outcomes examine gains, for instance, in critical thinking (including analytic reasoning) and written communication by using instruments such as the Collegiate Assessment of Academic Proficiency (CAAP, http://www.act.org/caap/), Measure of Academic Proficiency and Progress (MAPP, http://www.ets.org/portal/site/ets/menuitem.1488512ecfd5b8849a77b13bc3921509/?vgnextoid=ff3aaf5e44df4010VgnVCM10000022f95190RCRD&vgnextchannel=f9

8546f1674f4010VgnVCM10000022f95190RCRD), and Collegiate Learning Assessment (CLA, http://www.cae.org/content/pro_collegiate.htm). Each institution determines the release of the findings because the institution owns the information compiled and analyzed from these instruments.

## Conducting College, Program, and Course Assessment

When assessment focuses on student learning outcomes, it is carried out at the college or school, program, or course level. The assessment effort includes the development of an assessment plan, undertaking the assessment, and analyzing and using the findings. The development of college or school, program, or course assessment plans begin with developing a mission statement that, in part, is based on the institutional mission and the identified goals for general education learning. Once student learning goals are identified, faculty craft specific and measurable objectives and outcomes. Learning objectives are stated in terms of what students will know or be able to do, and those objectives are directly connected to the general education curriculum and related core competencies. Additionally, there is a distinction between learning goals and outcomes for a particular time (a course) and learning outcomes over time, such as students appreciating the need for life-long learning. Assessment tools might include supportive details such as timelines, rubrics, and an identification of who is responsible for conducting the assessment.

The gathering of evidence might rely on national or locally developed tests, papers and projects, and portfolio evaluation. When such methods provide insights into what students actually learned, they are known as direct methods. On the other hand, when data collection recounts self-reported perceptions, it is necessary to draw inferences and to rely on indirect methods of gathering evidence, especially student satisfaction surveys, exit interviews, focus group interviews, and, surveys of alumni and employers. It is likely that a mixture of direct and indirect assessments might be used. Additionally, the assessment might include course-embedded or stand-alone metrics and use qualitative (assessing student portfolios) or quantitative (numeric data on scores on examinations) methods.

Depending on the assessment need, evidence gathering might involve all students in a course or a sample of students selected to represent the program or the larger college or school. The information compiled is analyzed, and findings interpreted and reported, usually flowing internally up through the institutional hierarchy from the course level. The findings should be connected to the learning objectives; college, school, or program goals; core competencies; general education goals; and the goals expressed in the institutional mission statement. At the college, program, and course level, the findings provide feedback that should lead to decision making and improvement—a change in pedagogy or content, or a revision of learning goals and objectives.

On the institutional level, college or school, program, and course evaluation reviews and judges assessment as a system. In doing so, evaluation addresses whether assessment processes do what they are intended to do. Evaluators therefore ask questions such as:

• Do the institutional mission and related learning goals and expectations guide assessment?

• Are meaningful, manageable, and sustainable assessment practices created?

• Does assessment involve faculty, staff, and students in meaningful conversations about teaching, learning, and student progress?

- Do the faculty determine their program's mission, goals, objectives, and assessment priorities, and the implications of assessment results?

- Do the assessment tools used, and the findings, provide information concerning the extent to which the learning goals and objectives are met?

- Are identified general education goals and core competencies measured?

- Are the assessment findings used to guide decision making and to improve programs?

- Is assessment an ongoing process of improvement rather than an effort merely to meet accreditation or other external requirements?[15]

Assessment processes are applied to efficiency, effectiveness, performance, and impact, and the metrics and findings are stated in terms of inputs, processes, outputs, and aggregated program, services, and student outcomes. Faculty and others develop goals for general education and core competencies, which colleges or schools, programs, and departments adopted when they develop their own missions statements and assessment plans. Those plans identify measurable learning objectives and outcomes, which are incorporated into course syllabi. Course content is supported by pedagogy and is assessed by means of direct and indirect methods.

The evidence about the declared outcomes of a college education may not be consistently constructed, compiled, measured, and reported. Furthermore, there is no commonly used metric (or set of metrics) that determines effectiveness, when defined in terms of student learning, across all of higher education in the United States. As a result, making comparisons with an institution's peers is inexact.

## ACADEMIC LIBRARIES

Within the structure of most institutions of higher education, academic libraries are organizational units. To support organizational accountability, libraries apply assessment and evaluation processes to determine their internal status (by comparing results to measurable objectives and standards); to report their contributions to the institution and other stakeholders; and to serve as feedback for decision making and the improvement of operations, services, and programs. This section of the chapter focuses on evaluation and assessment for internal library use; chapter 7, which discusses stakeholders, presents an external focus on assessment and evaluation.

As with other organizations within the institution, academic libraries develop their mission statement and planning document based on the stated institutional mission, institutional education and service goals, and general education goals and outcomes. Libraries might also align their mission with a college, school, or program's mission statement and to student education and learning goals and core competencies. Library goals are written, and measurable objectives supporting the goals are identified, oftentimes indicating how the objectives will be measured. Information about activities, processes, functions, programs, and services are compiled, analyzed, and reported. Strengths and weaknesses are identified, and the findings from any assessment and evaluation effort are incorporated into the library's strategic plan. Libraries, as well as the institutional stakeholders to which they report, want to know how well they meet their goals—including learning goals—and objectives and how well they support the institution and its mission. Figure 3.3 illustrates the relationship between the mission statements of the institution and the academic library, the metrics gathered about library services and support, and reporting the findings concerning the library's contribution to the institution.

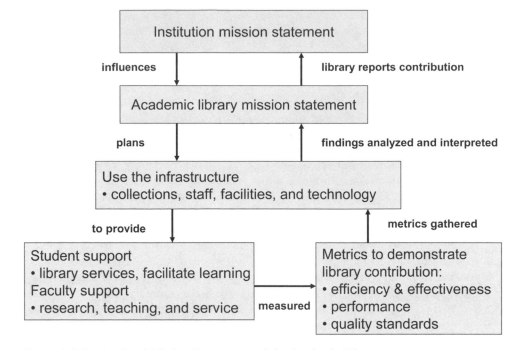

Figure 3.3  Institutional Mission Statement and the Academic Library

## Brief Definitions

The literatures of library and information science, management, and evaluation, as well as documents produced by professional associations (e.g., the American Library Association) define key terms relative to assessment and evaluation. For purposes of this chapter,

- Input metrics identify the resources provided to the library, including fiscal, staff, materials, equipment, and space. These metrics identify the total cost for operating the library as well as the mix of resources used to provide all of the library's services.[16] Input measures also represent the most traditional approach to assessing the quality of libraries and their resources and services.[17]

- Process metrics portray how efficiently resources are transformed into potential or capabilities to deliver services. Process measures usually quantify the time or costs involved in performing a specific task or activity and are often used for comparisons.[18] A focus on process involves looking at how something happens rather than, or in addition to, the product (an output).[19]

- Output metrics point to a degree to which the library and its services are used. Such metrics are usually counts that measure volume of activity. Some libraries use output metrics as an indication of success; the rationale being that the more the library is being used, the better the library is.[20]

- Outcome metrics indicate the impact or effects of library services on an individual and ultimately on the library's community. Outcomes include changes in attitude, skills, knowledge, behavior, status, or condition.

- Performance measurement comprises a process of determining progress toward achieving predetermined goals, including the efficiency with which resources are transformed into goods and services (outputs); the quality of those outputs, that is, how well they are delivered to customers and the extent to which customers' expectations are met (service quality and satisfaction); and the qualitative results of the service used in comparison to its intended purpose (outcome).[21]

While commonly used, most of these metrics are not proxies for accountability. Although input and output metrics have been used as success indicators, neither alone or jointly can they adequately indicate that a library actually accomplishes its mission.[22] Additionally, the lack of consistency in the data provided by information or other third-party vendors (log-ins, sessions, and pages viewed) may result in useless, year-to-year comparisons as portrayed in some output metrics.[23]

A composite of metrics, those combining two or more metrics including traditional and virtual counts, may be better illustrators of accountability than either traditional and virtual counts when they are used alone. For example, total library visits may include gate counts of those entering the library as well as virtual visits to use library resources.[24] Other accountability metrics may focus on cost-effectiveness, cost-benefit analysis, and benchmarks for making decisions.[25]

### Libraries and Evaluation

As an internal process, libraries use evaluation to support institutional accountability: understand, analyze, and explain what they do; inform decision making; support long and short-term planning efforts; and improve their operations, programs, and services by enhancing performance and increasing efficiency and effectiveness. Before libraries start their evaluation activities, they need to consider input, process, output, performance, and outcome metrics that cover the library's infrastructure (collections, facility, staff, and technology) and the services it provides. Additionally, an awareness of the evaluation tools and methods available, including those used internally or shared with other libraries, is helpful.

*The Library Infrastructure.* Libraries use evaluation more often than they do assessment. Evaluation involves an analysis of inputs, processes, and outputs, and it is often broadly characterized in terms of efficiency and effectiveness, including performance and quality. While much of this book discusses metrics for internal use by the library as well as ones that represent the customer, institution, and stakeholder, many of the metrics presented are aligned with the library's infrastructure and support the provision of information services and programs to the various stakeholders. Examples of the alignment include:

- The collections of the library comprise print, nonprint, and electronic sources. Inputs are the financial resources allocated to acquire new materials, processes include the staff to enable the purchased information resources to be available for their intended users (how long a book is in the processing area before it is placed on the shelf), and outputs refer to counts documenting the use of the resources (including circulations and log-ins). Inputs for the physical facility include the number of seats available for users and the availability of electricity. Processes may include the time it takes to make a repair such as replacing burned-out light bulbs, while outputs document the number of users entering the library. Technology inputs record the number of computer workstations available or the number of wired Ethernet jacks. Processes comprise the amount of computer time to transact a resource checkout in the circulation module, and an output may include the number of times a workstation is used. Staff inputs reflect the portion of the budget devoted to staff, and a process may relate to the time it takes staff to reshelve returned books. Outputs include the number of staff having participated in some type of professional development.

- The library's infrastructure supports services to the library's constituency and users. Inputs for services are the number of hours the library is open and the availability of staff assistance to meet user needs (involving, for instance, circulation, reference, and information technology support). Processes include the length of time to fill an interlibrary loan request or to retrieve a book from remote storage. Outputs may reflect the number of pages printed by users, the number of attendees at a library program, or the number of reference questions answered.

Evaluating academic libraries to illustrate how they support the institutional mission may require an examination of the infrastructure in terms of how it supports higher education's triad: research, teaching, and service to the community. What goals are found in the library's mission statement, and what objectives are included in the strategic or long-term plan to support the triad? Objectives and metrics to support research may relate to collection development and a focus on prioritizing interlibrary loan services for faculty. Teaching may engage the library in faculty development as well as in supporting the course-based information needs and skills of both faculty and students. Service may include having staff representation on a committee as well as supporting committees with pertinent information resources.

*Performance.* Evaluation is more than just counts of activities or transactions; it is more useful when its purpose is to review the relationships among operational performance and users.[26] Performance may be evaluated through activity counts, and metrics associated with efficiency and effectiveness. Performance evaluations relate to the performance of the library, its departments and programs, and individuals responsible for the operation of those departments and programs.[27] Most performance metrics that libraries use are internally focused; these input, process, and output metrics reflect what the library receives and converts into services that the community uses.

Efficiency metrics are better measures of performance than simple workload counts. Performance metrics concerning efficiency evaluate the amount of resources used to achieve results. Efficient operations demonstrate better results (higher levels of output for a given set of inputs or use of the minimum amount of inputs to achieve a preset output level). Common metrics include cost-per-item calculations. A decrease in the cost per item of output is interpreted as an increase in the efficiency of operations.[28]

Metrics documenting performance measure the extent to which an achievement is the result of a planned and implemented activity that supports a measurable objective.[29] Such indicators of effectiveness are directly related to a library's program or departmental objective and to the library's mission. An example of a performance metric based on effectiveness is the percentage of reference questions answered successfully.

Performance metrics concerning collections concentrate on accessibility, currency, depth and breadth of coverage, and availability. Accuracy and timeliness form the basis of performance metrics that cover routine tasks. Such metrics covering customer service deal with helpfulness, friendliness, and professionalism of staff. These counts, however, do not indicate if the learning and nonlearning objectives specified in the library's plan, and its support of the institutional mission, are met.

*Quality.* Another type of evaluative issue concerns quality. One way to view quality is from the customer perspective and perceptions of the ideal service in contrast to the public's actual experience. In this context, service quality becomes an area for the development of output metrics. Quality metrics may also be stated as measurable quality standards. A quality standard defines the level of performance that the organization is willing to accept for a particular service or activity. As such, a quality standard determines the degree to which that standard is met. Charles R. McClure and others state that quality standards differ from performance metrics. A performance metric, they note, might be "correct answer fill rate" whereas the quality standard might be "the digital reference service will have a correct answer fill rate of 65%."[30]

*Relationships between Two or More Metrics.* While some metrics may stand alone, the value of one metric increases when it relates to another one. A combination of inputs, throughputs (processes), and outputs can create meaningful ratios. An example involves the number of students and faculty in terms of inputs: library volumes, and student full-time equivalents (FTE). Used separately, some metrics reflect the size of the library and others characterize the student body. However, when combined into a ratio, library volumes to total student FTE, a context emerges, and the resultant metric can be used for internal trend analysis, benchmarking against internally established standards, and peer comparisons. Other commonly used library and student/faculty ratios include: FTE library staff to combined student and faculty FTE, usable library space (in square feet) to total student and faculty FTE, library seating to combined student and faculty FTE, circulation (excluding reserve) to total student and faculty FTE, and reference questions answered to total student and faculty FTE.

Ratios are useful for internal trend analysis over a period of time (e.g., years) because at least one of the variables involved in the calculation is likely to change (e.g., number of students enrolled, of volumes in the collection, or of reference questions answered). Plotting the ratios on a line chart helps to visualize trends over time. Figure 3.4 is an example of a graph illustrating the trend for the number of FTE library staff per 1,000 students over 10 fiscal years.

A library may also apply one or more standards as objectives. A standard is a guide or practice of a good library service or operations that a group of experts usually develops.[31] A standard may also be internally created. For example, an internal standard might be to expend no more than 40 percent of total library expenditures on staff costs. This standard can be benchmarked, which is a process that establishes a standard to which an internal operation can be compared by calculating the measure and then comparing the result to the expenditure for staff. Benchmarking can be applied internally to evaluate whether or not the standard was achieved.

The library may also want to compare its data, ratios, and information with those of its peers. Such evaluative comparisons, however, are only useful and effective

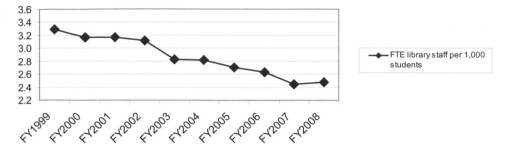

Figure 3.4    Trend Line: FTE Library Staff per 1,000 Students

when the metrics are identical in definition and compilation. Furthermore, comparative metrics are best limited to quantitative inputs, processes, and outputs.

Applying the percentage of total library budget expended for information resources, staff, and all other operating expenditures illustrates all three evaluative uses in trend analysis, internal benchmarking, and peer comparison. A simple table would be:

**Expenditures**

| on info resources | on staff | on all other operating | total expenditures |
|---|---|---|---|
| as a percentage | as a percentage | as a percentage | sums to 100 percent |

The data can be plotted on a line chart and viewed over years to discover trends (e.g., the expenditure on information resources increased as staff expenditures decreased). A library may have set an internal standard in which the percentage of expenditures on information resources is 50 percent of the total budget, staff expenditures are 40 percent, and all other operating expenditures are 10 percent. By calculating the percentages for the past fiscal year, the library can easily determine the status of the metric and evaluate whether or not it met the standard. Lastly, these metrics can be compared with those for other libraries providing there is identical definition and similar data collection and reporting. This peer comparison may result in the library confirming or revising its internal standard.

*Cost Metrics.* Another useful set of evaluative metrics relates to costs. Cost efficiency determines if the cost as an input metric is efficient in terms of a measurable end product, an output. For example, an academic library may seek to support no-fee student printing by holding the cost per page printed (the measurable relationship) as low as possible. Tactics may include buying used and rebuilt high-cycle-per-month printers, recycling laser toner cartridges, and purchasing reams of sheet paper in bulk.

Cost-effectiveness looks at alternative strategies involving cost as an input metric, and output metrics include the cost per item (the measurable relationship) based upon the objectives for which two or more items can be calculated and compared. As an example, to determine if it is more cost-effective to purchase an information resource as a print volume versus as an e-book, it is important to review the cost of each resource, the expected number of users, expected time of usage (the library would need to be open for a student to use a print volume), and time and labor to reshelve a referred-to print volume.

As a guide, Claire Hulme identifies and explains the steps necessary for a library to conduct a cost-effectiveness analysis (CEA). She also presents a case study that compares two library services (library staff providing information and mediated searching directly to clinicians on request and librarians training clinicians to search for information themselves) as a practical example.[32]

Another cost relationship, cost-benefit analysis, refers to the relationship between cost for an asset and the benefits derived from its use. Chapter 7 discusses cost-benefit analysis. Furthermore, Sage Publications (Thousand Oaks, CA, http://www.sagepub.com/home.nav) has produced different works that present economic efficiency analysis, including a discussion of cost-benefit analysis. One example is *Evaluation: A Systematic Approach,* first published in 1979 and now in its seventh edition (2003).[33]

## Evaluation Tools

Many of the evaluation processes that academic libraries use involve the review of compiled metrics, creating and reviewing ratios of two or more metrics, and trend analysis using a single metric or ratio. This section highlights a few evaluative tools that can be applied internally.

*The Balanced Scorecard.* The balanced scorecard is a strategic planning and management system that aligns business activities with the vision and strategy of an organization, improves internal and external communications, and monitors organization performance in relationship to strategic goals (see chapter 11). This framework for performance measurement adds strategic, nonfinancial performance metrics to traditional financial metrics, and it provides managers and executives with a more balanced view of organizational performance.[34]

Although it communicates performance metrics to stakeholders, one value of the balanced scorecard, and why it is included in this chapter, is that it can also be used to evaluate progress by collecting and comparing information to meet internally developed objectives. This internal evaluation identifies problems and encourages adjustments as part of an internal strategy for improvement. This evaluation-improvement activity can be undertaken prior to reporting to external stakeholders.

While the balanced scorecard was initially viewed as a business tool, Robert S. Kaplan found that the nonprofit sector can also deploy it. Unlike the business sector, financial considerations can play an enabling or constraining role but will rarely be the primary objective in a nonprofit environment. Success for nonprofits should be measured by how effectively and efficiently these organizations meet the needs of their constituencies. As such, the nonprofit's mission represents the accountability between it and society—the rationale for its existence. Strategy and performance measurement should focus on what outputs and outcomes the organization intends to achieve as stated in its mission statement, not what programs and initiatives are implemented. Therefore, the balanced scorecard can be used to evaluate the performance of the organization and its departments and thereby demonstrate how the organization and its departments contribute to the institutional mission.[35]

G. Stevenson Smith, a professor of accounting at West Virginia University, explains that the balanced scorecard provides a tool for managers to link financial and nonfinancial performance evaluation to the mission and strategic initiatives of the organization. The scorecard also allows for the monitoring of operating activities in a way to ensure that library staff perform daily activities that contribute to the achievement of those initiatives. The starting point for the development of the scorecard in a library begins with its mission statement and the objectives flowing from it.[36]

Smith explains the four performance objectives covered in the balanced scorecard from the perspective of a library:

1.  Financial: targets may mean ensuring the library is financially viable. Evaluators may include government budget dollars received and the number of patrons; an increase in budget funding from the previous year; the total cost of operations and the number of patrons; and total cost of operations and the total number of books in the collection.

2.  Customer: metrics of service quality and customer satisfaction. Evaluators may include the number and trend of customers using the library, satisfaction index scores on a customer survey, and the number and the trend of complaints.

3.  Internal processes: performance metrics to advance to the next level. Evaluators may include administrative cost and the total appropriation; new books and the total collection; dollars spent on new technology; and administrative cost per employee.

4.  Learning and growth—staff. Employees must be adequately trained and skilled. Evaluators may include the number of hours of technology training per employee; satisfaction index scores on an employee work survey; the number of part-time employees and the total employees; and employee turnover rate.[37]

Joseph R. Matthews, who offers an extensive treatment of the balanced scorecard in libraries, points out that the scorecard helps the library to demonstrate accountability by measuring its true performance beyond the simple counts of activities.[38] It can also help library management in selecting the most important performance metrics as well as understanding the relationship between them and in improving services. Improvement requires measurement to be effective. If library management is unaware of the current status of library programs and services, then it is difficult to measure progress and achieve intended objectives.[39]

At the bottom of the scorecard for Matthews is the financial perceptive, which identifies the financial and other resources provided to the library as well as to the infrastructure. Upwards is the organizational readiness perspective, which refers to staff. At the third level, there are two, side-by-side perspectives: the information resources perspective and the internal process perspective. The information resources perspective includes print and electronic collections, selected quality Web links, interlibrary loan, and document delivery. The goal of the internal process perspective is to understand the processes and activities critical to enabling the library to satisfy the needs and expectations of its customers and to add value that the customers can actually see. This perspective usually includes costs, quality, throughput, productivity, and time issues. Staff use the available tools provided by the financial perspective in an efficient manner (internal process perspective) to provide access to collections (information resources perspective). The combination of organizational readiness, information resources, and efficient internal processes deliver a mix of products and services upwards to the top of the balanced scorecard, which is the customer perspective. Figure 3.5 illustrates Matthews's model for a library balanced scorecard.[40]

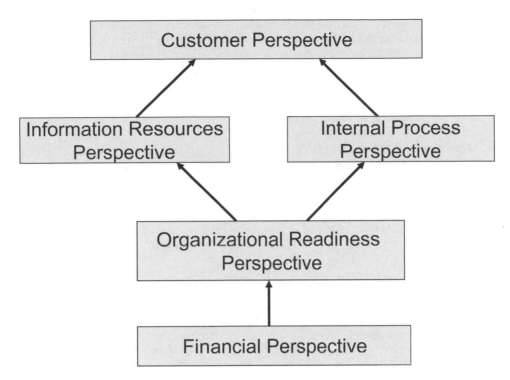

Figure 3.5    Matthews's Model for a Library Balanced Scorecard

Source: *Scorecard for Results* by Joseph R. Matthews. Copyright 2008 Carlsbad City Library. Reproduced with permission of ABC-CLIO, LLC and the Carlsbad City Library.

In summary:

- The financial perspective addresses what financial resources are required to be successful. The core values are budget, value, and accountability, and the performance metrics are inputs.

- The organizational readiness perspective deals with customer satisfaction and service quality, and the capability of staff and the infrastructure to deliver services. The core values are staff skills, innovation, and the availability and reliability of tools and how these relate to the library's infrastructure. The performance metrics are inputs, process, and outputs.

- The internal process perspective covers those business processes in which the library excels and that satisfy customers. The core values are productivity, time, and cost. The performance metrics are process (throughput) metrics.

- The information resources perspective examines whether the information resources provided satisfy customers. The core values are accessibility, relevance, accuracy, quality, depth, programs, and training. The performance metrics are inputs, process, and outputs.

- The customer perspective addresses what the library and its services will resemble to achieve the stated vision. The core values are purpose, service, and quality. The performance metrics are outcomes.[41]

An example of a mature process is found at the University of Virginia Library, where the scorecard has been in use since 2001 (see also chapter 11).[42] Each of the perspective's metrics contains two targets; one indicates complete success in achieving the metric, and the other suggests partial success.[43] Implementation of the balanced scorecard at the library is closer to Kaplan and Smith's structure and content with four perspectives than to Matthews's five perspectives.

The balanced scorecard, once embedded into the library's organization culture and operations, is used for discussion at the departmental and work team levels. The evaluative results enable library management and staff to monitor progress and use the findings to guide improvement.[44]

*The Report Card.* Another evaluation tool for internal use is the report card, which is a practical hybrid of the balanced scorecard. The report card takes the balance scorecard a step further (by doing less) and simplifies the way the organization looks at data. Rather than grouping the metrics by type of data as is done with the balanced scorecard, the report card focuses on how measurement is done rather than on what is measured. The report card is based on four categories of performance:

1.  effectiveness—the customer's view of the organization
2.  efficiency—the business view of the organization
3.  human resources—the worker's view
4.  visibility—management's need for more insight into the organization[45]

For anyone considering the use of the report card, the organization begins with effectiveness because it offers the greatest return for the investment required. If customers are ignored (effectiveness perspective) and the organization loses their support, it will not matter how efficient the organization is, how happy the workers are, or how much insight management has. When considering effectiveness metrics, the graded components are: delivery of service (quality of product), measured by availability, speed, and accuracy; usage; and customer satisfaction. To create a report card, it is important to identify the key services or products, and the metrics for each service or product. Each component is worth a portion of the final grade for the service or product. The values are weighted for each key service, and the aggregate of the grades becomes the organization's grade for the period measured. The organization may fail in one facet of effectiveness and excel in others.[46]

Providing a report card enables the organization to check its progress and overall performance, and to make adjustments accordingly. A report card using the effectiveness perspective will not inform management how efficiently the organization functions, but it gives the insights needed for identifying areas for improvement.[47]

*Data Envelopment Analysis (DEA).* Although there is an increasing need to measure effectiveness in terms of the impact that library services have on customers, efficiency measures should not be overlooked for internal evaluation. Efficiency measures the library's ability to transform its inputs (resources) into outputs (services), or to produce a given level of outputs with the minimum amount of inputs.[48]

Data Envelopment Analysis (DEA) measures the relative efficiencies of organizations with multiple inputs and outputs as opposed to other techniques such as ratio analysis or regression. Individual organizations, teams, or units are called decision-making units (DMUs). The inputs or outputs that the DMUs control are called *standard* or *discretionary* variables (e.g., total circulation, reference transactions; library visits, interlibrary loans, online searching, and the provision of information).

*Nondiscretionary* variables (e.g., population density, area size, resident population, nonresidential borrowers, and socioeconomic indices) are beyond the control of library administration.[49]

The basic purpose of DEA is to identify the efficient frontier (line on a graph) in some comparison set of DMUs. All units on the line presumably operate at 100 percent efficiency. A unit is evaluated by comparing its performance with the best performing units of the sample. DEA provides an efficiency score for each inefficient unit and a benchmark set of efficient units. Although the formula is too complicated to reproduce here, it is important to know that a model for measuring efficiency using multiple input and output variables exists and has been applied in libraries.[50]

Wonsik Shim used annual statistics (1996 and 1997) from 95 university research libraries in the United States with membership in the Association of Research Libraries (ARL). The input variables include the total volumes held, net volumes added during the period (two years), monographs purchased, in volumes, total number of current serial copies, number of full-time professional staff, number of full time support staff, number of full-time equivalents of hourly student employees, full-time student enrollment, full-time graduate student enrollment, full-time instructional faculty, library expenditures per full-time student, and library expenditures per faculty. The output variables are the total number of interlibrary loan lending transactions filled, total number of interlibrary loan borrowing transactions filled, number of people who participated in group presentations or instruction, total number of circulations including renewals, and reference transactions excluding directional questions.

Shim found that

- ARL libraries with large net volumes added and professional staff tend to have lower efficiency scores
- libraries producing more reference and circulation transactions are more efficient
- total circulation was a statistically significant predictor of efficiency
- the amounts of library expenditures per student and faculty were not significant predictors of efficiency
- the size of the library budget was a significant predictor
- none of the per-user activities, measured by the number of various service outlets per student, was a significant predictor of efficiency
- the number of reference transaction handled per professional staff was a significant predictor
- libraries with a larger proportion of total volumes circulated have higher efficiency[51]

Shim states that the results from the DEA study are suggestive rather than confirmatory, and need to be verified through other means such as in-library case studies. Instead of replicating a similar broad perspective, he recommends that future studies focus on a particular library operation or function (e.g., cataloging and reference).[52]

Gerhard Reichmann notes that library performance can be assessed by surveying library users' opinions (subjective component) and/or analyzing library performance indicators (objective component). He studied 118 university libraries in Europe and Australia, including ARL libraries in North America. The input variables are full-time equivalents of library staff and book materials held in volumes; these variables, he believes, serve as reliable proxies for current and capital resource use. Service outputs are the number of serial subscriptions, total circulations, regular hours open per week, and book materials added in a year. He found that the libraries surveyed had a mean efficiency of only 69 percent.[53]

A third DEA study, which involved public libraries in New York, uses 1992 data. Input variables include total holdings of all items (e.g., books, AV, and maps), total hours of operations per week, new books purchased, and total current serial subscriptions active. Output variables are limited to the total circulation of all library materials and the number of reference questions answered. Study author Donald F. Vitaliano calculated a mean efficiency score of 67 percent; the principal source of inefficiency was too many hours open per week. Public library resources could be cut by one-third without reducing any dimension of service quantity or quality, and the typical inefficient library could reduce weekly library hours by 20 percent without reducing measured output (actual mean number of hours per week).[54] Hours open is always an issue for managerial consideration in academic library operations.

DEA analysis estimates the relative operating efficiency of libraries irrespective of quality comparisons. Because DEA provides the precise corrective figure for every output and input deployed in the analysis, a library may use the calculations to improve the efficiency of a university library.[55]

## Libraries and Assessment

Generally, an academic library can assess impact and learning outcomes, and users (as opposed to use).

*Impact Outcomes.* Impact outcomes are oftentimes concerned with user satisfaction, opinion, and perceptions, including satisfaction with use of the library's services and programs. They may also include the impact or the effectiveness of library policies and management on services as well as the organizational culture. Data concerning impact outcomes are collected through formal and informal surveys as well as unsolicited comments delivered via a multiplicity of communication means. However, a library must be careful in differentiating outcomes from evaluations of library functions and activities.

The library's infrastructure may be assessed, before being evaluated, when a measurable objective or standard is replaced with subjective observation. Decisions are based upon the perspectives of those undertaking the review. As an example, the physical condition of the collection is assessed; a book in "poor" condition may be in "fair" condition based upon the reviewer's perspective. The following questions illustrate that one purpose of assessment is to make improvements: Is the collection strong or weak in a specific discipline? What is the physical condition of the facility? Is it good, in need of repair, or in need of replacement? Are staff members qualified to do what they are doing? Is the staff diverse? Is the technology sufficient for downloading and viewing course-related media via the Internet? Are books reshelved in a timely manner?

Other areas for an academic library to assess include:

- impact on external environments (Most of the library's attention on impacts from external environments has focused on costs for doing business. There is a trend toward assessing the library's impact on its external environment through economic impact analysis; see chapter 7.)

- changes in curriculum and how that influences library use, such as the increasing use of content management systems
- changes in technology infrastructure, such as students using or owning their own computers; use of proxy servers for off-campus database access coupled with the ubiquitous availability of wireless connections, and the relationship between visits to the physical library versus virtual use of library resources[56]

*Learning Outcomes.* Academic libraries may assess if students learn from their use of library resources and services. In this context, it is possible to assess the outcomes of an interaction between the library and the user to determine what has the student learned in terms of skills, values, and attitudes. Learning outcomes for libraries should parallel those of the academic departments. The library's learning objectives are stated in its assessment plan for student learning outcomes, which identifies measurable learning objectives and applies scoring rubrics, based in part upon the *Information Literacy Competency Standards for Higher Education* developed by the Association of College and Research Libraries (ACRL).[57]

A common assessment methodology involves measuring pre- and postinstruction skills to determine if there are statistically significant changes in what students learned. This methodology is best related to an experimental design that is rigorous and reduces the likelihood of interpretation error. Libraries may create and administer internally developed assessment methods such as pre- and postinstruction tests. The tests may be administered through testing software such as those available through course management systems or created using third-party software. Aggregate data can be gathered through the use of clicker software systems, with the data captured for analysis and reporting. Libraries might also review student portfolios that academic programs or departments require students to maintain throughout their program of study.

For those libraries or institutions not wanting to develop internal tests for assessing student learning outcomes, at least one internally developed test, Go for the Gold (James Madison University in Harrisonburg, Virginia), can be administered via the Web, and James Madison University can make available individual and aggregate student results at a cost (see https://www.lib.jmu.edu/gold/secure.aspx). Another test instrument available is the Project for Standardized Assessment of Information Literacy Skills (SAILS), a Kent State University initiative to develop an instrument for standardized assessment of information literacy skills. Test items are based on ACRL's Information Literacy Competency Standards for Higher Education. Many academic institutions find that the standards maximize the value of the instrument for internal and external benchmarking.[58] The Educational Testing Services (ETS) created and makes available the fee-based *iSkills* assessment. *iSkills* is intended to

- measure a student's ability to navigate, critically evaluate, and make sense of the information available through digital technology
- assess critical thinking in the digital environment
- test the range of literacy skills aligned with the ACRL information literacy standards
- identify where further curriculum development is needed so that the institution or library can make the necessary changes to narrow skill gaps and help students succeed[59]

Although not part of what is known as student learning outcomes, a related type of assessment identifies the impact of academic libraries on student learning.

A study on linking critical thinking to academic libraries involved the levels of time and effort that students invest in their college activities, as reported on the 1992–1993 College Student Experiences Questionnaire (CSEQ). Routine use of the academic library does not influence the development of critical thinking. However, students who engage in more focused library activities (checking citations in sources read, reading basic references or documents, finding materials by browsing in the stacks, and checking out books) report a significant impact on their critical thinking development.[60]

In another assessment study, postsecondary researchers George D. Kuh and Robert M. Gonyea asked: broadly defined, what does the library contribute to student learning? It is generally thought that quality of effort that students expend is the single best predictor of what they gain from attending college. The measure can also be used to estimate the effectiveness of an institution or its component organizations (e.g., the library) in promoting student learning.[61]

Kuh and Gonyea reviewed the responses of 300,000 students on the College Student Experiences Questionnaire (CSEQ), administered between 1984 and 2002, in order to answer the following:

- Has student use of various library resources changed during those years? Given the Web, are students using the library more or less (for studying and for finding information)?

- Is frequent use of the library associated with greater gains in information literacy? What does the library contribute to other desired outcomes of the college?

- Are students who frequent the library more likely to report increased contact with faculty members inside and outside the classroom? How does student use of library resources affect student engagement with effective educational practices?[62]

They found that a greater number of students use indexes and databases over the duration of the study. Furthermore, there was a decline in the proportion of students who use the library as a place to read or study. Additionally, there was a slight increase in number of students asking a librarian for help. However, the type of questions asked (e.g., technical assistance for using databases or mediated assistance in finding materials within the library) is unknown.

Focusing on understanding the relationship between student engagement and information literacy, in addition to student interactions with librarians or their library experiences, Bonnie Gratch-Lindauer and ACRL's Information Literacy's College Students Surveys Project Group facilitated the inclusion of 10 experimental items tested on some of the 2006 National Survey of Student Engagement (NSSE) questionnaires. A total of 12,044 students at 33 institutions completed questionnaires.[63] Many of the items included on NSSE are derived from other questionnaires, including the CSEQ, the Cooperative Institutional Research Program (CIRP) Freshman and follow-up surveys, and student and alumni surveys administered by the University of North Carolina system.[64] As Gratch-Lindauer notes, Robert Gonyea, Associate Director and Project Manager at the Indiana University Center for Postsecondary Research, finds that that the information literacy questions posed fit into NSSE's framework, although they produce too many questions. Until all of those questions or a subset of them are considered and included in NSSE, he encourages academic libraries to work with their institutional NSSE instruments to locally include questions that query students about their engagement with information literacy and the library.[65]

*Assessing Users.* Libraries are increasingly assessing students to learn more about them than just their search skills. For example, what do they use? The answer might focus on the library's Web site and the use of local digitized collections. It might also address why they use specific techniques or resources. Furthermore, do they use Google™ to search for course-based resources instead of, or before, examining the library's collections? Do they ask for help from library staff? How do they use the resources they find? It is thought that the more librarians know about the user, the more likely they can implement changes and improve services. Assessment methodologies for user studies often rely on indirect methods (e.g., focus group interviews, surveys, and observations).

A user study was conducted at the University of Rochester in 2005 and into 2006 using anthropological and ethnographic methods to examine how undergraduate students write their research papers and what services, resources, and facilities would be most useful to them. Among the study's many findings was the following:

> The reality is that the student body of each higher education institution is unique, for it is a reflection of a variety of factors including socioeconomic conditions, the ratio of residential to commuter students, local climate, and the robustness of the campus IT infrastructure, just to name a few. Consequently, to be truly student-centered we must be cognizant of the high-level student trends but truly fluent in the local campus situation.[66]

*Outcomes Assessment and Peer Comparisons.* Although desirable, assessment measures are less comparable than evaluation metrics, certainly when applied externally to peers. As with institutions, academic libraries are different and unique although their functions are similar and familiar. While standards for assessment exist, it is the differences in application that results in assessment metrics being less comparable among and between institutions. For example, although it may be accepted that use of Conspectus methodology can evaluate collection subject depth and produce metrics comparable to other library collections, the assessment of the physical condition of the collection differs from reviewer to reviewer. Some customers may find the library's computer technology adequate while others find it unacceptable because it cannot render art images realistically. Metrics associated with staff development in one library may not be possible in another library.

### Data Collecting and Sharing

The first point of data compilation for evaluation and assessment is internal—the library itself. While additional information about the library's organized effort to collect and store measures is discussed in chapter 10, it must be noted that libraries collect a variety of metrics and often share them with other libraries. Input, process, and output activities are counted, stored in spreadsheets for easier management and subsequent analysis, and reported internally through departmental, program, college or school, and institutional reports. The metrics and data compiled annually are oftentimes those collected historically. Other metrics and data might be necessary to support internal data collection for inclusion of the findings in fact books and other publications and reports of the library and the parent institution.

In addition to the metrics collected for internal use, academic libraries may collect data and counts of activities to be submitted to the Academic Library Survey undertaken biennially by the National Center for Educational Statistics (NCES) within the Department of Education. Libraries may also participate in surveys conducted by ACRL, which annually collects, organizes, and publishes *Academic Library Trends & Statistics.* The report is available in print and electronic formats and includes data on collections, expenditures, personnel, enrollment, electronic resources, networked electronic resources and services, and digitization activities.[67] ARL also makes publicly available the ARL Library Investment Index (previously named the ARL Expenditures-Focused Index). It is a summary measure of relative size among the university library members based on four variables: total library expenditures, salaries and wages for professional staff, total library materials expenditures, and professional plus support staff.[68]

Libraries collect and share data requested and used by consortia members for local and regional peer comparison, or for those library consortia based on other membership criteria, such as The Oberlin Group, which represents 80 libraries of selective liberal arts colleges. The consortium surveys, often undertaken annually, may mirror data (and use the same definitions) collected by ACRL and NCES, and they include additional data or information not collected, such as detailed salary information based on positions. Other information (e.g., gender and diversity) may be requested and collected as well. These surveys are often used because the reports generated by the NCES survey are frequently published two or more years after the data collection, and the detailed data measures available in the individual volumes in *Academic Library Trends & Statistics.* Libraries are also generous in responding to survey requests from individuals or groups who seek information to undertake research, identify and measure trends, or to review and analyze responses for focused peer comparisons.

## MOVING TOWARD STANDARDIZED STATISTICAL GATHERING

Evaluation and assessment processes are critical for organization accountability. The findings generated from any of the metrics complied and analyzed are essential for planning, understanding the current status of achieving goals and objectives, reporting progress, and making improvements. Many of the metrics involve inputs, processes, and outputs, but they may not fully address the following questions: Does the current state of evaluation and assessment demonstrate the value of the library's contribution to the institution and its mission? Are the findings from the assessment and evaluation efforts used to improve library operations, programs, and services? Does the library evaluate its assessment and evaluation processes?

Academic library administrators and practitioners may agree that developing standards and metrics that evaluate library resources, and assess their use and their impact on users, are critical to the continued centrality and success of the academic library.[69] However, it is difficult to define, never mind standardize, what and how much libraries measure, or how well they are doing it.

Academic libraries need to use clear and standardized definitions and instructions for compiling metrics so that the data collected are reliable and institutionally comparative, if possible. There is an additional need to ensure that the metrics, definitions, and compilation are simple so that they do not overcomplicate the library's data compiling resources and so that stakeholders can understand the language used in reporting the results. Efforts underway to standardize definitions come from the International Coalition of Library Consortia (ICOLC), ARL, and the National Information Standards Organization (NISO). For assessment and evaluation, the use of fewer statistics and performance metrics that are comparable, defined, and common are better than providing dozens of complicated and non-comparative statistics (see chapter 4).

Academic librarians need guidance in the methodologies and training concerning assessment and evaluation. Several library organizations that have formal statistic gathering programs also make training available to assist librarians in assessment and evaluation. For example:

- CAUL (Council of Australian University Librarians) statistics have been gathered and published annually since 1953. CAVAL Collaborative Solutions of Bundoora, Victoria, has managed the collection and compilation of the data since 1992, and offers training in assessment and evaluation.[70]
- SCONUL (Society of College, National and University Libraries) in the UK and Ireland has been collecting and publishing statistics from university libraries since 1987, with the aim of providing sound information on which policy decisions can be based. The Working Group on Performance Improvement (WGPI) provides a toolkit of data, as well as measurement techniques and instruments related to performance measurement, and libraries can use these resources to demonstrate their value and worth to senior stakeholders within their institutions.[71]
- ARL has been collecting, organizing, publishing, and analyzing its member statistics since its inception. In addition to providing annual statistical reports, the association has developed programs and methods, provided training and consultant services for libraries, and published reports about assessment and evaluation. Its programs include LibQUAL+™ (library service quality); DigiQUAL (assessing services provided by digital libraries); Mines for Libraries (data on user demographics and customer use of electronic resources); and, ClimateQUAL (staff perceptions about diversity as well as organizational policies and procedures). The Effective, Sustainable and Practical Library Assessment is an on-site team-based consultation with local library staff to identify assessment issues and needs and to provide recommendations to move local assessment forward.

## CONCLUSION

Librarians must have the will, organizational capacity, and interest to implement and use data effectively in library management. They have, however, been slow to standardize definitions and methods, develop guidelines and best practices, and to provide the benchmarks necessary to compare the assessed results across institutions. Successful ongoing assessment and evaluation require administrative support; the need to focus on fewer rather than many metrics; and the need to ensure that the staff have obtained basic skills related to research designs and methods, collection efforts, statistics (descriptive and inferential), data analysis, and data reporting. Further, assessment and evaluation require that the staff is organized to undertake evaluation; involve library information technology staff; and understand the need to organize and manage data.[72]

Assessment and evaluation efforts are worth it when they are integrated into the daily library operation, used to improve and to plan, are sustainable over a period of time, and get internal human and financial commitment because the effort has value to decision makers. Libraries must take their basic statistics and convert them into meaningful measurements.[73] However, there cannot be one set of universally standard impacts applicable to all academic libraries, as outcomes depend on and reflect the institution's unique nature and mission, as well as the areas that the faculty want to emphasize in whatever scoring rubrics emerge.

## NOTES

1. Carol A. Dwyer, Catherine M. Millett, and David G. Payne, *A Culture of Evidence: Postsecondary Assessment and Learning Outcomes* (Princeton, NJ: Educational Testing Service, June 2006), 1.

2. Paul Basken, "Accreditors Honor College—and Hope to Send a Message about Themselves," *The Chronicle of Higher Education* (February 1, 2008). Available at http://chronicle.com/weekly/v54/i21/21a01801.htm (accessed July 28, 2008).

3. Ibid.

4. Dwyer, Millett, and Payne, *A Culture of Evidence*, 8.

5. Ibid., 8–9.

6. Patrick Callan and John Immerwahr, "What Colleges Must Do to Keep the Public's Good Will," *The Chronicle of Higher Education* LIV, no. 18 (January 11, 2008): A 56.

7. For the application of outcomes assessment in public libraries, see Rhea Joyce Rubin, *Demonstrating Results: Using Outcome Measurement in Your Library* (Chicago: American Library Association, 2006); U.S. Institute of Museums and Library Service, "Grant Applications: Outcomes Based Assessment" (Washington, DC: Institute of Museums and Library Service, 2008). Available at http://www.imls.gov/applicants/learning.shtm (accessed October 6, 2008).

8. Christopher R. Foley, "Mission Statements: A Definition, an Assessment, a Call for Action." Available at http://www.uvm.edu/~vtconn/v16/foley.html (accessed September 8, 2008).

9. Jo Allen, *Assessing the Work of Higher Education: Institutional Effectiveness and Student Learning* (Philadelphia, PA: Middle States Commission on Higher Education, April 2008). Available at http://www.msche.org/documents/PRR_08-Presentation—Allen.ppt (accessed October 2, 2008).

10. Dwyer, Millett, and Payne, *A Culture of Evidence*, 6.

11. University of Albany, "Institutional and Student Learning Assessment." Available at https://wiki.albany.edu/display/middlestates/Institutional+and+Student+Learning+Assessment- (accessed October 3, 2008).

12. Dwyer, Millett, and Payne, *A Culture of Evidence*, 1, 16.

13. Voluntary System of Accountability Program, "Welcome to the VSA Online!" Available at http://www.voluntarysystem.org/index.cfm?page=homepage (accessed October 2, 2008). See also Christine M. Keller and John M. Hammang, "The Voluntary System of Accountability for Accountability and Institutional Assessment," in *Assessing and Accounting for Student Learning: Beyond the Spellings Commission,* edited by Victor M. H. Borden and Gary R. Pike, New Directions for Institutional Research [Series], Assessment Supplement (San Francisco, CA: Jossey-Bass, 2007), 39–48.

14. National Survey of Student Engagement, "Our Origins and Potential." Available at http://nsse.iub.edu/html/origins.cfm (accessed September 15, 2008).

15. University of Albany, "Institutional and Student Learning Assessment."

16. Joseph R. Matthews, *Scorecard for Results: A Guide for Developing a Library Balanced Scorecard* (Westport, CT: Libraries Unlimited, 2008), 64.

17. Ronald R. Powell, "Evaluation Research: An Overview," *Library Trends* 55, no. 1 (2006): 105.

18. Matthews, *Scorecard for Results,* xiv.

19. Powell, "Evaluation Research," 107.

20. Matthews, *Scorecard for Results,* xiv.

21. Ibid., 102.

22. American Library Association, Association of College and Research Libraries, ACRL's Task Force on Academic Library Outcomes Assessment, *Task Force on Academic Library Outcomes Assessment Report* (Chicago: American Library Association, 1998). Available at http://www.ala.org/ala/acrl/acrlpubs/whitepapers/taskforceacademic.cfm (accessed September 22, 2008).

23. Denise Troll Covey, *Usage and Usability Assessment: Library Practices and Concerns* (Washington, DC: Digital Library Federation and Council on Library and Information Resources, 2002), 42.

24. Ibid., 55.

25. Ibid., 53.

26. Powell, "Evaluation Research," 104.

27. G. Stevenson Smith, *Managerial Accounting for Libraries and Other Not-for-Profit Organizations,* 2nd ed. (Chicago: American Library Association, 2002), 203.

28. Ibid., 205.

29. Powell, "Evaluation Research," 106.

30. Charles R. McClure, R. David Lankes, Melissa Gross, and Beverly Choltco-Devlin, *Statistics, Measures and Quality Standards for Assessing Digital Reference Library Services: Guidelines and Procedures,* 60. Available at http://quartz.syr.edu/quality/Quality.pdf (accessed July 26, 2008).

31. Powell, "Evaluation Research," 110.

32. Claire Hulme, "Using Cost Effectiveness Analysis: A Beginners Guide," *Evidenced Based Library and Information Practice* 1, no. 4 (2006): 17–23. Available at http://ejournals.library.ualberta.ca/index.php/EBLIP (accessed December 12, 2008).

33. See Peter H. Rossi, Howard E. Freeman, and Sonia R. Wright, *Evaluation: A Systematic Approach* (Beverly Hills, CA: Sage Publications, 1979); Peter H. Rossi, Mark W. Lipsey, and Howard E. Freeman, *Evaluation: A Systematic Approach* (Beverly Hills, CA: Sage Publications, 2003).

34. Balanced Scorecard Institute, "What Is the Balanced Scorecard?" Available at http://www.balancedscorecard.org/BSCResources/AbouttheBalancedScorecard/tabid/55/Default.aspx (accessed September 28, 2008).

35. Robert S. Kaplan, "Strategic Performance Measurement in Nonprofit Organizations," *Nonprofit Management and Leadership* 11, no. 3 (Spring 2001): 353–70.

36. Smith, *Managerial Accounting for Libraries and Other Not-for-Profit Organizations,* 210–12.

37. Ibid., 211, 224.

38. Matthews, *Scorecard for Results,* xv.

39. Ibid., xvi.

40. Ibid., 5, 21.

41. Ibid., 56, 65.

42. The reports available on the library's Web site include the results for each fiscal year and a chart-based longitudinal report covering fiscal years 2002 through 2007. See University of Virginia Library, "Balanced Scorecard at UVa Library." Available at http://www.lib.virginia.edu/bsc/ (accessed October 1, 2008).

43. Ibid.

44. Matthews, *Scorecard for Results,* 75, 81.

45. Martin Klubeck and Michael Langthorne, "Applying a Metrics Report Card," *Educause Quarterly* 31, no. 2 (2008), 76–77.

46. Ibid., 76.

47. Ibid., 75.

48. Wonsik Shim, "Applying DEA Technique to Library Evaluation in Academic Research Libraries," *Library Trends* 51, no. 3 (Winter 2003), 312.

49. Stancheva Nevena and Vyara Angelova, "Measuring the Efficiency of University Libraries Using Data Envelopment Analysis," *Proceedings from INFORUM 2004* (May 25–27, 2004). Available at http://www.inforum.cz/archiv/inforum2004/english/prispevek.php-prispevek=93.htm (accessed August 23, 2008).

50. Shim, "Applying DEA Technique to Library Evaluation in Academic Research Libraries," 313.

51. Ibid., 329–30.

52. Ibid., 330–31.

53. Gerhard Reichmann, "Measuring University Library Efficiency Using Data Envelopment Analysis," *Libri: International Journal of Libraries and Information Services* 54, no. 2 (2004): 136, 139–40.

54. Donald F. Vitaliano, "Assessing Public Library Efficiency Using Data Envelopment Analysis," *Annual of Public and Cooperative Economics* 69, no. 1 (1998): 108, 112, 119.

55. Nevena and Angelova, "Measuring the Efficiency of University Libraries Using Data Envelopment Analysis."

56. Covey, "Usage and Usability Assessment," 59.

57. American Library Association, Association of College and Research Libraries, *Information Literacy Competency Standards for Higher Education*. Available at http://www.ala.org/ala/acrl/acrlstandards/informationliteracycompetency.htm (accessed September 27, 2008).

58. Project SAILS, "Overview." Available at https://www.projectsails.org/sails/overview.php?page=aboutSAILS (accessed October 1, 2008).

59. Educational Testing Service, "ETS iSkills Assessment: Overview" (Washington, DC: Educational Testing Service). Available at http://www.ets.org/iskills (accessed October 1, 2008).

60. Ethelene Whitmere, "Development of Critical Thinking Skills: An Analysis of Academic Library Experiences and Other Measures," *College & Research Libraries* 59, no. 3 (May 1998): 270.

61. George D. Kuh and Robert M. Gonyea, "The Role of the Academic Library in Promoting Student Engagement in Learning," *College & Research Libraries* 64, no. 4 (July 2003): 259.

62. Ibid., 258–9.

63. Bonnie Gratch-Lindauer, "Information Literacy-Related Student Behaviors: Results from the NSSE Items," *College & Research Libraries News* 68, no. 7 (July/August 2007). Available at http://www.ala.org/ala/mgrps/divs/acrl/publications/crlnews/2007/jul/infolitstudent.cfm (accessed December 14, 2008).

64. National Survey of Student Engagement, "Our Origins and Potential." Available at http://nsse.iub.edu/html/origins.cfm (accessed September 27, 2008).

65. See Gratch-Lindauer, "Information Literacy-Related Student Behaviors."

66. Nancy Fried Foster and Susan Gibbons (Ed.), *Studying Students: The Undergraduate Research Project at the University of Rochester* (Chicago: American Library Association, Association of College and Research Libraries, 2007), 83. Available at http://www.ala.org/ala/mgrps/divs/acrl/acrlpubs/downloadables/Foster-Gibbons_cmpd.pdf (accessed September 23, 2008).

67. American Library Association, Association of College and Research Libraries, "Academic Library Statistics." Available at http://www.ala.org/ala/mgrps/divs/acrl/publications/trends/academiclibrary.cfm (accessed September 30, 2008).

68. Association of Research Libraries, "Statistics & Measurement." Available at http://www.arl.org/stats/index.shtml (accessed September 30, 2008).

69. Steve Hiller and Cathie Jilovsky, "Measuring Value: A Comparison of Performance Quality Measures and Outcomes Identified by Australian and North American Libraries," at the conference on Evolution of Evidence: Global Perspectives on Linking Research with Practice. Available at http://conferences.alia.org.au/ebl2005/Hiller.pdf (accessed August 29, 2008). See also Covey, *Usage and Usability Assessment,* 53.

70. Council of Australian University Librarians, homepage. Available at http://www.caul.edu.au/ (accessed October 10, 2008). CAVAL, "Linking Leading Libraries." Available at http://www.caval.edu.au/home.html (accessed August 29, 2008).

71. SCONUL (Society of College, National and University Libraries), "The Performance Portal." Available at http://vamp.diglib.shrivenham.cranfield.ac.uk/ (accessed August 29, 2008).

72. McClure, Lankes, Gross, and Choltco-Devlin, "Statistics, Measures and Quality Standards for Assessing Digital Reference Library Services," 7.

73. Stephen Abram, "The Value of Libraries: Impact, Normative Data, & Influencing Funders" (May 5, 2005). Available at http://www.imakenews.com/sirsi/e_article00039 6335.cfm?x=b4TcM1g,b2rpmkgK,w (accessed August 18, 2008).

# 4

---

# THE LIBRARY PERSPECTIVE

Traditional metrics of library resources, activities, and use often rely on surrogates such as the number of items borrowed to reflect the amount of library use, the number of reference questions asked to represent the amount of assistance offered, the number of items cataloged to portray the size of the collection, or the average customer rankings on satisfaction scales to suggest the value of the library. These imprecise indicators do not really characterize a library and its contribution to the community it serves. Furthermore, these indicators provide managers with limited information to make decisions regarding the library's efficiency, effectiveness, and impact and to advocate for increased financial support on a competitive basis with other campus organizations.

College and university administrators engage in data-driven decisions about resource allocations and expect relevant information from their libraries to judge the importance of libraries in supporting the core activities of the institution. Accurate and clear library metrics increasingly are needed to communicate the library's value within campus fiscal discussions. Furthermore, as Douglas G. Birdsall notes, it is important to understand institutional politics and in whom both formal and informal power resides.[1] In other words, because metrics convey a political message whose purpose is to influence others, librarians need to consider what their metrics truly say and how they present the library in terms of competitive advantage. Complicating matters, metrics portraying the library perspective tend to comprise inputs and outputs that indicate how library managers allocate the budget and how much the library accomplishes. In effect, the metrics ask stakeholders to view the library on its own terms and not so much on how it advances the institutional mission. Metrics that deal with convergence and collaboration with other campus organizations, even when they reflect inputs and outputs, are useful and indicate how campus units work together to accomplish the institution's mission.

This chapter reviews major trends in library metrics that evolved in academic libraries, including long-standing metrics of inputs and outputs involving physical resources and activities, and newer initiatives that are evolving similar metrics for electronic resources. To a much lesser extent, the chapter reviews emerging trends that suggest metrics that address perceptions of satisfaction and service quality among library customers. Omitted here is any discussion of the impact of library services on student learning and faculty research and productivity. Readers interested in these topics should consult chapters 5 and 6.

## TRADITIONAL INPUTS AND OUTPUTS

Historians claim that librarians have gathered and reported statistics as far back as the ancient libraries in Alexandria and Pergamon.[2] In the early 19th century, the statistician Adriano Balbi attempted to determine the number of volumes held by major European libraries by comparing published reports. He was disheartened by what he speculated were the variations in counting methods, interpretations of metrics, and even the well-intentioned inflation of estimated counts. Some argue that these practices have not fully disappeared even today.

In 1908, James Thayer Gerould, Librarian at the University of Minnesota, began a series of published library statistics, which he continued when he moved to Princeton University in 1920. Staff at Princeton continued these reports after his retirement in 1938. Since 1961/62 the Association of Research Libraries (ARL) has published the *ARL Statistics*, which builds on Gerould's work. In *The Gerould Statistics 1907/08—1961/62*, Robert E. Molyneux discusses the historical compilations of what were first known as the "Princeton" statistics and which now cover ARL libraries from 1908 to the present;[3] these compilations represent "the oldest, most comprehensive, continuing library statistical series in North America."[4]

In this century-long gathering of library statistics, the consistently reported input and output metrics relate to the collection, its size, and expenditures to build it.[5] Gerould's statistics include eight factors, five of which were reported in all years: volumes held; volumes added; expenditures for materials, staff, and salaries; material expenditures; and total expenditures. Wages were not covered each year. Librarians have used the number of volumes held, or a derived ranking among comparable libraries, as a long-standing metric of how *good* a library is, even though in recent years there has been general recognition that this measure is actually not one of a library's quality. The presumption is that the greater the number of volumes held, the better the library is. Molyneux reports that 12 libraries have reported data consistently in *The Gerould Statistics*[6] and that their collections grew from an average of 107,425 volumes in 1907/08, to 1,772,831 by 1961/62 and to 5,334,620 by 1995/96.[7] The calculation of collection growth for these libraries is 6,778,375 as reported in the ARL Statistics for 2006/07.

Other statistics related to collections that have been long reported include the volumes added (gross and net) and expenditures for library materials and binding. In addition, appropriations or total expenditures, total staff, staff salaries, and student salaries (since 1949/50) have been consistently reported. All these metrics, similar to number of volumes held, have been viewed as indicators of the library's health and the commitment of the institution to the library.

The Association of College and Research Libraries (ACRL) also compiles statistics about library inputs and outputs for over 1,300 North American academic libraries, including but going beyond those in the ARL, with the intention of "providing the profession with timely data that will inform management decisions and facilitate comparative studies of library operations."[8] It publishes trends from gathered data that consist of metrics similar to those established by ARL, including information about collections, expenditures, electronic expenditures, personnel, public services, faculty, students, and degrees granted. Supplementary reports for networked electronic resources and digitization activities are also provided.[9] Free online access to statistical summaries of reported data for these metrics, compiled for institutions within similar Carnegie classifications are posted on the ACRL Web site.[10]

Similar efforts to gather data systematically about academic libraries have developed beyond North America. In the United Kingdom and Ireland, the Society of College, National and University Libraries (SCONUL) has collected, analyzed, and published statistics since 1987 for more than 170 national and academic libraries that comprise its membership. SCONUL performs this membership service to enable benchmarking and collaborative work to influence government agencies and advocate support for higher education. Since 1995 the Library and Information Statistics Unit (LISU) at Loughborough University maintains the collected data in back files from which trends can be inferred.[11] A Working Group on Performance Improvement has developed a Performance Portal, offering SCONUL members a tool kit of information and advice on data-gathering methodologies as well as a forum for discussing and sharing experiences and questions; the portal aims "to encourage a community of practice in library performance, measurement, assessment and evaluation."[12]

Based in Australia, CAVAL is a not-for-profit company established in 1978 to offer support services for academic and other *leading* libraries in Australia, New Zealand, and Asia. Among services to its membership of 11 universities and an additional 14 institutes, colleges, and government libraries, is the "collation and analysis of statistics for library benchmarking and performance reviews."[13] Collected data elements are based on those developed by the ARL. Other groups have also used the CAVAL services to manage regionally gathered statistics, such as the Asian Academic Libraries Online Statistics piloted by 15 members in order to be able to compare performance through input and output metrics used across continents.[14]

There are irregularities in the data reported, some of which are attributed to the lack of a universally accepted understanding of what a volume is; physical volume and bibliographic volume are two of the most widely utilized definitions. The ARL Statistics, as well as the U.S. HEGIS, now IPEDS,[15] library reports follow the ANSI Z39. 7-1983 (covering information services and use) definition of a volume: "a physical unit which has been cataloged, classified, and made ready for use."[16] Volumes added annually, however, indicate the number of volumes cataloged; the number of gross volumes added should be reduced by the number of withdrawn volumes. Applying regression analysis to data reports over numerous years, Kendon Stubbs identified statistically significant relationships between gross volumes added and cataloged monographs and serials; however, the relationships between gross volumes added and purchased monographs and serials are weaker.[17] Although there are standards and definitions for describing the resources comprising a library, there is not always common application in gathering data about them, even though they are direct measures and not surrogates of inputs. The difficulties of gathering accurate and complete statistics for comparisons across libraries are even greater when a global view is sought. Using data from UNESCO and Libecon sources, the International Federation of Library Associations (IFLA) made a first attempt to take "a snapshot of the world's libraries" in 2003 and acknowledge these difficulties in spite of following internationally accepted standards and definitions.[18]

When managers analyze data elements to draw insights into characteristics of a library's activities, they may be misled by other irregularities or statistical paradoxes. As Stubbs illustrates, some library metrics resulting from comparisons of unit costs, averages, rates, ratios, percentages, or proportions may produce counterintuitive results, thus illustrating occurrence of the Reversal or Simpson's Paradox. This statistical effect occurs when interpretations are drawn from frequency data—that represent counts of inputs, for example—taken from combining several groups of data that independently offer opposite conclusions. For example, comparing two libraries' average expenditure per volumes (monographs and serials) may result in one library having a lower percent payment than the other. When taken individually the expenditure per monographs and the expenditure per serials, however, may show the opposite: higher percent payment between the two libraries. A library manager may be confused about which conclusion to follow in reaching a decision about relative expenses among peer institutions. One explanation for these seemingly contradictory conclusions may be found in Stubbs' example of the *lurking* variable, the proportion of budget allocated for purchase of monographs and serials. He cautions managers to be watchful for the paradoxes inherent in using data, in particular in using solely input data (e.g., average expenditures) when drawing insights for management decisions such as identifying criteria for cutting categories of publications.[19]

In the late 1980s, a growing awareness of the limitations of relying on inputs led to interest in utilizing metrics that focus more on library performance and, in particular, in measures of access provided for students and faculty—or for public libraries in looking at their users and the frequency of their use. The numbers of items lent and borrowed through interlibrary loan and document delivery services, for example, were added to the set of gathered data as metrics of access. By the end of the 1990s, metrics of reference activity and instructional assistance to readers were also gathered and reported annually. Although this added interest in the relationship with the users of the library was measured in terms of these library service outputs, the emergence of electronic resources and interactive services required new metrics other than the traditional ones developed for activities utilizing physical resources.

## E-METRICS

Electronic resources and services evolved rapidly from the 1990s, requiring new definitions and data for collection management decisions. Although the statistical reports annually published by ARL primarily focus on the quantitative measures of inputs and outputs, the many footnotes accompanying the tables in these reports also offer a context for interpreting changes that are occurring.[20] The footnotes in the reports produced in the 1990s described changes resulting from the availability of electronic resources, suggesting that the traditional metrics were not enough to describe this new type of inputs and monitor their effect on library services and activities. Soon ARL began collecting additional data, primarily to support fiscal management of acquiring electronic resources and access services beginning in the early 1990s. The appearance of electronic resources, however, posed new challenges for library managers to develop library collections and responsive services, and these were only partially understood through trends and insights inferred from the existing input and output metrics.

In 2000 the ARL initiated development of the E-Metrics Project to gather "baseline data about efforts to measure the impact of electronic services and resources and also decision-making processes related to electronic materials."[21] The project recognized the complexities of the electronic environment, including the importance of capturing the user's perspective, and involved the development of both qualitative and quantitative metrics. Collectively, qualitative and quantitative methods provide a more robust view of the library and its newly added electronic services and resources.

The project aimed to address member libraries' needs, as identified by results of a survey and discussion of them among directors and ARL staff at a retreat in 2000. The major issues identified include the need for improved data (about use and vendor pricing) for making purchasing decisions about electronic resources and services, and for data to demonstrate the value of these resources to institutional decision makers. Some participants recognized the opportunity for new forms of data about the impact, cost effectiveness, and value of the electronic resources and services, while others sought to analyze Web transaction logs for helpful data.[22] An advisory committee helped frame a series of 18 electronic resource data elements gathered in *ARL Supplementary Statistics* reports for 2003–4 and affirmed the need for measures beyond the traditional inputs and outputs to understand electronic resources and services. Though still early in development, these e-metrics met some of the voiced needs by providing ways to collect vendor usage statistics consistently, to create a baseline for comparison and future studies of the impact of electronic resources, and to advocate good data-collection practices.[23]

Collecting data for these formulated e-metrics poses numerous challenges. Librarians depend on vendors for statistics about use, and since these suppliers do not share common methods of tracking use, inconsistencies in definition and what is actually counted made compiling a composite of usage difficult. For example, distinctions between resource types or format, content (full text, citation, or abstract), mode of access (browsing or searching), or condition of acquisition (freely on the Internet, free with print purchase or consortia purchasing packages) complicate the process of gathering data analogous to the types of mutually exclusive data captured in the print environment. As a result, reported data overlap, calling for the need to *deduplicate* records that in many cases are not easy to do across vendor reports.

Organizations other than the ARL have addressed similar problems since the 1990s. Within the American Library Association, for example, over a dozen committees are identified by the Science and Technology Assessment Team as involved with assessment, excluding groups concerned with statistics or evaluation related to a specific service or function. Even at this selected broad level of attention to measurement, the committees' foci range across such activities as collection development, accreditation and instruction, facilities development, and personnel management.[24] Innovators exploring e-metrics advocate the benefit and richness offered by using mixed methodologies to develop metrics for network services assessment.[25] Various initiatives have developed in different library settings to portray a range of e-metrics to reflect the usage of library network services and resources. Five innovations are summarized here.

1. **Equinox.** Funded by the European Commission for two years (1998–2000), this project aimed "to develop and use methods for measuring performance in the new networked, electronic environment, alongside traditional performance measurement, and to operate these methods within a framework of quality management."[26] The project prepared a set of performance indicators for electronic libraries that complemented the traditional ISO 11620 standard, Library Performance Indicators. Such metrics as "the number of sessions on each electronic library service per member of the target population," "percentage of total acquisitions expenditure spent on acquisition of electronic library services," and "number of attendances at formal electronic library service training lessons per member of the population served" illustrate this early attempt to measure the hybrid library in terms of both physical and virtual resources and services.[27]

2. **International Coalition of Library Consortia (ICOLC).** The Coalition has been an informal, self-organized international group since 1996. By 2006 it included nearly 200 library consortia, worldwide, members of which facilitate discussion on issues of common interest among all types of libraries, but primarily within higher education institutions. A key area of common interest has been information relating to vendor pricing practices for electronic resources and other e-collection topics. This group initiated vendor-based network statistics and reports standards through its 1998 guidelines.[28] Revised twice, the guidelines include reporting standards and endorse the NISO Standardized Usage Statistics Harvesting Initiative (SUSHI) protocol and use of XML as the standard delivery format for usage statistics. The required data elements for vendor reports are similar to traditional output metrics, but they emphasize the user interaction as an integral component of the library metric. For example, these include number of log-in sessions, number of search queries, number of menu selections, and number of full-content units supplied to users.[29]

3. **International Organization for Standardization (ISO).** Among the thousands of international standards that this organization publishes and maintains, several have developed and adopted standard e-metrics and definitions for both national and international reporting. Frequently cited are ISO/CD 2789 (Information and Documentation: International Library Statistics), issued in 2003; and ISO/CD 11620 (Information and Documentation: Library Performance Indicators) in 1998 and revised in 2003.[30] These evolved from the research and work of ICOLC and COUNTER.[31]

4. **National Information Standards Organization (NISO).** NISO built on ISO standards and the efforts of ICOLC, COUNTER (discussed subsequently), the U.S. National Center for Education Statistics (NCES), and others to develop e-metrics and contribute standard definitions and approaches for gathering data to understand and improve performance of current libraries. First published in 1968, reaffirmed in 1974, and revised in 1983 and 1995, ANSI/NISO Z39.7 (Information Services and Use) is a standard that evolves to provide "quantifiable information to measure the resources and performance of libraries and to provide a body of valid and comparable data on American libraries."[32] The categories of e-metrics provided in ANSI/NISOZ39.7-2004 are as follows:

   - reporting units (describing types of libraries and the context of their administrative and budgetary controls, as well as the population served)
   - human resources (describing all levels of staffing with each library type)
   - collections (describing broad categories in all formats)
   - infrastructure (describing facilities and technology)
   - finances (describing categories of revenues and expenditures)
   - services (describing categories of services provided by libraries)

Within these categories, links to e-metrics further distinguish data elements requiring different definitions (e.g., current serials received, information requests in virtual reference services, electronic document delivery, and use of electronic collections and Internet access).[33] This standard again illustrates the evolution of traditional input and output measures, incorporating those for collections as well as use, and offers new interpretations for understanding the electronic environment.

5. **Project COUNTER.** COUNTER (Counting Online Usage of Networked Electronic Resources) began as an initiative in 2002 and became incorporated in England in 2003 as a nonprofit company, Counter Online Metrics. It works closely with publishers, database aggregators, and academic libraries to develop codes of practice and standards to utilize vendor-generated data about use of online information products and services. For example, under review is the August 2008 Release 3 of the COUNTER Code of Practice for Journals and Databases, which specifies "the data elements to be measured, definitions of these data elements, usage report content, format, frequency and methods of delivery, protocols for combining usage reports from direct use and from use via intermediaries."[34] The list of definitions addresses functionality and activities that emerge from developments in technologies and organizations of information providers, as, for example, terms such as *aggregator, cache, federated search, gateway,* or *turn away.* This project has had a major effect on creating a set of criteria by which vendors can be designated as *COUNTER compliant* and thus acknowledge accountability of the performance of their product and service in the purchasing library's setting, and to do so in a standardized way to allow library managers to compare performance among competing vendors. Usage reports from COUNTER compliant vendors allow libraries to utilize traditional input and output metrics as well as ones that reflect the user and use of resources in the electronic environment.[35]

## DEVELOPMENT OF METRICS BASED ON PERCEPTIONS

The ongoing evolution of library metrics reflects the development of metrics in general, with most maturity found in the use of quantifiable inputs and outputs and more recent introduction of qualitative measures for addressing user perceptions of service quality. The challenges raised by the presence of electronic resources and services have resulted in the development of metrics that redefine the traditional input and output metrics, and that integrate the user perspective and interaction in usage as a defining element of library services.

ARL introduced the New Measures and Assessment initiatives to sponsor a framework of responses to these challenges that address the transitional measurement areas as well as to try to develop outcomes assessment models. The New Measures and Assessment program is an approach to help library managers enact local strategies for using library metrics toward the improvement of services, process efficiencies, and external support for their libraries. Most mature among the initiatives is LibQUAL+™ (http://www.libqual.org/). Others include ClimateQUAL™ (http://www.lib.umd.edu/ocda/index.html), DigiQUAL and E-metrics (http://www.digiqual.org/digiqual/index.cfm), and MINES (http://www.arl.org/stats/initiatives/mines/index.shtml). This section highlights each of the initiatives in the context of how they provide library managers with alternatives to use metrics for decision making.

### LibQUAL+™

Beginning in 1999, this suite of tools was developed through an extensive collaboration and exploration among library administrators at Texas A&M University

(Dean of Libraries Fred Heath, Executive Associate Dean Colleen Cook, and faculty member Bruce Thompson), as well as ARL staff (most notably Martha Kyrillidou, director of ARL's Statistics and Measurement Program). A Web-based questionnaire is central to the applications and analysis that fall under this ARL service. This service is the first that ARL offered that provides metrics beyond the traditions of inputs and outputs about library collection resources and services. It presents the self-reporting user-centric perceptions of library service performance and individualized indications of service expectations. Although there are debates over the interpretation of data resulting from the application of the LibQUAL+™, there is little doubt that library managers and administrators have welcomed and extensively embraced the offering of measures for the user's perspective as an important dimension to their work to understand, improve, and advocate their libraries.[36]

## ClimateQUAL™

Paralleling the important marketing interest in understanding the customer perspective to improve service quality in the 1990s was the equally important exploration among organizational development researchers to understand the impact of the climate and health of an organization on the service it provides. The theoretical work of Benjamin Schneider and his Service Climate Model relates the employee's perceptions of what behavior is rewarded and expected in an organization to customer experiences and satisfaction.[37] This model was tested and extended in the library context by the ClimateQUAL survey to understand how organizational procedures and policies effect customer perception of service quality in a library setting and "help in the development of a healthy organization."[38] The development work, undertaken at the University of Maryland, involved collaborative research with the library administration and staff; Paul Hanges, director of the Industrial/Organizational Psychology Department; and the ARL. Administered first in 2000 "as a means of collecting information about staff perceptions about how well the Libraries were doing in achieving the climate for diversity and organizational health," the survey was repeated in 2004 at the University of Maryland Libraries and then tested further by 14 other ARL libraries between 2007 and 2008.[39] This initiative offers library managers another way to gather data to help identify factors that affect delivery of services, but its relatively early stage of development does not present a set of metrics by which to gauge the importance of a library's climate on its service outcomes.

## DigiQUAL and E-metrics

This project is under development, with funding from the National Science Foundation, to repurpose the LibQUAL+™ protocol to evaluate the e-service quality provided for the user community. Five questions about services, functionality, and content are posed to users online while viewing a library Web site. The goal is to determine utility, reliability, and trustworthiness. Twelve themes are identified, of which five may be selected for development in a customized survey instrument for each library using this tool. There is greater reluctance among library managers to share results about customer perceptions of digital library services than there is to share data about library service quality in general. The results have not been analyzed to any extent across institutions, but individual libraries receive some diagnostic data different than what was available to them before.

### Measuring the Impact of Networked Electronic Services

Adopted in May 2003, the Measuring the Impact of Networked Electronic Services (MINES) is an online data gathering protocol involving a randomly triggered, short popup survey questionnaire to gather information about use of electronic resources viewed from the users' perspective. It goes beyond the more traditionally aligned output measures of COUNTER, for example, or the perceptions of how well resources are accessible as captured by LibQUAL+™ by identifying who is using the target electronic resources, from what location, at what time, and for what self-reported purpose. The methodology was developed by Brinley Franklin of the University of Connecticut and Terry Plum of Simmons College and implemented in several settings, including through a contract between ARL and the Ontario Council of University Libraries (OCUL). This Canadian consortium created the Scholars Portal, an infrastructure to deliver multiple disciplinary digital content and services of over 8.2 million articles from over 7,200 full-text electronic journals to the faculty and researchers of its 20 university library members.[40] By applying a customized version of the MINES protocol to the usage of the Scholar's Portal between May 2004 and April 2005, 16 participating member libraries in the consortium obtained data about the user linked to actual journal usage.[41] The speculation is that, "ultimately, this methodology, if ever combined with usage data for the specific resources, can provide a rich array of perspectives in evaluating digital collection or even specific publishable units, such as published scholarly articles."[42] As Toni Olshen, one of the OCUL project directors, mentions, the benefit of the new definition of usage that the MINES approach offers is that OCUL members "are not held 'hostage' to the limitations and inconsistencies of vendor statistics."[43]

In summary, these New Measures and Assessment initiatives have raised awareness and encouraged academic libraries to look beyond the counts of objects, products, and events and to explore less tangible factors that influence the understanding of libraries and their impact on the customers served or goals of their institutions. Through these efforts, methods to gather data have been developed, and, to varying degrees, analysis of data gathered have identified theoretical models that suggest metrics to gauge library success.

## STRATEGIES FOR USING LIBRARY METRICS

The use of library metrics is most important at the institutional level, where the director or mangers utilize data gathered to achieve specific, locally defined goals. Metrics often appear as measures for success or to track progress in achieving objectives outlined in a strategic plan. They bridge the outlined vision of what the library aims to become with the tactics or action plans employed to develop it. Nonetheless, at least three themes repeatedly appear in discussions about gathering data for managerial decision making in support of accountability, accreditation, and measuring organizational performance achievements. They suggest common strategies for the use of metrics in academic libraries. Summarized as follows, these will be reviewed here to highlight some of the key reasons for libraries to develop effective perspectives on metrics:

- to advocate support for libraries with influential stakeholders
- to make sound collection management and development decisions
- to improve services

Though each of these may utilize metrics discussed earlier along the historic continuum of traditional inputs and outputs, e-metrics, and perception-based measures, each reflects a prevalent use of specific types of metrics.

## To Advocate Support for Libraries with Influential Stakeholders

Advocacy is a required activity for library leaders and managers, to maintain or increase budgets, and to assure that the library is positioned to contribute meaningfully to the institutional mission. Historically, academic libraries have been an important part of the evaluation of universities and particularly in terms of the size of resources provided for research and teaching. Input metrics were, and still are, used to offer comparable evidence about size of collections and resource expenditures in support of the academic enterprise. Data are important in loosely applied benchmarking practices to compare or rank a library with other institutions deemed to be of like (or of aspired) character. Quantifiable measures of the library's assets and resources (inputs) and what the library achieves with them (outputs) are easily comparable, putting aside other factors that might differentiate the institutions, such as size of population served, complexity of service mission, or faculty recruitment and student admission criteria. Academic administrators encourage the application of the argument that to be a better institution of higher education, its library must have a collection and budget at least the size of its aspirational peers. The early development of e-metrics have tried to complement this approach and provide comparable metrics for what electronic resources are available to an institution's research community and how much is spent to achieve that environment. The actual use of these resources began to contribute to the development of arguments for greater library support based on contribution to the academic mission, with circulation and electronic usage metrics as surrogates for value. Satisfaction and perceived service quality among faculty and students are added qualitative metrics to advocate the merits of the library in seeking stakeholders' support.

Some libraries are explicitly developing local metrics to account for ways that the library supports university strategies. For example, the University of Illinois at Urbana Champaign Library has developed a set of diversity metrics to track its internal goals as well as contributions to the university's goals for creating a welcoming environment to its diverse academic community. Metrics illustrate the range of activities and resources involved in advocating this important area of contributions. Figure 4.1 illustrates the metrics associated with campus goals; the summary also offers a view of library metrics that supports arguments of how the library contributes to the campus interests. Such a listing of quantifiable goals with associated metrics can help managers identify what data need to be gathered and utilized to plan improvements, manage services, advocate for reciprocal support from the campus, and continuously learn about the activities central to the library's operations.

| Campus Goals | Metrics |
|---|---|
| Baseline Measures | Percentage of women faculty by rank |
| | Percentage of faculty from underrepresented populations by rank |
| | Percentage of student employees (undergraduate and graduate) from underrepresented populations |

| Unit Goals | Metrics |
|---|---|
| Provide a welcoming environment for all members of the community | Number of faculty/staff training and development programs incorporating diversity issues |
| | Number of Web sites (unit level or higher) incorporating images or content related to diversity programs or research |
| | Percentage of library facilities meeting accessibility standards |
| | Percentage of pages on library Web site meeting accessibility standards |
| | Number of library facilities making accessibility software available on public workstations |
| Enhance teaching, learning, and research across campus by improving access to information resources and services that serve the needs of a diverse academic community | Number of educational resources, exhibits, or public programs provided in support of research and teaching in diverse American cultures, disability studies, LGBT studies, or related fields |
| | Expenditures dedicated to the provision of access to content supporting research and teaching in diverse American cultures, disability studies, LGBT studies, or related fields |
| | FTE faculty assigned to developing collections and services in diverse American cultures, disability studies, LGBT studies, or related fields |

| | Number of participants in service programs designed for library users from underrepresented populations, national origins outside the United States, or LGBT communities, and for users with disabilities |
|---|---|
| Improve recruitment and retention of faculty from underrepresented populations and diverse ethnic and national origins | Number of faculty participating in mentoring programs at the college or campus level |
| | Percentage of successful recruitments of faculty from underrepresented populations |
| | Percentage of tenure-system faculty from underrepresented populations retained |
| | Number of faculty participating in regional or national professional development programs for faculty from underrepresented populations |

Figure 4.1    University Library Diversity Metrics*

*Source: The University of Illinois at Urbana-Champaign, Library Diversity Committee. Available at http://www.library.uiuc.edu/ugl/diversity/committee.html (accessed February 20, 2009).

Contributions to the academic enterprise are powerfully expressed when the importance of the library moves toward greater emphasis on the impact the library has on its customers and its parent institution. Outcomes or impacts assessment are difficult to design in part because suitable criteria and techniques to determine the benefit of library services and activities on customers are not fully developed. Bonnie Gratch-Lindauer, through her review of accreditation standards, brings attention to the important role librarians play in student learning and suggests reserving the use of the phrase *outcomes assessment* for measures of student learning and performance, and development of student mastery of information literacy skills.[44] The impact libraries have on their institutions is another focus for outcomes assessment, which Julia C. Blixrud suggests may be measured by such metrics as the number of patron accessible electronic resources, amount of use of networked resources and services, expenditures for networked resources and related infrastructure, digitization activities, and performance measures.[45]

## To Make Sound Collection Management and Development Decisions

A frequently described managerial context for seeking library metrics is to make sound collection development decisions. Among the reasons identified for using metrics are making decisions about whether to:

- rely exclusively on electronic journals or purchase both electronic and print subscriptions and, if so, at what price
- subscribe to or rely on single article demand for certain journals
- discard print issues or rely on them as a backup for archival purposes
- negotiate site licenses
- deal directly with publishers or rely on intermediary services (e.g., consortia, aggregators, and gateways) and, if so, at what price
- depend, in some cases, on information freely accessible on the Web as a substitute for costly electronic resources

These complex decisions require a sound economic underpinning as well as good judgment in applying economic information and metrics.[46] For example, in an attempt to better understand the *life-cycle* costs of collections, Stephen R. Lawrence, Lynn S. Connaway, and Keith H. Brigham analyzed data from ARL statistics reports and developed a methodology to determine the full range of acquisition and ownership costs to build library collections. The resulting data provide librarians information to compare options of acquiring information resources in print and alternative formats.[47]

These decisions illustrate how traditional measures found in libraries revolve around collection issues. Purposes for collection data gathering have moved from decision making as a way to support the objective that *more is better* to *more use is better*. Inputs (e.g., the number of volumes held, titles cataloged, or dollars spent on collection acquisitions) are easily used to gauge growth and size as indicators of success. As the customer interests and perspectives, however, have gained prominence in driving service management, metrics related to the use of library collections have been added to the manager's toolkit. Outputs (e.g., the number of items circulated, documents delivered, and interlibrary loans filled) describe what the library has provided with its resources. Researchers are exploring journal price data, content counts, and usage statistics to develop metrics that help collection managers make decisions about purchases and cancellations, particularly with the availability of content and usage metrics for electronic resources.[48]

## To Improve Services

Library managers are increasingly viewing the library as a service organization, which suggests that it provides benefit to those who use it, calling them *customers,* analogous to those seeking services in the world of business and marketing. Services are based on relationships with these customers, as discussed further in chapter 9. At least two categories of library metrics are emerging that help managers make decisions on improving services, and thereby nurture relationships with customers. One group of metrics helps monitor relationships with customers through gauging their expectations for service quality and perceptions of its delivery, and the other measures service performance in terms of meeting deliverable goals and of doing so efficiently. The first group relies heavily on qualitative data, mostly opinions and perceptions expressed by the users of libraries; the second consists of quantitative data that measure such service factors as speed, accuracy, and staff time to determine efficiencies and reliable service delivery. With either set of data, the manager is equipped with evidence to decide on making changes and to test the extent of resulting improvement in services, whether through the eyes of the customer or through observable activities.

The popularity of the LibQUAL+™ instrument has generated a large number of testimonies of how its use has changed the way libraries approach planning and improving services. For example, an issue of *Performance Measurement and Metrics* devoted to "The Maturation of Assessment in Academic Libraries: The Role of LibQUAL" (2000, volume 3, no. 2) has several articles describing how customer-generated data guided managers to focus on areas of customer concern. At the University of Nebraska, Lincoln Libraries, for instance, the accuracy of catalog information, access to the collections, and appearance of facilities were among targeted areas where librarians made changes as an intentional response to user perceptions of poor service quality, as analyzed from survey responses.[49]

However, reported interpretations of data sometimes illustrate confusion about the meaning of data gathered. For example, the account of analyzing data from a user survey at the university libraries at Virginia Tech suggests a lack of distinction between perceptions and observations of user behavior, specifically frequency of use.[50] How frequently people actually use library resources is a metric that is measurable from observation (or analysis of transaction logs in an electronic setting). The perception (or recall) by users is not a reliable method to measure frequency of use. And yet, managers progress from acknowledging that users are asked to identify such a behavioral issue to describing their opinionated responses as fact about the behavior. Other misleading examples easily are overheard in library conversations about services when, for instance, faculty perceptions of the lack of available workstations can be confirmed by an actual count of occupancy by hour or day of the week. Such data are important to collect but also to understand correctly in order to direct perceptions to the planning stages when insights and priorities are being identified, and to use observable facts in the evaluation of continuous improvement.

## PROFESSIONAL DEVELOPMENT IS NEEDED

The shortcomings of misunderstanding and incorrectly interpreting library metrics are important to minimize when data serve as evidence for making important decisions. Some work is underway to understand the level of preparedness libraries possess to implement a strategy of changing the managerial approach and fostering organizational cultures that encourage assessment and good practice of decision making based on data. Working with ARL sponsorship, Steve Hiller and Jim Self have visited over 24 libraries to identify, through conversations and review of institutional studies and reports, "organizational factors that facilitate and impede effective data use."[51] Although they found evidence of a number of assessment methods being used in libraries, including the LibQUAL+™, data mining of e-metrics and use statistics, usability testing, surveys, and process analysis, they repeatedly found several factors as being important to the utilization of the results, including library leadership, organizational culture, sufficiency of resources, and assessment skills and expertise. As they report, "while progress has been made in using evidence in decision making, many libraries still had trouble using data effectively in management."[52]

This leads to the increasingly apparent need for professional development and basic training of librarians in methods to gather data for meaningful application to management. But more important than teaching methodologies (e.g., designing a survey, orchestrating a focus group interview, or mining transaction log data) is the development of analytical skills to frame the questions for data and to interpret findings in a reasonable way that will generate the evidence needed for making decisions. Master's degree curricula provide inconsistent preparation for new library and information professionals in basic research and evaluation methods. Powell, Baker, and Mika found "that 58.6% of LIS practitioners stated that their LIS programs did not adequately prepare them to conduct research, and 36.9% said that their LIS programs did not adequately prepare them to read and understand research-based publications."[53]

Once in the profession, practitioners have various avenues to develop their skills. Beyond research and funded initiatives, discussions and renewed interest in assessment among library and information professionals are seen in the growing number of conference presentations and publications devoted to library performance measurement. The biennial Northumbria International Conference on Performance Measurement in Libraries and Information Services, begun in 1995, continues to gather academics and practitioners from around the world to address methods and experiences in monitoring performance of libraries and museums through research papers, panel discussions, poster sessions, and workshops.[54] In 2006 another biennial library assessment conference was launched, based in the United States, to complement the schedule of the Northumbria program; it has been jointly sponsored by the ARL, University of Virginia Library, and the University of Washington Libraries.[55] Specialized publications have also emerged. Advertised as the "only journal devoted solely to measurement of the performance of library and information services," *Performance Measurements and Metrics* offers an international forum for practitioners and academics in the information professions to publish theoretical and applied research, literature and book reviews, concept pieces, and case studies about measurement.[56] Workshops and continued education opportunities about assessment are few but increasing in frequency.

An alternative to training practitioners to conduct and interpret research is to contract the work to obtain the data. This approach still requires some basic understanding of data gathering methodologies to evaluate the validity of information obtained. Such demand for data about libraries generates a commercial market for library metrics. The Irish-based Research and Markets, for example, conducts surveys and then repackages information as promotion of its very extensive listing of the results of *The Survey of Academic Libraries*.[57] This company prepares more specific library benchmarking surveys (e.g., *The Survey of Library Database Licensing Practices*) that report findings from surveying 90 corporate, public, and academic libraries, in countries such as the United Kingdom, United States, and Canada. This compilation provides detailed, self-reporting metrics.[58] Client libraries use the assorted metrics from these reports to track progress on achieving internal goals.

## CONCLUSION

The library's perspective on metrics has evolved in ways that parallel a changing perspective on the organizing focus of the library. Danuta A. Nitecki and William Rando, from their explorations of the impact of using digital images in teaching, devised a service rubric that identifies three levels of service: collection building, information consulting, and knowledge transformation.[59] The role of the librarian is that of a collector who build comprehensive collections, responsive consultants who satisfy clients and provide service quality, and leaders who affect change through fostering collaborations. The organizational norms that they suggest align with these three phases of service and are similar to the values that underpin the categories of metrics described in this chapter. For collection building, value is placed on "more is better." The traditional inputs and outputs used to measure size of collections, expenditures, and volume of work or services a library produces echo this same principle. The emphasis on *access* over ownership and goals to teach skills fundamental to self-sufficiency and personal success characterize the information consulting role. This orientation parallels the paradigm shift away from measuring physical holdings to creating e-metrics for gauging accessible information resources that are provided when needed, *just in time,* rather than acquired *just in case.* And, finally, the knowledge transformation role calls for the library to join others to create ways to integrate individuals' collections of resources with those provided by the library; it recognizes that no institutional unit on campus can provide all resources needed to meet requirements for information in teaching, learning, or research, and expertise is drawn from multiple sources. Success is measured in terms of the impact the library has on the academic enterprise, the contribution it makes to the institution, and the learning outcomes of students. Metrics are complex and multifaceted, involving qualitative perceptions as well as quantitative observations.

A similar framework, though in four parts, is referenced in Kathlin Ray's philosophical review of the postmodern library over the past 20 years of assessment changes. She points out that "postmodern assessment will include traditional or 'scientific' methods and tools" as well as "newly emerging structures, viewpoints and attitudes."[60] Referencing Ralph Wolff, Ray places four values or paradigms along a time frame, summarized in Figure 4.2.

As she points out, "a library that organizes itself around learning looks and behaves differently than a library that is organized around access or students. A focus on learning as an ultimate goal changes organizational priorities, quality indicators and assessment programs."[61] Furthermore,

When learning is the organizing principle of an organization, assessment becomes an integral part of daily operations. It is assimilated into the daily work of each staff member. Assessment is no longer viewed as an externally imposed chore or a detour from normal routines. It becomes a self-organizing principle and helps create an organizational climate that encourages inquiry, exploration and reflection. We become full participants in the learning process, not mere observers.[62]

The evolution of the library perspective on metrics not only reflects changes in the value of the data gathered for managerial decisions, but the process itself transforms the culture through being one focused on assessment "to the creation of a true learning organization."[63] When academic libraries succeed in completing

| Time Frame | Values or Paradigm |
| --- | --- |
| Before 1980 | Resources or holdings |
| 1980 | Access |
| 1995 | Use (students) |
| 2010 | Learning transformation |

Figure 4.2   Wolff's Value Scheme*

*Source: Kathlin L. Ray, "The Postmodern Library in an Age of Assessment," ACRL Tenth National Conference, March 15–18 (Denver, CO: Association of College and Research Libraries, 2002), 250–54. Available at http://www.ala.org/ala/mgrps/divs/acrl/events/pdf/kray.pdf (accessed February 18, 2009). Adapted from Ralph A. Wolff, "Using the Accreditation Process to Transform the Mission of the Library," in "Information Technology and the Remaking of the University Library," edited by Beverly P. Lynch, *New Directions for Higher Education* [Jossey-Bass Publishers] 90 (Summer 1993), 83.

this transformation, they will become full partners in the educational activities of their institutions.

## NOTES

1. Douglas G. Birdsall, "The Micropolitics of Budgeting in Universities: Lessons for Library Administrators," *The Journal of Academic Librarianship* 21, no. 6 (November 1995): 427–37.

2. Robert E. Molyneux, *The Gerould Statistics 1907/08–1961/62* (Washington, DC: Association of Research Libraries, 1998). Available at http://www.arl.org/news/pr/arl-statistics-18dec08.shtml (accessed December 22, 2008).

3. Ibid. See chapter 1, "Introduction." Available at http://fisher.lib.virginia.edu/lib sites/gerould/ (accessed January 7, 2009).

4. Association of Research Libraries, "Press Releases: ARL Statistics 2006–07." Available at http://www.arl.org/news/pr/arl-statistics-18dec08.shtml (accessed December 22, 2008).

5. A review of the history of these data elements, detailed analysis about their use, and the evolution of the ARL Statistics reports can be found at Molyneux, *The Gerould Statistics 1907/08–1961/62*, http://fisher.lib.virginia.edu/libsites/gerould/ (accessed January 7, 2009).

6. These are university libraries at Berkeley, California; Champaign Urbana, Illinois; Indiana; Iowa; Kansas; Michigan; Minnesota; Missouri; Nebraska; Ohio State; Washington; and Wisconsin.

7. Molyneux, *The Gerould Statistics 1907/08–1961/62*.

8. Virgil E. Varvel, Jr., e-mail communication (to Danuta Nitecki), January 7, 2008. Available at http://libstats07.pbwiki.com/Email (accessed 13 February 2009).

9. American Library Association, Association of College and Research Libraries, *Academic Library Trends and Statistics* (Chicago: American Library Association, 2007). Available at http://acrl.telusys.net/trendstat/2007/index.html (accessed February 13, 2009).

10. American Library Association, Association of College and Research Libraries, *Publications: 2007 Statistical Summaries.* Available at http://acrl.telusys.net/trendstat/2007/index.html (accessed February 13, 2009).

11. SCONUL, Statistical Questionnaire Web site, http://vamp.diglib.shrivenham.cranfield.ac.uk/statistics/sconul-statistical-questionnaire (accessed February 14, 2009).

12. SCONUL, The Performance Portal Web site, http://vamp.diglib.shrivenham.cranfield.ac.uk/ (accessed February 14, 2009).

13. CAVAL Web site, http://www.caval.edu.au/ (accessed February 14, 2009).

14. "Asian Library Statistics," *Access* 61 (June 2007). Available at http://www.aardvark net.info/access/number61/monthnews.cfm?monthnews=05 (accessed February 14, 2009).

15. As summarized on the International Archive of Education Data Web site, "the Higher Education General Information Survey (HEGIS) Series, the predecessor to the Integrated Postsecondary Education Data System (IPEDS) Series, was designed to provide comprehensive information on various aspects of postsecondary education in the United States and its territories (American Samoa, Guam, Puerto Rico, the Virgin Islands, and the Marshall Islands) and Department of Defense schools outside the United States. Data are available for both public and private two-year and four-year institutions. There are eight components: Earned Degrees/Completions, Employees, Finance, Residence and Migration, Salaries, Fall Enrollment, Institutional Characteristics, and Libraries." Descriptions and reports of data gathering of library statistics for these surveys may be found at International Archive of Education Data, http://webapp.icpsr.umich.edu/cocoon/IAED/SERIES/00030.xml (accessed February 13, 2009).

16. Molyneux, *The Gerould Statistics 1907/08–1961/62.*

17. Kendon Stubbs, "Apples and Oranges and ARL Statistics," *The Journal of Academic Librarianship* 14, no. 4 (1988): 231.

18. International Federation of Library Associations, *Global Library Statistics 1990-2000: Draft (September 2003).* Available at http://www.ifla.org/III/wsis/wsis-stats4pub_v.pdf (accessed February 13, 2009).

19. Stubbs, "Apples and Oranges and ARL Statistics," 233–34.

20. Martha Kyrillidou and Sarah Giersch, "Qualitative Analysis of Association of Research Libraries' E-metrics Participant Feedback about the Evolution of Measures for Networked Electronic Resources," *Library Quarterly* 74, no. 4 (2004): 425.

21. Ibid., 432.

22. Ibid., 430.

23. Ibid., 432.

24. American Library Association, Science & Technology Section, STS Assessment Committee, homepage. Available at http://www.ala.org/ala/mgrps/divs/acrl/about/sections/sts/committees/assessment/assesscommlist.cfm (accessed February 14, 2008).

25. Joe Ryan, Charles R. McClure, and John Carlo Bertot, "Choosing Measures to Evaluate Networked Information Resources and Services: Selected Issues," in *Evaluating Networked Information Services,* edited by Charles R. McClure and John Carlo Bertot (Medford, NJ: American Society for Information Science and Technology, 2001), 111–35.

26. EQUINOX, homepage. Available at http://equinox.dcu.ie/index.html (accessed February 13, 2009).

27. Peter Brophy, Zoe Clarke, Monica Brinkley, Sebastian Mundt, and Roswita Poll, "EQUINOX, Performance Indicators for Electronic Library Services" (November 2000). Available at http://equinox.dcu.ie/reports/pilist.html (accessed February 13, 2009).

28. International Coalition of Library Consortia, "Revised Guidelines for Statistical Measures of Usage of Web-based Information Resources" (revised in 2001 and 2006). Available at http://www.library.yale.edu/consortia/webstats06.htm (accessed December 23 2008).

29. For more information, see International Coalition of Library Consortia, http://www.library.yale.edu/consortia (accessed February 18, 2009).

30. John Bertot, "E-metrics Information" (Tallahassee, FL: Florida State University, School of Information Studies, Information Use Management Policy Institute). Available at http://www.ii.fsu.edu/emis/resources.cfm?display=subject&subject_key=49 (accessed November 27, 2008).

31. For more information see International Organization for Standardization, http://www.iso.org/iso/home.htm (accessed February 18, 2009).

32. See National Information Standards Organization, *ANSI/NISO Z39.7-2004: Information Services and Use: Metrics & Statistics for Libraries and Information Providers—Data Dictionary* (Baltimore, MD: National Information Standards Organization). The forward is available at http://www.niso.org/dictionary/foreword/ (accessed December 23, 2008).

33. See National Information Standards Organization, *ANSI/NISO Z39.7-2004: Information Services and Use: Metrics & Statistics for Libraries and Information Providers—Data Dictionary* (Baltimore, MD: National Information Standards Organization). Available at http://www.niso.org/dictionary/emetrics_elements/ (accessed December 23, 2008).

34. COUNTER, Release 3 of the COUNTER Code of Practice for Journals and Databases (August 2008), "Introduction to the Release." Available at http://www.projectcounter.org/r3/r3_intro.pdf (accessed January 2, 2009).

35. For more information, see COUNTER, http://www.projectcounter.org/ (accessed January 10, 2009).

36. For discussion of the LibQUAL+™ see Michael J. Roszkowski, John S. Baky, and David B. Jones, "So Which Score on the LibQUAL+™ Tells Me If Library Users Are Satisfied?" *Library & Information Science Research* 27, no. 4 (2005): 424–39; Xi Shi and Sarah Levy, "A Theory-guided Approach to Library Services Assessment," *College & Research Libraries* 66, no. 3 (May 2005): 266–77; Danuta A. Nitecki and Peter Hernon, "Service Quality, A Concept Not Fully Explored," *Library Trends* 49, no. 4 (Spring 2001): 687–708.

37. Benjamin Schneider and Susan S. White, *Service Quality: Research Perspectives* (Thousand Oaks, CA: Sage Publications, 2004), 117.

38. Association of Research Libraries, "ClimateQUAL™" (Washington, DC: The Association, 2009). Available at http://www.climatequal.org/ (accessed May 12, 2009).

39. See Association of Research Libraries, *ClimateQUAL TM-Organizational Climate and Diversity Assessment* (Washington, DC: Association of Research Libraries). Available at http://www.lib.umd.edu/ocda/ (accessed January 4, 2009).

40. Association of Research Libraries, *MINES for Libraries™: Measuring the Impact of Networked Electronic Services and the Ontario Council of University Libraries' Scholars Portal,* Final Report (Washington, DC: Association of Research Libraries, 2005), 6–8. Available at http://www.libqual.org/documents/admin/FINAL%20REPORT_Jan26mk.pdf (accessed September 10, 2008).

41. Ibid., 11.

42. Kyrillidou and Giersch, "Qualitative Analysis of Association of Research Libraries' E-metrics Participant Feedback about the Evolution of Measures for Networked Electronic Resources," 437.

43. Toni Olshen, "Outcome Assessment Tools for the Library of the Future: MINES at OCUL" (Washington, DC: Association of Research Libraries, April 7, 2005). Available at http://www.libqual.org (accessed January 2, 2009).

44. Bonnie Gratch Lindauer, "Comparing the Regional Accreditation Standards: Outcomes Assessment and Other Trends," *The Journal of Academic Librarianship* 28, no. 1/2 (January–March, 2002), 20.

45. Julia C. Blixrud, "Assessing Library Performance: New Measures, Methods, and Models." Libraries and Education in the Networked Information Environment: 24th International Association of Technological University Libraries (IATUL) Conference, June 2–5, 2003, Middle Eastern Technical University, Düsseldorf, Germany. Available at http://

www.iatul.org/doclibrary/public/Conf_Proceedings/2003/BLIXRUD_fulltext.pdf (accessed October 16, 2008).

46. Donald W. King, Peter B. Boyce, Carol H. Montgomery, and Carol Tenopir, "Library Economic Metrics: Examples of the Comparison of Electronic and Print Journal Collections and Collection Services," *Library Trends* 51, no. 3 (Winter 2003): 376–405.

47. Stephen R. Lawrence, Lynn S. Connaway, and Keith H. Brigham, "Life Cycle Costs of Library Collections: Creation of Effective Performance and Cost Metrics for Library Resources," *College & Research Libraries* 62, no. 6 (November 2001): 541–53.

48. See for example, Karla L. Hahn and Lila A. Faulkner, "Evaluative Usage-based Metrics for the Selection of E-journals," *College & Research Libraries* 63, no. 3 (May 2002): 215–27; Carol Tenopir and Donald W. King, "Designing Electronic Journals with 30 Years of Lessons from Print," *Journal of Electronic Publishing* 4, no. 2 (December 1998), available at http://quod.lib.umich.edu/cgi/t/text/text-idx?c=jep;view=text;rgn=main;idno=3336451.0004.202 (accessed February 15, 2009).

49. Beth McNeil and Joan Giesecke, "Using LibQUAL+™ to Improve Services to Library Constituents: A Preliminary Report on the University of Nebraska-Lincoln Experience," *Performance Measurement and Metrics* 3, no. 2 (2002): 96–99.

50. Eileen E. Hitchingham and Donald Kenney, "Extracting Meaningful Measures of User Satisfaction from LibQUAL+™ for the University Libraries at Virginia Tech," *Performance Measurement and Metrics* 3, no. 2 (2002): 48–58.

51. Steve Hiller, Martha Kyrillidou, and Jim Self, "When the Evidence Is Not Enough: Organizational Factors That Influence Effective and Successful Library Assessment," *Performance Measurement and Metrics* 9, no. 3 (2008): 223–30.

52. Ibid., 227.

53. Ronald R. Powell, Lynda M. Baker, and Joseph J. Mika, "Library and Information Science Practitioners and Research," *Library & Information Science Research* 24, no. 1 (2002): 61.

54. 8th Northumbria International Conference on Performance Measurement in Libraries and Information Services. Available at http://www.northumbria.ac.uk/sd/academic/ceis/re/isrc/conf/prn8/?view=Standard (accessed February 15, 2009).

55. See Library Assessment Conference, *Building Effective, Sustainable, Practical Assessment* (Seattle, WA, August 2008). Available at http://www.libraryassessment.org/ (accessed February 15, 2009).

56. Emerald, *Performance Measurement and Metrics* [Information Page]. Available at http://info.emeraldinsight.com/products/journals/journals.htm?id=pmm (accessed February 15, 2009).

57. Research and Markets, *The Survey of Academic Libraries,* 2006–07 ed. (Dublin, Ireland: Research and Markets). Available at http://www.researchandmarkets.com/report info.asp?report_id=444575 (accessed January 11, 2009).

58. Illustration of the range of metrics gathered for this commercial product is the following quote from the company's Web site: "Metrics provided include: percentage of licenses from consortiums, spending on consortium dues, time spent seeking new consortium partners, number of consortium memberships maintained; growth rate in the percentage of licenses obtained through consortiums; expectation for consortium purchases in the future; number of licenses, growth rate in the number of licenses, spending on licenses for directories, electronic journals, e-books, and magazine/newspaper databases; future spending plans on all of the above; price inflation experienced for electronic resources in business, medical, humanities, financial, market research, social sciences and many other information categories; price inflation for e-books, electronic directories, journals, and newspaper/magazine databases; percentage of licenses that require passwords; percentage of licenses that have simultaneous access restrictions; spending on legal services related to licenses, percentage of libraries that have threatened to sue a database vendor; percentage of libraries that have been threatened with suits by database vendors; number of hours spent in reviewing license con-

tracts; percentage of contracts that require contract terms be kept secret; level of awareness of the terms of other libraries contracts; contract terms regarding inter-library loan; success rates in seeking changes in license contracts; percentage of libraries that have paid an article processing fee or received a rebate as compensation for open access; number of articles obtained through digital repositories; planned development of digital repositories; use of journal archives provided for free after an embargo period; use of Google Scholar; percentage that report loss of perpetual access to journal archives; percentage of journal contracts that guarantee perpetual access; use of grants for financing databases; use of charge backs and departmental contributions to finance database licensing; percentage that outsource copyright clearance; plans for the elimination of paper-base course reserves; expectations for renewing current database subscriptions; number of databases tried on a free trial basis; rated reliability of usage statistics obtained from database vendors; staff time spent on service interruption issues." See Research and Markets, *The Survey of Library Database Licensing Practices* (Dublin, Ireland: Research and Markets, December 2007). Available at http://www.researchandmarkets.com/reportinfo.asp?report_id=586437&t=d&cat_id=(accessed November 2, 2008).

59. Danuta A. Nitecki and William Rando, "Evolving an Assessment of the Impact on Pedagogy, Learning and Library Support of Teaching with Digital Images," in *Outcomes Assessment in Higher Education Views and Perspectives,* edited by Peter Hernon and Robert E. Dugan (Westport, CT: Libraries Unlimited, 2004), 175–96.

60. Kathlin L. Ray, "The Postmodern Library in an Age of Assessment," ACRL Tenth National Conference, March 15–18 (Denver, CO: Association of College and Research Libraries, 2002), 250–54. Available at http://www.ala.org/ala/mgrps/divs/acrl/events/pdf/kray.pdf (accessed February 18, 2009).

61. Ibid., 253.

62. Ibid.

63. Ibid.

# 5

---

# THE CUSTOMER PERSPECTIVE

At one time, librarians defined quality in terms of collections and the extent of their growth under a particular director. Now, many librarians view collections as part of the services they provide and look at the totality of the services offered from a human perspective, namely, that of the customer. The public operates largely within the digital world of the Internet and its Web 2.0 environment, while still relying in a number of instances on the physical library. In such a context, librarians are searching for new ways to gauge the quality of their activities and the impact of those activities on their customers. This chapter examines the customer perspective and identifies a number of metrics that libraries could develop to gauge the effectiveness of their services and the impact of the library on its user communities. Some metrics could conceivably relate to the information needs and information-seeking behavior of those using libraries. Examples might focus on the purpose for which the library is used, the types of resources used, and the age of those resources. The problem with developing such metrics is that the context might be ignored. In other words, for undergraduates (or for those in middle and high school), purpose might relate to the type of classroom assignment they are working on or whether they are visiting the library to meet friends.

This chapter asks, "What matters to customers?" but before addressing that question, the chapter offers a characterization of customers and illustrates different metrics that might be of importance to them. It is up to individual libraries to decide which metrics they want to develop and how often to gather data. The chapter identifies a number of writings that might serve as models for data collection. It also suggests that meaningful data might not always be reduced to a simple ratio and percentage. Furthermore, which metrics are compiled is less important than how any data gathered are actually used for service improvement.

## TYPES OF CUSTOMERS

A customer is the recipient of any product or service provided by the organization. That recipient might be *internal*, such as a coworker in the same or another unit, or *external,* such as someone in the community visiting the library physically or remotely. Internal customers use library services and might have thoughts about what external customers would appreciate. They also have their own set of expectations and use library services (e.g., search databases, consult reference sources, peruse periodicals and newspapers, and borrow books). Perceptions of internal customers are useful to document and improve processes supporting the delivery of services to external customers. Having satisfied employees, combined with an organizational commitment to the provision of outstanding customer service, leads to empowerment and a willingness to resolve problems when they arise. Moreover, satisfied employees deliver better services to their customers.

External customers might be seeking materials or information, or using the library as a social center or to attend a workshop or program. Such customers vary in the frequency of their use, from occasionally to regularly. There are also *never-gained* customers (e.g., incoming college freshmen who have not yet experienced the services of a particular library), *lost* customers (who are dissatisfied with the services provided and unwilling to revisit), and *noncustomers* (who are unwilling to visit under any circumstances; they either perceive no need for a visit or had an unpleasant experience that makes them adamant in their refusal to revisit). Figure 5.1 characterizes the different groups and reminds us that a survey of an undifferentiated population likely yields only very frequent and perhaps satisfied customers.

Perusal of the figure suggests some metrics (reported as mere numbers) that libraries might gather about their customers. For example, they might determine the number of never-gained or lost customers they attracted during a given time period. The number might be subdivided by subgroups such as the number of never-gained faculty (perhaps by discipline: humanities, social sciences, behavioral sciences, and sciences) and students (perhaps by class year).

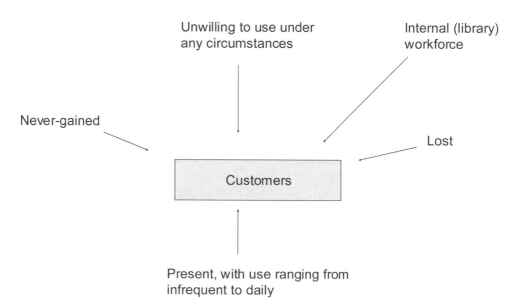

Figure 5.1    Depiction of the Community Served

The business literature, which focuses on employees but does not necessarily characterize them as internal customers, notes that "there is nothing as frustrating or expensive as having to retrain a new person to be as good as the person who just left you. In fact, one of the most significant costs to any company is that of turnover and retraining new employees. It can take one to two years to get a new employee 'up to snuff'."[1] In addition to improving worker productivity and retention, good customer service, as noted in the literature on the topic, improves staff morale, the service provided to external customers, and, for the private sector, profitability. There are instances in which some in the current workforce do not support the organization's mission and vision and do not work collaboratively. Still, productive workers merit retention, but at the same time, there may be no advancement opportunities within the organization.

Employees need to understand their role in the organization and how their work fits in (or serves) others in the organization. The development of employees involves learning new skills, abilities, and ways to assume tomorrow's responsibilities. Employees need encouragement to engage in problem solving, to be innovative, and to take reasonable risks to achieve the organization's mission and goals. In this context, questions (e.g., "What does an employee do to support the delivery of high-quality service?") become important and help to identify what to measure.

Businesses seek to create a culture whereby their "people and their passion for making a difference" view themselves as a family (e.g., the Nordstrom family) and want members of that family to practice good listening skills, exercise good judgment, feel empowered, "be honest," "be recognized," "be a good neighbor" ("support community organizations through contributions, outreach programs, special events, and volunteerism"), "be kind," realize that "it's your business" ("our employees have a personal, financial, and professional stake in the success of our company"), "have fun," and so on.[2] Clearly, there is a direct link between internal and external customer satisfaction. Both types of satisfaction lead to organizational loyalty. Furthermore, surveys have shown that the reasons customers give for not returning for repeat business are the following: they moved, 3 percent; other friendships, 5 percent; competition, 9 percent; dissatisfaction, 14 percent; and employee attitude, 68 percent.[3] Reinforcing these general findings is the fact that "30–40 percent of the time when a customer problem occurs it is a result of poor internal customer service."[4]

## EXCELLENCE IN CUSTOMER SERVICE

During the 1990s and the early 21st century, some public and private sector organizations, including a few academic and public libraries, pledged to provide excellent customer service and perhaps to make an organizational commitment to:

- provide courteous, prompt, and accurate service to everyone (They might promise to welcome customers courteously and with a smile.)
- listen carefully to customer needs and respond to them appropriately
- do their best to provide resources to meet customer research needs
- offer opportunities for instruction about library resources and services
- provide an environment that is conducive to information gathering, study and reflection, and research

- provide the assistance customers need, or put them in contact with someone who can
- ensure that service is the library's top priority

In some instances, organizations have posted a pledge so that customers could know what to expect from any of the services they might use. In other instances, a pledge might not be shared with the public; rather, it is incorporated in strategic planning and staff development. The purpose is for the staff to review the pledge, to make whatever changes it wants, and, for the administration and staff, to view that revised pledge as a basis for the service provided. Customer service could therefore be framed within the context of that pledge. More importantly, staff across the organization might meet and review the types of statements highlighted in Table 5.1. In their review, they might change the wording, fill in the blank time period, and replace statements or add new ones. The critical issue is for the staff to develop measurable statements, ones for which management could develop objective and quantifiable means of collecting data. Perhaps at randomly selected times, someone holding a stop watch or tally sheet might compile data about the speed or amount of service, which could be reviewed and any necessary service improvements enacted. For example, the length of time for which computer workstations and printers are inoperative might be recorded and the results factored into service improvement.

**Table 5.1**
**Quantitative Metrics for Staff Review**

## GENERAL SERVICES

Acknowledge you immediately at any service desk and serve you within __ minutes or call additional staff

Call you back if we need to ask you to hold on the phone for more than __ minutes

Report photocopier problems immediately

Respond personally to your signed suggestions within __ days

Make the names and phone numbers of department managers available at all service points (and on the library's homepage)

Provide users with the tools and training to enable access to the library collections and to resources available nationally

Maintain designated quiet study areas

Maintain designated noisy study areas

Provide a clean and comfortable study environment

## COLLECTIONS AND ELECTRONIC INFORMATION SERVICES

Ensure easy and efficient navigation of the library Web site
— Navigation can be accomplished within __ clicks of the mouse

No public workstation will be down longer than __ (minutes, days)

Ensure that workstations are capable of efficient printing and/or downloading

Catalog materials accurately and promptly

(*Continued*)

**Table 5.1**
**Quantitative Metrics for Staff Review (*Continued*)**

Make new books available within __ weeks of receipt and provide rush delivery when necessary

Locate acceptable substitutes immediately or provide copies within __ hours when requested materials are at the bindery

Respond to faculty book orders within __ working days

## INFORMATION AND RESEARCH SERVICES

Respond to online reference inquiries within __ working day(s)

Respond to e-mail questions within __ hours

## INFORMATION DELIVERY SERVICES

Check out and check in all books and materials with __ % accuracy

Maintain an error-free fine system

   — If mistakes are made, then _____

Shelve books within __ hours of use and regularly maintain shelf order

Shelve bound periodicals within __ hours of use and regularly maintain shelf order

Shelve current periodicals within __ hour(s) of receipt

Reshelve current periodicals within __ hour (s) of use

Respond to requests for book purchases within ___ hours

Ensure that no equipment is out of service more than ___ (minutes, hours, days)

Initiate searches for missing materials within __ (hours or days)

Ensure that no ILL request goes unfilled longer than ___ days

*Adapted with permission from the Lehigh University Information Resources Services Standards, which appears in Peter Hernon and Ellen Altman, *Assessing Service Quality: Satisfying the Expectations of Library Customers* (Chicago: American Library Association, 1998), 39–41.

## TYPES OF QUESTIONS RELEVANT TO MEASUREMENT

Peter Hernon and Ellen Altman identify 11 questions that outline the different *hows* of measurement and that encompass the different types of metrics discussed in this book, namely, inputs, outputs, and outcomes. Those questions, they note, "can be used singly or in groups. In fact, some of the 'hows' are calculated by using data derived from other 'hows'. This list of measuring rods progresses from the highly quantitative to the highly qualitative. The focus shifts from a library or internal perspective to a customer or external perspective."[5] All 11 questions suggest metrics that address the customer perspective:

1. *How much?* Cost might focus on affordability from the customer perspective. For instance, questions that might be of interest to customers relate to the cost of making photocopies, downloading papers, or borrowing CDs or videos.

2. *How many?* Most often, relevant questions relate to outputs from the perspective of the organization (e.g., the number of reference questions asked or of visitors to the

library, either in person or remotely). Associated questions might include "How many people does it take to reserve a room for group study?" "How many times can a book be renewed?" or "How many books can be borrowed at one time?"

3. *How economical?* Thrift is the focus, and this question most often is approached from an organizational perspective. Customers might ask themselves, "How economical is it for me to borrow a book, especially one that the customer needs for an extended period of time, as opposed to purchasing it?"

4. *How prompt?* For this chapter, this question does not pertain to speed in completing processes or functions (e.g., the average time to catalog items) unless there is a customer request or demand for prompt receipt of an item. Rather, the focus is on promptness in receiving service. This question might also address the length of the waiting line at a circulation or reference desk.

5. *How accurate?* This question relates to the accuracy of outputs constituting a service deliverable, for example accuracy of shelving material, answering reference questions, or records in an online catalog or in databases.

6. *How responsive?* As Hernon and Altman note, responsiveness is associated with the extent to which "the library anticipates customer questions and problems and works to eliminate or ameliorate them. . . . Data about responsiveness are usually binary, in that the element or service is either available or not, and these service elements are also countable in terms of the numbers available." More detailed analysis of responsiveness might incorporate customers' judgments on the degree to which the library is responsive along a continuum, thereby the metric of responsiveness looks at "how well" the service is delivered. In addition, "*helpfulness* is another indication of responsiveness. Customers perceive staff members who actively assist them, rather than pointing or shrugging, as responsive."[6]

7. *How well?* Typically this question is defined in terms of effectiveness or how successfully a service accomplishes its stated objectives and furthers library goals. Customers, however, might characterize this question in terms of other questions identified here (e.g., how promptly): "Customers and staff perceptions may differ sharply about how well a function or a service performs. These perceptions are subjective, but have validity because they influence perceptions and attitudes about the library."[7]

8. *How valuable?* Customers might view this question in terms of their willingness to pay for a service, or they might evaluate the value of a visit to the library in terms of the relationship of cost (expenditure of time, effort, or money) and of benefit (received information, helpful treatment, or ease of use). Clearly, this question involves a judgment call of the highest order in that the public places an economic value on the services received. Table 5.2 identifies a number of writings in the literature of library and information science associated with value.

9. *How reliable?* Businesses see reliability as the likelihood that a product performs as expected and does not malfunction within a given time period. For libraries heavily reliant on automation, reliability applies to predictable technology and the avoidance of malfunction. It might also apply to the information received and the consistency of staff over time in providing accurate answers to the same customers.

10. *How courteous?* A number of organizations (e.g., The Ritz-Carlton) view courtesy as underpinning every interaction among staff members as well as between them and the public they serve. Realizing that employees treated internally with respect most likely extend that same treatment to customers, excellent service organizations provide specific and ongoing training in courtesy. In essence, these organizations practice servant leadership, whereby the servant-leader serves his or her employees by providing support needed for each person in the organization to grow both professionally and personally.

**Table 5.2**
**Public Library Value: Selected Readings**

Aabø, Svanhild. "The Value of Public Libraries," presented at World Library and Information Congress: 71th IFLA General Conference and Council, "Libraries—A Voyage of Discovery," August 14–18, 2005, Oslo, Norway. Available at http://www.ifla.org/IV/ifla71/papers/119e-Aabo.pdf (accessed March 22, 2008).

Barron, Daniel D., Robert V. Williams, Steven Bajjaly, Jennifer Arns, and Steven Wilson. *The Economic Impact of Public Libraries on South Carolina.* Colombia, SC: University of South Carolina, School of Library and Information Science, 2005. Available at http://www.libsci.sc.edu/SCEIS/final%20report%2026%20january.pdf (accessed March 3, 2008).

Berk & Associates. *The Seattle Public Library Central Library: Economic Benefits Assessment.* Prepared for the Seattle Public Library Foundation, 2005. Available at http://www.spl.org/pdfs/SPLCentral_Library_Economic_Impacts.pdf (accessed March 3, 2008).

Elliott, Donald S. *Measuring Your Library's Value: How to Do a Cost-benefit Analysis for Your Public Library.* Chicago: American Library Association, 2007.

Fitch, Leslie, and Jody Warner. "Dividends: The Value of Public Libraries in Canada." Canada Book and Periodical Council, 1999. *Australasian Public Libraries and Information Services* 12, no. 1 (1999): 4–24.

Griffiths, José-Marie, Donald W., King, D., and Thomas Lynch. "Taxpayer Return on Investment in *Public Libraries*" (funded under the provisions of the Library Services and Technology Act, from the Institute of Museum and Library Services, administered by the Florida Department of State, State Library and Archives of Florida), 2004. Available at http://dlis.dos.state.fl.us/bld/roi/pdfs/ROISummaryReport.pdf (accessed March 3, 2008).

Holt, Glen E. "On Becoming Essential: An Agenda for Quality in Twenty-first Century Public Libraries." *Library Trends* 44, no. 3 (1996): 545–71 (see the entire issue).

Holt, Glen E., and Donald Elliott. "Measuring Outcomes: Applying Cost-benefit Analysis to Middlesized and Small Public Libraries," *Library Trends* 51, no. 3 (2003): 424–40 (see the entire issue).

Holt, Glen E., and Donald Elliot. "Proving Your Library's Worth: A Test Case." *Library Journal* 123, no. 18 (1998): 42–44.

Holt, Glen E., Donald Elliott, and Amonia Moore. *Placing a Value on Public Library Services.* St. Louis, MO: St. Louis Public Library, n.d. Available at http://www.slpl.lib.mo.us/libsrc/restoc.htm (accessed March 3, 2008).

Imholz, Susan, and Jennifer W. Arns, *Worth Their Weight: An Assessment of the Evolving Field of Library Valuation.* New York: Americans for Libraries Council, 2007. Available at http://www.actforlibraries.org/pdf/WorthTheirWeight.pdf (accessed March 3, 2008).

Kamer, Pearl M. *The Economic Value of the Port Jefferson Free Library in Suffolk County, NY.* Available at http://www.actforlibraries.org/pdf/PortJeffersonEcoVal2006study.pdf (accessed March 3, 2008).

McCallum, Ian, and Sherrey Quinn. "Valuing Libraries." *The Australian Library Journal.* Available at http://www.alia.org.au/publishing/alj/53.1/full.text/mccallum.quinn.html (accessed March 3, 2008).

*(Continued)*

**Table 5.2**
**Public Library Value: Selected Readings (*Continued*)**

McClure, Charles R., Bruce T. Fraser, Timothy W. Nelson, and Jane B. Robbins. *Economic Benefits and Impacts from Public Libraries in the State of Florida* (Final report to the State of Florida, Division of Library and Information Services). Tallahassee, FL: Florida State University, Information Use Management Policy Institute, n.d. Available at http://dlis.dos.state.fl.us/bld/Research_Office/final-report.pdf 9 (accessed March 3, 2008).

Morris, A., J. Sumsion, and M. Hawkins. "Economic Value of Public Libraries in the UK." *Libri* 52 (2002): 78–87.

Urban Libraries Council. *Making Cities Stronger: Public Library Contributions to Local Economic Development*. Chicago: Urban Libraries Council, 2007. Available at http://www.urbanlibraries.org/files/making_cities_stronger.pdf (accessed March 3, 2008).

Wisconsin Department of Public Instruction. *Economic Impact of Public Libraries*. Madison, WI: Department of Public Instruction, 2008. Available at http://dpi.wi.gov/pld/econimpact.html (accessed March 3, 2008). This site provides "links to various studies designed to measure the economic impact or taxpayer return-on-investment for public libraries, as well as resources for conducting local studies."

11. *How satisfied?* This question deals with customers' expectations of a service and their perceptions of how well the service meets those expectations. Typically, this question relates to one or more experience with a service. Satisfaction focuses on customer opinions emerging from an experience—a visit to the library, its online catalog, or one of its other digital services. On the other hand, satisfaction might relate to a collective set of experiences (e.g., use of the library or one of its services over the past week, month, or year).

   Beyond perceptions, customers form attitudes about a service over time or after having multiple experiences with it. Expectations about what they would like to see in the services and resources provided evolve. The degree to which they perceive that the service meets these ideals for service excellence becomes the basis for metrics associated with *service quality*.

Perhaps one of most important of all the questions from a customer perspective is the last one, *How satisfied?* However, satisfaction is not an end unto itself. Rather, the resolution of an information need or the question of *How valuable?* become more important. Undoubtedly, aspects of the other questions contribute to meeting customer expectations and to making library customers satisfied and willing to use a service or the library again. The goal is not merely to meet their expectations; it is to exceed them—forming customer loyalty or individuals who constantly recommend the library and its services to friends, colleagues, and acquaintances.

## CUSTOMER EXPECTATIONS

Expectations for either internal or external customers are desired wants, or the extent to which customers believe a particular service attribute is essential for an excellent service provider. To complicate matters, expectations change over time, and there might be substantial differences among (and within) generations regarding expectations. Expectations can be viewed from one of two perspectives: satisfaction and service quality. In essence, service quality is subordinate to satisfaction; service quality should lead to satisfied or delighted customers.

## Satisfaction

Satisfaction, which is defined as the extent of contentment that arises from an *actual* experience in relation to an *expected* experience, might be envisioned as a perception of a particular service experience or of encounters over a period of time (e.g., week, month, or year). Satisfaction is transaction specific. *Service-encounter satisfaction* is how much a customer likes or dislikes an actual service encounter, whereas *overall service satisfaction* is the customer's feeling of satisfaction or dissatisfaction based on all of that person's experiences with the library. Librarians should be cautious in attributing causality to any experience of satisfaction or dissatisfaction.

Most customers have preconceived notions of what they expect from a library, but they have probably not thought very much about those expectations and probably would not do so unless and until some kind of *positive surprise* takes place. An event that significantly deviates from expectations is a satisfaction surprise. On the other hand, an untoward service surprise, otherwise known as a *service failure,* can have a severely damaging effect on an organization's reputation, and too many organizations respond to such events poorly. How the organization responds to service failures can make or break its reputation with the affected customers and have a ripple effect through word of mouth. A standout response in the case of a service failure can do wonders to maintain and even enhance an organization's reputation.

Table 5.3 illustrates questions that might be asked in either an overall service or a specific service encounter. Regardless, prior experience is the most important antecedent of satisfaction. Although not directly part of a satisfaction study, an examination of service encounter satisfaction might ask:

Please indicate all of the services of this library you used today:

- borrowed items (books and other materials)
- used materials while in the library (read, viewed, listened to, browsed)
- used the library's equipment (e.g., computers, workstations, audiovisual equipment, printers, and copiers)
- attended a program
- used library facilities (e.g., chairs, tables, rooms, or bathrooms)
- accessed library services from a location other than the library
- accessed the Internet while at the library
- accessed an online database at the library
- asked a question of library staff
- other (please specify)

A follow-up question then might be, "How valuable was that service?" with the scale being 1 (no value) to 10 (very valuable). An alternative way to frame the

**Table 5.3**
**Satisfaction Questions: Examples for Service Encounter and Overall Service***

| Service Encounter Satisfaction | Overall Service Satisfaction |
|---|---|
| Please indicate how long you have been using the services of this library.<br><br>OR<br><br>Please indicate how often you have used the services of this library in the past [month, school term, or year]. | Please indicate how long you have been using the services of this library.<br><br>OR<br><br>Please indicate how often you have used the services of this library in the past [month, school term, or year]. |
| Overall, how satisfied are you with today's library visit?<br><br>Name specific services or facilities and ask which they use and how satisfied they are with the service provided. For instance, "Did you request assistance of a library staff member? Yes__ No___.<br><br>If yes, when dealing with library staff,<br><br>    They respond in a professional manner.<br>    They answered your questions in a timely manner.<br><br>Did you experience any problems in the use of the library? Yes__ No__.<br><br>    If yes, what was the problem?<br><br>    Was the problem resolved to your satisfaction?<br><br>Will you use the library again?<br>OR<br>How likely are you to recommend us to a friend or colleague? (If the question appeared with a scale of 1–10), if you indicated 8 or lower, why? | Please indicate your overall satisfaction with this library compared with the following information providers:<br><br>• Bookstore<br>• Colleague, friend, or instructor<br>• Information available across the Internet (not from the library)<br>• Media<br>• Other libraries<br>• Other<br><br>Based on past experience with this library, how satisfied are you with its services?<br><br>Based on past experience, what are we doing that you particularly like?<br><br>Based on past experience, what are we doing that you particularly dislike?<br><br>If we could do *one* thing to improve, what should it be?<br><br>Will you use the library again?<br>OR<br>How likely are you to recommend us to a friend or colleague? (If the question appeared with a scale of 1–10), if you indicated 8 or lower, why? |

*A number of the questions require the use of a scale, most likely one ranging from 1 to 10, with 1 being very unlikely or very unimportant to 10 being very likely or very important.

question might be, "If you were given 100 money bills to distribute across the services you used today, how much would you spend on each?" Or, a different question becomes, "Was it worth your time to come to the library today?"

For overall service satisfaction, a question that involves value might be, "How much would you support library services overall if the university introduced a student fee to support the library (or if you were asked to vote for a budget increase for the library)"? As this example illustrates, a question might have significance for more than 1 of the 11 evaluation question.

Service levels among internal customers in different departments or work areas, as Charles D. Kerns notes, can be measured in terms of:

- Helpfulness: Was the issue or problem resolved or was valuable progress made (in its resolution)?
- Responsiveness: Was the request (for assistance) received and answered promptly?
- Respectfulness: Were sincere interest and cooperation shown?[8]

To his list, we add accuracy: Was the work performed or the answer given correct? As Kerns observes,

"The [four] service level measurement factors—helpfulness, responsiveness . . . respectfulness, [and accuracy]—need to be rated by members of the various departments within an organization. A simple Likert type scale can be used. The following eight-point rating scale has worked well in many settings:

1–2 = Consistently fails to reach my expectations in this area.

3–4 = Meets some of my expectations in this area.

5–6 = Meets a majority of my expectations.

7–8 = Exceeds my expectations in this area.

When one department's personnel have had no interaction with another department for the period being rated, a zero is recorded on the rating form. A recurring pattern of zeros may be significant, especially when there is a perceived high level of interdependence between the two departments in question. A string of zeros may reflect conflict avoidance or other dysfunctional issues. The manager who supervises the various department heads or team leaders is responsible for collecting the data. This person usually holds a collaborative orientation session at the onset of the program to establish rating performance targets, reporting periods/timeframes, and interaction expectations. A four to six week baseline of ratings is useful to determine current perceptions of service levels across the three dimensions being measured. In terms of reporting periods, it is recommended that initially the data across functional areas be collected on a weekly basis and reported back to the various departments. After the process of rating and reporting is working, a biweekly reporting period may be sufficient. The feedback timeframe should never extend beyond one month. Based on experience, it is apparent that organizations tend to pay less attention to this important area of internal customer service when it is measured and discussed infrequently."[9]

An example of an instrument intended for internal customers appears in *Delivering Satisfaction and Service Quality*,[10] whereas *Assessing Service Quality* offers an extensive array of questions such as those listed in Table 5.3.[11] Additionally, survey forms for external customers can be found in *Delivering Satisfaction and Service Quality*.[12] As part of outcomes assessment, institutions of higher education might use the National Survey of Student Engagement, which includes some questions related to the educational experience, how supportive students find the campus environment, satisfaction with library collections and services, and the effectiveness of information literacy instruction.[13]

## Service Quality

The most cited conceptual model of service quality, known as the Gap Model of Service Quality, sets up metrics for managers to diagnose where a service design and performance weakly meet customer expectations for service excellence. The model includes five discrepancies:

Gap 1: Between customers' expectations for excellent service and management's perceptions of those expectations (i.e., the extent to which managers know what customers expect)

Gap 2: Between management's perceptions of customers' expectations and service quality specifications (i.e., the extent service standards are designed to meet understood service-quality expectations)

Gap 3: Between service quality specifications and service delivery (i.e., the service performance in terms of its standards)

Gap 4: Between service delivery and external communications to customers about the service (i.e., the degree to which service promises are delivered)

Gap 5: Between customers' expectations for service excellence and their perceptions of service delivered (i.e. the operational definition of service quality)[14]

As A. Parasuraman explains, "improving the quality of service experienced by customers (i.e., closing Gap 5) required diagnosing the causes of and correcting the internal deficiencies (i.e. Gaps 1–4)."[15] Together with his colleagues (Leonard L. Berry and Valarie A. Zeitmal), Parasuraman develops instruments to measure each of the five gaps. The instrument designed to measure Gap 5 is the SERVQUAL, which has become the most popular tool to measure service quality since it was first introduced in the 1980s.

A number of academic libraries use LibQUAL+™, a variation of SERVQUAL, to review service quality. To date, more than 1,000 libraries in the United States, Canada, the United Kingdom, South Africa, and Europe ("including colleges and universities, community colleges, health sciences libraries, law libraries, and public libraries-some through various consortia, others as independent participants") have participated in a survey of their customers.[16] Furthermore, LibQUAL+™ "has expanded internationally, with participating institutions in Canada, the U.K. and other European countries as well as Australia and South Africa. It has been translated into several languages, including French, Swedish, Dutch, Afrikaans, German, Danish, Finnish, and Norwegian."[17] The purpose of the survey is to produce comparable data to enable benchmarking and comparison among libraries, but it does provide some data useful for local service review and improvement.

Turning to electronically delivered service, Parasuraman redefines service quality as e-SQ, "the extent to which a Web site facilitates efficient and effective shopping, purchasing and delivery of products and services. The dimensions on which customers assess e-SQ are access, ease of navigation, efficiency, customization/personalization, security/privacy, responsiveness, assurance/trust, price knowledge, site aesthetics, reliability, flexibility, and efficiency."[18] Each of these dimensions contains a number of specific attributes.

As an alternative (or complement) to LibQUAL+™, libraries might use a variation of SERVQUAL, in which the staff select those statements most relevant to
local conditions from an extensive pool of assertions that define quality services.
Through an iterative process, a set of statements might be developed and inserted
into a SERVQUAL-like instrument. Customers would be invited to indicate both
the degree of their agreement that each is important for excellent service and then
the extent to which they perceive the library service under review to possess these
characteristics of quality services. Calculations involving the difference or gap between these two measures provide a SERVQUAL score. An example of the basic
instrument evolved in this fashion was published in *The Journal of Academic Librarianship* in 2000.[19] Building on A. Parasuraman's writings on e-SQ, Hernon
and Philip Calvert produced an extensive set of statements relevant to the digital
environment that could be inserted into the framework described by Danuta A.
Nitecki and Hernon.[20]

StatsQUAL™, which operates under the auspices of Association of Research Libraries (ARL), serves as a gateway to library assessment tools that describe the role,
character, and impact of physical and digital libraries (http://www.digiqual.org/).
One of the tools is DigiQUAL™, which modifies and repurposes LibQUAL+™
to assess the services provided by digital libraries (http://www.digiqual.org/
digiqual/index.cfm). Thus, it serves as an alternative to the statements that Hernon and Calvert developed.[21]

Still, Hernon and Calvert caution that neither LibQUAL+™ nor the existing
variations of SERVQUAL apply to special populations such as individuals with disabilities, recipients of library services who represent different racial and ethic groups
(ones for whom English is a second language), and students requiring remedial
services. With the assistance of experts within the United States and New Zealand,
they developed and pilot-tested two versions of a special SERVQUAL instrument
relevant to the expectations of persons with disabilities.[22] Anyone using the prevail-
ing versions of LibQUAL+™ and SERVQUAL should consider the limitations of
generalizing the results across a population such as college freshmen, since that
group may contain a number of students with disabilities, from different racial and
ethnic groups, or from cultures other than the United States.

Because the statements included in the various instruments can be converted to
a quantitative metric, the choices exceed the number of metrics presented in this
chapter. At the same time, librarians might explore the use of library spaces and convert some of the findings into statements that could be inserted into a SERVQUAL-
like instrument.[23]

## RELIABILITY AS A CUSTOMER EXPECTATION

SERVQUAL includes a set of statements that encompass interrelated dimensions
that customers most value when, regardless of the service provided, they evaluate
the service quality provided by an organization. Service quality, to repeat, refers
to the gap between service expectations and the service actually provided. As Hernon and Altman point out, "these expectations may or may not match what the
library thinks appropriate, but nevertheless *they represent reality for the customer.*"[24]
One dimension associated with service quality is reliability, which refers to the
ability to perform the promised service dependably and accurately. In those instances in which SERVQUAL has been applied in a library setting, "except for a
study of reference services, all applications identified reliability as the single most

important service dimension."[25] LibQUAL+™, which defines and measures library service quality across institutions and creates a general picture of such service for use in individual libraries, places reliability as a subset of "affect of service," along with "empathy," "responsiveness," and "assurance." The reports of libraries using this instrument that the authors examined, view "affect of service" as the dominant dimension. Some of those reports address dependability, but not accuracy, except somewhat through statements such as "employees who have the knowledge to answer user questions." Apparently the dimension, as some libraries envision, focuses on selected aspects of customer service, such as "willingness to help users," staff courtesy, and dealing with users "in a caring fashion." A number of the statements under "affect of service" are subjectivity, for instance, "employees who deal with users in a caring fashion." What does this actually mean?

Some of the other library reports examined cover both responsiveness and reliability, with reliability addressing certain statements:

- providing service at the promised time
- performing services right the first time
- accuracy in the catalog, borrowing, and overdue records
- dependability in handling users' service problems
- providing service as promised

Such statements do not address issues such as response time in terms of queuing or standing in line to receive a service.

Since the early years of the 21st century, there have been efforts to document consumer perceptions of e-service quality. The evidence suggests that reliability is the most important service dimension for those making purchases over the Internet, whereas "Internet non-purchasers consider 'security' as their most critical concern."[26] An examination of e-service and the provision of virtual reference in libraries do not produce statistically significant differences along three dimensions: timely response, reliability, and courtesy.[27] In their study of e-service quality in libraries, Hernon and Calvert find that reliability trails ease of use and collections as the most important dimension.[28] Furthermore, in their development of an instrument to measure service quality for student with disabilities, they note that reliability is not a significant dimension.[29]

Given the general findings of the literature highlighted in this section, libraries might choose to omit addressing reliability in the nondigital environment.

## METHODS OF DATA COLLECTION

### Overview

The choices for gathering data that document customers interaction with library services become asking customers for self-reports, viewing and reacting to comments that customers make, observing performance and estimating what customers expect, and determining where problems exist and making corrections based on those problems. Self-reporting relies on a survey of employees or existing, new, or lost-customers. Customers might also respond to comment cards or be subject to interviewing, including focus group interviews, or make complaints. Viewing and reacting to customer comments focuses on an examination of a library's blog or complaints and comments that customers make. Observation might involve the use of mystery shoppers (unobtrusive testing), which is the process of asking reference questions for which answers have been determined of library staff members who are unaware that the trained individuals who ask the questions are evaluating their demeanor and responses.

Additionally, there might be a review of captured data (logs of customer online transactions and employee field reporting). Library staff might also draw inferences from a review of databases or the use of customer advisory panels, sometimes called customer listening groups. Libraries might also monitor waiting times.

An advantage of using methods that directly involve customers in data collection is the opportunity to demonstrate that library staff members listen to them. Listening is an underrated tool for obtaining information and, ultimately, evaluating customers' experiences. Listening means communication and developing a relationship of trust. It does not mean doing everything that customers request.

Using a multidimensional approach for Web evaluation, librarians might:

- engage in usability testing (e.g., site navigation and user friendliness)
- gather used feedback (expectations, use, and impact)
- compile performance data (e.g., page download time)
- collect usage data (e.g., pages viewed and total visits)

## Advice

As libraries prepare to investigate the extent of satisfaction among the communities they serve, they might remember some of the suggestions that the Office of the Legislative Auditor offered to Minnesota state government agencies:

- "Two concepts are particularly important in conducting valid customer surveys: (1) random sampling and (2) representativeness. Random sampling is the process of selecting random subsets of customers in order to draw conclusions about all customers of given types . . . Representativeness means that those who respond share important characteristics with all customers of given types."

- "Customer satisfaction surveys are a form of 'feedback' from those who have received services. But feedback may assume many forms, and the conclusions one can draw from feedback depend on the strength and types of controls that have been placed over the collection of information. For example, casual comments from customers can offer insights that improve services, but a scientific, rigorous survey of all or a sample of a customer population is needed to yield results that can be generalized with reasonable certainty to customers as a whole."

- "To minimize nonresponse bias, staff of federal agencies . . . told us they work to achieve response rates of at least 70 or 75 percent. When sound methods and techniques are used, . . . experts suggest that response rates of 60 to 70 percent can be achieved."[30]

Lesser response rates, as the Office of the Legislative Auditor notes, serve as a warning that nonresponse error—the respondents could be systematically different from the rest of the population—and nonsampling error—data gathered from a sample can be inaccurate not only as a result of an inaccurate or nonrepresentative sample but also due to errors of measurement—might pose problems.[31]

## Quantitative Metrics

A number of metrics can be presented as numbers, ratios, or percentages and reflect the interests and concerns of library customers. These customers might be relying on digital services or services available through the physical library. The actual metrics discussed in this chapter are not comprehensive for every service a library offers; rather, they are suggestive. It is possible to develop metrics for the length of queuing (wait time) at service points. Whatever metrics are adopted, however, they might include some qualitative components.

### Qualitative Data Collection

As Table 5.3 illustrates, some of the questions related to overall service satisfaction might be open-ended and give respondents an opportunity to offer written comments. Some of the quantitative metrics might even be framed as questions to pursue in focus group interviews.

## CONCLUSION

As this chapter illustrates, libraries can compile a number of metrics, either quantitative or qualitative, that represent the customer perspective. The majority of those metrics, be they for service quality or satisfaction, are outputs. Service quality is a multidimensional term with two critical facets: content and context. *Content* refers to obtaining what prompted the physical or virtual visit, and *context* covers the experience itself: interaction with staff, ease or difficulty in navigating the system, and the comfort of the physical environment. As first characterized by developers of the SERVQUAL, service quality consists of interrelated dimensions that customers most value when they evaluate a service industry:

* *tangibles* (appearance of physical facilities, equipment, personnel, and communication material)
* *reliability* (ability to perform the promised services dependably and accurately)
* *responsiveness* (willingness to help customers and provide prompt service)
* *assurance* (knowledge and courtesy of employees and their ability to inspire trust and confidence)
* *empathy* (caring, individualized attention that a firm provides its customers)[32]

Within library and information science, assorted research studies have reviewed and amended those dimensions so that they can be more applicable to libraries.[33] Further, as previously discussed, Parasuraman shows that a different set of dimensions applies to e-SQ, and the previous discussion of reliability merits consideration.

Satisfaction can be cast in terms of service encounter satisfaction or overall service satisfaction. Customer-related metrics can be used for demonstrating accountability and showing the extent to which libraries exceed their customers' expectations and provide superior customer service. These metrics should also be used to improve the quality of service that customers receive. In this instance, quantitative metrics should be accompanied by qualitative ones that provide more in-depth insights into problem areas.

Today's libraries function in a very competitive marketplace that contains assorted providers of digital and nondigital resources. As customer expectations change, the marketplace will adapt and create new services and products. Libraries, however, will have to remain competitive. At the same time, it is important that internal customers not be neglected. As a result, it is important to compile data over time and make comparisons for benchmarking (see chapter 8).[34] Still, the

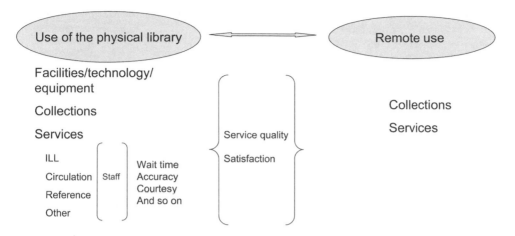

Figure 5.2   Customer Areas for the Development of Metrics

most critical issue is to select those metrics most essential for service improvement and strategic planning. Figure 5.2 identifies the areas from which customer metrics might be selected. It is critical to recognize that service quality and satisfaction are not interchangeable terms and that the figure should not be viewed exclusively from the perspective of external customers.

## NOTES

1. Business Resource Center, "Want to Deliver 'Outrageous Service'? Then You Must Keep Turnover Low," Available at http://www.mandtbank.com/smallbusiness/brc_management_outrageous.cfm (accessed September 18, 2007).

2. Nordstrom Careers, "Our Culture." Available at http://www.recruitingsite.com/csbsites/nordstrom/company/culture/index.asp (accessed September 18, 2007).

3. Adams Six Sigma, "Customer Satisfaction and Customer Loyalty Are the Best Predictors of Customer Retention." Available at http://www.adamssixsigma.com/Newsletters/customers_results.htm (accessed September 18, 2007), 2 (of 4).

4. Mid-America Regional Council, Government Training Institute, "Serving the 'Invisible' Internal Customers: Explore Sunken Treasure." Available at http://www.marc.org/gti/Customer_Service_Skills/cs-invisiblecustomers.htm (accessed September 18, 2007).

5. Peter Hernon and Ellen Altman, *Assessing Service Quality: Satisfying the Expectations of Library Customers* (Chicago: American Library Association, 1998), 51.

6. Ibid., 53.

7. Ibid.

8. Charles D. Kerns, "Serving Each Other on the Inside: Proven Methods for Improving Internal Customer Service," *Graziadio Business Report* [Pepperdine University, Graduate School of Business and Management]. Available at http://gbr.pepperdine.edu/002/inside.html (accessed September 18, 2007).

9. Ibid., 3 (of 7).

10. Peter Hernon and John R. Whitman, *Delivering Satisfaction and Service Quality: A Customer-based Approach for Libraries* (Chicago: American Library Association, 2001), 109–10.

11. Hernon and Altman, *Assessing Service Quality,* 182–7.

12. Hernon and Whitman, *Delivering Satisfaction and Service Quality,* 101–04, 113–14.

13. For information about the National Survey of Student Engagement, see http://nsse.iub.edu/index.cfm (accessed August 6, 2007).

14. A. Parasuraman, "Assessing Improving Service Performance for Maximum Impact: Insights from a Two-decade-long Research Journey," *Performance Measurement and Metrics* 5, no. 2 (2004), 45.

15. Ibid., 50.

16. For information on LibQUAL+™, see http://www.libqual.org/About/Informa tion/index.cfm (accessed August 6, 2006).

17. See University of Colorado at Boulder, "2006 Summary." Available at http://ucbli braries.colorado.edu/libqual/2006.htm (accessed September 20, 2007).

18. Parasuraman, "Assessing Improving Service Performance for Maximum Impact," 45.

19. Danuta A. Nitecki and Peter Hernon, "Measuring Service Quality at Yale University's Libraries," *The Journal of Academic Librarianship* 26, no. 3 (July 2000): 259–73.

20. Peter Hernon and Philip Calvert, "E-service Quality in Libraries: Exploring Its Features and Dimensions," *Library & Information Science Research* 27, no. 3 (2005): 377–404.

21. MINES for Libraries™, another assessment tool under the umbrella of StatsQUAL™, "is an online transaction-based survey that collects data on the purpose of use of electronic resources and the demographics of users" (http://www.digiqual.org/mines/index.cfm).

22. Peter Hernon and Philip Calvert, *Improving the Quality of Library Services for Students with Disabilities* (Westport, CT: Libraries Unlimited, 2006).

23. See Lisa M. Given and Gloria J. Leckie, "Sweeping the Library: Mapping the Social Activity Space of the Public Library," *Library & Information Science Research* 25 (2003): 365–85; Nitecki and Hernon, "Measuring Service Quality at Yale University's Libraries."

24. Hernon and Altman, *Assessing Service Quality,* 8.

25. Nitecki and Hernon, "Measuring Service Quality at Yale University's Libraries," 265.

26. Minjoon Jun, " 'Consumer Perception of E-service Quality' from Internet Purchaser and Non-purchaser Perspectives," *Journal of Business Strategies.* Available at http://fin darticles.com/p/articles/mi_hb3254/is_200203/ai_n7952947 (accessed February 22, 2008).

27. Pnina Shachaf, Shannon M. Oltmann, and Sarah M. Horowitz, "Service Equity in Virtual Reference," *Journal of the American Society for Information Science and Technology* 59, no. 4 (2008): 535–50.

28. Hernon and Calvert, "E-service Quality in Libraries."

29. Hernon and Calvert, *Improving the Quality of Library Services for Students with Disabilities.*

30. Minnesota Office of the Legislative Auditor, *Program Evaluation Division. State Agency Use of Customer Satisfaction Surveys* (St. Paul, MN: Office of the Legislative Auditor, 1995), x–xiii. Later in the report, they qualify response rate and recommend one of at least 50 percent (p. 14).

31. Ibid, 12–13.

32. Peter Hernon and Danuta A. Nitecki, "Service Quality: A Concept Not Fully Explored," *Library Trends* 49, no. 4 (Spring 2001): 693.

33. See, for instance, C. Colleen Cook, *A Mixed-methods Approach to the Identification and Measurement of Academic Library Service Quality Constructs: LibQUAL+™,* Ph.D. diss. (College Station, TX: Texas A&M University, 2001), available from *Dissertations & Theses: Full Text,* AAT 3020024 (accessed August 7, 2007); University of Memphis, "LibQUAL+™," available at http://exlibris.memphis.edu/about/reports/libqual/usr_dim. html (accessed September 19, 2007); University of Colorado at Boulder, "LibQUAL+™ 2006 Survey," available at http://ucblibraries.colorado.edu/internal/assessment/libqual/ 2006results.pdf (accessed September 20, 2007).

34. For a good introduction to data collection regarding satisfaction, see Terry G. Vavra, *Improving Your Measurement of Customer Satisfaction: A Guide to Creating, Conducting, Analyzing, and Reporting Customer Satisfaction Measurement Programs* (Milwaukee, WI: ASQ Quality Press, 1997).

# 6

―――•◦•――――

# THE INSTITUTIONAL PERSPECTIVE

Academic institutions, in part through their offices of institutional research, compile and report an extensive set of metrics internally and to departments of education at the state and federal level, accreditation organizations, and a host of other stakeholders including their boards of trustees. States might require annual accountability reports of public institutions that include performance metrics and that, for instance, provide evidence that funds are spent efficiently and that learning indeed occurs. Some metrics might also provide taxpayers, students, and parents with useful information upon which to make informed decisions about the choice of a college.

Many performance metrics focus on data that are easy to obtain and report. Examples include graduation and retention rates, percentage of dollars spent on instruction, credit hours taught per faculty member, number and amount of research grants received, length of time to complete undergraduate programs (e.g., within four or six years), and percentage of class sections taught by full-time faculty. These metrics, however, do not focus on the purpose of higher education—learning or, in the case of research-oriented institutions, the quality of research and scholarship. Seldom do learning measures appear in lists of state-wide performance metrics.

Performance metrics typically encompass inputs and outputs, and they reflect an institution's activities and accomplishments. Such metrics demonstrate a level of performance that an institution has achieved or planned, or, in the case of public institutions, the level that legislative directives require. Furthermore, some metrics might be labeled *efficiency metrics,* meaning they are indicative of the resources required to produce a given output. Efficiency metrics measure resource costs in dollars, employee time, or equipment used per unit of product or service output. They relate institutional efforts to institutional outputs.

For a given metric, a legislature, a board of trustees, or another stakeholder might set performance targets, a quantitative performance standard. The metrics discussed in this chapter are ones for which libraries might contribute and assist institutions in meeting their missions, but no attempt is made to identify targets.

## INSTITUTIONAL METRICS (IN GENERAL)

In the United Kingdom, Australia, New Zealand, and elsewhere, there are efforts to evaluate the research quality of universities and their departments and faculties. In these countries, there is "general agreement that a range of indicators, subjective and objective, are necessary in any research assessment process, particularly when the outcome will determine the distribution of significant amounts of research funding" that the government provides to higher education in support of research.[1] The indicators used in the Research Assessment Exercise (RAE, http://www.rae.ac.uk/), which was first used in 1986 to "produce quality profiles for each submission of research activity made by institution. The four higher education funding bodies intend to use the quality profiles to determine their grant for research to the institution which they fund."[2] Those indicators tend to comprise outputs and to convey the extent to which faculty are productive, defined as producing scholarly works, receiving research grants, and so on. A key metric, one with recognized limitations, focuses on citation counts and the extent to which individuals are cited and which of their works are most cited. The reporting of citation rate might recast individuals as part of a given university or broad faculty grouping (e.g., for the social sciences) for comparisons across departments or universities in a given country.

An alternate perspective emerged in Saudi Arabia, where there is a perceived need for performance metrics to ensure that academic departments "meet their set objectives and foster an environment of continuous improvement."[3] The suggested metrics are mostly outputs; however, the few suggested metrics to measure outcomes are, in fact, subjective (e.g., "percentage of alumni surveyed who agree or strongly agree that graduates perform . . . very well"), except for those relying on student scores taken from professional examinations.

Table 6.1, which identifies assorted metrics that various institutions use, indicates that many of those metrics might be classified as performance metrics. Depending on the situation, such metrics might be used for benchmarking performance. In the case of the Oregon University System, during the fall of 1997, institutional research staff in the central office of the system developed a set of peer comparators for the state's public universities, with input from the university presidents, members of the board of trustees, legislators, and the governor's office.[4] Given the importance of the metrics covered in the table, libraries should develop qualitative indicators that gauge how library resources and services contribute to the accomplishment of institutional metrics. For instance, how do library collections and services contribute to the retention and transfer rates? Going beyond the set of performance measures, the question arises, "How does the library assist in accomplishing student learning outcomes and the research production of faculty and graduate students?"

**Table 6.1**
**Typical Institutional Metrics Gathered and Reported (Examples)***

---

**Input**
  **Number (and percentage)**
Accredited programs
Degrees awarded (bachelor's, master's, doctoral)
    Time to degree

---

*(Continued)*

**Table 6.1**

**Typical Institutional Metrics Gathered and Reported (Examples)\* (*Continued*)**

Facilities (classrooms)
    Occupancy rate

Faculty
    Gender
    Race/ethnicity
    Rank
    Research dollars per faculty
    Courses taught, committees serving on, thesis/dissertation committees
    Activities (e.g., publications, inventions, grants received, and software developed)

Students
  Enrollments in
    Distance education courses
    Internships (by department)
  Graduate instructional cost per full-time equivalent student (master's, doctoral)
  Student credit hours
    Courses completed (rate at which courses are dropped)
    Per full-time equivalent institutional faculty

**Output**

**Number (and percentage)**

Graduation rate (overall, by major, race/ethnicity)
    Four-year graduation rate
    Six-year graduation rate

Retention (overall, major, race/ethnicity)

Students
    Freshman persistence rate
    Class level
    Race/ethnicity
    Satisfaction with institution, its offerings and services
    Transfer rate (and transfer graduation rate)

Transfers (overall, race/ethnicity, by state, community colleges within the state)

**Outcome**

**Number and percentage**

Students at time of graduation
    Those taking and successfully passing teacher certification or licensure examination for entry into a profession (e.g., engineering, law, and nursing)

---

\*For additional examples, see University of California, *Higher Education Compact Performance Measures, 2005–06* (2007), available at http://www.ucop.edu/budget/compact/CompactReport-final-2005–06.pdf (accessed October 22, 2007); Minnesota Office of Higher Education, *Minnesota Measures: 2007 Report on Higher Education Performance* (2007), available at http://www.ohc.state.mn.us/pdf/MinnesotaMeasures.pdf (accessed October 22, 2007); Oregon State University, *Strategic Plan for the 21st Century: Performance Metrics. Sources and Definitions* (Corvallis, OR: Oregon State University, 2006), available at http://oregonstate.edu/leadership/strategicplan/11_02_06_University PerformanceMetrics.pdf (accessed October 22, 2007); Oregon University System, *Monitoring Performance* (2007), available at http://www.ous.edu/factreport/mp/ (accessed October 22, 2007); University of Texas System, Office of Strategic Management, "Index of Performance Measures" (Austin, TX: University of Texas System, available at http://www.utsystem.edu/osm/accountability/2004/mea sures.pdf (accessed October 23, 2007).

## INSTITUTIONAL METRICS TO WHICH LIBRARIES CAN CONTRIBUTE

"Libraries, by function," as Elizabeth M. Mezick writes, "are an integral part of the college experience."[5] Today, they are more than a place where resources and research assistance are available for the completion of coursework and the conduct of formal scholarship. Students also use library space for group and individual study, for social purposes, to meet with faculty outside the classroom, as a place to relax—read, reflect, or use computers for personal reasons—and to complete course work.[6] Because libraries can assist students in making a connection to the institution, they can contribute to various metrics relevant to the entire institution.

The *Standards for Libraries in Higher Education,* which the Association of College and Research Libraries (ACRL) adopted in June 2004,

provide[s] both a quantitative and a qualitative approach to assessing the effectiveness of a library and its librarians. They advocate the use of input, output, and outcome measures in the context of the institution's mission statement. They encourage comparison of these measures with those of peer institutions; they provide statements of good library practice, and they suggest ways to assess that practice in the context of the institution's priorities. They address libraries only, not other components of a larger organization (e.g., computing).[7]

Furthermore, metrics should serve as "points of comparison," whereby

each library is encouraged to choose its own peer group for the purpose of comparisons. Peer groups may already be identified for benchmarking purposes by the institution. If not, a peer group could be identified using criteria such as the institution's mission, reputation, selectivity for admission, size of budget, size of endowment, expenditure for library support, and/or size of collection. Once a peer group has been determined, "points of comparison" can be made to compare the strength of the library with its peers. Suggested points of comparison for input and output measures are provided. This list is not to be considered exhaustive; other points of comparison can be determined by the institution. If comparisons are going to be conducted on an annual or other regular basis, the same categories should be used each time to assure a consistent and usable result.[8]

As a consequence, metrics might be useful for benchmarking performance; however, with some exceptions, those points of comparison focus entirely on inputs. The assessment portion of the standards tends to focus on the library but without adopting an institutional perspective. For example, the section on services includes questions such as:

• How do student and faculty expectations affect library services?
• How well do interlibrary loan and document delivery services support the needs of qualified users?
• Does the library maintain hours of access consistent with reasonable demand?
• How are students and faculty informed of library services?[9]

The section on instruction does not examine the changes, over time, in students due to their contact with the library; rather the questions probe what programs and services the library offers, with the exception of "How does the library apply the *Information Literacy Competency Standards for Higher Education*?" The remaining sections have similar foci and therefore do not relate to the following sections of this chapter.

Also adopted in 2004 by the ACRL, the *Guidelines for Distance Learning Library Services* includes two precepts:

1. Access to adequate library services and resources is essential for attaining superior academic skills in postsecondary education, regardless of where students, faculty, and programs are located. Members of the distance learning community are entitled to library services and resources equivalent to those provided for students and faculty in traditional campus settings.
2. The instilling of lifelong learning skills through general bibliographic and information literacy instruction in academic libraries is a primary outcome of higher education. Such preparation and measurement of its outcomes are of equal necessity for the distance learning community as for those on the traditional campus.

Yet, the documentation to demonstrate achievement of the points covered in the guidelines includes 18 points:

1. Printed user guides
2. Statements of mission and purpose, policies, regulations, and procedures
3. Statistics on library use
4. Statistics on collections
5. Facilities assessment measures
6. Collections assessment measures
7. Needs and outcomes assessment measures
8. Data on staff and work assignments
9. Institutional and internal organization charts
10. Comprehensive budget(s)
11. Professional personnel vitae
12. Position descriptions for all personnel
13. Formal, written agreements
14. Automation statistics
15. Guides to computing services
16. Library evaluation studies or documents
17. Library and other instructional materials and schedules
18. Evidence of involvement in curriculum development and planning[10]

The 7th point, which relates to this chapter, does not sufficiently suggest the extent to which instruction is a shared partnership with teaching faculty framed around metrics and assessment rubrics developed together.

## Retention Rate

Using fall-to-fall retention rates available from the Integrated Postsecondary Education Data System (IPEDS) of the National Center for Education Statistics (see http://nces.ed.gov/ipeds/web2000/viewNarrativeEdits.asp?instID=148), Mezick analyzed the relationship between library expenditures (or the number of professional library staff) and student persistence. She found the strongest correlations between student retention and total library expenditures, total library materials costs, and serial costs for institutions categorized as baccalaureate according to the Carnegie Classification of Institutions of Higher Education™ (http://www. carnegiefoundation.org/classifications). She discovered a positive correlation between the number of library professional staff and student persistence at doctoral-granting institutions.[11]

Mezick's research shows that selected library inputs have a positive correlation to student retention. Other research has shown a positive correlation between library use, as evidenced by the circulation of library materials, and persistence among college freshmen.[12] Furthermore, aesthetically pleasing and well-equipped libraries contribute to helping students select a college or university and, later, in influencing their decision to stay at that institution.[13] Brent Mallinbckrodt and William E. Sedlacek found that library use is related to retention for African American, international, and white students and that use of nonacademic facilities is particularly important for retention of African American students.[14]

As Mezick points out, Vincent Tinto's model of the student persistence/withdrawal process is "a major theoretical advance in attrition research," which "assumes persistence/withdrawal is largely determined by student integration into the social and academic systems of an institution." The model also considers "the importance of libraries in encouraging retention."[15]

Retention might also focus on faculty, those whom an institution would want to retain, and the contribution of the library to retention. Historically, regarding libraries, recruitment and retention have centered on collection strength in their areas of research and scholarship. In such instances, the focus is often on relevant inputs that document expenditures on matters of concern to the faculty (e.g., for books and periodicals).

Libraries contribute to student retention, but that contribution might not be evident from an examination of selected inputs and outputs. By conducting personal interviews or focus group interviews, librarians generate a dialogue with students and compile their stories. After all, everyone loves a good story, and those stories become a good way of promoting the library as a learning and social space. They show what individuals think and the impression that librarians have made on them.

Those stories draw on anecdotal evidence and make direct inferences about the library's contribution to retention or, for that matter, the reasons for transferring to an institution. The types of inferences drawn, however, as Steven Bell points out, are not the same as merely saying

that an information literacy program enhances a student's ability to successfully research and write papers—and that academic success contributes to retention. That's a nice thought, but does that increase retention? We can point to libraries participating in freshman year experiences, but can that be connected to improving retention? I don't think so. In fact, some schools are already looking beyond freshmen to sophomores as the critical year for retention. What we really need are methods that can be quantified and measured so as to allow us to say something along the lines of "The library was responsible for a 10 percent increase in the number of students who persisted to graduation." But can we ever achieve that and document it?[16]

Bell goes on to recommend that librarians "develop better assessment tools and metrics to capture the impact of the library on student retention."[17]

Perhaps the closest set of relevant metrics addresses student satisfaction, with the target population of lower-division undergraduates, and the expectation that those who are more satisfied (or loyal—"extremely satisfied") will stay and graduate. Surveys such as the National Survey of Student Engagement (NSSE; http://nsse.iub.edu/html/quick_facts.cfm) document the extent of satisfaction with any institution, including its library. Further, the Beginning College Survey of Student Engagement (BCSSE), a companion to NSSE, measures entering first-year students' precollege academic and cocurricular experiences, as well as their interest in and expectations for participating in educational activities.[18] There might also be surveys directed at use of a learning or information commons, or of the library as place.[19] Those surveys might contain a section that addresses satisfaction (see chapter 5). In addition, a series of personal interviews might produce student stories or narratives, whereas focus group interviews provide an interactive discussion among a group of students. Narratives might be written and submitted to higher administration or be included in Facebook. There might also be a library blog that, among other things, probes the library's contribution to retention.

## Graduation Rate

There have been various efforts to assess the validity of different indicators as well as the quality of education that an institution offers.[20] Some argue that the graduation rate is becoming increasingly important as a measure of effective undergraduate education and for institutional accountability, whereas others disagree. Even others believe there is a gap in persistent rates by race/ethnicity. The *Journal of Blacks in Higher Education* considers graduation rate as an important indicator of a university's commitment to attracting a student body:

in making college decisions, young African Americans face a uniquely complicated and stressful decision. The racial climate at the schools they are considering is a matter of prime concern. We intend to give our institutional rankings wide publicity with the hope that our information will help college-bound African Americans identify universities that suit their goals and expectations.[21]

This section of the chapter neither reviews different studies nor takes a position about the role of persistence rates. Rather, it focuses on the library's contribution to any set of figures. Some assume, as does the provost at Kansas State University, that

an up-to-date, top-quality library is essential to ensuring that all members of our academic community, both students and faculty, have the fullest opportunity to succeed in their endeavors and remain innovators in their fields of expertise and beyond. The Library deserves special attention to ensure that it preserves and expands current, archival, and electronic holdings that are essential to student and faculty scholarship.[22]

The library contribution might be viewed in terms of volume count or expenditures. For instance, Florence A. Hamrick, John H. Schuh, and Mack C. Shelley II include institutional characteristics (e.g., Carnegie classification) as part of a statistical model to predict undergraduate graduation rates. That model does factor in library expenditures as an institutional characteristic. They conclude that

library resource allocations may be expended disproportionately on digital technology and information retrieval systems rather than on periodical subscriptions and book purchases. In such cases, it is not possible to separate the effects of traditional library resources on graduation rates from the effects of advanced technological resources that libraries on many campuses increasingly house. Nonetheless, higher library allocations and instructional expenditures are associated strongly with higher student graduation rates. As mentioned in the discussion of independent effects above, expenditures on student affairs is a significant independent predictor of graduation rates, but its effects are negligible when analyzed as one variable within the context of the full model.[23]

Since various stakeholders rely on graduation rate, as well as retention rate, it is useful for libraries to try to document their contribution. The same suggestions discussed in the previous section apply here: "The use and power of stories is consistent with the growing body of literature on the role of emotions in learning and its inextricable connection with the intellect." Stories therefore become a way "to make connections to larger themes and patterns."[24]

Documenting the contribution of the library calls for qualitative data in that quantitative metrics cannot explain that contribution. After all, no student enters or graduates with a major or degree in the library. Librarians need to remind others constantly that quantitative metrics do not tell the entire story.

## Affordability

Typically, federal and state governments view higher education in terms of affordability and its availability to the American citizenry. Affordability includes the cost of gaining an education related to tuition, fees, and indirect costs to students and their families. A key component in maintaining affordability is the institutional commitment to providing financial aid; institutions, however, want to limit the amount of assistance granted. Availability refers to the opportunity for more individuals to earn a degree. Community colleges seek inclusiveness, whereas many other institutions tend to focus on selectivity and how the student body selected impacts the reputation of a program or institution and quality of the educational experience.

When institutions offer a breakdown of the various fees they charge each term, they might identify the portion going to support library services. It would be possible to calculate the portion of fees (and perhaps tuition) going to the library. For example, as discussed in chapter 7, the Mildred F. Sawyer Library, Suffolk University, has among its FAQs (frequently asked questions), "How Can I Get My Tuition Money's Worth from the Library?" Table 6.2, which reprints part of that FAQ, shows the dollar amount that students receive in library services for the tuition dollars expended.[25]

Another input-directed metric might focus on the money that students could save when copies of course textbooks are placed on reserve. Libraries might obtain one or two copies of each textbook and place them on reserve, thereby lessening the need for each student to purchase all of the textbooks needed per academic term. Such a service could be promoted as one way in which institutions try to manage some of the other expenses that students might incur.

## Student Learning

As the Council for Higher Education Accreditation noted,

For institutions and programs, information about student learning outcomes is central to any claim of intellectual authority that they may offer. For faculty, the primary value of evidence of student learning outcomes is to aid in the improvement of teaching and learning. Such a commitment to improvement is not only a key aspect of scholarship and intellectual responsibility, it is essential to claims of academic quality as well. Part of the task of accreditation is to help institutions, programs, and faculty substantiate their claims to quality.[26]

Academic librarians have tended to focus their contributions on information literacy, but, as Figure 8.2 indicates, there are other options. Most typically, program and institutional accrediting organizations have encouraged member institutions and organizations to pursue student learning outcomes, but they have not offered a road map about how to proceed. The Middle States Commission on Higher

**Table 6.2**
**Getting Your Tuition Money's Worth from the Library***

| Service | What You Can Do During the Academic Year | Value of the Service |
| --- | --- | --- |
| Study in the library | Study in the library for one hour every week | $16.62** |
| Borrow reserve books | Borrow three reserve books | $129.90 |
| Ask a question of the reference staff OR Use a subject guide created by the reference staff to answer a question | Ask one reference question OR Use one reference-developed subject guide | $40.27 |
| Use the reference collection | Consult two reference books | $84.07 |
| Borrow a laptop computer | Borrow a laptop once | $10.00 |
| Use a desktop computer to search for information | Use a desktop computer once | $10.00 |
| View a VHS or DVD for a course | View a video in the library once | $4.00 |
| Access and download full text scholarly articles and print them out | Download and print 12 articles averaging five pages per article | $123.00 |
| Use the library's proxy server to access and download full text articles while at home OR while at work | Use library resources from off-campus and save two subway trips to the library | $6.80 |
| Borrow a book from the circulating collection | Borrow two books | $24.98 |
| **TOTAL VALUE DURING THE ACADEMIC YEAR** | | **$449.64** |

*Suffolk University, Mildred F. Sawyer Library, "How Can I Get My Tuition Money's Worth from the Library?" (Boston: Suffolk University, 2007). Available at http://www.suffolk.edu/sawlib/faq.htm#anchor13273 (accessed January 7, 2009).

**Suffolk University, Mildred F. Sawyer Library, "Calculations" (Boston: Suffolk University, 2007). Available at http://www.suffolk.edu/files/SawLib/ay2008-9-value.pdf (accessed January 7, 2009).

Education, however, has produced two textbooks that provide an introduction to outcomes assessment, calling for it to be a partnership among teaching faculty, librarians, and administrators. These works, together with different approaches to outcomes assessment, have been discussed elsewhere.[27]

Outcomes assessment, as a consequence, offers different foci for developing rubrics that provide a framework to assess the ongoing development of students throughout their program of study.[28] Since the choices for setting outcomes and rubrics are vast, this section is not comprehensive. However, because outcomes assessment is linked to active learning, outcomes are framed around verbs such as the ability to *synthesize, differentiate, demonstrate,* or *develop.* For example, the *Information Literacy Competency Standards for Higher Education,* which ACRL approved in 2000, calls for "the information literate student" to extract, record, and manage information and its sources." One of the indicators then asks for students to "differentiate between the types of sources cited and understand the elements and correct syntax of a citation for a wide range of resources."[29] The challenge is for librarians and teaching faculty who accept this outcome and indicator as one they want to embrace to forge a partnership and to develop rubrics that measure student progress over time.

A quick scan of different search engines for the other areas of student learning outcomes (e.g., oral/written communication skills, analytical thinking, problem solving, and global citizen) produces examples of rubrics. For instance, there is a "capstone portfolio rubric," which covers the "global citizen." The points covered, however, will have to be developed into a more extensive set of rubrics.[30] Any metric related to a student learning outcome might be viewed quantitatively or qualitatively depending on such factors as the method of data collection used and the sample size.

### Other

As previously discussed, qualitative indicators can indicate how the library contributes to metrics prized at the institutional level. Examples include:

- Has access to library collections and services contributed to faculty achievement and productivity (e.g., acceptance of a research paper in a peer-reviewed journal or the receipt of a prize for scholarship or research from a professional association)? However, a key question is, "How might access to those collections and services influence a faculty-productivity index, which addresses the number of faculty in a given program; the number of publications they generated; the number of scholars citing those works; and the awards, honors, and grant dollars they have received?"[31]

- What is the role of the library in donor relations? What are the endowments for library programs, and how does the library use the financial resources it gains to support projects important to classroom learning and student and faculty research? For example, the library might offer financial support to the digitization of collections important to the accomplishment of the institutional mission. As a result of that support, the library might hire students to work on projects and faculty to serve in a consulting capacity.

- What is the role of the library in labor relations? As a major employer of clerical staffs at some institutions, libraries contribute to the overall institution's workplace environment. Research libraries hire individuals with a variety of skills (e.g., language) that may result in employment for students and their partners, or graduates of academic programs. These individuals might also contribute to diversity on campus. Consequently, there might be a link between library metrics on recruitment and diversity representation and institutional interests. Clearly, there might be additional input metrics, which remind the institution of the role of the library as an employer.

## CONCLUSION

The metrics that are of interest to higher education might be either internally or externally driven. For instance, in October 2005, U.S. Secretary of Education Margaret Spellings established the National Commission on the Future of Higher Education to lead a national debate on issues of access, affordability, quality, and accountability. Commission members from higher education, business, and not-for-profit organizations, together with ad hoc members from a number of federal agencies, addressed questions such as the following:

• How can we ensure that college is affordable and accessible?
• How well are institutions of higher education preparing students to compete in the new global economy?

Appropriate metrics deal with economic efficiency, the impact of learning on students and their ability to contribute to globalization, and to engage life-long learning. Any metrics might become part of an

accountability system that defines an organization's mission, goals, priorities, initiatives, where it intends to add value, and lays out measures or indicators of progress toward those goals. Most simply, accountability means taking responsibility for and measuring the effectiveness of what you do. An effective accountability system makes it possible to answer these questions:

• Where do . . . institutions seek to excel?
• How . . . [do institutions] intend to act strategically to accomplish . . . [their] goals?
• How well are . . . institutions doing to achieve their goals and add value; what needs to be done next?[32]

In summary, librarians too often rely on metrics that indicate what they do, how they expend resources, and how often they do different things. Clearly, they are busy, but we should not forget that others within the institution make important contributions—ones in which the library might (and often does) play a role. As a consequence, the library contributes to the institution's success in accomplishing its mission in many different ways. The library has a great story to tell, but traditional library inputs and outputs do not portray the entire story effectively to its stakeholders.

## NOTES

1. Linda Butler and Ian McAllister, "Metrics or Peer Review? Evaluating the 2001 UK Research Assessment Exercise in Political Science" (Canberra, Australia: Australian National University, 2007), 1. Available at http://repp.anu.edu.au/papers/2007_ukresearchassess.pdf (accessed October 23, 2007).

2. Umar Al-Turki and Salih Duffuaa, "Performance Measures for Academic Departments," *International Journal of Educational Management* 17, no. 7 (2003): 330–38.

3. See Research Assessment Exercise, "RAE2008" (2008). Available at http://www.rae.ac.uk/ (accessed March 4, 2008).

4. See S. F. Weeks, D. Puckett, and R. Daron, "Developing Peer Groups for the Oregon University System: From Politics to Analysis (and Back)," *Research in Higher Education* 41, no. 1 (February 2000): 1–20.

5. Elizabeth M. Mezick, "Return on Investment and Student Retention," *The Journal of Academic Librarianship* 33, no. 5 (September 2007), 561.

6. See Council on Library and Information Resources, *Library as Place: Rethinking Roles, Rethinking Space,* CLIR Report 129 (Washington, DC: Council on Library and Information Resources, 2005). Available at http://www.clir.org/pubs/reports/pub129/contents.html (accessed October 24, 2007); Logan Ludwig and Susan Starr, "Library as Place: Results of a Delphi Study," *Journal of the Medical Library Association* 93, no. 3 (2005): 315–24; Harold B. Shill and Shawn Tonner, "Does the Building Still Matter? Usage Patterns in New, Expanded, and Renovated Libraries, 1995–2002," *College & Research Libraries* 65, no. 2 (2004): 123–50.

7. American Library Association, Association of College and Research Libraries, *Standards for Libraries in Higher Education* (Chicago: American Library Association, 2004), 2 (of 10). Available at http://www.ala.org/ala/acrl/acrlstandards/standardslibraries.cfm (accessed October 27, 2007).

8. Ibid.

9. Ibid., 4.

10. American Library Association, Association of College and Research Libraries, *Guidelines for Distance Learning Library Services.* Available at http://www.ala.org/ala/acrl/acrlstandards/guidelinesdistancelearning.cfm (accessed October 27, 2007).

11. Mezick, "Return on Investment and Student Retention."

12. Lloyd A. Kramer and Martha B. Kramer, "The College Library and the Drop-out," *College & Research Libraries* 29, no. 4 (July 1968): 310–12. See also Maurie Caitlin Kelly and Andrea Kross, *Making the Grade: Academic Libraries and Student Success* (Chicago: Association of College and Research Libraries, 2002).

13. See David Cain and Gary L. Reynolds, "The Impact of Facilities on Recruitment and Retention of Students," *Facilities Manager* (March/April 2006): 54–9. Available at http://www.appa.org/files/FMArticles/fm030406_f7_impact.pdf (accessed October 24, 2007).

14. Brent Mallinbckrodt and William E. Sedlacek, "Student Retention and the Use of Campus Facilities by Race," *NASPA Journal* 24, no. 3 (Winter 1987): 28–32. See also George D. Kuh and Robert M. Gonyea, "The Role of the Academic Library in Promoting Student Engagement Learning," *College & Research Libraries* 64, no. 4 (July 2003): 256–82; Alberto F. Cabrera, Amaury Nora, and Maria B. Castaneda, "College Persistence: Structural Equations Modeling Test of an Integrated Model of Student Retention," *Journal of Higher Education* 64, no. 2 (March–April 1993): 123–39.

15. Mezick, "Return on Investment and Student Retention," 562.

16. Steven Bell, "What's Our Contribution to Retention," ACRLog [Association of College & Research Libraries]. Available at http://acrlblog.org/2006/10/02/whats-our-contribution-to-retention/ (accessed October 24, 2007). See also Steven Bell, "Keeping Them Enrolled: How Academic Libraries Contribute to Student Retention," *Library Issues [Briefings for Faculty and Administrators]* 29, no. 1 (September 2008), 4 pages.

17. Bell, "What's Our Contribution to Retention."

18. National Survey of Student Engagement, "What Is BCSSE?" (Bloomington, IN: Indiana University, 2007). Available at http://bcsse.iub.edu/about.cfm (accessed October 24, 2007).

19. See note 6.

20. See, for instance, Constance C. Schmitz, "Assessing the Validity of Higher Education Indicators," *Journal of Higher Education* 64, no. 5 (1993): 503–21; Douglas C. Bennett, "Assessing Quality in Higher Education," *Liberal Education* 87, no. 2 (2001): 40–5.

21. "Ranking America's Leading Universities on Their Success in Integrating African Americans," *The Journal of Blacks in Higher Education* (2002). Available at http://www.jbhe.com/features/36_leading_universities.html (accessed October 30, 2007).

22. Kansas State University, Office of the Provost and Senior Vice President, "A Vision for the Future of Kansas State University, 2000–2005" (Manhattan, KS: Kansas State University, 2006). Available at http://www.k-state.edu/provost/planning/strategy/vision99.htm (accessed October 27, 2007).

23. Florence A. Hamrick, John H. Schuh, and Mack C. Shelley II, "Predicting Higher Education Graduation Rates from Institutional Characteristics and Resource Allocation," *Education Policy Analysis Archives,* 12, no. 19 (May 4, 2004). Available at http://epaa.asu.edu/epaa/v12n19/ (accessed October 27, 2007).

24. See Peter Frederick, "The Power of Student Stories: Connections that Enhance Learning," *Essays on Teaching Excellence: Toward the Best in the Academy* 16, no. 2 (2004/2005). Available at http://www.colorado.edu/ftep/research/protected_memos/powerstude.html (accessed October 27, 2007).

25. Suffolk University, Mildred F. Sawyer Library, "FAQ: How Can I Get My Tuition Money's Worth from the Library?" (Boston: Suffolk University, 2007). Available at http://www.suffolk.edu/sawlib/faq.htm#anchor13268 (accessed October 30, 2007).

26. Council for Higher Education Accreditation, "Student Learning Outcomes Workshop," *The CHEA Chronicle* 5, no. 2 (2002), 2 (of 4). Available at http://www.chea.org/Chronicle/vol5/no2/Chron-vol5-no2.pdf (accessed October 24, 2007).

27. See Peter Hernon and Robert E. Dugan, *Outcomes Assessment in Higher Education: Views and Perspectives* (Westport, CT: Libraries Unlimited, 2004); Peter Hernon, Robert E. Dugan, and Candy Schwartz, *Revisiting Outcomes Assessment in Higher Education* (Westport, CT: Libraries Unlimited, 2006); Linda Suskie, *Assessing Student Learning Outcomes: A Common Sense Guide* (Bolton, MA: Anker Publishing, 2004). See also publications from Stylus Publishing, LLC (Sterling, VA, http://styluspub.com/Books/Features.aspx) and the home page of the Middles States Commission of Higher Education, in particular, http://www.msche.org/publications_view.asp?idPublicationType=5&txtPublicationType=Guidelines+for+Institutional+Improvement (accessed January 7, 2009).

28. See, for instance, DePaul University, Office for Teaching, Learning, and Assessment, "Assessment Resources: Rubrics" (Chicago: DePaul University, 2007). Available at http://condor.depaul.edu/~tla/html/assessment_resources.html#rubrics (accessed October 30, 2007).

29. American Library Association, Association of College and Research Libraries, *Information Literacy Competency Standards for Higher Education* (Chicago: American Library Association, 2000), 21 (of 27). Available at http://www.ala.org/ala/acrl/acrlstandards/informationliteracycompetency.cfm (accessed October 30, 2007).

30. Indiana University East, Division of Education, "Appendix D: Capstone Portfolio Rubric" (Bloomington, IN: Indiana University East, 2006). Available at http://webdev.iue.edu/departments/doe/appendix_d1_07.pdf (accessed October 30, 2007). See also Christy R. Stevens and Patricia J. Campbell, "Collaborating to Connect Global Citizenship, Information Literacy, and Lifelong Learning in the Global Studies Classroom," *Reference Services Review* 34, no. 4 (2006): 536–56.

31. Paula Wasley, "Faculty-productivity Index Offers Surprises," *The Chronicle of Higher Education* (November 16, 2007): A10, A12.

32. University of Texas System, Office of Strategic Management, "Accountability" (Austin, TX: University of Texas System). Available at http://www.utsystem.edu/osm/accountability/homepage.htm (accessed October 23, 2007).

# 7

---·•◦•·---

# THE STAKEHOLDER PERSPECTIVE

Parents, students, alumnae, employers, government officials at the state and federal levels, and regional and program accreditation organizations are examples of stakeholders that share a concern about higher education and what individual institutions are doing. As this chapter illustrates, that concern does not exempt academic libraries from addressing the needs and expectations of those stakeholders. The libraries might do so directly or indirectly (provide information to the parent institution) as they help their institutions explain the investment that society makes in the higher education system. They can do so by assisting their institutions in answering five important how questions:

1. How well does the higher education system serve the public?
2. How can affordability be ensured?
3. How well are students learning?
4. How cost-effective is the library operation?
5. How can we ensure that the library is globally competitive?[1]

Perhaps a sixth question, one that is more narrowly focused on accountability, applies: "How do libraries demonstrate their contribution and value given the investment that institutions make in them?"[2]

While these questions are critical to individual stakeholders, they might also appeal across stakeholder groups. After all, different stakeholders may be interested in the same aspects of accountability, want comparative information, and demand transparency. The discussion in this chapter views the institution as an important stakeholder for the academic library, one to which the library must demonstrate its value and relevancy as a dependent organizational unit.

Academic libraries advocate their contributions to the institution and other stakeholders as active participants in meeting stated educational goals and objectives. They also measure their effectiveness and efficiency, especially concerning costs and individual/community impacts as librarians manage resources and provide services, and compile and analyze input, process, and output metrics to use in reporting as well as for comparative purposes to confirm the progress of academic libraries toward complying with benchmarks and standards, and implementing best practices. Librarians, as part of their professional culture, transparently make available information for stakeholders and others to review.

## ACCOUNTABILITY

Accountability is a visible and often discussed expectation of stakeholders that want to know about costs and the relationship between those costs and their investment; in other words, is the cost worth their investment? One of the most important products of higher education is students and what they learn. Learning might be defined in terms of how well prepared they are to contribute to society as knowledgeable, engaged, and active citizens, as well as the extent to which they become employed upon graduation. Stakeholders might even compare institutions to see if some are more successful than others in advancing learning.

Although the quality of student learning is important, stakeholders are also interested in other impacts (e.g., how the institution contributes to and improves the quality of life in the locality, region, and state). Some stakeholders, in particular government and accreditation organizations, are interested in how the institution identifies, assesses, and determines it standing with internally established benchmarks and standards, and how that information gathered guides continuous internal improvement.

Accountability for higher education institutions includes a variety of metrics and explanations about what has, and is, occurring. An institutional culture that embraces a willingness for being accountable to stakeholders (to engage in assessment and to communicate and report the results to stakeholders) is critical to creating and maintaining successful and productive relationships between institutions and stakeholders. Additionally, the institution must frame the metrics and their explanations so that the stakeholder for whom the communiqué is intended understands the content. Accountability therefore has both vertical and horizontal planes. Accountability on the horizontal plane includes a multiplicity of metrics and explanations for all stakeholders to select for review and meeting their information needs. For example, a metric of interest to parents, government officials, and accreditation organizations is the institution's graduation rate. Accountability on the vertical plane includes specific metrics and explanations that are targeted to specific stakeholder perspectives. For instance, job placement for graduates from a specific academic program is of interest to prospective students and their parents. They are also interested in passage rates on any relevant licensure examinations.

The information needs of stakeholders also change depending on their at-the-time perspective. For instance, prospective students and their parents want cross-institutional, comparative information so that they can develop a list of preferred colleges or universities to which they make application. Once their son or daughter is enrolled at an institution, however, the parents' focus shifts as they become acquainted with a specific institution and prepare for the transition to campus life.

For parents and other stakeholders, affordability is a broad accountability issue. As the costs to attend college increase, some stakeholders perceive higher education as becoming less accessible. The causes for cost increases include decreasing support from state governments as well as institutions trying to meet increasing student expectations, such as those related to high-quality facilities and spaces, advanced information technologies, and the availability of a qualified and personally responsive faculty and staff. Those paying the bills (e.g., parents, students, and government) ask institutions, and the academic library, to demonstrate value for the dollars invested as well as to present metrics that demonstrate cost-efficiency and cost-effectiveness. Accrediting organizations want evidence of an institution's financial management—planning and auditing—to support its expenditures.

Complicating affordability is the fact that, with the recession of 2008 and 2009, institutions face unanticipated costs (e.g., a substantial decline in the endowment and the annual interest they earn from that endowment, increased operating expenses such as from the added cost of building heating and benefits paid for staff such as for health care). They may see a decline in student enrollment as more families and individuals may be unable to afford the cost of earning a degree. Students and their parents might find that students can enter the program but have insufficient funds to complete it.

Two other broad accountability issues concern transparency and the availability of comparative information. Stakeholders seek comparative information for a multiplicity of reasons, including cross-institutional decision making that necessitates the use of aggregate input, output, and outcome metrics (e.g., retention and graduation rates, and costs). Higher education institutions are increasing being pressured to provide current information in a transparent manner and in a multiplicity of communication means and formats, which a variety of stakeholders can use for comparative purposes.

The National Center for Public Policy and Higher Education releases a biennial national report card that covers past 10 years. Known as *Measuring Up,* it focuses on results, outcomes and improvement by evaluating and reporting upon the performance of all 50 states in six key areas:

1. preparation for college (How well are high school students prepared?)
2. participation (Are opportunities for college and training beyond high school accessible to all?)
3. affordability (How difficult is it to pay for college considering family income, college costs, and financial aid?)
4. completion (Do students complete certificate and degree programs?)
5. benefits (How do college-educated and trained residents contribute to the economic and civic well being of the state?)
6. learning (How do college-educated residents perform on a variety of measures involving knowledge and skills?)

The report informs stakeholders (the public, education leaders, elected officials, and business and civic leaders) about the status of the six aforementioned areas and the progress, or regression, made toward achieving the educational opportunity, effectiveness and quality of the higher education system necessary for the United States to compete globally.[3]

Institutions may interpret the demand for increased accountability as a threat to their autonomy, that is, as an effort on the part of stakeholders to manage higher education. Higher education remains self-regulated; it depends on a collective of federally approved program and regional accreditation organizations to ensure institutional integrity and quality. Supporters of the American higher education system do not want critics to force Congress to federalize accreditation. As a consequence, supporters ask higher education to improve its advocacy role by becoming more communicative and transparent concerning the amount and type of information it provides, its educational achievements, and its contributions to society, culture, and the economy.[4]

## The Institution and the Academic Library

Accountability begins with the institution and its response to stakeholder requests for information about student retention, learning, costs, satisfaction, engagement, graduation, career placement, and many other issues. In turn, the academic library is asked to demonstrate (or is willing to do so voluntarily) its contribution to the institution and the successful meeting of the institutional mission.[5] If the academic library is not asked for specific information and metrics, it may benefit from reviewing the metrics that the institution uses to demonstrate accountability and in highlighting its contributions. Those metrics might include ones produced by the Voluntary System of Accountability (VSA, http://www.voluntarysystem.org/index.cfm?page=about_cp) and U-CAN (University & College Accountability Network, http://www.ucan-network.org/).

The VSA and its College Portrait (discussed subsequently in the chapter) are sponsored by the American Association of State Colleges and Universities (AASCU) and the National Association of State Universities and Land-Grant Colleges (NASULGC). More than 80 higher education leaders from 70 public institutions developed the College Portrait. Managed by the National Association of Independent Colleges and Universities (NAICU), U-CAN, which is also discussed later in the chapter, is a free Web-based resource that gives prospective students and parents, as well as policymakers, information on nonprofit, private colleges and universities in a common and therefore cross-institutional comparative format.

In 2008, the University of California issued *Accountability Framework: Draft for Discussion,* which demonstrates the university system's effort to support transparency and public accountability; strategic planning, and decision making; budgeting; and the evaluation of management performance. The goal is to report, on an annual basis, metrics of campus and university-wide performance related to research, teaching, and public service. An annual report will include metrics concerning access and affordability, student success, research impact and funding, and faculty diversity and quality.[6]

Selected university indicators, together with campus comparisons, address:

- undergraduate student success (graduation rates, retention rates, and undergraduate degrees awarded by discipline)

- undergraduate affordability (estimated cost of total attendance, percent need-based aid recipients, estimated per capita gift aid and net cost of attendance for need-based aid recipients, net cost of University of California attendance by family income, undergraduate income distribution, undergraduate hours worked per week by family income, and percentage of graduating seniors with student loan debt)

- undergraduate access (freshman applicants, admits, and enrollees; SAT scores;[7] and high school and college grade point average)

- undergraduate student profile (entering freshman and transfer students, full- and part-time undergraduate enrollment, undergraduate enrollment by race/ethnicity, female undergraduate enrollment, and age of undergraduate students)

- undergraduate student experience and proficiencies (group and active learning experiences, student satisfaction, student interaction with campus faculty and staff, and self-reported gains in thinking, writing, and effectively understanding a specific field of study)
- graduate and professional student profile (graduate and professional enrollment such as by race, ethnicity, and gender; and graduate degrees awarded by discipline)
- faculty (full-time ladder-rank faculty by race, ethnicity, and gender; student-faculty ratios; average faculty salaries; and faculty recipients of awards and honor)
- research (total research and development expenditures, the number of patents and inventions, and trend in the number of active licenses)
- campus rankings (U.S. News and World Report)
- finance, capital, and development (revenue by source, expenditure by function, per-student average expenditures for education, total assignable square feet, average hours per classroom use, average hours per laboratory use, and endowment per student)[8]

## Academic Library Reporting to the Institution

A review of the literature on higher education and institutional metrics for accountability shows that that there has been little discussion about the role and contribution of academic libraries. At most, institutional data might refer to a few inputs or outputs for which libraries might contribute. Since institutions, as reflected in that literature, do not appear to offer guidance or direction, it is the library's responsibility to demonstrate its contributions and to identify its metrics. The contributions reflected through those metrics should contribute to the accomplishment of the institution's mission, and not focus solely on unique services and resources.

Most academic libraries demonstrate institutional accountability through their annual reports. These reports typically include a variety of input and outputs metrics and ratios based on these metrics. A series of ratios, for example, might compare student FTE to the library's infrastructure—collections, staffing, technologies deployed, and facilities: student FTE to print volumes, student FTE to usable library space in square feet, student FTE to expenditures and student FTE to available student-used computer workstations. Other examples include the number of FTE staff and the data may be arranged according to function (e.g., the number of FTE staff in public services, the number of computer workstations available for student use, and the number of seats for studying in the library). Any of these ratios represent input and output metrics, and they are especially useful when they chart longevity trend analysis. For example, charting the library's expenditures over the past decade, as well as the number of student FTE, may disclose a trend line. When viewed as a ratio of library expenditures per FTE student over 10 years, the trend line may show an increase or decrease of expenditures per FTE student. As an example, Figure 7.1 is the expenditures per FTE student trend line over 10 years of the Mildred F. Sawyer Library at Suffolk University in Boston.

Because the percentage of acquisition dollars expended for electronic resources has risen dramatically over the past decade, academic libraries tend to use metrics that provide the institution with information that justifies these expenditures and that argues for increases in funding for those resources.[9] The Association of Research Libraries (ARL) recommends that libraries collect and report statistics about:

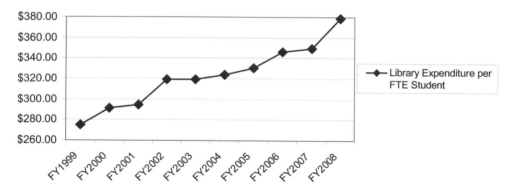

Figure 7.1    Trend Line: Expenditures per FTE Student (Mildred F. Sawyer Library)

- patron accessible electronic resources (the number of electronic full-text journals, the number of electronic reference sources, and the number of electronic books)
- use of networked resources and related infrastructure (the number of electronic reference transactions, the number of log-ins (sessions) to electronic databases, the number of queries (searches) in electronic databases, the number of items requested in electronic databases, and the number of virtual visits to library's Web site and catalog)
- expenditures for networked resources and related infrastructure (the cost of electronic full-text journals; the cost of electronic reference sources; the cost of electronic books; library expenditures for bibliographic utilities, networks, and consortia; and external expenditures for bibliographic utilities, networks, and consortia)
- library digitization activities (the size of library digital collection, the use of library digital collection, and the cost of digital collection construction and management)
- other (the percentage of electronic reference transactions of total reference, the percentage of virtual visits of all library visits, the percentage of electronic books to all monographs, and the percentage of electronic journals to serial subscriptions)[10]

Data about library usage are also found in various reports that the library makes to the institution. Those data might be cast in terms of metrics displaying the number of items in the reserve collection used by students, the number of reference questions asked and answered, the number of interlibrary loans requested and delivered, and the number of students attending library instruction sessions.

In addition to usage metrics, academic libraries frequently report cost measures to support accountability, or at least to display their awareness of the importance of costs. The costs frequently reported include the total expended, which might be stated as a ratio (e.g., the total expended by the library per student FTE). Reported cost-efficiency metrics include the staff costs to circulate a book or the cost for reference staff to answer a question. Cost effectiveness is also reported, perhaps as the percentage of all expenditures dedicated to information resources, staffing, and other operating costs. Based on the library's mission, the goal might be for total staff expenditures to be less than the amount expended on information resources.

These traditional metrics, along with the metrics supporting the adoption of electronic resources, are important to compile and analyze. The academic library, however, needs to plan and collect additional metrics for the purpose of accountability and to demonstrate its managerial contributions to the institution.

A means of demonstrating its contribution and value is for the academic library to compare already attained metrics with expected internal standards and benchmarks (as identified in the library's planning documents). The differences between the metrics achieved and expected can be reported to the institution, together with brief explanations. Those explanations might revise expectations or indicate how the library will improve in order to meet internal expectations. Additionally, external sources of comparative metrics might be used for the library to compare attained metrics with similar data from other academic libraries. Most of the comparative metrics are quantitative inputs and outputs.[11]

## Academic Libraries and User Surveys

A critical set of output metrics address customer satisfaction. Measuring such satisfaction helps the library learn how content customers are with what they get, regardless of the degree to which the service could be better. Satisfaction is a perception of a particular stakeholder/group but not the only metric of "how well?" Businesses view satisfaction as developing an accurate indication of well-being or knowing how well the business process works; where to make changes to enact improvements, if changes are needed; and the extent to which changes lead to improvements.[12] Before focusing on satisfaction, libraries should ascertain the needs and expectations of students, faculty, and other stakeholders in order to plan for and deliver high-quality programs, services, and functions. Next, they can determine the effectiveness of service delivery and the extent of customer satisfaction with those programs, services, and activities.[13] One common method for examining customer satisfaction is a survey. However, before engaging in that methodology, it is advisable to review the literature on satisfaction surveying.[14]

An example of a relevant survey occurred in 2005, when the Library Research Service, in association with the Colorado Academic Library Consortium, studied undergraduate and faculty use of the library. The findings of the study have implications for understanding

- when and how both groups gain access to library resources on site and remotely
- the reasons for using the college or university library
- the most utilized library services
- how undergraduates learn to locate resources and information in the libraries as well as how successful they are in their efforts
- use of library Web sites
- when and why students seek assistance[15]

A separate faculty survey addresses the following:

- use of bibliographic instruction/information literacy sessions, of links to electronic resources available from their library, of reserve services, of instructors recommending print and electronic resources to their students, of suggesting titles for purchase by the library, of onsite and remote library access, and of access to library catalogs other than to the catalog of their library
- how instructors use the library and its Web site
- the availability of resources through the immediate libraries, as well as the accessibility and availability of materials from other college and university libraries

- which library services and resources instructors used during the preceding year
- ways in which the library supports the development of faculty instructional plans[16]

## Academic Libraries Contributing to Recruitment, Retention, and Reputation

Academic libraries demonstrate their contribution and value to the institution by means of input and output metrics as well as ratios of cost and usage data. Based on the University of California accountability framework, however, academic libraries should demonstrate that their educational and cultural mission and services support the institution's mission. One example concerns recruitment. When prospective students consider where they will attend college, they have rated the library second in importance, right behind the facilities related to the student's major.[17] Academic libraries may want to remind the institution of this finding and to ensure that they are included on the campus tour for prospective students and that photographs of the library as a physical facility are visible on the institutional Web site.

At the institutional level, other important considerations include student retention and persistence. For institutions that rely heavily on tuition and fees to support academic programs and services, including the library, student retention is fundamental to the ability of an academic institution to carry out its mission. Yet, the question arises, "How does an academic library demonstrate its contribution to retention?" Insights into the answer can be derived from a study of 586 higher education institutions in the United States that uses fall-to-fall institutional retention rates from the Integrated Postsecondary Education Data System (IPEDS) of the National Center for Education Statistics (NCES), 2002–2003 library data from ARL, and ACRL's 2003 annual statistics report. The study found a statistically significant relationship between student retention and total library expenditures, total library materials expenditures, and serial expenditures at baccalaureate colleges. Academic libraries, it is suggested, can maintain and expand their role in fostering student persistence by interacting as much as possible with the university community, providing library hours for as long as possible, extending the hours of reference service, providing alternative service formats (e.g., chat reference for research assistance), and using technology to provide electronic delivery of interlibrary loan materials.[18]

In 2006, the California State University, Bakersfield, studied the library's contribution to retention by asking students what library initiatives are important in helping them accomplish their academic work successfully and efficiently.[19] Authors Ying Zhong and Johanna Alexander identified the 10 most cited factors students stated as helping them to succeed; they also identified the five least cited factors.[20] Students think library services and resources directly and positively impact their academic work, and they therefore conclude that library services contribute to academic success. Interestingly, there is a gap between factors that the librarians think are important to students and those factors students actually choose.

One study has explored whether academic libraries contribute to the institution's reputation. Using the reported 2004 U.S. News and World Report Peer Assessment Score (PAS) of institutional reputation as the dependent variable, Sharon Weimer examined the relative importance of selected independent performance variables of doctoral institutions (grants; expenditures for instruction, research, and student services; and alumni, corporate, and foundation giving) and service-based library indicators (library expenditures, library instruction presentations, number of participants at library presentations, reference transactions, and library professional staff) using several models. Her findings show that the role of the library is important, as are other cross-institutional functions included in the study, in contributing to an institution's reputation. The variable of library expenditures is consistently a significant predictor of reputation in all of the appropriate models studied.[21]

## Academic Library Support for Faculty

The academic library demonstrates its value by illustrating how it supports faculty teaching, research, and community service. Metrics of library support for faculty community service include fulfillment of information requests from program, school, or institution committees on which faculty members discharge their responsibilities. Metrics relating to teaching support for faculty might show an improvement in the quality of information resources referenced in papers and projects submitted for grades (e.g., the number of librarian-led information skills instruction classes conducted), as well as the number of library-developed and maintained subject or topic-based help guides. Library staff might also assist faculty in preparing course syllabi, especially with the inclusion of course-based persistent URLs to required and recommended lists of articles, e-books, or other information sources available through library-funded subscription databases. The documented usage of these articles is an indicator of course support.

Metrics that support faculty research may include inputs and outputs (e.g., the number of interlibrary loan requests filled, the number of times the library provided assistance to locate research materials, and the usage of library print and electronic collections in research projects). However, because few metrics directly show the library's role, determining an indirect linkage between library use and research output may be relevant. These surrogate measures include:

- the amount of research and development expenditures
- the number of Ph.D. degrees awarded annually
- the number of postdoctoral appointments
- the number of research awards per year[22]

## Student Learning

Student learning outcomes are of particular value to an institution, and to its regional and program accreditors. However, it is becoming increasingly clear that employers are also interested in student learning outcomes and not just aggregate student outcomes (e.g., graduation rates and test scores). Libraries can help the institution and its programs in understanding, applying, gathering, and reporting relevant metrics and data. Still, it is critical to demonstrate how the faculty and librarians use the data collected to improve the educational experience.

Academic libraries contribute most directly to the achievement of student learning outcomes through their collection development efforts and instruction programs, the measurement of the results, the reporting and analysis of the findings, and relating those results to the learning goals stated in the library's educational support plans, which are oftentimes based on the Association of College and Research Libraries' (ACRL) *Information Literacy Competency Standards for Higher Education* (http://www.ala.org/ala/mgrps/divs/acrl/standards/informa tionliteracycompetency.cfm). The creation of the instruments, their application, data compilation, and the evaluation of the results are oftentimes conducted by the library internally or through externally developed and administered assessment programs such as the Project for Standardized Assessment of Information Literacy Skills (SAILS) (https://www.projectsails.org/sails/overview.php?page=aboutSAILS) and the Educational Testing Services (ETS) *iSkills* assessment (http://www.ets. org/iskills).[23]

The topic of academic libraries and student learning outcomes is discussed in chapter 3, as well as in the literatures of library and information science and management.[24] From a brief examination of student reports of student learning outcomes made available by academic libraries via their Web sites, it appears that self-reported student learning outcomes compiled from in-class surveys is the most common methodology used.[25]

Complicating matters, employers are starting to question what their workforce has gained from their college or university experience. In one instance, a survey of 301 employers of companies with at least 25 employees found that, while recent college graduates demonstrate adequate skills in the areas of teamwork, ethical judgment, and intercultural skills, the employers are less convinced about staff preparedness in terms of global knowledge, self-direction, and writing. They maintain that assessments of real-world and applied-learning approaches are more effective than tests of general content, particularly multiple-choice instruments. Assessments that employers hold in high regard include evaluations of supervised internships, community-based projects, and comprehensive senior projects.[26] What employers want is much more focused on the individual; they are not demanding tools that allow for comparisons of colleges on how they perform in certain areas.[27]

The Boeing Company matched internal data from employee evaluations in 2007 with information about the colleges its engineers attended. The results reveal differences in individual skills and quality (e.g., the ability to communicate and work well in teams), which might correlate to the college that workers attended. This analysis was used to create a ranking system of which colleges produced the workers that Boeing considers most valuable to meeting its mission. The aerospace company plans to use the ranking system as a guide for recruiting and hiring.[28]

Although the Boeing study summarizes it findings at the institutional level, both of the studies mentioned suggest that aggregated institutional outcomes compiled from a standardized and comparative test may not be viewed as an effective recruitment and hiring tool for employers. Employers are interested in the individual and his or her learned knowledge, skills, and values.

Given this situation, the question arises, "How might the academic library demonstrate its contribution to the employer as a stakeholder?" One means of doing so is for the library to collaborate with faculty to assist students as individuals and as members of teams to meet the information needs necessary to support class projects, particularly those that become products in the portfolios that employers would later review as part of the hiring process. The metrics compiled and reported may include the number of portfolios in which the library is used for support as well as the number of courses for which such assistance is provided. Course-based library instruction on the retrieval, analysis, and application of information is also a contributing factor. Student satisfaction with the library concerning project assistance could be measured through surveys and interviews, including focus group interviews; however, accreditation organizations tend not to recognize satisfaction as an outcome. They see it as an output.

A less direct but important contribution involves those students working for the library. If the library cannot provide student assistants with skills directly related to their discipline, program, or career, it might foster in them a work ethic, an understanding of the value and need for information in day-to-day situations outside of their course work, and an awareness of the need for lifelong learning. Students might learn these values from the members of the library staff who become role models and mentors.

## AFFORDABILITY

An important and especially visible accountability issue facing institutions of higher education is that of affordability. The cost of college tuition and fees, which are rising faster than inflation, is increasingly becoming a personal and national concern.[29] Opinion research shows that 62 percent of the public believes that qualified students are denied the opportunity to gain a college education and that 56 percent thinks that colleges could spend less without compromising educational quality.[30] The public has asked Congress to put pressure on higher education to do something about college costs, and members of Congress have found a way to influence institutions to contain costs; they created and publicize federal watch lists.

Written into the Higher Education Opportunity Act signed into law in August 2008 (P.L. 110–315), Section 132, "Transparency in College Tuition for Consumers," requires that "College Affordability and Transparency Lists" be made available and updated annually through the U.S. Department of Education's public Web site after July 1, 2011. The lists will identify:

- the 5 percent of institutions that have the highest tuition and fees for the most recent academic year for which data are available
- the 5 percent of institutions with the highest net price for the most recent academic year for which data are available
- the 5 percent of institutions that have the largest increase, expressed as a percentage change, in tuition and fees over the most recent three academic years, for which data are available
- the 5 percent of institutions that have the largest increase, expressed as a percentage change, in net price over the most recent three academic years for which data are available (using the first academic year of the three-year period as the base year to compute such a percentage change)
- the 10 percent of institutions that have the lowest tuition and fees for the most recent academic year for which data are available
- the 10 percent of institutions that have the lowest net price for the most recent academic year for which data are available

Those institutions that make the list of the largest increase, expressed as a percentage change, in tuition and fees or creating a new price, will be required to submit a report explaining the costs. If institutions qualify for either list in consecutive years, they must file a report describing the progress made to reduce the costs (section 132[e][][2]). The thinking behind the tuition and price lists is that if the colleges with excessive tuition increases are publicly exposed, they will take steps to contain their costs. The lists would hold colleges accountable for rapidly escalating tuition and enable consumers to compare colleges based on price.[31]

Moving from the institution to the library, the library's budget and expenditures incur, in reality, a small portion of the institution's total costs, likely less than 3 percent. Despite its minor impact on tuition and fees,

- How does the library demonstrate value for the funding it receives?
- How does (and would) the library measure and demonstrate its contributions to affordability?

While there are formal and informal metrics for costs and affordability, many of the studies conducted, and much of the literature, involve public libraries. Still, many of the formal and informal techniques used by and on behalf of public libraries can, and have been, applied by academic libraries and higher education institutions. Through ACRL, the academic library community views return on investment (ROI) metrics as a way to demonstrate how the library adds value to the institution.[32]

For accountability purposes, based on the funds allocated by the institution, the library needs to assign or estimate a cost or economic value to the services and resources it provides. Such an effort is difficult for two reasons. First, most of the services have an intangible value; they are educational- and cultural-based and are often unique in that they are not duplicated by the for-profit sector. The direct costs for acquiring a book and making it available for use can be determined. Its value, though, to the user is more difficult to measure. Would the cost of the book if purchased by the user be its value? What is the value of the book for the user who states it has changed his or her life? What is the value of a user sitting at a table in the library? Would the value differ for a seat in the same library for a poetry recital?

Second, the benefits from library services can be grouped into direct and indirect. Direct benefits refer to the direct value for those who use or have access to library services. On the other hand, indirect benefits reflect what third parties or the population as a whole derive when they use library services.[33] An example of an indirect benefit is a geopolitical area (e.g., a state) in which a person uses library resources to become informed about a referendum issue appearing on the ballot, and then votes on that issue.

In the effort to demonstrate affordability to their stakeholders (e.g., the institution, parents, students, accreditors, and community members), academic libraries measure or estimate and report their costs, economic value, and impact.[34] These libraries cannot depend on for-profit business practices for demonstrating economic value because of the educational, cultural, and social nature of their services, resources, and use.[35] Nonetheless, they can apply formal and informal cost and economic benefit techniques to discover the value of library services.

## Return on Investment

Typical input and output library statistics focus on productivity and efficiency. While library expenditure and other cost metrics are critical for accountability to the institution, library return on investment measures demonstrate how the library supports institutional affordability. Return on investment (ROI) is one of the most applied measures for demonstrating a library's value concerning costs and affordability to its stakeholders. Simply, it is a ratio: for each dollar invested in the library, the stakeholder receives $nnn in benefits from library services. There are several approaches to ROI, and three will be discussed here: a simple calculation, cost-benefit analysis, and economic impact analysis.

The first analysis, which the Americans for Libraries Council refers to as cost/benefit analysis, calculates the benefit of a library service based upon the use of that service. For example, the value of circulated materials is based on the cost of the volume times the number of circulations.[36] Although referred to as cost/benefit analysis, the Americans for Libraries Council's definition differs from the explanation of Glen Holt et al., which is addressed later in the chapter. Despite the moniker applied, this calculation is frequently used, and the metric is easily explained to stakeholders. If the library circulates 10,000 books, and each book is valued at $20, then the value of this service to the stakeholders is $200,000. The dollar value assigned to the book is the only variable, and it can be manipulated; if circulation decreases, would one be tempted to increase the value of each book?

This ROI metric is used when libraries determine the value of electronic database use. For example, using vendor-supplied data, the library documents that students downloaded 100,000 electronic articles. A value is assigned to each article at $10.00, the fee that customer would paid to download an individual article from a third-party information supplier. The library then states that students receive $1,000,000 in benefits from the availability of these databases.

Another frequently calculated metric involves library consortia and economy of scale. The consortia contracts with vendors for licensing several electronic databases and then provides access to the databases for all of the students at member institutions. The subscription cost and availability of the databases across the consortia are less than if each library acquires the subscriptions itself. Value therefore is calculated at what the consortia paid for access against the cost of the same databases paid for by each member library. One consortium, for instance, reports that for each dollar paid by the consortia for databases, member libraries received seven dollars in cost savings if they had subscribed individually.[37]

Cost-benefit analysis (CBA) is a frequently applied ratio, especially by public libraries, although it has application for demonstrating academic library cost and affordability to a stakeholder. Glen Holt of the St. Louis Public Library and his associates are often cited when researchers apply CBA to libraries. The CBA methodology determines the worth of the library to end users, or how much value the library adds to the lives of those served based on the measured costs to the library for providing those services.[38] The CBA valuation methodology reflects the users', rather than the library's, perspective, and the library's stated mission. CBA results are unique to that library; they are not useful for comparing libraries. Because CBA methodologies are transferable, other libraries can use them.

The costs of providing library services are relatively easy to measure. Placing a value on as many direct services and benefits as possible is fundamental to the goal of assessing the economic benefits that stakeholders receive for the dollars they spend on libraries. These benefits are far more complex to define and measure. Because many library services have no market price to gauge their values, the benefit to the users for those library services must be imputed based on the closest substitute that has a market price.

Contingent valuation is a CBA survey methodology developed to assign value to nonmarket goods (e.g., those produced by educational and environmental organizations). In the case of library services, value is explored by presenting stakeholders with various funding scenarios and service levels and asking them to make hypothetical funding decisions. The resulting estimates of "willingness to pay" more to receive services or the "willingness to accept" less service, can be developed through stakeholder surveys or questionnaires.[39]

A variation of contingent valuation is the consumer surplus approach. The economic theory of consumer surplus holds that, in a market economy, most consumers are willing to pay more than the market price (where supply equals demand). The difference between what consumers would have been willing to pay and the market price is called *consumer surplus,* because most consumers are able to enjoy a relative bargain at the market price. In other words, they would have been willing to pay more than the market price. If a good or service is free, then the bargain (the consumer surplus) is even greater. The goal of the approach for valuing free library services is to ascertain the additional consumer surplus that results from providing priced goods for free.[40]

To measure the benefits of using library services, Donald S. Elliott, Glen E. Holt, Sterling W. Hayden, and Leslie E. Holt prefer consumer surplus and willing to pay contingent valuation.[41] Combined, the two concepts indicate the value that an individual user places on a good or service, and that individual's willingness to pay for a good or service rather than do without it. This measure is therefore based on private market value substitution if a library service no longer exists (e.g., borrowing books). An example of a question posed to the end user being surveyed is, "How many books a month that you borrow from the library would you purchase if the library was not available?"[42] A table is created and it lists the service, the substitute, the price range, and the average price, as well as a more conservative substitution price.[43] The total value of library services is equal to the value of the closest substitute—the *price*—multiplied by the number of times a library provides the service (or event)—the *quantity*. Price times quantity equals value.[44]

The value of services to the stakeholder is derived from a formula:

$$\frac{\text{annual dollar value of direct benefits (as compiled from the users surveyed)}}{\text{cost of operating outlays (excluding capital outlays)}} = \$\_\_\_\_$$

The outcome from the formula is a statement: for each dollar spent in the library, the stakeholder receives $_____ in benefits from library services. The net benefit of the library is the value of annual benefits minus the annual operating costs.

A third ROI is economic impact analysis, which includes direct and indirect benefits to the broader geopolitical community. The direct economic impact is measured from the funds that are returned to the community. An example is the cost to purchase supplies from a local business. Economic analysts have devised a number of formulas and algorithms for assessing the secondary economic impacts by using multipliers as indirect economic impact measures. The employment contribution that libraries make to their local economies is an example. Indirect benefits accrue when library employees who live locally spend their wages in their community and thereby contribute to local prosperity. As the wages are spent, they multiply the effect of the original expenditures.[45] The measurement of economic impact is inexact and may not be an effective measure for explaining the library's contribution to affordability.

## Examples of Cost Impact Studies

Another cost/affordability measure is value-in-use. In the profit sector, value-in-use is the measured positive gain that accrues to a business customer as a result of using a product or service. The measure documents the benefits and costs realized by business users, estimates worth of net benefits in monetary terms, and shapes the cost and affordability message that resonate worth for both the product/services users as well as managers.[46]

Leslie Simmel and Colleen Anderson applied value-in-use to discover the monetary impact and benefits of information literacy instruction to faculty and the institution. They examined:

- the net benefit of librarian-provided information literacy instruction to faculty who incorporate the service into their curricula
- the net worth of librarian-provided information literacy instruction to institutions of higher education[47]

The benefits to the faculty include improved course quality because of the higher quality of student deliverables (papers, projects, and in-class discussion); better productivity because of the increased knowledge of relevant resources; improved curricula through the provision of customized resources; and saved faculty time. The cost element to the faculty is the time spent interacting with the librarians who conduct information literacy instruction.

Demonstrating worth to the institution includes calculating cost savings (e.g., time saved for the faculty in class preparation and interacting with students about information resources; calculating a financial savings by deploying part-time faculty rather than full-time faculty; worth in employer hiring rates; and satisfaction with graduates because of saved employer training costs). Additionally, employer satisfaction with graduates contributes to the institution's student recruitment. The related costs to the institution are for librarian time and training expenditures.[48]

Value-in-use is an interesting cost measure, one that demonstrates library contributions to students, faculty, and the institution. Librarians can assign a monetary value to a service (e.g., information literacy instruction) from the faculty perspective (i.e., by saving them time in teaching information literacy skills); this leaves them more time to engage in other activities and ideally to receive better papers that take less time to grade. The institution benefits because faculty are more productive and the graduates have gained better information literacy skills. Presumably there is also an increase in institutional reputation, which aids student recruitment, and student retention improves as students feel they are learning something worthwhile for their future careers.

Not all studies focus on value in terms of the academic library generating cost savings. For the University of Illinois at Urbana–Champaign (UIUC) library, a goal of a return on investment study is to create a quantifiable measure and a compelling position that demonstrates economic value to the university administration. The objective is to state that for every dollar spent on the library, the university receives $_____ dollars in return. The need to identify a return on the university's investment, however, led to linking the library to income generation rather than cost savings. Recognizing that faculty use citations in their grant proposals, the study connects the use of citations in successful proposals to library resources.[49]

Linking the use of library resources to successful grant proposals assumes that faculty necessarily use citations in writing grant proposals, citations are important in the grant awards process, and citations come from resources provided by the library. UIUC used a faculty survey to determine the extent to which each factor applies, and the study highlights the use of library resources in securing grant income for research, which is one part of a larger set of benefits and costs that include tuition revenue related to teaching, the value of time saved by types of users, the external value of university research to the community, and use of library space by student groups. In all, 95 percent of responding faculty state that citations are important in securing grant awards, 94 percent of responding faculty use citations in grant proposals, and 94 percent of responding faculty obtained citations via the campus network or Library Gateway. Using these factors, Judy Luther shows a return of $4.38 in grant income to the university for every dollar invested in the library in 2006.[50]

An economic impact study conducted for the state of Indiana includes public and academic libraries. In contrast to most other studies that have attempted to measure the economic impact of public libraries, this investigation also focused on the role that public libraries play in supporting business and economic development in their communities. Designed to help Indiana libraries identify and quantify their benefits in a systematic and objective manner, the study focused on three general questions: What are the measurable economic benefits of public and academic libraries? How well are libraries playing an active role in economic development? How can Indiana libraries take a more active role in economic development and business growth?[51]

The greater the degree to which libraries contribute to economic development, the stronger the case that they provide a significant return on their expenditures. It is possible, therefore, to estimate the direct and measured economic benefits of spending taxpayer dollars on libraries as well as to evaluate the contribution of libraries in developing the local economy.[52]

According to the National Center for Education Statistics, in 2004, Indiana's college and university libraries had a combined staffing of 2,216 full-time equivalent employees. The academic libraries were responsible for $136.1 million throughout the state economy in the form of wages and expenditures on goods and services. As an indirect, secondary impact, expenditures on academic libraries supported 638 additional jobs and approximately $112.1 million in additional economic activity that year throughout the state.[53]

## Informal Cost and Affordability Metrics

There are also informal means for academic libraries to demonstrate affordability and cost management to stakeholders. A Web-based "Library Use Value Calculator" helps public library stakeholders to learn how much the services that the library provides would cost if users had to pay for them directly.[54] Individuals insert the number of times they use a specific library service in one column, and the calculator determines the value for that service and sums the total value of library use.[55] The calculator could be adopted for academic library use by revising the Perl Script that is the basis for the calculator and its calculations.

Another approach includes identifying those services that can be attributed to saving fees and other costs for the stakeholders, and obtaining direct cost and usage measures. For example, the Mildred F. Sawyer Library at Suffolk University in Boston purchases two copies of every text (other than course packets) required by every undergraduate and graduate course, except for those in the university's law school. A relevant metric is the number of times that students use each reserve book multiplied by the cost of the volume. A second metric is the number of no-fee pages printed by students using the library's printers multiplied by the cost per page as if photocopied (see Figure 7.2).

Another informal means to demonstrate cost information and affordability to stakeholders is based on a chart that the Mildred F. Sawyer Library has used since 1999. Titled "How Can I Get My Tuition Money's Worth from the Library?" the chart identifies the 10 most student-used services provided by the library, a minimal usage figure for the service, the value of the service for the academic year based upon the minimal level of usage, and a conservative estimated market value or the calculated actual cost for the service (see Table 6.2). The calculations for that table are updated annually based upon the prior year's expenditures and related workload measures. A spreadsheet is linked from the table so that anyone can review the market value calculations. Figure 7.3 displays three of the costs from the spreadsheet used to develop the Web-based chart.[56]

| | Pages Printed | | | Student Savings |
| Fiscal Year | Fall Semester | Spring Semester | Total Pages Printed | for printing at $.05 per page |
|---|---|---|---|---|
| FY2002 | 264,723 | 517,389 | 782,112 | $39,106 |
| FY2003 | 253,206 | 342,998 | 596,204 | $29,810 |
| FY2004 | 329,872 | 293,003 | 622,875 | $31,144 |
| FY2005 | 253,776 | 276,282 | 530,058 | $26,503 |
| FY2006 | 296,279 | 254,841 | 551,120 | $27,556 |
| FY2007 | 415,207 | 541,459 | 956,666 | $47,833 |
| FY2008 | 667,607 | 689,551 | 1,357,158 | $67,858 |

Figure 7.2  Costs Savings to Students (Mildred F. Sawyer Library's No-Fee Printing Policy)

| Service | Factors | Measure Applied | Value Academic Year |
|---|---|---|---|
| Studying, which requires the library to be open | - hours open during year = 4,294<br>- $1,057,770 expended for all \|salaries, wages, and benefits<br>- 453 seats (excluding B1 & Zieman rooms)<br>- $1,057,770/4294 = $246.34/ hour to open<br>- $246.34/453 seats = $0.544/ seat/hour | - use the library for 1 hour every week during the academic year<br><br>- that's 30 hours/year x $0.554/ seat/hour = $16.62 | $16.62 |
| Borrow a reserve book | - expended $121,684 for reserve books<br>- acquired approx 2,810 volumes<br>- average = $43.30/volume | - borrow three reserve books during the the academic year | $129.90 |
| Ask a question of the reference staff<br><br>OR<br><br>Use a subject guide created by the reference staff to answer a question | - answered 9,340 questions in FY2008<br><br>- reference salaries = $295,356 plus benefits (27.4%) = $80,809   for a total = $376,165<br>- cost per question = $40.27 | - ask only one reference question during the academic year<br><br>OR<br>- use one reference-developed subject guide during the academic year | $40.27 |

Figure 7.3  Example of Affordability Calculations (Mildred F. Sawyer Library)

Value of Services at the Mildred F. Sawyer Library
Academic Year 2008–2009

| Service | What You Can Do During the Academic Year | Value of the Service for the Academic Year |
|---|---|---|
| Study in the library | Study in the library for 1 hour per week | $16.62 |
| Borrow reserve books | Borrow three reserve books | $129.90 |
| Ask a question of the reference staff | Ask one reference question | $40.27 |
| OR | OR | |
| Use a subject guide created by the reference staff to answer a question | Use one reference-developed subject guide | |
| Use the reference collection | Consult one print reference book | $84.07 |
| Borrow a laptop computer | Borrow a laptop once | $10.00 |
| Use a desktop computer to search for information | Use a desktop computer once | $10.00 |
| View a VHS or DVD for a course | View a video in the library once | $4.00 |
| Access and download full text scholarly articles AND print them out | Download and print 12 articles averaging five pages per article | $123.00 |
| Use the library's proxy server to access and download full text articles while at home OR while at work | Use library resources from off-campus and save two subway trips to the library | $6.80 |
| Borrow a book from the circulating collection | Borrow two books | $24.98 |
| TOTAL VALUE DURING THE ACADEMIC YEAR | | $449.64 |

Figure 7.4    Value of Services for Academic Year 2008–2009 (Mildred F. Sawyer Library)

The table and the figure provide students with general data about library costs and the library's efforts to increase affordability for students. Library expenditures per FTE student are calculated based on the audited costs of the prior fiscal year. That metric, stated as "$_____ of your tuition directly supports the library," is usually a surprise to students who, when asked how much of their tuition is allocated to the library overestimate the cost by several hundred dollars. Expenditure per FTE student is the base figure. Students are encouraged to *take advantage* of the library: use more library services presented on the chart than they paid in tuition dollars. The chart (recreated as Figure 7.4) of 10 services is set at a minimum activity level (e.g., ask one question of the reference librarians, use two reference books, and borrow one circulating book).

The cumulative dollar value of using the minimum activity level of all 10 services exceeds the FTE costs contributed by the student to the library. Affordability is therefore demonstrated to students in terms of library usage. The data also help them to understand how the institution applies some of their tuition dollars.

## The Balanced Scorecard as a Demonstration of Value for Stakeholders

While providing stakeholders with information and metrics about affordability is important for the academic library, other impacts need to be considered. One approach, known as social return on investment (SROI), expands the traditional cost-benefit analysis and includes the economic value of cultural, social, and environmental impacts. SROI links the library to the welfare and good-will of the institution and the general community. The library organizes and provides access to collections that are of value to researchers and offers space for cultural and educational programming as well as a place for students to gather and deliberate, both of which are difficult to cost as to value to the user.[57]

The balanced scorecard, a strategic management process that typically conceptualizes organizational performance from a set of perspectives, is a means of capturing and measuring SROI. As discussed in chapter 11, those perspectives include financial, customer, internal processes, and learning and growth. As Robert Kaplan, one of the developers of the scorecard, states, the balanced scorecard demonstrates how an organizational unit contributes to the institutional mission.[58] It therefore provides a framework for presenting information about the performance and value of the library.

Depending on the library and its support of the institutional mission, the metrics focus on:

- financial (budget dollars received/the number of patrons, total cost of operations/the number of patrons and total cost of operations/total books in the collection)
- organizational readiness (hours of technology training per employee, satisfaction index scores (on employee work satisfaction survey), the number of part-time employees/total employees, and employee turnover rate)
- internal processes (administrative cost/total appropriation, the average time for decisions in days, new books/total collection, dollars spent on new technology, and administrative cost per employee)
- customer perspective (the number and trend of patrons using the library), satisfaction index scores (on patron service satisfaction survey), and the number and trend of complaints[59]

Figure 7.5, which represents a version of a traditional nonprofit balanced scorecard, identifies selective library metrics.

Joseph R. Matthews reconceptualizes the balanced scorecard into five perspectives (see also chapter 10). The financial perspective identifies the financial and other resources provided to the library as well as the infrastructure as the score card's base, then upward to organizational readiness perspective (staff). The scorecard then splits into two parallel perspectives. Staff use the available tools in an efficient manner (internal process perspective—understanding the costs, quality, throughput, productivity, and time processes and activities critical to satisfy library customer and add value from their perspective) to provide access to collections (information resources perspective—print and electronic collections, selected quality Web links, and interlibrary loan (ILL) and document delivery). The combination of organizational readiness, information resources, and efficient internal processes delivers a mix of products and services to the customer, who represents the top and the most important perspective of the scorecard.[60]

The balanced scorecard at the University of Virginia Library (as discussed in chapter 11) provides a view of an organization from the four traditional perspectives. Although the internal processes, financial and learning/growth potential perspectives are important, the university's customer perspective is a good example of

<u>Customer Perspective</u>
• number of patrons using the library
• patron satisfaction index scores
• number and trend of user complaints

<u>Internal Process Perspective</u>
• administrative cost/total allocation
• average time for decision in days
• new books added per total volumes in collection

<u>Organizational Readiness Perspective</u>
• hours of technology training per employee
• employee satisfaction index scores
• employee turnover rate

<u>Financial Perspective</u>
• funds allocated per number of users
• cost of operations per number of users
• cost of operations per total volumes in collection

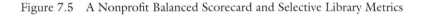

Figure 7.5    A Nonprofit Balanced Scorecard and Selective Library Metrics

metrics that demonstrate value to stakeholders by measuring how well the library meets their needs and expectations. This perspective is arranged as follows:

*Goal 1.* Provide excellent service to users of the University of Virginia Library. Metrics: Overall rating in student and faculty surveys, customer service rating in student and faculty surveys.

*Goal 2.* Educate users in the skills necessary to fulfill their information needs. Metrics: Overall instruction rating in user education participant surveys and satisfaction rating with library instruction in student and faculty surveys.

*Goal 3.* Develop high quality collections that reflect the needs of the Library's users and support the university's mission. Metrics: Circulation of new monographs and the use of special collections' materials.

*Goal 4.* Provide convenient and timely access to the library's collections. Metrics: Turnaround time for searches, LEO (which provides service to faculty by delivering library material to departmental offices), instructional scanning (for local resources), turnaround time for new book and ILL requests (external resources), and reduce the number of recalls placed each year

For each goal and metric, the target and method of data collection are given.[61]

The balanced scorecard, which relies heavily on the use of surveys, is used internally to evaluate progress (see chapter 3). As an external tool, it demonstrates continuous improvement as a result of evaluative feedback by showing progress toward meeting goals and targets, and by identifying the organization's strengths and weaknesses. A completed balanced scorecard is informative and should be made available annually to stakeholders.

## Examples of General Community Impacts

The academic library may demonstrate its value to the institutional mission through its good-will. Although good-will has many meanings in the profit world, in this context it is an intangible value that people place on the library as a result of its community efforts.

In 2005, the Pittsburgh and Allegheny County conducted an economic impact analysis. The findings of that study indicate that the public libraries sustain more than 700 jobs and more than $63 million in economic output in Allegheny County annually and that, for every dollar provided by the City of Pittsburgh and the Allegheny Regional Asset District, the library provides more than $6 worth of benefits. The study also examined other factors, including access to electronic databases (e.g., JSTOR) that the public could not gain access to elsewhere.[62]

The San Francisco Public Library, which conducted a study in 2007, identifies qualitative benefits that library services provide to the community. These benefits include:

- enriching personal learning and recreation
- fostering economic and workforce development
- enhancing the image and identity for the city
- partnering for education and early literacy[63]

The study assigned a dollar value to quantifiable benefits related to the library's direct services for which the library tracks usage data. The value of most of these services is estimated by determining the market cost of a comparable service or other means of acquiring the same benefit. This market value is multiplied by the number of uses by San Francisco Public Library customers during the 2005–2006 fiscal year. An example is the value for use of a public access computer, estimated by multiplying the cost of using a comparable machine for an hour in an Internet café by the total number of computing hours that library customers used during the one fiscal year.[64]

The quantifiable benefits that the library provided are placed in context by considering the cost to the community of funding the library. In fiscal year 2005–2006, the San Francisco Public Library had operating expenditures of $62 million, primarily supported through property tax and other general funds, with additional resources coming from state grants, gifts and bequests, interest, and fees. Using operating cost as the denominator, a cost-benefit ratio for the library is calculated. It was found that, for every dollar spent supporting the library, the citizens of the city see a return in the range of $1.40 to $3.34.[65]

A study was conducted in Florida during 2000 to identify and describe the economic impacts and benefits on the state's community and taxpayers as provided by its public libraries. Study results indicated that patrons believe libraries contributed to their financial well-being, provided economic benefits to local businesses, and supported the community by offering financial information, job and career resources, computer technology and services, businesses resources, educational support for the community, and support for public services.[66]

Small, high-tech startup companies face a challenge in getting essential scientific and technical information because many scientific journals are too costly for them to purchase. The New Jersey Knowledge Initiative of the New Jersey State Library helps to overcome this challenge by providing a portal to free and unlimited access to expensive proprietary informational resources (including millions of articles published in the top scientific, medical, technology and business journals), to high-tech startups, entrepreneurs, small businesses, researchers, and students. This information is not available in bookstores and is accessible online but only through costly fees and subscriptions. This central access point to these resources saves small business startups millions of dollars and serves as a major catalyst to economic development growth in the state. Through 2007, the initiative has provided over 300 small startup companies and every college and university in New Jersey with access to databases that would have cost nearly $75 million if each site had to purchase them individually.[67]

Examples of an academic library's good-will include allowing the general public to search the academic library's online public access catalog and to borrow the identified needed resource via ILL, or to use the library's government depository collection. Many academic libraries open their educational- and cultural-based special events (e.g., a poetry reading) to the general public. Additionally, academic libraries may allow the public to use their resources and collections on-site; both entry to the libraries and use might otherwise be prohibited. Academic libraries are also converting local collections of unique sources (e.g., letters and photographs) into digital form and enabling electronic access to anyone.

## TRANSPARENCY AND COMPARATIVE METRICS

Stakeholders want institutions of higher education and their organizational units to be accountable. As discussed in chapter 11, they want meaningful information presented in an understandable manner. Furthermore, they want that information to be transparent when possible and comparative when feasible. It should be noted that because an institution or library is accountable does not mean that information about it is also transparent or comparative. It may be that only the information required for compliance is provided, that the information provided is not accessible or made available to stakeholders in an understandable way, or that the information is presented in such a way that it is comparable to similar information available from other institutions.

Institutions participate in accountability systems that have differing degrees of transparency and comparability. The Collegiate Learning Assessment (CLA), sponsored by the Council for Aid to Education, is an example of a performance-based examination that focuses on the institution's contribution to student learning. The metrics and results are comparable among the participating institutions. The results from the CLA, however, are reported only to the institutions and made public only by institutional discretion. As a result, the institution is accountable and the CLA metrics are comparative, but the availability of the results is not transparent.

Another example of an institutional accountability tool is U-CAN, which include college and university profiles. These profiles provide statistical data that are supported by narrative descriptions and subject-specific links to relevant campus Web pages. The information covers admissions, enrollment, academics, student demographics, graduation rates, most common fields of study, transfer of credit policy, accreditation, faculty information, class size, tuition and fee trends, price of attendance, financial aid, campus housing, student life, and campus safety. U-CAN also gives site visitors access to information from the U.S. Department of Education's IPEDS survey and the Common Data Set about average loans at graduation, undergraduate class-size breakdown, and net tuition for hundreds of colleges.[68] Institutional student learning outcomes are excluded because there is no stakeholder demand for that information and because there is no common set of measures that cut across institutions and academic fields of study. Another free Web-based institutional accountability tool is the College Portrait. Designed as an effort to thwart impositions of accountability on institutions by government or accreditation organizations, it focuses on four-year public institutions. The tool includes graduation and retention rates as well as a requirement that participating institutions conduct and release results from standardized tests as a means of measuring learning.[69] The College Portrait has three parts: student and family information, student experiences and perceptions, and student learning outcomes. The student and family information section includes a variety of standard demographic categories; a college cost calculator, which will allow prospective students to get an idea of net price; and the student success and progress rate, which is an alternative to the federal graduation rate.[70]

For student experiences and perceptions, participating institutions will report data from one of the following surveys: the College Student Experiences Questionnaire (http://dpb.cornell.edu/documents/1000093.pdf); the College Senior Survey (http://www.gseis.ucla.edu/heri/cssoverview.php); the National Survey of Student Engagement (NSSE, http://nsse.iub.edu/index.cfm); or the University of California Undergraduate Student Experience Survey (http://www.universityofcalifornia.edu/studentsurvey/about/history.html). Survey results focus on six areas: group learning, active learning, experiences with diverse groups of people and ideas, student satisfaction, institution commitment to student learning and success, and student interaction with faculty and staff.[71]

The phased-in testing requirement in the College Portrait requires participating colleges to provide data from state licensure examinations and other tests taken by graduates of certain programs so that prospective students can see passage rates, and measures of broad cognitive skills (e.g., critical thinking, analytic reasoning, and written communication). Participating colleges will also be required to report results from one of three measures: the Collegiate Assessment of Academic Proficiency (from ACT; http://www.act.org/caap/); the Measure of Academic Proficiency and Progress (MAPP from the Educational Testing Service; http://www.ets.org/portal/site/ets/menuitem.1488512ecfd5b8849a77b13bc3921509/?vgnextoid=ff3aaf5e44df4010VgnVCM10000022f95190RCRD&vgnextchannel=f98546f1674f4010VgnVCM10000022f95190RCRD); or the CLA (http://www.cae.org/content/pro_collegiate.htm). Students take the examination as freshmen and as seniors so that results indicate both test scores and any gains achieved during their undergraduate education. The College Portrait therefore serves as a means of accountability after participating institutions phase in student testing, and, most importantly, its Web-based information is transparent and institutionally comparative.

The National Center for Education Statistics (NCES), in the Institute of Education Sciences (part of the U.S. Department of Education), provides institutional stakeholders with access to free Web-based information through the College Navigator (http://nces.ed.gov/collegenavigator/), which is compiled from various reporting and statistical programs on the federal level. The navigator enables site visitors to build a list of higher education institutions for side-by-side comparisons. Users can save their Web sessions for later referral and export search results into a spreadsheet. The search options and information are available by state, program or major, level of degree, institutional type, tuition and fees, undergraduate student enrollment, whether housing is available through the institution, campus setting, the percentage of applicants admitted, test score (25th percentile for the SAT critical reading and math; ACT composite), varsity athletic teams by gender, extended learning opportunities, religious affiliation, and specialized mission (single sex, historically black, or tribal).[72]

The federal government has mandated an expanded role for the College Navigator as an important tool for accountability and comparative information for years to come. As legislated in section 132 of the Higher Education Opportunity Act, information gathered as required by this section must be made publicly available through the College Navigator. The Act also requires the Secretary of Education to make available on the College Navigator Web site, for each institution receiving student assistance, a comprehensive profile that is updated annually. That profile includes more than two dozen information points or statistics including:

- the institution's mission
- the number of undergraduate students who applied to, are admitted by, and enrolled in the institution
- for institutions that require SAT or ACT scores to be submitted, the reading, writing, mathematics, and combined scores on the SAT or ACT, as applicable, must be available for the middle 50 percent range of the institution's freshman class
- the number of first-time, full-time, and part-time students enrolled at the institution, at the undergraduate and (if applicable) graduate levels
- the percentages of first-time, full-time, degree or certificate-seeking undergraduate students enrolled at the institution who obtain a degree or certificate within the normal time for completion of, or graduation from, the student's program; 150 percent of the normal time for completion of, or graduation from, the student's program; and 200 percent of the normal time for completion of, or graduation from, the student's program
- the number of certificates, associate degrees, baccalaureate degrees, master's degrees, professional degrees, and doctoral degrees awarded by the institution
- the student-faculty ratio, the number of full-time and part-time faculty, and the number of graduate assistants with primarily instructional responsibilities
- the cost of attendance for first-time, full-time undergraduate students enrolled in the institution who live on campus and those living off-campus
- the average annual grant amount (including federal, state, and institutional aid) awarded to a first-time, full-time undergraduate student enrolled at the institution who receives financial aid
- the availability of alternative tuition plans, which may include guaranteed tuition plans (section 132[i][1]-[2])

Additional institutional information (i.e., tuition and fees and net price for each of the three most recent available academic years) will appear on the College Navigator's Web site in a sortable and searchable format beginning on July 1, 2010 (section 132[i][5][A]).

Most of the institutional accountability tools identified in this section of the chapter do not include academic library statistics or metrics. Many academic libraries, however, include statistics, trends analysis, input and output metrics, and other information in their annual reports, many of which are accessed via their homepages. Nonetheless, academic libraries tend to provide more information about their operations and costs than what appears in annual reports. For example, the Mildred F. Sawyer Library, as previously discussed, provides a chart aimed at students, via the FAQ section on its Web site that divides the previous fiscal year's expenditures into staffing, information resources, and other operating costs. The chart answers questions from prospective and enrolled students about how the library spends their tuition money.[73]

Academic libraries also share input and output statistics with other libraries, library consortia, and library associations (e.g., ARL and ACRL). Consortia may then compile and include the information on their membership Web sites; that information may or may not be publicly available. Some of ARL's statistical compilations are available through its Web site (http://www.arl.org), while ACRL's print statistical publications can be purchased through the American Library Association.

It is doubtful that many stakeholders of academic libraries closely review library metrics, trends, and data. The data, which are mostly inputs and outputs, may be of little interest to prospective students and parents, and may be of only passing interest to enrolled students. It is doubtful that the data are useful to stakeholders for decision-making purposes. The physical presence of the library is likely to be more impressive to prospective students and their parents than the number of books circulated. Additionally, comparative library statistical data are not easy to find; measures of library-based student learning outcomes are even more difficult to locate. Furthermore, the measures and trends about the library are likely to be more important to the institution for accountability purposes and to the accrediting organizations as part of the accrediting process. Internally, academic libraries frequently apply the metrics for comparing their services and resources with other academic libraries within, and outside of, their peer group as determined by the library or the institution.

If stakeholders want comparative input and output metrics, they can turn to NCES which collects data biennially (Academic Libraries Survey, ALS) from more than 3,000 degree-granting postsecondary institutions in order to provide an overview of academic libraries nationwide and by state.[74] The survey collects information on about three dozen inputs and outputs (e.g., library staff, expenditures, collections, and services). Compiled and available about two years following data collection via its Web site, the reports include a summary of findings and tables, mostly arranged by type (private and public), highest degree level offered, FTE enrollment size, and the Carnegie classification of institutions as developed by the Carnegie Foundation for the Advancement of Teaching or by state.

NCES also provides an online tool for comparing two or more academic libraries based upon the compiled ALS data.[75] After choosing a base library, the user selects "Choose Similar Libraries (Comparison Group) by Variable," which leads to a comparison group based on one or more variables (e.g., city, state, collection size, or income per capita) or to "Choose Specific Academic Libraries for Your Comparison Group," which lets the person choose specific academic libraries for comparison by name, city, state, zip code, and/or distance from zip code.[76] Clearly, the metrics and data about academic libraries are transparent, and, together with information from several print sources and through the NCES Web site, comparative.

## ADVOCACY

It may no longer be adequate just to inform and report to stakeholders on many of the accountability issues of importance to them (e.g., costs), to do so in a transparent manner, and to provide comparative points of measures. It may be that institutions and academic libraries need to demonstrate their value and contributions by mounting marketing and public relations programs. Accountability may also require the institution and library to bring their stories to the stakeholders rather than just providing them with the metrics, trends, and analysis they want and need.

There are some excellent examples of advocacy efforts using input and output metrics (e.g., economic impact). The Atlanta Regional Council for Higher Education (ARCHE), for instance, produced a report to give civic and business leaders information that they can use to leverage college and university resources in economic and community development. This report highlights Atlanta's place in ARCHE's national statistical profile of the higher education capacity among the largest metropolitan areas. The report ranks metropolitan areas by students enrolled, degrees awarded, and college and university finances. The city ranks among the top higher education centers in each instance. Leveraging the size and scope of the city's colleges and universities is important to promoting economic prosperity, educating a skilled workforce, advancing scientific discovery, expanding the arts and improving quality of life.[77] Local colleges and universities also give the region a competitive edge in fields that support business growth. That is an advantage for businesses in the Atlanta area and for those considering relocating.[78]

ARCHE also conducted an economic impact analysis of Atlanta-area private and public institutions based upon FY 2003 data and expressed in FY 2005 dollars. The results of the study, which were widely publicized in the state, show the spending impact from the colleges and universities in the region: students, employees, and visitors account for $10.8 billion and the institutions contribute 130,000 jobs to the state's economy annually.[79]

One institution of higher education has claimed success with its student learning outcomes. The University of Nebraska at Omaha issued a news release headlined "UNO First in U.S. for Value-Added Education," because it "contributes more to the learning gains made by students than any other institution that participated in a recent national examination." University officials based the claim on their students' performance on the CLA examination. The report that the Council for Aid to Education (sponsors of the CLA) prepared mentioned that the university "contributes more to the learning gains made by students than 100 percent of the 176 four-year undergraduate institutions participating in the 2007–2008 CLA."[80]

As discussed in chapters 2, 10, and 11, the Minnesota State Colleges and Universities System advocates its accountability and transparency through a Web-based dashboard, http://accountability.mnscu.edu/workspace/index.jsp. The dashboard displays indicators concerning:

- access and opportunity (percent change in enrollment and net tuition and fees as percent of median income)
- quality programs and services (licensure exams pass rate, persistence and completion rate, high quality learning, and student engagement)
- state and regional economic needs (partnerships and related employment of graduates)
- innovation and efficiency (innovation and facilities condition index)

The metrics can be displayed as a system summary, an all institutions summary, and by institutional detail. The dashboard visually provides information on how each college and university performs by applying color-coded categories of "exceeds expectations," "meets expectations," and "needs attention" to each indicator.

Academic libraries advocate their value to the institution and its stakeholders. One example comes from the Partnership among South Carolina Academic Libraries (PASCAL), which collected testimonials from users about which library services (e.g., book delivery and shared database access) help them in their coursework.[81] PASCAL plans to use the testimonials to demonstrate the quantitative and qualitative value of its services as described by users (who are also taxpayers). The testimonials are aimed at the state legislature, which did reduce the library budget by 90 percent in fiscal year 2009.[82] Another example is the aforementioned Mildred F. Sawyer Library's chart displaying ways in which students can recoup tuition funds by taking advantage of library services.

It is not enough for libraries to compile, analyze, and report their activities; the availability of metrics and their significance must be widely publicized to the stakeholders in a planned effort that demonstrates how, and how well, the library contributes to the institutional mission and the value and benefits provided to its constituencies.

## CONCLUSION

Stakeholders demand information about costs and affordability, graduation rates, and institutional demographics presented transparently and in a comparative way. They then use that information for decision making and accountability. Libraries are not immune from the pressures of accountability and they need to demonstrate their contributions and value to stakeholders, especially their own institution which shapes their mission statement and is the source of most of their funding.

Tensions between the stakeholders and the institution concern accountability. Institutions want autonomy in defining and meeting their missions and in conducting the operations that support their educational programs. Stakeholders may not understand or appreciate the uniqueness of each institution as stated in its mission and educational goals. Institutional culture may result in differences when defining, compiling, analyzing, and reporting inputs, outputs, and outcomes. As a result of these differences, stakeholders may overestimate the reliability of cross-institutional comparative metric.

The Association of American Colleges and Universities, which represents 1,100 public and private colleges and focuses on liberal education, and the Council for Higher Education Accreditation, an association of colleges that coordinates accreditation nationally, issued "New Leadership for Student Learning and Accountability: A Statement of Principles, Commitments to Action." This paper states that the primary responsibility for setting quality student learning standards and achieving excellence falls on the institutions, and not on external stakeholders. Internally, every school and program should develop goals for student learning to support the institution's stated mission. Then, evidence of learning should be gathered and the results used to improve institutional performance. Conclusions should be shared with stakeholders in an effort to inform as well as educate them about higher education institutions and learning.[83] The paper also suggests that institutions and stakeholders reconsider developing comparable ways of measuring student learning. The immediate need is to create tools that can be used to measure outcomes; comparative measures can be derived later from the assessment practices.[84]

Little information about the library is collected by the major, institutional instruments (e.g., the CLA and the NSSE), while neither the College Portrait nor U-CAN cover the library. At the same time, academic libraries would comprise a small, if even measurable, factor in area economic impact analysis models. And, while academic libraries have used return on investment, cost-benefit analysis, and value-in-use to help discover their program and institutional contribution and value, none of these produce viable cross-institutional or cross-library comparative metrics. Because libraries have social and cultural benefits, measuring libraries as if they are a for-profit business will not generate *bottom line* measures of success or failure.

Academic libraries have a difficult time in demonstrating their value and contribution to all of their stakeholders in a measured and comparative manner regardless of the transparency of their annual reports and the availability of the traditional suite of input and output metrics. Library valuation is hampered by a lack of standard definitions and data gathering practices. Furthermore, little guidance accompanies the request for valuation metrics directed from the institution to the library. As a result, there is a need to adopt an effort similar to that of the Association of American Colleges and Universities and the Council for Higher Education Accreditation and to create a varied set of tools that are useful in identifying and measuring the academic library's valuation and contribution to the institution, and reporting resulting information to stakeholders. A suite of tools is necessary to capture a variety of metrics (e.g., return on investment; student learning outcomes; customer satisfaction; and faculty research, teaching, and service). One tool will not suffice to capture the metrics and data to value systematically the libraries' contribution to improvements in education, civic participation, and the quality of life.[85]

While and until the tools are developed, academic libraries should continue their accountability efforts, remaining vigilant of the stakeholders' perspectives and information needs. Assessment and evaluation processes should be applied to identify, gather, and analyze data; to use the results and conclusions to measure progress toward achieving stated objectives and benchmarks; and for demonstrating the library's contributions to meeting the goals found in the institutional mission statement. The reports generated should be as transparent as possible, and present comparative data when meaningful. Accountability as an effort is ongoing; it is not the results of a onetime measure nor should it be limited to an accountability day or undertaken just in time for the writing and submission of accreditation self-studies.

## NOTES

1. David Breneman, "Elite Colleges Must Stop Spurning Critiques of Higher Education," *The Chronicle of Higher Education* (February 15, 2008): A40.

2. Kathryn J. Deiss, "ARL New Measures: Organizational Capacity White Paper" (Washington, DC: Association of Research Libraries, April 21, 1999), 1. Available at http://www,arl.org/bm~doc/capacity.pdf (accessed October 8, 2008).

3. The National Center for Public Policy and Higher Education, *Measuring Up 2008: The National Report Card on Higher Education,* 4 (San Jose, CA: The National Center for Public Policy and Higher Education, 2008). Available at http://measuringup2008.higher-education.org/print/NCPPHEMUNationalRpt.pdf (accessed December 15, 2008).

4. Doug Lederman, "Warning from a Friend," *Inside Higher Ed* (January 31, 2008). Available at http://www.insidehighered.com/news/2008/01/31/lamar (accessed October 13, 2008).

5. American Library Association, Association of College and Research Libraries, Research Committee, "Environmental Scan 2007" (Chicago: American Library Association, January 2008), 16–17, available at http://www.ala.org/ala/mgrps/divs/acrl/acrlpubs/whitepapers/Environmental_Scan_2.pdf (accessed October 12, 2008); Julia C. Blixrud, "Assessing Library Performance: New Measures, Methods, and Models," Libraries and Education in the Networked Information Environment: 24th IATUL Conference, Middle Eastern Technical University, June 2–5, 2003 (Düsseldorf, Germany: International Association of Technological University Libraries, 2003), 10, available at http://www.iatul.org/doclibrary/public/Conf_Proceedings/2003/BLIXRUD_fulltext.pdf (accessed October 16, 2008).

6. University of California, *University of California Accountability Framework: Draft for Discussion* (Oakland, CA: University of California, September 21, 2008), 11. Available at http://www.ucop.edu/ucal/accountability/documents/accountabilityframework_draft.pdf (accessed November 21, 2008).

7. The SAT Reasoning Test (formerly Scholastic Aptitude Test and Scholastic Assessment Test) is a standardized test for college admissions in the United States. The College Board owns and publishes the SAT.

8. University of California, *University of California Accountability Framework,* 3–9.

9. Blixrud, "Assessing Library Performance," 4.

10. Ibid., 10.

11. Print resources of comparative metrics include those from ARL and the Association of College and Research Libraries. See Association of Research Libraries, "Statistics and Measures: Annual Surveys, ARL Statistics" (Washington, DC: Association of Research Libraries), available at http://www.arl.org/stats/annualsurveys/arlstats/index.shtml (accessed November 4, 2008); American Library Association, Association of College and Research Libraries, "Academic Library Statistics" (Chicago: American Library Association), available at http://www.ala.org/ala/mgrps/divs/acrl/publications/trends/academiclibrary.cfm (accessed November 4, 2008). Academic and other libraries, and others, might subscribe to ACRL's annual data and access them via the Web. A free Web-based tool for comparing academic library measures is available from the Department of Education's National Center for Education Statistics, "Compare Academic Libraries" (Washington, DC: Department of Education). Available at http://nces.ed.gov/surveys/libraries/compare/index.asp?LibraryType=Academic (accessed on November 4, 2008).

12. Bob E. Hayes, Measuring *Customer Satisfaction and Loyalty: Survey Design, Use, and Statistical Analysis Methods* (Milwaukee, WI: ASQ Quality Press, 2008), 1.

13. John B. Harer and Bryan R. Cole, "The Importance of the Stakeholder in Performance Measurement: Critical Processes and Performance Measuring for Assessing and Improving Academic Library Services and Programs," *College & Research Libraries* 66, no. 2 (March 2005): 158, 160.

14. See, for instance, Hayes, *Measuring Customer Satisfaction and Loyalty;* Peter Hernon and Ellen Altman, *Assessing Service Quality: Satisfying the Expectations of Library Customers* (Chicago: American Library Association, 1998); Peter Hernon and John R. Whitman, *Delivering Satisfaction and Service Quality: A Customer-based Approach for Libraries* (Chicago: American Library Association, 2001).

15. Don Dickenson, *How Academic Libraries Help Faculty Teach and Students Learn: The Colorado Academic Library Impact Study* (Denver, CO: Colorado State Library, Library Research Service, 2006), iii–iv. Available at http://www.lrs.org/documents/academic/ALIS_final.pdf (accessed October 18, 2008).

16. Ibid., iv–vi.

17. American Library Association, Association of College and Research Libraries, "Environmental Scan 2007," 18.

18. Elizabeth M. Merzick, "Return on Investment: Libraries and Student Retention," *The Journal of Academic Librarianship* 33, no. 5 (2007): 561–66.

19. Ying Zhong and Johanna Alexander, "Academic Success: How Library Services Make a Difference" (Bakersfield, CA: California State University, Bakersfield), slides 2–4. Available at http://www.eshow2000.com/acrl/2007/handouts/735_CPZhong_Ying_093852_031607050311.pps (accessed November 4, 2008).

20. Ibid., slides 37 and 41.

21. Sharon Weiner, "The Contribution of the Library to the Reputation of a University," *The Journal of Academic Librarianship* 35, no. 1 (2009): 4, 5, 8, 9.

22. Julia C. Blixrud, "Assessing Library Performance: New Measures, Methods, and Models," 12, Libraries and Education in the Networked Information Environment: 24th IATUL Conference, Middle Eastern Technical University, June 2–5, 2003. Düsseldorf, Germany: International Association of Technological University Libraries, 2003. Available at http://www.iatul.org/doclibrary/public/Conf_Proceedings/2003/BLIXRUD_fulltext.pdf (accessed October 16, 2008).

23. Other examples can be found in Peter Hernon, Robert E. Dugan, and Candy Schwartz, *Revisiting Outcomes Assessment in Higher Education* (Westport, CT: Libraries Unlimited, 2006).

24. See Ibid; Peter Hernon and Robert E. Dugan, *Outcomes Assessment in Higher Education: Views and Perspectives* (Westport, CT: Libraries Unlimited, 2004).

25. An example is the University of Maryland Libraries' summary of their Library Day program. See J. Hatleberg, *Summary: Assessment of Library Day Learning Outcomes* (College Park, MD: University of Maryland Libraries, 2007). Available at http://www.lib.umd.edu/UES/engl101/onlineassessment0607.pdf (accessed November 19, 2008).

26. Peter D. Hart Research Associates, Inc. *How Should Colleges Assess and Improve Student Learning? Employers' Views on the Accountability Challenge* (Washington, DC: The Association of American Colleges and Universities, 2008), 1. Available at http://www.aacu.org/leap/documents/2008_Business_Leader_Poll.pdf (accessed November 7, 2008).

27. Scott Jaschik, "Mixed Grades for Grads and Assessment," *Inside Higher Ed* (January 23, 2008). Available at http://www.insidehighered.com/news/2008/01/23/employers (assessed October 8, 2008).

28. Paul Basken, "Boeing to Rank Colleges by Measuring Graduates' Job Success," *The Chronicle of Higher Education* (September 19, 2008). Available at http://chronicle.com/weekly/v55/i04/04a00102.htm (accessed October 13, 2008).

29. Goldie Blumensyyk, "The $375-Billion Question: Why Does College Cost So Much?" *The Chronicle of Higher Education* (June 5, 2008). Available at http://chronicle.com/weekly/v55/i06/06a00101.htm (accessed October 8, 2008).

30. John Immerwahr and Jean Johnson, *Squeeze Play: How Parents and the Public Look at Higher Education Today* (New York: Public Agenda for the National Center for Public Policy and Higher Education, 2007), 3, 6. Available at http://www.highereducation.org/reports/squeeze_play/squeeze_play.pdf (accessed October 8, 2008).

31. Kelly Field, "Congress's Cost Cure May Have Side Effects," *The Chronicle of Higher Education* (February 8, 2008): A1.

32. American Library Association, Association of College and Research Libraries, Research Committee, "Environmental Scan 2007," 17.

33. Indiana Business Research Center, *The Economic Impact of Libraries in Indiana* (Indianapolis, IN: Indiana State Library, 2007), 10.

34. Ibid., 7.

35. Americans for Libraries Council, *Worth Their Weight: An Assessment of the Evolving Field of Library Valuation,* 11 (New York: Americans for Libraries Council, 2007). Available at http://www.actforlibraries.org/pdf/WorthTheirWeight.pdf (accessed October 8, 2008).

36. Ibid., 15.

37. Partnership among South Carolina Academic Libraries, "Letter to Senator Hugh K. Leatherman Sr. of South Carolina" (Columbia, SC: Partnership among South Carolina Academic Libraries, 2008). Available at http://pascalsc.org/component/option,com_docman/task,doc_download/gid,390/ (accessed November 8, 2008).

38. Donald S. Elliott, Glen E. Holt, Sterling W. Hayden, and Leslie E. Holt, *Measuring Your Library's Value: How to Do a Cost-benefit Analysis for Your Public Library* (Chicago: American Library Association, 2007), 119.

39. Americans for Libraries Council, *Worth Their Weight,* 16.

40. Indiana Business Research Center, *The Economic Impact of Libraries in Indiana,* 13–14.

41. Elliott et al., *Measuring Your Library's Value,* 23, 75.

42. Ibid, 72–74.

43. Ibid., 76–79.

44. Indiana Business Research Center, *The Economic Impact of Libraries in Indiana,* 16.

45. Americans for Libraries Council, *Worth Their Weight,* 15–16.

46. Leslie L. Simmel and Colleen D. Anderson, "Why Services Matter: Building Your Value Story & Business Case," presentation delivered at NERCOMP 2007 Annual Conference (Worcester, MA, March 21, 2007), 9. Available at http://net.educause.edu/ir/library/pdf/NCP07062.pdf (accessed October 12, 2008).

47. Ibid., 11–12.

48. Ibid., 16.

49. Judy Luther, "University Investment in the Library: What's the Return? A Case Study at the University of Illinois at Urbana-Champaign," *LibraryConnect* (San Diego, CA: Elsevier, 2008). Available at http://libraryconnect.elsevier.com/whitepapers/0108/lcwp (accessed May 14, 2008). See also Paula T. Kaufman, "The Library as Strategic Investment: Results of the Illinois Return on Investment Study," *LIBER Quarterly: The Journal of European Research Libraries* 18, no. 3–4 (2008): 424–36.

50. Luther, "University Investment in the Library," 11.

51. Indiana Business Research Center, *The Economic Impact of Libraries in Indiana,* 4.

52. Ibid., 7.

53. Ibid., 53.

54. This online calculator, created by Brian Herzog of the Chelmsford Public Library, was adapted from the downloadable spreadsheet (xls) created by the Massachusetts Library Association, Legislative Committee, and posted by a member of the Northeast Massachusetts Regional Library System. See http://www.chelmsfordlibrary.org/library_info/calculator_custom.html (accessed November 9, 2008).

55. Chelmsford Public Library, "Library Information: The Value of Your Library" (Chelmsford, MA). Available at http://www.chelmsfordlibrary.org/library_info/calculator.html (accessed November 9, 2008).

56. Suffolk University, Mildred F. Sawyer Library, "FAQ: How Can I Get My Tuition Money's Worth from the Library?" (Boston: Suffolk University). Available at http://www.suffolk.edu/sawlib/faq.htm (accessed November 13, 2008).

57. Americans for Libraries Council, *Worth Their Weight,* 26.

58. Robert S. Kaplan, "Strategic Performance Measurement in Nonprofit Organizations," *Nonprofit Management and Leadership* 11, no. 3 (Spring 2001): 366.

59. G. Stevenson Smith, *Managerial Accounting for Libraries and Other Not-for-Profit Organizations* (Chicago: American Library Association, 2002), 224.

60. Joseph R. Matthews, *Scorecard for Results: A Guide for Developing a Library Balanced Scorecard* (Westport, CT: Libraries Unlimited, 2008), 5, 21.

61. University of Virginia Library, "Balanced Scorecard at UVa Library" (Charlottesville, VA: University of Virginia, 2007). Available at http://www.lib.virginia.edu/bsc/metrics/all0708.html (accessed November 11, 2008).

62. Carnegie Mellon University, Center for Economic Development, *Carnegie Library of Pittsburgh: Community Impact and Benefits* (Pittsburgh, PA: Carnegie Mellon University, 2006), 2, 11.

63. Friends of the San Francisco Public Library, *Providing for Knowledge, Growth, and Prosperity: A Benefit Study of the San Francisco Public Library* (San Francisco: Friends of the San Francisco Public Library, 2007), 2.

64. Ibid., 46.

65. Ibid.

66. Charles R. McClure, Bruce T. Fraser, Timothy W. Nelson, and Jane B. Robbins, *Economic Benefits and Impacts from Public Libraries in the State of Florida* (Tallahassee, FL: Florida State University, School of Information Studies, Information Use Management and Policy Institute, 2000 [revised January 2001]), vii–viii.

67. "New Jersey State Library's Knowledge Initiative Wins National Award" (Trenton, NJ: New Jersey State Library, October 10, 2007). Available at http://www.njstatelib.org/News/news_item.php?item_id=817 (accessed October 18, 2008).

68. UCAN: University and College Accountability Network, "Commonly Asked Questions about U-CAN." Available at http://ucan-network.org/commonly-asked-questions-about-u-can-2 (accessed October 13, 2008; November 13, 2008).

69. Scott Jaschik, "Accountability System Launch," *Insider Higher Ed* (November 12, 2007). Available at http://www.insidehighered.com/news/2007/11/12/nasulgc (accessed October 13, 2008).

70. Ibid.

71. Ibid.

72. U.S. Department of Education, National Center for Education Statistics, *College Navigator* (Washington, DC: Department of Education). Available at http://nces.ed.gov/collegenavigator/ (accessed October 14, 2008).

73. Suffolk University, Mildred F. Sawyer Library, "FAQ: What Does the Sawyer Library Do With All of My Tuition Money?" (Boston: Suffolk University). Available at http://www.suffolk.edu/sawlib/faq.htm (accessed November 14, 2008).

74. U.S. Department of Education, National Center for Education Statistics, *Library Statistics Program: Academic Libraries* (Washington, DC: Department of Education). Available at http://nces.ed.gov/surveys/libraries/Academic.asp (accessed October 18, 2008).

75. U.S. Department of Education, National Center for Education Statistics, "Welcome to Compare Academic Libraries" (Washington, DC: Department of Education). Available at http://nces.ed.gov/surveys/libraries/compare/index.asp?LibraryType=Academic (accessed October 18, 2008).

76. Department of Education, National Center for Education Statistics, "Choose Comparison Group" (Washington, DC: Department of Education). Available at http://nces.ed.gov/surveys/libraries/compare/PeerVariable.asp (accessed October 18, 2008).

77. Atlanta Regional Council for Higher Education, *The Atlanta Region: National Leader in Higher Education* (Atlanta, GA: Atlanta Regional Council for Higher Education). Available at http://www.atlantahighered.org/default.aspx?tabid=627&Report=5&xmid=557 (accessed October 8, 2008).

78. Atlanta Regional Council for Higher Education, *Study: Atlanta a National Leader in Higher Education Growth Region Ranks in Top 10 Across All Measures* (Atlanta, GA: Atlanta Regional Council for Higher Education, 2008). Available at http://archednn.webtransit.com/Newsroom/FeatureStoryDetail/tabid/604/xmid/632/Default.aspx (accessed October 8, 2008).

79. Atlanta Regional Council for Higher Education, *Atlanta Higher Ed Adds Spending, Jobs, Talent to Georgia and Atlanta Economies* (Atlanta, GA: Atlanta Regional Council for Higher Education, 2006). Available at http://www.atlantahighered.org/Portals/12/ArcheImages/Reports/Docs/ARCHEeconimpactrelease.pdf (accessed October 8, 2008).

80. Doug Lederman, "Let the Assessment PR Wars Begin," *Insider Higher Ed* (August, 18, 2008). Available at http://www.insidehighered.com/news/2008/08/18/cla (accessed October 8, 2008).

81. Partnership among South Carolina Academic Libraries, "PASCAL Testimonials" (Columbia, SC: Partnership among South Carolina Academic Libraries). Available at http://pascalsc.org/content/view/170/1/ (accessed November 17, 2008).

82. Partnership among South Carolina Academic Libraries, "PASCAL's Funding Crisis" (Columbia, SC: Partnership among South Carolina Academic Libraries, 2008). Available at http://pascalsc.org/content/view/173/1/ (accessed November 17, 2008).

83. Doug Lederman, "Calling out Colleges on Student Learning," *Inside IIigher Ed* (January 31, 2008). Available at http://www.insidehighered.com/news/2008/01/31/aacu (accessed October 13, 2008).

84. Ibid.

85. Americans for Libraries Council, *Worth Their Weight*, 32–34.

# 8

———◆———

# BENCHMARKING AND
# BEST PRACTICES

Various definitions and perspectives have been offered on both benchmarking and best practices. One of these perspectives advances benchmarking as leading to the enactment of best practices, and another maintains that the terms are interchangeable.[1] The authors of this book, however, see the concepts as building from each other but fulfilling different purposes. A benchmark, as used here, is a measure of progress taken at intervals toward meeting or complying with an objective or a standard. It can also be viewed as a measurable performance goal against which a library's success is measured. As is evident, an organization self-defines and self-determines a benchmark. A best practice, on the other hand, is an activity or procedure that has produced outstanding results in a situation that could be adopted through replication to improve either effectiveness or efficiency in a similar situation. Furthermore, a best practice

- is a technique or methodology that, through experience and research, has been shown to lead reliably to a desired result
- tends to be broadly used throughout a field or industry after a success has been demonstrated
- may lead to the development of a standard

Within the context of this discussion, a standard is a predetermined ideal expressed in terms of which something can be measured or judged. That ideal, which serves as a basis for comparison, becomes a reference point for taking a measure and then comparing it to the standard to evaluate whether that measure meets, exceeds, or fails to meet the standard. Another way to explain a standard is by viewing it as an acknowledged and predetermined measure of comparison for a quantitative or qualitative value that may be created, identified, or developed internally within an organization, or created, identified, and developed externally by an association or some other form of informal or formal governance that is then established as a model of excellence.

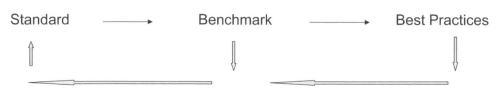

Figure 8.1    The Process: Standards, Benchmarks, and Best Practices

As Figure 8.1 illustrates, a standard, which is set, is developed internally or externally. It leads to a benchmark, which can be measured repeatedly over time and compared against the standard to measure progress in meeting that standard. Taking this another step, those measures that become accepted measures of quality, and the process to produce them, are in fact best practices. If those best practices are replicated externally, they may become a standard.

Many academic libraries engage in benchmarking and should regularly use the results to make continuous quality improvements. Benchmarking enables a library to focus on two questions:

1.  In the context of a standard, goal, and objective, how good do we want to be with the service we offer?
2.  Is our performance meeting, exceeding, or failing to meet the standard?

Best practices, on the other hand, address three questions:

1.  How do others do it?
2.  Are others doing it better than we are?
3.  How can we adapt our library to what others do?

The answers to the five questions often address time, cost, and perceived quality, as measured against that library's previous performance, other libraries or professions, or the so-called best in class. As the U.S. Department of the Defense explains,

Organizations that accomplish a particular activity at the highest value, that is, at the lowest cost and/or highest quality or efficiency, are considered "best-in-class." In determining what qualifies as world-class, benchmarking asks the question: "who are we now, and who do we want to be?" The best benchmarking efforts don't simply match the performance of others; they exceed it.[2]

To ensure that comparisons with other organizations are valid and provide useful insights, the department reviews "how leading organizations perform specific process(es)," compares "their methods with its own," and uses "the information to improve upon or completely change its processes." As a reminder, the department notes that "it is important when benchmarking with stellar organizations that you gain a clear understanding of the scope of their project, the methodology they used, the critical success factors they identified, the challenges and opportunities they faced in implementation, and the important lessons they learned."[3] As is evident, both benchmarking and the application of best practices have value for managing change and improving the quality of service provided.

## DIFFERENTIATING MORE BETWEEN BENCHMARKING AND BEST PRACTICES

The types of benchmarking, as discussed in the popular and scholarly literatures, are called internal, competitive, customer, and functional or comparative. Internal benchmarking can be conducted in organizations in which several departments or units conduct similar processes. It reinforces an inward focus that can engender complacency or set up rivalries within the library that become counterproductive. Such benchmarking addresses questions of how many, how economical, how prompt, how responsive, and/or how well, and it compares new processes with old ones.

Competitive benchmarking generally focuses on direct (so-called peer libraries and institutions) or indirect (related organizations, such as bookstores) competitors. Historically, comparisons relate to resource allocation and workload measures. Before embarking on such benchmarking, it is critical to determine the degree of comparability—comparing like, not unlike, items. Customer benchmarking applies when value-added structures of the supplier and the customer are aligned and comparable.

Benchmarking might be functional—targeted at organizations in other fields to see how a particular function is carried out—or generic—going beyond a particular function and identifying the ways in which other organizations operate. Functional or industry benchmarking is similar to competitive benchmarking, except that the group of competitors is larger and more broadly defined. Generic benchmarking uses the broadest application of data collection from different industries to apply the best operational practices available.

The five questions highlighted earlier are divided into ones relating to benchmarking and best practices. Viewing the set of questions in terms of the different types of benchmarking illustrates that internal benchmarking is the most consistent with only the first two questions. The other types of benchmarking actually address some of the questions related to best practices. Anyway, according to different scholarly literatures, the selection of the benchmarking type depends on the process(es) being analyzed, the availability of data, and the available expertise at the institution.

### Example Areas from the Literature

Benchmarking, which can be undertaken in almost any area of the library, provides insights useful for planning new services and service improvements. In 1998/1999, California State University, Long Beach, together with other libraries in the system and selected other libraries across the nation, called their activity benchmarking. They produced benchmarking data in 22 areas. The data include survey findings from a study of students and faculty. Those findings cover student satisfaction and information needs, but they were not widely comparable given the use of different methods of selecting participants and tabulating the results.[4]

In 2007, Roswitha Poll reported on a group of libraries in different countries that tried to reach consensus on a common set of input and output metrics that provide insights into the quality of service provided. She maintains that the metrics selected for benchmarking should:

- "Mirror the full extent of library services
- Consider electronic as well as traditional services

- Help to demonstrate the importance and impact of libraries
- Further comparison between the participating libraries
- Avoid unfair treatment of individual libraries
- Allow for special conditions in the libraries (every library seems to be unique)
- Yield results that are easily understandable, even for politicians
- In spite of all that, consist of only a few measures that should preferably be collected from the normal library statistics."[5]

Any set of metrics should also be comparable to ISO Standard 11620 on performance measurement in libraries to ensure their standardization and utility globally. Poll finds that "24 of the 54 indicators are more or less identical to those of the ISO standard. This means that using internationally standardized methods results can be compared between projects."[6]

The metrics fall within four general categories: resources and infrastructure, usage, efficiency, and development and potentials. More precisely,

- The perspective on resources/infrastructure includes 16 indicators, 6 of which several projects use. "The library's role as place for learning and research is defined by the size of the user area, the availability of study places and workstations and of course by the opening hours. Indicators for the quality of information provision are expenditure and media per capita, the renewal rate of the collection and the availability of media. There is only one indicator for the library's teaching role (training lessons per capita) and one for staff resources (staff per capita)."

- For the perspective on usage, there are 16 indicators, 7 of which more than one project use. "Market penetration (percentage of active users of the population), user satisfaction, and the number of visits are used as general indicators for user-oriented services. The quality of the collection is assessed by loans and the number of interlibrary loans compared to total loans. Three indicators measure the use of electronic services (sessions on e-media and online catalogue, downloads per electronic journal). . . . [One library] intends to use an additional indicator for electronic services: 'web site visits per capita'. The data collection method for this indicator is in the test phase." "The use of the library's information services is evaluated in terms of attendances at user trainings and information requests per capita. Only one project (Sweden) evaluates the library's cultural role by counting attendances at cultural events per capita."

- The perspective on efficiency, "which shows the importance of demonstrating 'value for money' to the funding institutions. There are fourteen indicators and two of them are used twice, one ('cost per user') even thrice. 'Costs' in most cases mean the total annual operating expenditure of the library." "The expenditure for information provision is compared to staff costs and to total expenditure in order to assess whether a sufficient part of the budget is spent on the collection. Staff hours are set in comparison to opening hours, staff costs to users, and the allocation of staff resources to background and user services . . . [Such metrics are] meant to show whether user services have priority." "The efficiency of processes is evaluated in terms of speed (of acquisition, media processing, and interlibrary loan) and correctness (of shelving and interlibrary loan delivery). . . . [Two libraries] use the example of media processing to assess employee productivity (media processed per year per full- time equivalent staff involved in processing)."

- The perspective on development/potentials was introduced in quality assessment by the balanced scorecard (see chapter 11). That perspective "assesses the library's capability to cope with such change. It has not been easy, however, to find performance indicators for this perspective, as is shown by the small number of projects (only eight)." "The potential for development is assessed on one hand using electronic services (expenditure on the electronic collection, percentage of staff in electronic services), on the other hand using staff development and motivation (time and money spent on staff training, availability and fluctuation rate of staff). The library's success in obtaining funding from its institution and other sources is also seen as important for coping with the future."[7]

Poll cautions about employing user surveys in benchmarking projects. For instance, she notes that user/use surveys reflect perceptions and that other methodologies might produce different results. Further, there is a need for reliable data and a realization that conditions outside the library (e.g., the amount of funding given the library) might impact the services that libraries offer. She also mentions an important study limitation: "No indicators for the impact or outcome of libraries on users or on society are as yet used in the projects. Such indicators are still in the testing phase and therefore not ready for benchmarking with standardized data collection methods."[8]

The only usage metric requiring input directly from customers, in the study about which Poll reports, is a general one entitled *user satisfaction*. What such satisfaction comprises is not specified. As chapter 5 indicates, because satisfaction has many facets and also incorporates service quality, it merits more consideration especially if the intent is to generate data useful for service improvement. It is likely that satisfaction is more of a primary metric, or series of metrics, and the other metrics she highlights are subordinate; nonetheless satisfaction is not an outcome metric. Customer service involves meeting or exceeding the needs and expectations of the customer as defined by the customer. This means that libraries know what their customers want (knowledge of their information needs) and expect (satisfaction and service quality) and provide it to them on a consistent basis. Such insights do require interaction with customers and listening to what they say. Additional insights, however, emerge from observation and an analysis of completed transactions. At the same time, the importance of staff, their satisfaction and empowerment, should not be ignored.[9]

Although the literature does not sharply distinguish between benchmarking and best practices, the scholarly writings make an important contribution. Still, it is critical to keep the five questions raised earlier in the chapter in mind as librarians pursue benchmarking and best practices.

## BEST PRACTICES

### Overview

The U.S. General Accounting Office, now called the Government Accountability Office, has viewed best practices in terms of "best management practices," which refers to the processes, practices, and systems identified in public and private organizations that performed exceptionally well and are widely recognized as improving an organization's performance and efficiency in specific areas. Further, "successfully identifying and applying best practices can reduce business expenses and improve organizational efficiency."[10]

Anne Wilson and Leeanne Pitman note that best practices and quality are not used synonymously; however, they note that best practices emerge in "the pursuit of world class performance. It is the way in which the most successful organisations manage and organise their operations. It is a moving target. As the leading organisations continue to improve the 'best practice' goalposts are constantly moving. The concept of continuous improvement is integral to the achievement of best practice."[11]

## Application

For the purposes of this chapter, best practices apply to efforts to connect libraries to broader institutional programs and the standards set by accreditation organizations, be they institutional or program. To make that connection, we explored the literature of other disciplines to see how they define best practices, and if libraries might provide relevant data so that any metrics that emerge have relevancy across settings: libraries and academic departments, and libraries and accreditation.

As Linda Suskie explains, institutional effectiveness is defined as "how well an institution is achieving its mission and major institutional goals. Since student learning is the heart of most [academic] institutional missions, the assessment of student learning is a major component of the assessment of institutional effectiveness."[12] She recognizes that other factors contribute to institutional effectiveness:

Such as research and scholarship, community service, building a diverse community, or modeling certain values, and other major institutional goals, such as providing financial support to those without sufficient means to attend college, providing facilities and infrastructure that promote student learning, or developing collaborative partnerships with basic education.[13]

Within the context of institutional effectiveness, best practices might relate to areas associated with:

- Student outcomes, which are aggregate statistics on groups of students (e.g., graduation rates, retention rates, transfer rates, course and program completion rates, and job placement: employment rates for a graduating class). Such outcomes are institutional outcomes and are used to compare institutional performance. They do not measure changes in students due to their college experience, and these outcomes are in fact outputs that reflect what the institution has accomplished; they do not reflect what (or how much) students learned.

- Learning, which is defined as encompassing not only knowledge leading to understanding, but also abilities, habits of mind, ways of knowing, attitudes, values, and other dispositions that an institution and its programs and services assert they develop.[14] The so-called educational experience might focus more specifically on active learning, which engages students in activities that force them to think about, react to, and comment on the information presented. Students do not simply listen; they develop the ability to handle concepts by analyzing, synthesizing, and evaluating information in discussion with other students, through asking questions or through writing. In short, they engage in activities that force them to reflect upon ideas and upon how they are using those ideas.

  - Student learning outcomes focus on the development of students over time, such as the duration of an undergraduate or graduate program of study. Such outcomes focus on active learning, the demonstrable acquisition of specific knowledge and skills, and how well do students transfer and apply concepts, principles, ways of knowing, and problem solving throughout their program of study; integrate their core curriculum, general studies, or liberal studies into their major program or field of study; and develop understanding, behaviors, attitudes, values, and dispositions that the institution asserts it develops.

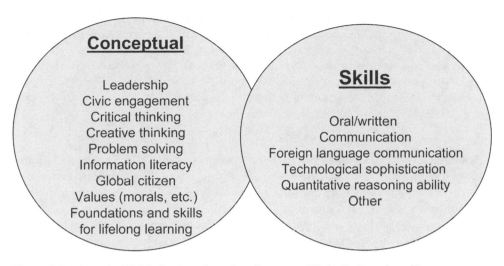

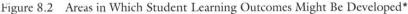

Figure 8.2    Areas in Which Student Learning Outcomes Might Be Developed*

*See also National Leadership Council for Liberal Education & America's Promise, *College Learning for the New Global Century* (Washington, DC: Association of American Colleges and Universities, 2007). Available at http://www.aacu.org/leap/documents/GlobalCentury_final.pdf (accessed January 2, 2009).

Figure 8.2 illustrates different areas where academic programs might develop student learning outcomes. For some of those areas, Sandra Bloomberg and Melanie McDonald offer ways for viewing student progress over time. It is possible for others to review their rubrics and adapt them for local use.[15] Furthermore, *Outcomes Assessment in Higher Education* and *Revisiting Outcomes Assessment in Higher Education* identify a range of methodologies and tools that educators can use to conduct those measurements.[16] One tool that emerged after publication of these books is the *iSkills*™ assessment (the former ICT Literacy Assessment), a comprehensive test of information and communication technology (ICT) literacy that uses scenario-based tasks to measure cognitive skills in a technological environment.[17]

## CONVERGENCE

By engaging in benchmarking and best practices, libraries search for ways to improve and to make connections to other libraries and to the broader institution. Applying best practices, as highlighted in this chapter, marks a continuation in the trend among academic libraries to cooperate and engage in convergence with partners across (and beyond) campus. An aspect of convergence involves the sharing of collaborative space, either physically or virtually, and the partnerships might extend, for instance, to instructional technology departments; academic departments; campus centers for learning, teaching, or writing; and student and food services.

Such efforts suggest additional metrics, which might be characterized as inputs, outputs, aggregated outcomes, or student learning outcomes. For instance, how much revenue is generated from a café located in the library (based on selling food and beverages as well as a percentage for renting the space)? Another example would be the number of students using the writing tutor in the library for their class papers (output) or the extent of improvement in their written work over the school year (outcome). Additional outputs might relate to use of the reference collection and services or the use of technology, both hardware and software. Any set of outcomes, and their corresponding scoring rubrics, align the library with the classroom and student learning over time.

## QUANTITATIVE METRICS

Academic libraries as well as program and institutional accreditation organizations often focus on information literacy and the application of the guidelines developed by the Association of College and Research Libraries (ACRL). By having students complete the *iSkills*™ assessment or another standardized test, perhaps one linked to the ACRL guidelines and standards, it is possible to generate metrics relevant to any specified competency.[18]

As an example, knowledge about the use of Boolean operations (use of AND, OR, and NOT) helps to reduce or refine the number of hits (retrievals) per search of almost every electronic database. This skill, once learned and applied, saves students time by increasing the effectiveness of the search process; their retrievals become "more on-target," resulting in less information overload and less time reading through abstracts of articles or sources that do not meet their needs. Librarians can gather data about the application of Boolean searching by conducting a pretest and posttest of freshmen receiving formal searching instruction and by retrieving the statistics from vendors supplying the databases to track the number of retrievals per search for each month of an academic term.

Librarians retrieve the monthly statistics for number of searches and number of hits and then calculate the number of hits per search. The Boolean operator AND might be emphasized during the instructional sessions because it is used to combine two or more keywords, thereby reducing the number of results. If the number has dropped, the library might infer that its efforts at instructing students on this specific operator have reduced the number of retrievals per search. To support the claim, librarians might obtain such statistics before implementing the instruction program. They want to determine if there is an observable/measurable change during the academic term.

The example above focuses on benchmarking when evaluators measure progress over time and determines whether the organization meets or complies with an objective or standard. The same example has best-practice implications when one library looks externally and addresses the following questions:

- How do others do it?
- Are others doing it better than we are?
- How can we adapt our library to what others do?

## QUALITATIVE METRICS

For purposes of accountability, the federal government, state governments, and accreditation organizations expect institutions of higher education to compile student outcomes such as graduate rates. This metric has been labeled a "distorted" statistic because it ignores life changes and the issues that might force students to proceed at a slower pace.[19] Nonetheless, institutions continue to gather and report these statistics. Libraries might use surveys or other indirect methods of data collection to show their role in contributing to an institutional statistic.

The concept of the library as a place might contribute to student retention or even graduation rate.[20] Perhaps quiet study facilities enable nursing students to prepare for their licensing examination, and the presence of a learning commons or information commons contributes to student retention, or that presence might have been a contributing factor for students transferring to the institution. Clearly, libraries might collect success stories and argue that they have a positive impact on student outcomes.

## PLANNING FOR THE FUTURE

Academic libraries are experiencing a period of uncertainty and transition due to the changes created by information technologies, the rapidly expanding digital environment, and changing information-seeking patterns. Partially as a result, they are seeking to "find and articulate their roles in the current and future information ecology."[21] As David W. Lewis writes, "if we cannot or will not do this, our campuses will invest in other priorities, and the library will slowly but surely atrophy and become a little used museum of the book."[22]

Accepting Lewis's premises, some question what an academic library should be, and they create scenarios that lay out alternative futures for the profession to review, to use for identifying strategic priorities, and to reflect on how to achieve the most realistic futures.[23] Lewis offers a road map that consists of five components:

1. Complete the migration from print to electronic collections
2. Retire legacy print collections
3. Redevelop library space
4. Reposition library and information tools, resources, and expertise
5. Migrate the focus of collections from purchasing materials to curating content[24]

As Lewis explains,

Three of the parts of the model . . . [points 1, 2, and 5] . . . represent a change in how the collecting activity is conceived. The third part is a new way of thinking about space [point 3]. The fourth modifies the way librarians employ their expertise [point 4]. In all cases, there is a blurring of the boundaries that separate the library from the rest of the campus and the external information environment. The library becomes less of a distinct place.[25]

The achievement of the road map requires the creation of new metrics to address the five questions raised at the beginning of this chapter. Those metrics will have to focus on cost savings to the library (e.g., systems costs and personnel), restructuring the work performed, use of space for new purposes, taking advantage of new naming opportunities, staff training, the ability to hire new staff with the prerequisite knowledge and skills, and the shifting of funds from collection-building to curation. As Lewis concludes, "on balance . . . it is not unreasonable to expect most libraries to manage without increases in funding, beyond the general rate of inflation."[26]

Any metrics adopted will have to be linked to the planning process and create an organizational culture that values change and learning. Libraries will need to develop succession management plans that offer strategies for hiring and retaining staff with the required knowledge, skills, and abilities. In addition, the library will have to invest in staff development. Over time, the number of relevant metrics covering benchmarking and best practices will increase appreciatively.

## CONCLUSION

Benchmarking and best practices serve as a reminder that libraries, like other organizations, should explore different methods to engage in service improvement and demonstrate accountability. An advantage of engaging in such endeavors is that library managers and leaders can see what works well in their own organization and elsewhere and incorporate the findings into change management and influencing the organizational climate as the library seeks to meet its mission and to challenge itself through a creative and challenging vision. Change management focuses on the infrastructure of libraries (facilities, staffing, collections, and technology) and the relationship of the organization to its broader environment. Most likely, organizational change affects more than one part of the infrastructure.

## NOTES

1. U.S. Department of Defense, "Best Practices & Benchmarking." Available at http://www.defenselink.mil/comptroller/icenter/learn/bestprac.htm (accessed August 7, 2007). For an excellent overview and background on benchmarking, see Norman Jackson, "Benchmarking in UK HE: An Overview," *Quality Assurance in Education* 9, no. 4 (2001): 218–35; Ian Smith, "Benchmarking Human Resource Development: An Emerging Area of Practice," *Library Management* 27, no. 6/7 (2006): 401–10; Sarah M. Pritchard, "Library Benchmarking: Old Wine in New Bottles?" *The Journal of Academic Librarianship* 21, no. 6 (1996): 491–5.

2. U.S. Department of Defense, "Best Practices & Benchmarking."

3. Ibid.

4. California State University, Long Beach, "Measuring Quality and Satisfaction." Available at http://www.csulb.edu/library/WASC/Q1_CSS_Report.pdf (accessed August 7, 2007). It merits mention that Thomas J. Hennen, Jr., maintains a Web site entitled "Hennen's American Public Library Ratings" that covers benchmarking and types of measures that might be included. See http://www.haplr-index.com/backtobasics.html (accessed August 7, 2007); Thomas J. Hennen, Jr., "Hennen's American Public Library Ratings 2008," *American Libraries* 39, no. 9 (October 2008): 56–61; Thomas J Hennen, Jr., "Public Library Ratings Corrected," *American Libraries* 39, no. 10 (November 2008): 54–5.

5. Roswitha Poll, "Benchmarking with Quality Indicators: National Projects," *Performance Measurement and Metrics* 8, no. 1 (2007), 42.

6. Ibid., 45.

7. Ibid., 45, 49.

8. Ibid., 49.

9. Anne Wilson, Isabella Trahn, Leanne Pitman, and Gaynor Austen, "Best Practice in Australian University Libraries: Lessons from a National Project," a paper presented at the 3rd Northumbria Conference on Performance Measurement in Libraries and Information Services (1999). Available at http://info.library.unsw.edu.au/libadmin/conf/bestprac.html (accessed August 10, 2007).

10. U.S. General Accounting Office, *Best Practices Methodology: A New Approach for Improving Government Operations*, GAO/NSIAD-95–154 (Washington, DC: General Accounting Office, 1995). Available at http://www.gao.gov/archive/1995/ns95154.pdf (accessed August 10, 2007).

11. Anne Wilson and Leeanne Pitman, *Best Practice Handbook for Australian University Libraries* (Canberra Department of Education, Training and Youth Affairs, Evaluations and Investigations Programme, Higher Education Division, 2000). Available at http://www.dest.gov.au/archive/highered/eippubs/eip00_10/00_10.pdf (accessed August 10, 2007).

12. Linda Suskie, *Assessing Student Learning: A Common Sense Guide* (Bolton, MA: Anker Publishing, 2004), 9.

13. Ibid., 10.

14. Peggy L. Maki, *Assessing for Learning: Building a Sustainable Commitment across the Institution* (Sterling, VA: Stylus Publishing, 2004), 3.

15. Sandra Bloomberg and Melanie McDonald, "Assessment: A Case Study in Synergy," in *Outcomes Assessment in Higher Education: Views and Perspectives*, edited by Peter Hernon and Robert E. Dugan (Westport, CT: Libraries Unlimited, 2004), 274–88.

16. See Hernon and Dugan, *Outcomes Assessment in Higher Education*; Peter Hernon, Robert E. Dugan, and Candy Schwartz, *Revisiting Outcomes Assessment in Higher Education* (Westport, CT: Libraries Unlimited, 2006).

17. Educational Testing Service, "iSkills™—Information and Communication Technology Literacy Test." Available at http://www.ets.org/portal/site/ets/menuitem.435c0b5cc7bd0ae7015d9510c3921509/?vgnextoid=b8a246f1674f4010VgnVCM10000022f95190RCRD (accessed August 8, 2007).

18. See American Library Association, Association of College and Research Libraries, *Objectives for Information Literacy Instruction: A Model Statement for Academic Libraries* (Chicago: American Library Association, 2001). Available at http://www.ala.org/ala/acrl/acrlstandards/objectivesinformation.cfm (accessed August 10. 2007); American Library Association, Association of College and Research Libraries, *Information Literacy Competency Standards for Higher Education* (Chicago: American Library Association, 2000). Available at http://www.ala.org/ala/acrl/acrlstandards/informationliteracycompetency.cfm (accessed October 14, 2007).

It is critical to note that accreditation organizations and academic programs do not confine outcomes assessment to information literacy.

19. See Paul Attewell and David E. Lavin, "Point of View: Distorted Statistics on Graduation Rates," *The Chronicle of Higher Education* LIII, no. 44 (July 6, 2007): B16.

20. For a discussion of library as a place, see Logan Ludwig and Susan Starr, "Library as Place: Results of a Delphi Study," *Journal of the Medical Library Association* 93, no. 3 (2005): 315–24; Harold B. Shill and Shawn Tonner, "Does the Building Still Matter? Usage Patterns in New, Expanded, and Renovated Libraries, 1995–2002," *College & Research Libraries* 65, no. 2 (2004): 123–50.

21. David W. Lewis, "A Strategy for Academic Libraries in the First Quarter of the 21st Century," *College & Research Libraries* 68, no. 5 (September 2007), 421.

22. Ibid.

23. See, for instance, Jerry D. Campbell, "Changing a Cultural Icon: The Academic Library as a Virtual Destination," *EDUCAUSE Review* 41, no. 1 (January/February 2006): 16–31; "Changing Roles of Academic and Research Libraries," Roundtable on Technology and Change in Academic Libraries, convened by the Association of College and Research Libraries on November 2–3, 2006, in Chicago. Available at http://www.ala.org/ala/acrl/acrlissues/future/changingroles.cfm (accessed March 25, 2008); Duane E. Webster, "Scenarios for Contemplating Research Library Futures," reconceived in July 2007, for use in the UCLA Senior Fellows Program (unpublished).

24. Lewis, "A Strategy for Academic Libraries in the First Quarter of the 21st Century," 418.

25. Ibid., 428.

26. Ibid., 429.

# 9

---·◆·---

# METRICS FOR MARKETING
# AND PUBLIC RELATIONS

Marketing is an approach to management, and public relations, which refers to a form of communications, is an important component of this approach. Marketing is a holistic process by which an organization's objectives are achieved through the voluntary use of programs designed and offered for target audiences. Public relations refers to the "planned and sustained communication of your messages to your target markets using the public media."[1] Both are disciplines that focus on the relationships of service-providing organizations with their customers, and both involve the purposeful use of systematically gathered information. In the past, both were related to selling a product or service to a targeted audience. Selling is distasteful to managers of nonprofit organizations,[2] including many librarians, who strongly hold values that libraries are intrinsically a public good, that there is no question but that everyone should use them, and that monetary exchanges have no place among librarians and users who benefit from *free* services and products. During the past quarter century, these business-oriented concepts have shifted to emphasize a relationship whereby the organization and customer share mutual benefit. The client orientation of library services has aligned with this emphasis, and, over the past decade, the shift has influenced the library and information science profession's philosophy of managing customer relations and product development.

Marketing is linked to planning. Both are management tools first developed in the business world but now also utilized by nonprofit organizations. Librarians give more attention to planning, and they narrowly associate marketing with publicity or promotion. In the past, it seemed enough to tell people what the library offers and that people *should* use it. In today's dynamic and changing environments, however, this passive promotional approach is no longer successful when libraries need not only to survive but also to thrive in an environment of rapid changes, diminishing fiscal resources, and increasing options for individuals to obtain information and assistance.[3] As Darlene E. Weingard argues, there is interdependence between the two activities. Planning provides a theoretical framework answering the question, "where are we going?" whereas marketing provides practical solutions, answering the concern "how do we get there?" Keith Hart characterizes marketing as requiring a "focus on what you do, why you do it, who you do it for, and how you do it. If you want to be successful you must know these things, either by instinct, or by planning."[4] Integrated together, the two approaches to manage organizational ambitions create a marketing plan, for which data are needed. Such a plan typically begins with an analysis of the community or customer segments served; together with an internal audit of the organization's strengths and weaknesses, the market audit provides data for developing and improving the service design. The marketing plan continues with establishment of mission and goals, pricing analysis, distribution channels, action strategies, promotion, and an evaluation of success, and it concludes with a review of the missions and goals.

In the 1970s, Philip Kotler, who articulated the principles of marketing, defined marketing as:

the analysis, planning, implementation, and control of carefully formulated programs designed to bring about voluntary exchanges of values with target markets for the purpose of achieving organizational objectives. It relies heavily on designing the organization's offering in terms of the target market's needs and desires, and on using effective pricing, communication, and distribution to inform, motivate, and service the markets.[5]

Hart gives a simpler clarification of what marketing does: "marketing anticipates and meets customer demand."[6] The Association of Research Libraries (ARL) offers definitions of marketing and public relations that focus more on the results of these activities:

- Public relations: "Any organized effort or activity created or performed primarily to enhance prestige or goodwill for an individual or an organization. Individuals involved in public relations are typically responsible or may be responsible for issues management, crisis management, promotions, image enhancement, publicity (media of all types), public awareness, fund raising, government lobbying. . . . and education."
- Marketing: "The organized process of planning and executing the conception, pricing, promotion, and distribution of ideas, goods, and services to create exchanges that will (if applicable) satisfy individual and organizational objectives. Marketing collects and uses demographic, geographic, behavioral, and psychological information. Marketing also fulfills the organization's mission and, like public relations, inspires public awareness and educates."[7]

In nonprofit organizations, both management and planning address the need to be accountable to funding agencies as well as to proactively respond to customer interests. Research data, and the metrics defining them, are important in gauging not only the impact of marketing efforts—centered on the communications of product and service to customers and prospective audiences—but also the markets themselves. In libraries, a change in managerial approach is required to redefine a relationship between the library and its customers. A server-client relationship has ceased to exist as there are no longer *free* services; multiple sources of revenue in fact might fund those services. Managers with a vision of thriving libraries realize that the problems facing libraries (e.g., securing sufficient funding, growing usage, and asserting the library provide essential services) are marketing ones that the profit sector has successfully resolved through the use of marketing principles and practices.

In this chapter, information to evaluate the effectiveness of marketing activities to gain customers and the use of libraries, as well as to gather information to help understand customers, will be reviewed in terms of types of metrics, methods of evaluation, and strategies for using such metrics. The chapter concludes with an agenda for further research.

## TYPES OF METRICS

Many Web sites and print publications offer advice and describe tools about marketing and the need for data of use to small-business owners; entrepreneurs; and people working in marketing, advertising, and public relations. It is less often, however, that one can find specific information about actual metrics used in marketing research or to evaluate marketing efforts. An exception is Joe Roy, who offers a list of metrics used in marketing to respond to activities associated with the marketing effort and the customer. The metrics are organized around two purposes:

1. "navigation: what you did [ad placements and media coverage] and what they thought [mental states]
2. evaluation: what they did [behavior]"[8]

Michele Eggers suggests four dimensions to categorize metrics:

1. marketing process efficiencies
2. marketing program effectiveness
3. nonprogram measures that offer context for evaluating the marketing program
4. the customer[9]

There is no single way to organize marketing metrics, but the various purposes represent what some authors refer to as *marketing research*: the interest in evaluating the marketing program itself, addressing what is actually done, and examining the corresponding cost and value, on one hand, and the impact of marketing on customer behavior, on the other hand. An evaluation of the impact of marketing is closely linked to the measured success of the product or service being marketed. Each effort differs in that it is associated with the goals and mission of a specific organization.

Marketing metrics overlap with, but are not identical to, various indicators of library operational efficiencies or performance. For example, the following list of indicators is among those metrics in use at La Trobe University, Victoria, Australia, to tell the story of the library to different audiences:

**General**

- selected indicators from CAUL (Council of Australian University Libraries, http://www.caul.edu.au/; http://www.caul.edu.au/stats/) annual statistics (e.g., salary expenditure as a percentage of total expenditure)
- selected indicators from library annual statistics, primarily use metric (e.g., building use and number of reference transactions)
- customer satisfaction survey (use of the Rodski survey)[10] (e.g., the level of satisfaction level, quality assessment, and gaps between importance and performance)
- client feedback from print and electronic suggestion boxes

**Services**

- information desk surveys (adequacy of support for library users)
- Web usability survey (ease of access and use of electronic library services)
- information literacy evaluation (impact on user)

**Information resources (access and availability)**

- materials availability survey (collection adequacy, shelving accuracy, catalog error rate, and library skills of user)
- intercampus loans and document delivery (turnaround time and fill rate)
- reshelving survey (turnaround time)
- new book order placement and receipt (turnaround time)
- electronic database usage statistics

**Facilities**

- study seating usage survey, including computer workstation usage (adequacy of study space)
- opening hours surveys (adequacy of access to the library building)

**Efficiency**

- unit cost (monograph and serial processing)
- intracampus loans (between the library and academic departments) and document delivery (turnaround time)
- reshelving (turnaround time)
- order placement (turnaround time)[11]

## Market Share

The most frequently used metric to gauge the success of a program is the brand or product's market share. Defining the market "is never a trivial exercise."[12] In the business sector, this process starts with defining the market in terms of sales or revenues for a specific list of competitors, geographic area, customers, and time period. The market share measures whether the company is gaining ground in the marketplace. In nonprofit settings, the quantifier might be the number of uses of the specific service or product (e.g., circulation volume of fiction books) compared to all uses or transactions with the organization (e.g., the number of all circulation transactions). One research library director suggests that "the most effective way to promote the [library's] value is to improve the services."[13] For example, users want direct and convenient links to full-text materials they need. The competition is the simple accessibility to online information via search engines such as Google™. To gain and maintain market share, measured in units of access to the online resources, libraries need to target customer segments to use the online sources that they made possible with the expenditure of library funds. The percentage of all searches that are to library resources is an application of using market share to gauge success.

## Marketing Research: What Is Done

Evaluating what is done to market the product or service is closely related to public relations, as this activity assesses the use of media: where advertisements are placed, news stories, or type of media coverage. Among the metrics often used by marketing professionals are the following:

- reach
- frequency
- gross rating points
- target rating points
- impressions
- cost per thousand
- number of clips
- accuracy of coverage
- advertising value equivalency[14]

Interviews with marketing professionals in various industries have identified a variety of metrics they use to determine the effectiveness of the marketing effort. These include the following:

- overall response rate to the media
- percentage of completed fill-out reply cards
- hits to a landing page on the Web
- referral links from the homepage to other informational Web pages
- return on investment
- additional business or market share such as quality of call-out and telemarketing
- brand awareness
- number of e-mails broadcast
- number of *click-throughs* (when the link is embedded in e-mail messages)[15]

## Market Research: What Has the Customer Thought or Done

Central to marketing research is information about the customers. One of the first steps to developing an effective marketing plan is to clarify the target population or customer segments in order to project who is served. Customer segmentation is the process by which the target audiences for whom a service or product is developed are identified and understood. Hart suggests the following customer characteristics are shared across library types and may illustrate the types of data points to consider in developing specific metrics for measuring customer needs or library success in serving them:

- age (e.g., early readers, teenagers, or adults for public libraries)
- location (e.g., on-site customers or those accessing the library remotely)
- frequency of use (e.g., regular customers or noncustomers)
- day and/or time of use (e.g., daytime or evening visitors, or weekday or weekend customers)
- ability or willingness to pay (e.g., crucial if developing services are offered for cost recovery)
- job function or status (e.g., researchers, policy advisors, product managers, undergraduate or graduate students, tenured or adjunct faculty)

- subject interest (e.g., academic libraries cover different academic disciplines, and public libraries include nonfiction and fiction)
- information delivery mechanism (e.g., face-to-face contact, telephone, e-mail, or any of a number of Web-based social networks)
- specific needs and problems (most customers do not think in terms of having needs rather they have a task or a facet of a problem for which there may be a need for information to resolve it)
- Critical success factors (i.e., factors critical to the customer's success)[16]

Segments need not be mutually exclusive, but they represent major populations for which a targeted service is designed. For example, in the academic setting, three major segmentations exist: students, faculty, and staff. These may be subdivided, depending on the service promotion plan to include specific interests, as for example,

- international and domestic students
- faculty members with tenure or seeking it, and those with no opportunity to exercise such permanent employment security
- disciplines and fields of study (e.g., humanities and colonial American history)
- staff by status (professional, managerial, clerical, and technical)
- staff by function (e.g., admissions, career services, facilities, administration, and budgeting)[17]

Some evaluators simply use a nonprobability sample, such as one based on convenience, to identify differ user segments. For example, in an art library there are the following segments:

- museum's staff
- history of art students
- fine arts students
- guides (docents)
- university teachers
- local artists, especially those who collaborate with a museum on exhibits
- gallery owners
- researchers
- general public[18]

The library staff might examine the extent of satisfaction that these customer segments have with different services. Eggers argues that, in nonprofit organizations, customer opinion about the extent of satisfaction is the key metric for service success.[19] The purpose of a satisfaction study is to analyze areas for improvement that are essential to meeting the library's objectives, as seen by the customer.

Targeted segments of customers are investigated for what they think and what they do, in relation to the product or services marketed. Some libraries categorize customers according to models of awareness and behavior, and they use these categories to see which segment came more or less frequently to a library and for what purpose. Flemish public libraries, for example, identify four different segments of customers. First, cultural elite or *cultural univores* are people who participate predominantly in activities that have a high cultural value; value is associated with people who go to museums or who attend opera and theaters. Second, univores participate in activities that belong to the fun world of bars, discos, sports events, and movie theaters; they prefer popular newspapers and media as sources for information. Third, omnivores tend to go both to theater and classical concerts, but also to bars, sports, and other popular entertainment venues; their media preference is more similar to cultural univores than to the fun action univores. Fourth, nonparticipants have no participation in any form of outside leisure, and popular media are predominant sources of information for them.[20]

The metrics used for measuring what customers think of the marketing communications address such questions as did they notice the advertisement, did they remember the ad, did they understand the messages in the press coverage, and did they believe the messages?[21] Probing what contributes to the decision-making process by which customers choose one service or brand over another has led to measures of awareness, attitude, and usage.[22] These factors are studied in terms of customer knowledge, perceptions, beliefs, intentions, and behaviors. Marketers use these tracking metrics to project changes in market share. Customer satisfaction data are perhaps the most often collected metrics of market perceptions, and studies indicate that satisfaction is probably the best indicator of customers' likelihood to make future purchases.[23] To gauge satisfaction, companies ask customers if their expectations are met or exceeded. Another key metric relating to customer satisfaction is willingness to recommend.

Measures of mental state give important information to understand if the marketing activities have reached the customers, in general, but they do not provide data about the customer's actions. Actions might include, for example, requesting a bibliographic instructional class session, initiating an interlibrary loan, referring students to a collection, or sending an e-mail or instant-messaging reference query. Measures of behavior are evaluative and useful for accountability among nonprofit organizations, and they can help calculate profitability or return on investment, developed primarily in the business sector. Metrics for library use habits and behaviors include measures over time of the percentage of registered library users within a community, number of document loans, document use rate, percent of titles requested in the collection, average search time for direct access documents, and search success rate by catalogue subject.[24] These are all aggregate numbers, gathered to draw a general picture of the customers' activities related to the library.

Typically, libraries conduct user studies, and staff analyze the data gathered to identify such metrics as characteristics of users (their status, department affiliation, age, and gender), frequency of library visit (in terms of number of visits per week, month, or some other time frame), duration of library visits, equipment used while in the library, activities conducted in the library, and desired changes in library services.[25]

Antonia Arahova and Sarantos Kapidakis identify several public library customer behavior metrics that are based on criteria related to participation or completion of a task. These include:

- evaluation criteria based on objectives for performance metrics
- number of eligible participants identified in respect to all eligible participants
- number of registrants to participate in a workshop with at least half participating during a six-month period

- time from initial request to answer per e-mail and live chat sessions turnaround time
- subject categories requested per requested subject categories ranked from most to least[26]

To prepare and evaluate a market plan, librarians should identify so-called marketing metrics. Even though discussions in the literature present the data elements of such metrics, no standard for these elements has emerged. Ksibi Ahmed highlights Canada's National Core Library Statistics Program, which provides fundamental data regarding the broad impact of library services on Canadian society. He also discusses indicators that are similar to metrics, defining indicators as

statistically significant data, either synthetic or analytical, used as standards for measuring or evaluating programs, projects and interventions in terms of resource count and methods. They define concepts and classifications that specify the measurements and data that can be collected and analyzed. The indicators to be used describe what data to collect and at what frequency.[27]

## METHODS OF EVALUATION

Traditionally, libraries have used press releases, annual reports, posters, brochures, direct reports, and giveaways (e.g., bumper stickers, bookmarkers, and buttons) to implement and evaluate their marketing techniques.[28] Friends groups use personal letters and special events to recruit new members; this strategy helps to build a target public relations group. In recent years, surveys and use of the Web have increased as channels to gather data for measuring marketing efforts. As more use of libraries is through the Internet, use of transaction log analysis is a method to evaluate if customers find resources, navigate through the marketing strategies offered on Web sites, and find appropriate information in efficient ways. Marketing professionals also use transaction logs to study click-throughs and landings on Web sites of importance to their efforts to improve awareness and choices to use resources offered through the Internet.

These techniques study customer behavior, which differs from measuring customer attitudes, opinions, and thoughts. Survey questionnaires and focus group interviews seem to be the most popular methods used to gather these data. Questions are sometimes presented through pop-up surveys to those using online services and who are willing to answer questions about their extent of satisfaction,[29] their affiliation, or the reasons for using the online service. Although the identification of responses is helpful in understanding behavior and opinions, the results from such self-selected respondents cannot be generalized to the population or customer segment targeted for the marketing effort.

Hart reviews the advantages and disadvantages of different evaluation methods used to ask customers for opinions and perceptions of marketing activities. Surveys reach many people, are inexpensive, and enable managers to compare results over time. They are, however, relatively inflexible in that there is little or no opportunity to deviate from standard questions asked. Since responses are self-reported, it is easy for respondents to be less than truthful, and the response rate is generally low; 10 percent is high in some settings. Telephone surveys include open questions, and response rates vary widely. Such surveys are labor intensive, and it is often difficult to contact respondents at convenient times. Face-to-face interviews offer flexibility to allow for more probing of open-ended questions. The interviewer can note body language and, when appropriate, show marketing materials; however, this approach is very labor intensive, and sometimes concerns about confidentiality arise. Focus group interviews have many of the same advantages as personal interviews. When participants make a commitment to provide relevant insights, a true understanding of their thoughts, beliefs, and opinions emerges. In spite of growing popularity of focus group interviews, conducting them requires skills such as the ability to facilitate a group discussion and to maintain neutrality throughout the session. It might also be difficult to get customers to attend sessions.[30]

Typically, reports of using metrics to evaluate marketing efforts in libraries fall short of the underlying principle of gauging success in terms of performance against a predetermined goal. At the University of Illinois, Urbana-Champaign, several methods were used to gather data for indicators that evaluate success of marketing efforts. For example, Yoo-Seong Song reports that the number of requests for individual consultations per year among graduate business students rose 8 percent. This was interpreted to be a marked increase as a result of a marketing effort. Similarly, the "number of attendees in workshops grew from 42 to 126 in two years."[31] What is missing, however, is any indication of the targeted activity level for which the marketing effort was designed to reach as a success measure.

Elena Roseras Carcedo established three types of assessment associated with the goal-achievement approach of using marketing metrics. First, *ex-ante* or a priori assessment establishes objectives for the results expected to be attained. Second, *concurrent* assessment provides information to make decisions about whether to continue operations based on the extent to which actions help attain the objectives during the implementation. Third, *ex-post* or a posteriori assessment defines the level to which established objectives have been attained.[32]

Carcedo identifies metrics used by a public library in Lexington, Kentucky, to view marketing success. However, these reported measures lack targeted goals for achievement. They include increases in both the number of reference transactions over a seven-month period and attendance for family programs, total bookings of program and small meeting room spaces, and constant use of 24 computers without waiting lines.[33]

Several software applications are gaining popularity for use in analyzing and presenting metrics. Among these is the dashboard, which presents multiple data points with thresholds identified as part of the market plan. The dashboard uses role-based permissions (a systems security approach allowing users to perform specific tasks depending on the level of authorization they are assigned) and live connectivity to feeds of data sources, which thus are current and strive for transparency. Small and large organizations use dashboards, which have evolved to provide Web 2.0 methods of sharing business intelligence not only among a few leaders, but throughout organizations.[34] One example of use of the dashboard for accountability and continuous improvement is found in Minnesota among the state colleges and universities. The board of trustees and other policymakers set directions in a strategic plan and then used the dashboard as an accountability system and reporting tool to monitor performance. Data on the 10 most important outcomes that gauge if the institutions are achieving their strategic directions are displayed showing placement within thresholds of success. Four success thresholds were developed based on the nature of the measure, existence of targets, and the availability of comparative benchmarking data. Thresholds are set based on specified goals or targets, external references, expected values, and historic performance. Colors are typically used on dashboards to reflect performance categories, and in the Minnesota case, these indicate whether each educational institution or the state system as a whole "exceeds expectations" (gold), "meets expectations" (blue), or "needs attention" (red). This system of reporting data to show achievements is maintained in such a way that decision makers can review current or previous reporting periods.[35]

Traditionally, marketing metrics have been purely quantitative, tracking such countable actions as views, calls, and Web click-through data. It may be worth mentioning that Web statistical programs are useful in making adjustments on the Web pages to help visitors, that Web statistical counts have become sophisticated, and that some universities use Google Analytics (http://www.google.com/analytics/) as a source of Web page data. Marketing analysts also find qualitative information important when they examine more deeply the root customer needs and try to understand quantitative results. They tend to use large samples of respondents to draw conclusions, be they based on quantitative or qualitative information. The assumption often expressed in marketing literature is that "ultimately, if the base of qualitative information is large enough, it can often be converted into statistical results and trends for quantitative reporting."[36]

It is not unusual to find response rates to marketing surveys below 20 percent and to have marketing researchers accept these under the pretense that large samples were used to seek opinions. Similarly, in applying qualitative methods such as interviews, marketing researchers go beyond targets of finding repetitive patterns in responses among no more than 25 participants, and they draw large target samples similar to what they do when they apply quantitative methods. *Marketing research* is sometimes a loosely applied term for the systematic gathering of data, but it does not always use validated methodologies concerned about the extent to which data can be used to draw insights about customers in general.

Another approach to capturing customer data involves building relationships with customers, for the purpose of seeking their trust and loyalty. Marketing researchers interact with customers during the evaluation phases of marketing plans. Nottingham Trent University, in the United Kingdom, calls this approach *customer value research* and bases it on customer discovery workshops and interactive value modeling. Sue McKnight notes that this approach

is an ideal methodology to use to gauge customer satisfaction where service improvement is necessary and where it is vital to engage library staff in the change process that will result. However, this methodology is not helpful if the customer satisfaction research is to be used, primarily, for across industry benchmarking, as the results of the research are valid only for that particular library service and cannot be used for direct comparisons with other library services.[37]

The approach is based on the customer having a hierarchy of values, progressing from anger to delight and moving beyond the unanticipated. There is no single metric of total customer satisfaction, but rather, this approach illustrates that given the complexity of services, some customers are angry and others are delighted with their interactions with services, staff, and resources. A value or total score can be calculated, and that score equals delighted (value) factors minus the irritation factors. For example, students seeking information for an assignment may be irritated by an inconsiderate staff member who speaks offhandedly, but they are pleased that they obtained the information they needed. The net value to the customer is the value of the information minus irritation caused by a rude staff member.

For customers of traditional libraries, basic services include those where customers find information by way of books and journals, and they expect to have access to electronic information sources as well. If these services are delivered, customers are neither annoyed nor delighted, they simply got what they believed should be available. Customers' perceptions are reality, so if customers perceive something is not there when it actually is, then the feedback about that service is not well communicated. Further, the public relations portion of the marketing plan needs to be addressed. As part of the methodology, customers write down irritants, vision a time in the future when the library contributes to their success, and discuss and rate the library performance. Similar to the expectations and perceptions found in the gap analysis of service quality (using SERVQUAL, see http://www.12manage. com/methods_zeithaml_servqual.html), value propositions—like expectations of excellence—remain static, and irritants change as improvements to services affect the extent of irritation experienced.[38]

After consolidating data received from customer discovery workshops, staff are brought together in a final workshop, and they consider actions to reduce irritants and/or improve value factors. The engagement of customers and staff, and use of software to plot likely changes in customer satisfaction, by targeted service improvements, improves quality of decision making.[39]

Sources of general information also can be found in published reports of research on user behaviors. The following annotations supplied in an article for the Association of College and Research Libraries (ACRL)[40] highlight some major studies that offer both generalized insights as well as methodological suggestions for conducting local studies:

- *Perceptions of Libraries and Information Resources* (2005). It "summarizes findings of an international study on information-seeking habits and preferences. With extensive input from hundreds of librarians and OCLC staff, the OCLC Market Research team developed a project and commissioned Harris Interactive Inc. to survey a representative sample of information consumers. In June of 2005, we collected over 3,300 responses from information consumers in Australia, Canada, India, Singapore, the United Kingdom and the United States" (available at http://www.oclc.org/reports/2005perceptions.htm).

- Academic and Research Library Campaign Research (KRC Research, Washington, DC). It "conducted a series of interviews and focus groups within the academic library community and with students, faculty, and administrators to determine the best way to communicate about the value of academic and research libraries and librarians in the 21st century. Key messages and talking points were developed by KRC, based on that research and further discussion with ACRL members."[41]

- The Big Picture Statistics and Studies. "The ALA Office for Research and Statistics (ORS) has compiled a variety of statistics on academic and research libraries. ORS also has put together a summary of three studies released in 2002 that focus on who uses academic libraries, as well as offer a summary of studies that reflect the Academic and Research Library Campaign's key messages."[42]

- *Library Advocate's Handbook.* It offers tips for developing a library advocacy plan and network @ your library™. It also includes communication planning strategies, how to generate key messages and prepare spokespeople, and a checklist of advocacy activities.[43]

- *MLS Marketing Library Services.* "This bimonthly newsletter from Information Today, Inc., provides information professionals in all types of libraries with specific ideas for marketing their services, including suggestions for planning programs, making money, increasing business, and proving your value to your administrators" (available at http://www.infotoday.com/MLS/default.shtml).

- *The Shy Librarian:* Promoting Libraries, Librarians and Books. "*The Shy Librarian* is a quarterly, ad-free, print magazine, which focuses on promoting libraries, librarians, and books, with many articles on library marketing, public relations, and programming. Also featured are over 50 original reviews of new books for children and young adults, as well as reviews of professional books written by librarians and teachers" (see http://www.shylibrarian.com/).

- *A Student's Guide to Evaluating Libraries at Colleges and Universities* from ACRL. This "brochure from ACRL . . . provides high school students with suggestions on how to evaluate libraries at . . . [the] colleges and universities they are considering, including services, facilities, and resources."[44]

## STRATEGIES FOR USING METRICS

Marketing metrics have a common purpose. They provide the management of an organization with evidence about direct services to customers and indirect services (through availability of products and resources). That evidence is useful for planning purposes. Marketing ultimately is about formulating goals, planning strategies to accomplish them, communicating the results of doing both, evaluating the process and the impact of the efforts, and revisiting the goals and strategies. At each stage, metrics are important to gathering the right information to support management's needs for accountability and improvement. The major applications of marketing metrics are to gauge the performance of the company as a result of a marketing effort, to evaluate financial results of that effort, and to understand the impact on customers. Accountability and improvement call for the alignment of goals and operations with customer needs and interests, and to do so in financially responsible ways.

Numerous examples exist of how libraries have gathered feedback from customers and then used it to develop or improve their services.[45] These examples illustrate first steps to gather and use information, but few libraries have reported a systematic and intentional marketing plan whereby they articulate and evaluate targeted metrics of success. Librarians often report satisfaction with increased numbers of people coming to the library or using a service, but they have not identified metrics for planning success that aimed to have targeted increased levels of use.

One popular strategy for gathering and utilizing data about customers' perceptions of services is the LibQUAL+™ set of services aimed to help librarians improve their service offerings based on service quality metrics. Sponsored by ARL, LibQUAL+™ has evolved from the SERVQUAL.[46] Through extensive empirical testing, Valerie Zeithaml, A. Parasuraman, and Leonard Berry designed the SERVQUAL questionnaire to examine service quality as the difference between customers' expectations for excellent services and their perceptions of actual service delivered; they assess this difference or gap from customer ratings on 22 statements.

The SERVQUAL dimensions of what are most important to customers were not specifically adapted to library services. Texas A&M University partnered with the ARL to convert SERVQUAL into LibQUAL+™. The challenge in this development has been to balance the interest in creating an evaluation tool that addresses both a global understanding of customer expectations and perceptions across libraries, and a local understanding related to specific services that a library can use to improve its delivery of services. The tool's widespread appeal among many types of libraries has been further supported by staff training and discussions about how to create a culture of assessment or active approach to use data to make improvement changes.

Marketing metrics do not all involve customer feedback. Jim Payne, for example, illustrates three functions regarding the application of marketing metrics:

1. Direct measurement correlates the marketing performance as a direct result (effect) of the marketing activities (cause). The measurements include such metrics as "marketing spend on acquisition," "spend on growth," and "spend on retention or attrition risk households."

2. Econometric modeling analyzes the effect on financial results with respect to the marketing activities. The key metrics focus on revenue and profitability from newly acquired customers, revenue and profit growth from existing customers, projected saved revenue, and profit from at-risk customers.

3. Customer touch-point interactions focus on analyzing the effect of marketing activities on customer impact. The customer impact metrics are "customer lifetime value," "percent of wallet share," and "customer loyalty metric for tenured and new customers."[47]

The importance of these functions differs between business and nonprofit organizations. Both settings, however, have direct interest in customers, seeking to align goals and actions with them. For libraries, there are numerous reasons to obtain customer feedback. Among these are the following:

- Libraries are service organizations and should understand and respond to customers' needs (customers matter).

- Library staff make assumptions about what customers require, and these assumptions are not always accurate.

- If library management does not know where to put resources (staff and funds), the result can be a waste of time and effort because no value is added to the customer's experience.

- Acting on the feedback from customers can be a powerful tool in achieving cultural change within an organization and in making the change more customer focused and responsive.

- Monitoring the action plans that are developed in response to customer feedback enables performance monitoring and encourages a culture of continuous quality improvement.[48]

Specific to the academic library setting, a key customer segment whose feedback is important to seek for planning and improving services is students. Understanding students' perceptions and expectations of the library are critical to the development of marketing strategies. At the Business Library at the University of Illinois, Urbana-Champaign, for example, survey results from 2002 and 2004 were used to understand customer demographics, satisfaction with various services, and use of the Internet. The findings produced the following insights that support marketing efforts:

- Library instruction changed students perceptions of library services.

- Students, especially international ones, are more motivated to use library services after receiving library instruction.

- Space for personal study was the most important library service to most respondents.

- Students showed little interest in using virtual reference services via e-mail and online chat.
- The length of stay at the College of Business did not correlate with frequency of library use.
- Students generally did not have a clear understanding of the roles of subject librarians and did not have confidence in their knowledge of the discipline of business.
- International students had much less experience with electronic business information resources in their home countries than did U.S. students.
- Some 80 percent of graduate business students had broadband access to the Internet, and the telecommunication infrastructure was not a barrier to using electronic information.
- Over 80 percent of international students had broadband Internet access.
- About half of the respondents spent most time using career-related Internet sites.[49]

The staff at the Business Library used the results to form a marketing plan. They identified library instruction as a critical opportunity to promote library services and to provide students with career-related information. To align the plan with customer needs and interests, the staff conducted workshops about career opportunities and using e-resources to identify such opportunities; the number attending the sessions was a metric of success. More specifically, the staff developed the classic 4Ps of a marketing mix: product, price, promotion, and place.[50] The product was both resources (a collection of electronic information resources) and services (staff help). The place related to the computer labs and classrooms where the instruction was given. The promotion strategy was to use library instruction in the form of workshops, seminars, and guest lecturers. Since the marketing metrics indicated that most graduate business students have broadband access to the Internet, the price element of the marketing mix required no extra cost.

Carole Moore, University of Toronto chief librarian, identifies instruction integrated with the curriculum and presented through work with faculty as a strategy to promote the value of the library to customers. Some of the most successful outreach activities on campus to raise customer awareness of library services have been special electronic newsletters that subject specialists send to users in their disciplines. She illustrates an entrepreneurial, marketing approach when she advises others to seek to understand stakeholders and to rely on metrics. She encourages librarians to recognize the issues with which campus administrators struggle and to "make it clear how the library can help advance the overall priorities." Librarians should "be willing to adjust library practice in creative ways" and to gather "as much concrete evidence as possible about the real impact of potential budget cuts before they happen, and try to communicate this information in constructive ways."[51]

In developing a library marketing plan, objectives should reflect those of the institutions. On many campuses, the library's aim, from the perspective of the college or university administration, is to be used and to maximize the satisfaction of its users. The library will become and will remain successful if it operates to satisfy both current and future user requirements with maximum efficiency. To do so requires utilizing metrics about both the user's requirements and the library's operations.[52] As Eileen Elliott de Sáez succinctly summarizes, the cycle of gathering information and implementing strategies for using metrics involves collecting information, developing forecasting trends, consulting all concerned, understanding the markets, formulating objectives, planning a marketing strategy, implementing that strategy, evaluating everything relevant, and communicating with all concerned.[53]

## AN AGENDA FOR CONDUCTING FURTHER RESEARCH

Most discussions of library marketing and public relations are pragmatic and relate to specific situations and institutions. Few writings on these topics involve rigorous research, and even fewer suggest research topics for further exploration. Those who have, however, share a common theme that the agenda for further research should be about outcomes. What impact do libraries make on society, and what evidence should be gathered and used to promote the answer to that question? Another set of topics relates to evaluating a marketing strategy for managing libraries. Do libraries create and implement marketing plans, and are they effective in raising awareness and gaining support for services, resources, and products offered?

A fair amount of activity is reported in Australia and the United Kingdom about marketing research and managing with metrics. Helen King suggests that the major task facing Australian university libraries, for example, is to go beyond the evaluative activities currently undertaken and to move to more outcome-focused activities. She observers that there is growing pressure "to demonstrate the value that academic libraries add to the Australian higher education system. . . . as the proportion of government funding available to universities continues to contract."[54] More specifically, John Crawford wonders about the importance of information literacy to employers. He finds varying opinions about this and notes that the primary outcome for university students is to find jobs more than to pursue scholarly pursuits. He advocates the need for metrics on how the library makes an impact on the employability of college graduates. There is a definite link between information literacy and employability.[55] Some other research questions are as follows:

- What skills that librarians teach extend to the workplace?
- What refinements to information literacy skills are needed to benefit future employees?
- What characterizes the workplaces where college graduates are employed, and what information skills are needed to succeed in them?
- What attitudes do employers hold about information literacy skills and developing these skills on the job or in college? What factors predispose employers, one way or another, toward information literacy? What are the barriers to teaching such skills after college? Do public libraries have a role to help teach such skills to post college graduates?
- Does information literacy have a direct value to employers and employees that can be calculated?[56]

Not to be overlooked is a societal dimension to the impact libraries make and to the need for greater documentation and understanding of that contribution. Ksibi Ahmed argues for a need for metrics about the information society and the role of libraries in it. For example, he wants metrics that present the relationship of technologies to changes in lifestyle, culture, and economy. He views youths as strategic partners in designing and managing information systems.[57] His perspective suggests a series of research questions:

- What lifestyle changes are associated with technologies among young people?
- What are the social and professional profiles of the majority of users of libraries and online information systems? What are their cultural and information behaviors?

- What characterizes information-disadvantaged customers of public libraries? What percentage of a local community falls within this profile?
- What library marketing metrics appear in official statistics at municipal, state, and national levels?

## CONCLUSION

Marketing and promotion take on increased importance as institutions of higher education engage in branding or image campaigns that are intended to create visibility and distinction for them in an increasingly competitive marketplace. These campaigns also aim to convince more alumni and corporate donors to add to the college's or university's endowment. The purpose is to attract students, faculty, and others to a world-class institution. Libraries are expected to be part of the campaign, to reinforce the image projected, and to show how they add to the value and strengths of the academic programs.

How this is done is changing and calls for contemporary skills in market research and marketing. The image of the library itself has changed and includes the importance of people and what they do within the library, whether in physical or virtual spaces. The many types of interactions people have with library resources as well as the services provided to respond to customer needs become the new sources of *added value* to the academic enterprise. Modern concepts of marketing go beyond the public relations notion that the academic library, and especially its rich collections or beautiful spaces, adds value merely by existing. Marketing tasks—understanding customers, gathering data about their expectations, setting goals, performing excellent services, measuring service quality, and communicating to everyone with an interest in the library—are part of strategies to create mutually beneficial interactions between libraries and their customers. Libraries deliver customer-focused products and services; customers deliver usage, appreciation, loyalty, and support of the library.

The metrics needed to gauge the success of marketing efforts and ultimately the library as a service organization are no longer limited to counting inputs and outputs. Behaviors, attitudes, opinions, and thoughts also are measured and incorporated into metrics used in telling the library's story as a place where valued changes occur among those who use it. As this chapter illustrates, the assorted metrics discussed in this chapter also apply to accountability and improved services and programs. Clearly, those metrics become critical as libraries support the institutional mission and reinforce their role as partners in helping the institution achieve its goals and objectives.

## NOTES

1. Keith Hart, *Putting Marketing Ideas into Action* (London: Library Association Publishing, 1999), 47.

2. Darlene E. Weingand, *Marketing/Planning Library and Information Services.* 2nd ed. (Englewood, CO: Libraries Unlimited, 1999), xi.

3. Ibid., 2.

4. Hart, *Putting Marketing Ideas into Action*, 7.

5. Philip Kotler, *Marketing for Nonprofit Organizations* (Englewood Cliffs, NJ: Prentice-Hall, 1975), 5.

6. Hart, *Putting Marketing Ideas into Action*, 7.

7. Association of Research Libraries, Office of Leadership and Management, *Marketing and Public Relations Activities in ARL Libraries* (Washington, DC: Association of Research Libraries, 1999), 3.

8. Joe Roy, *Marketing Metrics Made Simple*. Available at http://www.marketing.metrics.made.simple.com/marketing-meterics-list.html (accessed July 13, 2008).

9. Michele Eggers, "The 'Holy Grail' of Marketing Metrics," *Chief Marketer*. Available at http://chiefmarketer.com/crm_loop/roi/holy_grail_metrics (accessed June 20, 2008).

10. Rodski Survey Research, now known as Insync Surveys (Flinders Lane, Australia, http://www.insyncsurveys.com.au/) conducts surveys of external and internal customer surveys for libraries and other organizations (see, e.g., http://www.insyncsurveys.com.au/Info/?content=ExternalCustomerResearch). The surveys provide a means of highlighting areas where improvement is required, making comparisons to other university libraries, and tracking progress in making improvements between surveys. For a discussion of Rodski Survey Research and its survey, see Grace Saw, "Reading Rodski: User Surveys Revisited" (Queensland, Australia: University of Queensland, n.d.). Available at http://www.library.uq.edu.au/papers/reading_rodski.pdf (accessed July 26, 2008).

11. Helen King, "Evaluating Library Services—Best Practice Initiatives in Australian University Libraries," in *Management, Marketing, and Promotion of Library Services Based on Statistics, Analyses, and Evaluation*, edited by Trine Kolderup Flaten (IFLA Publication 120/121) (Munich: Germany: K. G. Saur, 2006), 297–98.

12. "Marketing Metrics: Where to Get Them? Which Ones Work?" *Advertising & Marketing Review*, 3–9. Available at http://www.ad-mkt-review.com/publics_html/docs/fs059.html (accessed July 13, 2008).

13. "Measuring Library Value: Interview with Carole Moore, Chief Librarian, University of Toronto, ON, Canada," *Library Connect* [Elsevier newsletter]. Available at http://libraryconnect.elsevier.com/lcn/0103/lcu010302.html (accessed June 20, 2008).

14. Roy, *Marketing Metrics Made Simple*.

15. "Marketing Metrics."

16. Hart, *Putting Marketing Ideas into Action*, 26.

17. Adapted from Yoo-Seong Song, "Marketing Library Services: A Case Study at University of Illinois at Urbana-Champaign USA," in *Management, Marketing, and Promotion of Library Services Based on Statistics, Analyses, and Evaluation*, 258.

18. Elena Roseras Carcedo, "Management and Marketing in the Library and Coumentation Centre of Artium Basque Centre-Museum of Contemporary Art," in *Management, Marketing, and Promotion of Library Services Based on Statistics, Analyses and Evaluation*, 220.

19. Eggers, "The 'Holy Grail' of Marketing Metrics."

20. Bart Vercruyssen, "The Library as a Part of Cultural Behavior. Summary of a Large Scale Survey to Identify User Trends and Reading Behavior in Flanders Libraries," in *Management, Marketing, and Promotion of Library Services Based on Statistics, Analyses, and Evaluation*, 271.

21. Roy, *Marketing Metrics Made Simple*.

22. "Marketing Metrics," 4.

23. Ibid., 42.

24. Ksibi Ahmed, "Statistical Indicators on Reading and Literacy for the 'Information Society' versus ITU's 'Technicist' Indices," in *Management, Marketing, and Promotion of Library Services Based on Statistics, Analyses, and Evaluation*, 349.

25. Elizabeth Kennedy Hallmark, Laura Schwartz, and Loriene Roy, "Developing a Long-range and Outreach Plan for Your Academic Library: The Need for a Marketing Outreach Plan," *College & Research Libraries News* 68, no. 2 (February 2007): 92–95.

26. Antonia Arahova, and Sarantos Kapidakis, "Promoting Library Services, Designing Marketing Strategies, Evaluating Our Past and Our Present, Feeling More Optimistic about

Our Libraries' Future," in *Management, Marketing, and Promotion of Library Services Based on Statistics, Analyses and Evaluation*, 384.

27.  Ahmed, "Statistical Indicators on Reading and Literacy for the 'Information Society' versus ITU's 'Technicist' Indices," 343.

28.  Weingard, *Marketing/Planning Library and Information Services*, 130.

29.  Arahova, and Kapidakis, "Promoting Library Services, Designing Marketing Strategies, Evaluating Our Past and Our Present, Feeling More Optimistic about Our Libraries' Future," 383.

30.  Hart, *Putting Marketing Ideas into Action*, 93–94. It merits mention that Sage Publishing (Thousand Oaks, CA, http://www.sagepub.com/home.nav) publishes a number of excellent books on the research process, including different methodologies.

31.  Song, "Marketing Library Services," 263–64.

32.  Carcedo, "Management and Marketing in the Library and Coumentation Centre of Artium Basque Centre-Museum of Contemporary Art," 231.

33.  Ibid., 244.

34.  iDashboards, "Turn Your Data into Insight" (product advertisement). Available at http://www.idashboards.com/?gclid=CJ_Dsfv2vZQCFQRJFQodSB2VUQ (accessed July 13, 2008).

35.  Minnesota State Colleges and Universities, Office of the Chancellor Research and Planning, *Overview Accountability Dashboard*. Available at http://www.mnscu.edu/board/accountability/index.html (accessed July 7, 2008).

36.  Jim Payne, "Marketing Metrics—More Than Just ROI," *S-Market Strategies* (January 2008). Available at http://www.adhub.com/columns/jimpayne03.html (accessed May 11, 2008).

37.  Sue McKnight, "Customers Value Research," in *Management, Marketing, and Promotion of Library Services Based on Statistics, Analyses, and Evaluation*, 206–7.

38.  Ibid., 209.

39.  Ibid., 214.

40.  American Library Association, Association of College and Research Libraries, *The Campaign for America's Libraries @your library TM: Toolkit for Academic and Research Libraries* (Chicago: Association of College and Research Libraries, 2007). Available at http://www.ala.org/@yourlibrary (accessed June 20, 2008).

41.  American Library Association, *Academic and Research Libraries Campaign Research* (Chicago, American Library Association, 2009). Available at http://www.ftrf.org/ala/issuesadvocacy/advocacy/publicawareness/campaign@yourlibrary/academicresearch/academicresearchlibraries.cfm (accessed May 12, 2009).

42.  See American Library Association, Office for Research and Statistics, "Statistics about Libraries" (Chicago, American Library Association, 2009). Available at http://www.ala.org/ala/aboutala/offices/ors/statsaboutlib/statisticsabout.cfm (accessed May 12, 2009).

43.  Print copies cost $2 from the ALA Public Information Office, or download it free at http://www.ala.org/ala/advocacybucket/libraryadvocateshandbook.pdf. It is free when it is distributed as part of ALA's Library Advocacy Now! Training. Call 800–545–2433, ext. 5044 to order. E-mail: advocacy@ala.org.

44.  Up to five copies are available in brochure form at no charge. Additional copies may be purchased from ACRL for $1 each or $35 for 50. See http://www.ala.org/ala/acrl/acrlissues/marketingyourlib/studentsguide.htm.

45.  See "ALA @ your library" and its use of focus group interviews. For other methodological choices, see Barbara Whitney Putruzzelli (ed.), *Real-Life Marketing and Promotion Strategies in College Libraries: Connecting with Campus and Community* (Binghamton, NY: The Haworth Information Press, 2005). This work was copublished simultaneously as *College and Undergraduate Libraries* 12, no. 1–2 (2005).

46.  See: Valarie A. Zeithaml, A. Parasuraman, and Leonard L. Berry, *Delivering Quality Service: Balancing Customer Perceptions and Expectations* (Toronto: The Free Press, 1990).

47. Payne, "Marketing Metrics—More Than Just ROI."

48. McKnight, "Customers Value Research," 206.

49. Song, "Marketing Library Services," 259.

50. Ibid., 263.

51. "Measuring Library Value: Interview with Carole Moore, Chief Librarian, University of Toronto, ON, Canada."

52. Carcedo, "Management and Marketing in the Library and Coumentation Centre of Artium Basque Centre-Museum of Contemporary Art," 217.

53. Eileen Elliott de Sáez, *Marketing Concepts for Libraries and Information Services*, 2nd ed. (London: Facet Publishing, 2002), 1–2.

54. King, "Evaluating Library Services—Best Practice Initiatives in Australian University Libraries," 293.

55. John Crawford, "The Use of Electronic Information Services and Information Literacy: A Glasgow Caledonian University Study," in *Management, Marketing, and Promotion of Library Services Based on Statistics, Analyses, and Evaluation*, 338.

56. Ibid., 338–39.

57. Ahmed, "Statistical Indicators on Reading and Literacy for the 'Information Society' versus ITU's "Technicist' Indices," 348.

# 10

———•••———

# MANAGEMENT INFORMATION SYSTEMS

There is a need for a management information system (MIS) for which the various metrics discussed in previous chapters can be stored, organized, retrieved, and prepared for delivery in reports, presentations, or dashboards (see also chapter 11). A MIS is useful for planning purposes (e.g., creating obtainable objectives); assessment and evaluation, including determining the current status of services and progress toward improvement (e.g., identifying weaknesses, applying a solution, and measuring change); managerial decision making (e.g., fund allocations or a change in hours open); responding to surveys from the institution, other libraries, library consortia, organizations, and the federal government; and communicating conclusions, results, and information through reports and presentations with an emphasis on improving accountability to meet stakeholder information needs.

Briefly, a MIS assists in accomplishing the following activities:

- gathering—looking for information as data or metrics (e.g., counting how many books circulated)
- collecting—organizing or otherwise compiling the information to store and to use to meet a variety of information needs (Instruments, e.g., forms, are often used to gather and collect metrics.)
- storing—maintaining the data and metrics gathered and collected in formats (e.g., tables or spreadsheets, on hard drives, and backed up to other devices)
- analyzing—using tools to sort, retrieve, and manipulate the data collected and stored to create results and draw conclusions
- disseminating—reporting or otherwise presenting the data and the analysis to stakeholders (This may involve the use of text, tables, charts, graphs, images, and dashboards.)[1]

Prior to the existence of MISs, the preparation of reports and presentations that contain different metrics required reams of tally sheets, count summaries, and other paper files. Using the paper files to develop a specific metric could be time consuming. Once librarians began to use microcomputers and software that included spreadsheet, statistical analysis, and word-processing applications, and once the integrated library systems (ILSs) improved their statistical and reporting functions, it became possible and feasible to collect, manage, analyze, and report additional metrics. These improvements in capacity and capability were timely because of the increasing need for libraries to demonstrate their contributions (effectiveness, efficiency, and value) and their ability to meet evolving accountability demands for, and by, their institutions and the assorted stakeholders discussed in chapter 7.

## CHARACTERISTICS OF METRICS

Libraries collect data concerning inputs, processes, outputs, and outcomes, and they typically organize the data in the form of performance and process metrics. The former refers collectively to metrics that reflect the performance of the organization, namely, inputs or resources used; processes or measures reflecting internal operations; productivity or the ratio of outputs to inputs; outputs (i.e., the extensiveness and effectiveness of services delivered); and outcomes, the effects of the services on users.[2] Information about performance measurement is helpful in setting performance goals, allocating and prioritizing resources, informing managers to either confirm or change current strategies or program directions to meet their goals, and reporting on the success of meeting those goals.[3]

Turning to process metrics, Sara Laughlin and Ray W. Wilson find that a task is a single action and that a process is a series of interrelated tasks that converts inputs into outputs.[4] If the library is to improve a process, it must gather data on that process. They argue that every process must have at least one measure to track how it is performing over time. They also identify five categories for process metrics:

1. time (elapsed time, wait time, cycle time, and response time)
2. cost (or cost savings)
3. quality (accuracy and error rate)
4. customer satisfaction (complaints, suggestions, and compliments)
5. quantity (productivity, throughout, and capacity)[5]

Additionally, they differentiate between measures and measurements. Some measures are measurements. These are generally distinguished by the fact that the degree of precision can be selected. For example, when measuring time, intervals concerning minute, hour, and day can be employed. Other measures are counts, and examples include the number of data entry errors, overdue notices sent, and customers served. Counts may be further delineated as counts of events (e.g., number of requests) and counts of items.[6]

Joseph Matthews explores the characteristics of selected library metrics for application to the balanced scorecard (see also chapter 11). Those characteristics include:

• strategic (The metric assesses the strategies selected for the balanced scorecard.)
• customer focused (reflects the views of customers and other stakeholders)
• timeliness (uses current data that reflect existing conditions)
• accuracy (not open to bias, interpretation, or inaccuracies)
• meaningfulness (Important metrics relate to the library's vision and choice of strategies.)
• understandability (easily explained)

- balanced (encompasses several types: input, process, output, and outcomes)
- comparability (useful for making comparisons over time and with other libraries)
- impact (shows the impact of strategies and actions over time, identifies trends, and can be compared to a baseline)
- cost-effective (Data collection is not expensive.)
- simplicity (Metrics are easy to calculate, interpret, and understand.)[7]

## MIS ACTIVITIES

If a library does not have a MIS, or the system is informal, establishing a formal yet simple MIS is easy and will prove its value over the years. Gathering the relevant metrics into a MIS helps to organize the data for use throughout the year.

Researchers use instruments to collect data. For the purposes of this chapter, instruments are devices used to collect data, while tools store, organize, sort, and manipulate or otherwise analyze the data collected. Instruments to collect data include a simple tally sheet one may find at a reference desk; the hash marks are counted at some time, and the sum is entered into a spreadsheet. The integrated library system is an instrument because it collects transaction data as well as feeds into institutional-based systems that are rich sources of information. Another instrument is a survey in print and electronic forms. Surveys may originate from an internal or external source, and the data collected may be numbers, facts, opinions, or perceptions. Many library consortia and associations use survey forms to collect data from their members. The U.S. Department of Education's National Center for Education Statistics (NCES) Academic Library Survey (ALS, http://nces.ed.gov/surveys/libraries/Academic.asp) form is an example, as well as the form used by the American Library Association's (ALA) Association of College and Research Libraries (ACRL) to collect data for its annual publication of *Academic Library Trends and Statistics* (e.g., http://staging.ala.org/ala/mgrps/divs/acrl/acrlpubs/nonserialtitles/06trendsstats.cfm). The individual responses from the information placed on the survey form (by hand or entered through an input device) are likely entered into a spreadsheet or table and eventually summed by question. Another instrument is the interview, either one-on-one or in groups. Information from interviews can also be entered into a document or spreadsheet.

There are several sources from which the library may begin its collection of information for inclusion in its MIS. Internal library data will likely be the most bountiful source. Oftentimes, the data collected have been counted either manually or by machine, resulting in a summed total. When considering which data and metrics to place in a MIS, start with the input and output metrics already collected for the library's annual report, as well as those metrics used for making comparisons with previous years to identify and analyze trends (e.g., expenditures and the number of full-time equivalent (FTE) students to create an annual ratio of expenditures per FTE student over a specific number of years). Another important source of internal data and metrics are those gathered from the integrated library system. Many transaction counts are collected by the software, and the library may query the ILS for a report of counts as well as linking it to other characteristics (e.g., the number of books lent to graduate students).

A second source of data is the institution. The library may request information concerning students and their characteristics from the registrar's office (e.g., learning how many students are enrolled in a specific course). Another institutional information source is the office or department that files the required report with the federal government stating the number of FTE students along with credit hours. Other metrics to collect are those that the institution requests of the library and uses to prepare an academic catalog to inform prospective students or to respond to the external surveys it receives. The self studies undertaken by the institution and its organizations to meet the information and compliance needs from regional and program accrediting organizations is another source of data and information.

A third source is the metrics and data requested on survey forms used by library consortia and organizations (e.g., the local consortia for which the library is a member). Other examples of survey forms include the previously mentioned *Academic Library Trends and Statistics* and the Academic Library Survey.

Once these metrics are inserted into the MIS, the library should turn its attention to determining which additional metrics are needed to demonstrate the library's contribution to the institution. These metrics may include data gathered from user surveys or student test results from library instruction. When a missing value-added metric is identified, its inclusion expands and improves the value of the MIS.

In designing its MIS, the Mildred F. Sawyer Library at Suffolk University, Boston, first created a spreadsheet with the data and metrics used to respond to the biennial NCES ALS (also known as IPEDS before becoming ALS) request. Although the NCES surveys academic libraries only every other year, the Sawyer Library collects the data annually for inclusion in the MIS. Additional worksheets are included in the spreadsheet, and they cover information requested by the institution (e.g., "how many computer workstations are available for student use in the library?" and "how many study seats are available for student use?") that are gathered from a variety of publications. Worksheets covering the facility (e.g., the number of square feet and the number of group study rooms) are also added.

The MIS worksheets include data concerning seven areas: expenditures, collections, circulation, reference and document delivery, facility, technology, and staffing (e.g., see Figure 10.1). The data included in the MIS have been standardized. Understandable and executable definitions are an important requirement for standardization. Counts for titles cannot be mixed with volume counts; this must be differentiated by the definition of the metric. Additionally, for a metric to be useful from year to year, variations in the means to collect the data must be minimized. Second, the source of the data must be authoritative. If it lacks authority, the metric is questionable. An example is the number of log-ins generated by statistical systems supporting Web services because each statistical system may define and count log-ins differently than its competitors.

Figure 10.2 is a worksheet for electronic database usage. The data are collected from either the integrated library system or the library's information vendors. The reliability of much of the data, however, is questionable. For example, the number of log-ins via the proxy server increased from 467,141 in FY2005 to 4,648,098 in FY2006, rendering the metric's value as questionable. A similar increase occurred with the total number of log-ins, and both metrics are no longer collected. Reviewing the range of total number of records used from FY1999 through FY2002 also raises questions concerning the value of that metric.

As a reminder, the information collected may include a multiplicity of formats. Although a MIS most often collects numeric data, text and audiovisual information, including sound and images, may also be gathered.

Sawyer Library: **Management Information Statistics**
Reference and Document Delivery

| | FY1999 | FY2000 | FY2001 | FY2002 | FY2003 | FY2004 | FY2005 | FY2006 | FY2007 | FY2008 |
|---|---|---|---|---|---|---|---|---|---|---|
| Document Delivery | | | | | | | | | | |
| interlibrary loans borrowed | | | | | | | | | | |
| returnable | 620 | 441 | 471 | 476 | 1,165 | 320 | 390 | | 388 | 427 |
| nonreturnable | 784 | 742 | 691 | 617 | 417 | 827 | 527 | | 856 | 800 |
| Total borrowed | 1,404 | 1,183 | 1,162 | 1,093 | 1,582 | 1,147 | 917 | 0 | 1,244 | 1,227 |
| interlibrary loans loaned | | | | | | | | | | |
| returnable | 487 | 478 | 370 | 395 | 447 | 436 | 425 | | 460 | 471 |
| nonreturnable | 698 | 728 | 603 | 585 | 608 | 635 | 568 | | 685 | 768 |
| Total loaned | 1,185 | 1,206 | 973 | 980 | 1,055 | 1,071 | 993 | 0 | 1,145 | 1,239 |
| Net borrows/loans ( "-" = borrows > loans) | -219 | 23 | -189 | -113 | -527 | -76 | 76 | 2,390 | -99 | 12 |
| Instruction Sessions | | | | | | | | | | |
| number of instruction sessions provided | 124 | 140 | 152 | 99 | 126 | 103 | 109 | 108 | 141 | 145 |
| total attendance at instruction sessions | 1,635 | 1,709 | 1,855 | 1,268 | 1,570 | 1,497 | 1,598 | 1,763 | 2,352 | 2,757 |
| Reference | | | | | | | | | | |
| total reference transactions | | 7,949 | 10,032 | 11,002 | 10,056 | 9,961 | 10,218 | 10,774 | 9,340 | |
| reference transactions in a typical week | | not gathered | not gathered | not gathered | not gathered | not gathered | not gathered | not gathered | not gathered | not gathered |

Figure 10.1   Selected Metrics for the Past Decade (Mildred F. Sawyer Library MIS)

Sawyer Library: **Management Information Statistics**
Reference and Document Delivery

| | FY1999 | FY2000 | FY2001 | FY2002 | FY2003 | FY2004 | FY2005 | FY2006 | FY2007 | FY2008 |
|---|---|---|---|---|---|---|---|---|---|---|
| Electronic Databases, Leased | | | | | | | | | | |
| total number of logins | 87,976 | 182,605 | 204,456 | 169,573 | 221,074 | 204,978 | 264,468 | 6,071,737 | 336,210 | |
| via proxy server | 35,669 | 41,647 | 92,422 | 66,439 | 121,721 | 668,810 | 467,141 | 4,648,098 | | |
| total number of records used | 431,016 | 20,821,259 | 114,568,782 | 56,957,020 | | | | | | |
| total number of pages, documents, images, etc. | | | | | | | | | 14,886,090 | 18,720,959 |

Figure 10.2   Electronic Database Metrics (Mildred F. Sawyer Library MIS)

Once the data have been gathered, application tools organize, sort, retrieve, analyze, and report them in the MIS. Electronic documents, image files, relational databases, and spreadsheets on hard drives have all replaced the use of manila file folders and file cabinets to store data and information. The ILS also stores the transaction data it creates. Organizing or sorting the data can be undertaken using a spreadsheet or a database. With a single spreadsheet or database field serving as the sort point (e.g., sort by month or day, or general circulation or reserve), it is easier to retrieve a specific measure or datum. Once the data are stored and organized, they can be manipulated. Again, for a simple MIS, the data organized and sorted in a spreadsheet are manipulated and yield measures of central tendency (mean, mode, and median) and ratios (where it is possible to create a numerator and denominator). Advanced statistical manipulation can be accomplished through specific software applications, including programs from SPSS, SAS, and Minitab.[8] Such manipulation might also involve data mining, which is an analytical process of discovering patterns among a multiplicity of fields in the MIS. The process goes beyond simple analysis to seeking trends. Depending on the software utilized, non-statisticians can do the data mining.

The manipulated and analyzed data are reported or presented to the intended audiences. As discussed in the next chapter, there are various ways to report the data. Libraries must be aware of the way that stakeholders prefer to receive information (perhaps through a printed report or dashboard), and the content and context must be understandable to the reader. A report or presentation might include an easy-to-find summary, and all presentations must be organized so that as much information as feasible can be easily scanned by the stakeholder for relevance to their information needs.

The data and information contained in annual reports and supporting presentations are likely to state activity during the past year and currently and to present relevant results, analysis, and conclusions. Numbers included in a report may be contained in paragraphs, charts, graphs, tables, and figures. Context may discuss characteristics (e.g., demographics of the student body), status, usage, services, costs, learning, trends, and perceptions and opinions. To communicate the information, numbers and text may be combined into charts for presentation/reporting. For example, a text-based chart for presenting information may be structured as follows:

*Goal:* improve the library's collection

*Fiscal Year Objective:* strengthen the physics collections by adding new monographs published during the last five years

*Inputs:* $10,000 allocated for project in fiscal year

*Processes* acquire, catalog, and shelve books

*Outputs:* 100 purchased books

*Indicators:* increased size of the physics collection; decreased the average age of copyright dates for the monographs in the physics collection; physics faculty satisfaction with the new books

*Sources/Methods:* physical count of physics collection; collection age report generated by the integrated library system; physics faculty survey response

An increasingly popular visual presentation format is a dashboard (see chapter 11). Such a presentation takes several forms. A common format is a bar or line chart, oftentimes based on a time series. Another is a grouping of small, trend line charts in rows and columns; each chart displays a single measure. Visually, this presentation appears as a series of gauges; the Merrill-Cazier Library at Utah State University employs this style of presentation (see Figure 11.3).[9] The Minnesota State Colleges and Universities system visually displays the performance of selected key metrics as gauges such as those found in a car (see Figure 11.4).[10]

Librarians should be cautious about the metrics they report, and they should review the content for accuracy before presenting the information to stakeholders. Thomas J. Hennen Jr. produces the Hennen's American Public Library Ratings (HAPLR), which rates, scores, and ranks municipal and county public libraries on 15 input and output metrics. The HAPLR ratings receive newspaper, magazine, and television coverage all over the United States. The 2008 HAPLR edition was featured in *American Libraries* in the October 2008 issue. However, as reported on Hennen's Web site, "On October 1st, I incorrectly published data [in the October issue of *American Libraries*]. I referred to the wrong dataset in my computer files. The result was republishing the last edition, scoring and ranking every library the same for the 2008 edition as for the 2006 edition."[11]

## THE SAWYER LIBRARY

As previously mentioned the Mildred F. Sawyer Library maintains a simple, spreadsheet-based management information system of input, process, and output data elements. Data elements are collected and compiled using manual and automated internal and external logs and records. Quantitative metrics from the MIS, which are critical when demonstrating accountability, include the following:

- inputs—the resources used to support the library's infrastructure (collections, staffing, the physical facility, and installed information technologies)
- processes/throughputs/activities—the library's use of the inputs to support the institution and its mission
- outputs—the direct products of the processes/throughputs/activities (Metrics identify how much work is performed and/or how many units of service are provided, e.g., the number of books circulated or of reference questions answered.)

Inputs and outputs are an invaluable type of metric for administrative and operational decisions concerning the provision of library services, while data about processes/throughputs and activities help when reviewing efficiency.

The Sawyer Library uses its MIS to answer quantitative questions involving inputs and outputs that the institution and its organizations, students, and library consortia raise. In many instances, the data request can be answered with the same data or metrics collected as responses to the Academic Library Survey (ALS). If a metric that is not collected is requested, the library makes every effort to gather the data and to incorporate them into the MIS.

The information is also used for selective inclusion in the library's annual report, and to openly inform students about how the library expends the funds it is allocated. The MIS is frequently used for trend analysis concerning a wide range of issues. It is also possible to compare selective metrics to other academic libraries and with national averages.

Trend information is also used to gauge progress toward meeting internally established benchmarks. For instance, a benchmark was set in FY1999 (July 1998 to June 1999) to rebalance the annual expenditure for salaries, information resources, and other operating costs as relative percentages of total expenditures in the library. The purpose is to show that more funds are spent on information content and resources than on salaries and wages. The components of these major categories followed the definitions from the NCES ALS.

The benchmark sought was 50 percent for resources, 42 percent for salaries, and 8 percent for other operating. Figure 10.3 displays the 10-year trend line from FY1999 to FY2008. As relative percentages, salaries have trended downward, information resources have trended upward, and the two trends lines crossed in FY2008. This figure is an effective illustration of the library meeting the benchmark.

Figure 10.4 deals with usage. Trend lines for three major circulation activities are graphed over the nine years for which data are reliable. General circulation per FTE student is increasing (the number of FTE students is collected annually as a data element). The Sawyer Library purchases two copies of every book required for all undergraduate and graduate courses other than for the law school to place on reserve. The figure illustrates that reserve transactions per FTE student are decreasing.

One may conjecture that reserve transactions increase, rather than decrease, per student over time. In FY2003, however, the institution introduced a Web-based course management system (CMS). It may be that faculty are including more links on their electronic syllabi to articles in the library's subscription databases and

Major Library Expenditures Categories Expressed in Percentages

| | FY1999 | FY2000 | FY2001 | FY2002 | FY2003 | FY2004 | FY2005 | FY2006 | FY2007 | FY2008 |
|---|---|---|---|---|---|---|---|---|---|---|
| **As a percentage of total expenditures** | | | | | | | | | | |
| Salaries | 54.1% | 51.7% | 51.4% | 52.0% | 50.8% | 51.0% | 49.3% | 47.3% | 45.8% | 43.3% |
| Information resources | 35.2% | 35.2% | 36.7% | 35.2% | 37.4% | 39.5% | 42.8% | 41.8% | 42.7% | 49.1% |
| Other operating | 10.7% | 13.1% | 11.8% | 12.8% | 11.8% | 9.5% | 7.8% | 10.9% | 11.5% | 7.6% |

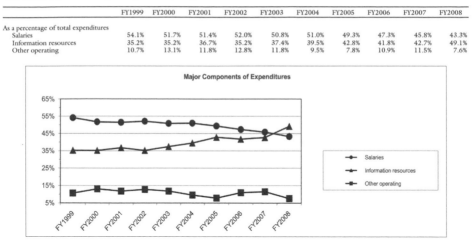

Figure 10.3   Calculated Ratios from the Past Decade and Chart of the Major Components of Expenditures (Mildred F. Sawyer Library)

CALCULATED RATIOS

| | FY2000 | FY2001 | FY2002 | FY2003 | FY2004 | FY2005 | FY2006 | FY2007 | FY2008 |
|---|---|---|---|---|---|---|---|---|---|
| Circulation transactions per FTE student | 3.3 | 2.2 | 2.4 | 2.4 | 1.7 | 1.5 | 1.4 | 2.2 | 2.7 |
| Reserve transactions per FTE student | 4.9 | 5.6 | 6.9 | 7.2 | 6.3 | 4.9 | 4.6 | 4.7 | 4.2 |
| Laptops loaned per FTE student | 0.3 | 1.2 | 2.2 | 2.6 | 2.5 | 4.6 | 5.3 | 5.9 | 6.0 |

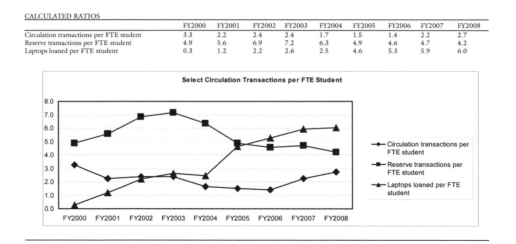

Figure 10.4   Calculated Ratios and Chart for Selected Circulation Activities (Mildred F. Sawyer Library)

decreasing the number of required print texts. That supposition could be tested by reviewing the data concerning the number of reserve books shelved each year (decreasing or increasing) per course and the number of log-ins to the library's article databases. Unfortunately, the number of log-ins into the library's subscription databases is still not adequately reliable to be used confidently.

A local modification was the inclusion of a worksheet using the NCES ALS expenditures information categories (e.g., "one time purchases of books, serial

| | | | | | | | |
|---|---|---|---|---|---|---|---|
| Total Library Operation (nonpersonnel) | $638,163 | $704,225 | $772,773 | $850,712 | $976,325 | $1,071,952 | $1,318,461 |
| Total of information resources, one-time | $79,975 | $94,750 | $107,895 | $118,201 | $133,233 | $146,870 | $219,057 |
|   monographs | $75,640 | $89,245 | $100,711 | $98,811 | $120,134 | $127,621 | $208,540 |
|   serial backfiles | | | | | | | |
|   microform backfiles | $2,415 | | | | $993 | | |
|   electronic | | | | | | | |
|     e-books | $0 | | | $14,486 | $9,295 | $15,262 | $5,451 |
|     e-journals | $0 | | | | | | |
|     aggregate databases | $0 | | | | | | |
|   audiovisual | $1,765 | $4,436 | $6,648 | $3,847 | $1,668 | $2,578 | $4,781 |
|   replacements | $155 | $1,069 | $535 | $1,057 | $1,143 | $1,410 | $286 |
| Total of information resources, ongoing | $387,849 | $451,349 | $526,082 | $608,536 | $643,589 | $737,929 | $926,302 |
|   serials | $195,529 | $210,614 | $223,582 | $243,501 | $255,207 | $275,451 | $260,076 |
|   microforms | $24,164 | $25,917 | $28,121 | $29,305 | $27,752 | $29,259 | $30,760 |
|   electronic | | | | | | | |
|     e-books | | | | $9,690 | $10,677 | $11,468 | $12,477 |
|     e-journals | $1,500 | $12,671 | $8,215 | $8,725 | $17,690 | $20,971 | $23,518 |
|     aggregate databases | $166,655 | $202,148 | $266,164 | $317,314 | $332,262 | $400,780 | $599,471 |
|   audiovisual | | | | | | | |
| Total of information resources, other | $222 | $132 | $370 | $624 | $141 | $300 | $513 |
|   document delivery/ILL | $222 | $132 | $370 | $624 | $141 | $300 | $513 |
|   preservation | | | | | | | |
|   other materials | | | | | | | |
| Total other operating | $170,117 | $157,993 | $138,426 | $123,351 | $199,361 | $186,852 | $172,589 |
|   furniture and equipment | $14,663 | $2,588 | $5,387 | $1,720 | $8,558 | $8,286 | $3,471 |
|   computer hardware and software | | | | | | | |
|     users | $39,132 | $38,061 | $31,237 | $29,496 | $80,705 | $13,095 | $70,390 |
|     staff | $2,886 | $20,683 | $10,207 | $11,667 | $2,520 | $10,125 | $5,555 |
|   bibliographic utilities, network, and consortia | $14,295 | $14,901 | $10,328 | $2,937 | $19,654 | $9,498 | $4,787 |
|   supplies | | | | | | | |
|     users | $17,543 | $12,087 | $6,729 | $6,984 | $9,059 | $11,732 | $23,440 |
|     staff | $7,879 | $8,039.38 | $14,519 | $11,331 | $9,702 | $15,726 | $18,060 |
|   equipment maintenance | $37,329 | $30,210 | $38,753 | $40,927 | $40,614 | $41,449 | $34,821 |
|   bindings | $3,692 | $3,140 | $8,669 | $4,613 | $10,423 | $10,082 | $4,290 |
|   travel | $1,235 | $2,411 | $627 | $1,595 | $1,839 | $2,506 | $1,214 |
|   printing | $1,683 | $393 | $1,155 | $579 | $358 | $559 | $609 |
|   mail | $4,371 | $4,082 | $1,709 | $1,922 | $4,394 | $1,905 | $1,556 |
|   memberships | $5,510 | $8,875 | $9,105 | $9,678 | $9,667 | $5,885 | $4,062 |
|   Millennium payments | $19,898 | $12,522.50 | | | | | |
| Business office end-of-year credit card payment charged to supplies | | | | | $1,869 | | |
| Business office errors: payments charged to the wrong accounts | | | | | | | $332 |
| Capital Expenditures | $11,488 | | $15,000 | | | | |
|   Computer hardware | | | | | | | |
|     users | | | | | | $40,172 | |
|     staff | | | | | | $15,830 | |

Figure 10.5  Mildred F. Sawyer Library Expenditures of Suffolk University Allocations Only (MIS Chart Formatted Based on NCES ALS Categories and Subcategories)

backfiles and other materials") but limiting expenditures to only those funds allocated by the institution. The survey requests expenditure information inclusive from all sources such as research grants, gifts, and fees (see http://nces.ed.gov/surveys/libraries/academic.asp). Additionally, the Sawyer Library separates staff costs from user costs for computer and supplies expenditures on this worksheet (see Figure 10.5).

The Sawyer Library used the data about the expenditures allocated as income from the institution to calculate the support from student tuition dollars (expenditures per FTE student via tuition) for the library (see Figure 10.6).

## OTHER APPLICATIONS

The data included in a MIS can be applied when conducting a cost benefit analysis (CBA), such as those studies that librarian Glen Holt and his associates undertake and report.[12] The full cost to operate the library is the denominator in the formula, and the perceived value (the summed benefit) of the library's services is the

**FY2008 Expenditures From University-only Allocation**
July 1, 2007 to June 30, 2008

| FTE students—as of October 1, 2007 | 6,454 | | | |
|---|---|---|---|---|
| | Subtotals | Total Expended | Subtotals per FTE Student | Total Expended per FTE Student |
| Staffing | | $1,057,770 | | $163.89 |
| Information Resources | | $1,145,873 | | $177.54 |
| Books, AV, and document delivery | $219,571 | | $34.02 | |
| Subscriptions (print/microform journals and serials) | $326,831 | | $50.64 | |
| Electronic databases | $599,471 | | $92.88 | |
| Other Operating and Capital | | $172,588 | | $26.74 |
| Travel | $1,214 | | $0.19 | |
| Furniture | $3,471 | | $0.54 | |
| Computers and software for student use | $70,390 | | $10.91 | |
| Computers and software for staff use | $5,555 | | $0.86 | |
| Supplies for student use (paper, toner, etc.) | $23,440 | | $3.63 | |
| Library supplies (supplies, binding, etc.) | $22,350 | | $3.46 | |
| Mail | $1,556 | | $0.24 | |
| Equipment maintenance | $34,821 | | $5.40 | |
| Printing | $609 | | $0.09 | |
| Bibliographic utilities, consortia, and memberships | $9,182 | | $1.42 | |
| **TOTAL** | | $2,376,231 | | $368.18 |

Figure 10.6    Chart Used by the Mildred F. Sawyer Library to Calculate Expenditures per FTE Student (Suffolk University-Only Allocations)

numerator. A CBA cannot be calculated with knowing the operating costs, which can be collected and stored in a MIS.

Data Envelopment Analysis (DEA) is an efficiency measure, more thoroughly discussed in chapter 3. Efficiency measures the library's ability to transform its inputs (resources) into outputs (services), or to produce a given level of outputs with the minimum amount of inputs.[13] DEA measures the relative efficiencies of organizations using multiple input and output variables as opposed to other techniques such as ratio analysis or regression.[14] The inputs or outputs may include simple data from a MIS such as total circulation, reference transactions, library visits, and interlibrary loans.

The data in a MIS can also be used for decision making. A published cost-benefit study assessed the economics of a library's electronic collection services in comparison to its print collection services. Using input, output, performance, usage, effectiveness, cost-effectiveness, and outcome metrics detailing library services, the study found that, from the library's perspective:

- The electronic collection and services yield benefits in requiring lower prices per title, less time of staff, and potentially substantial savings in space. Resources can therefore be reallocated into additional user services.

- Users benefit in flexibility of access, saving substantial time in searching, locating, and obtaining the articles.[15]

Factor analysis, which explores the interrelationships and commonalities among a set of variables, is another statistical application used for decision making. The main applications of factor analytic techniques are to reduce the number of variables, and to detect structure in the relationships between variables. A study applied factor analysis to allocate library book funds to academic departments (detect relationships between variables: in this study, the departments) based on the:

- total enrollment in courses offered by the department or program, which was likely downloaded from the institution
- number of regular faculty positions plus 1/4 of the number of adjunct instructors and other part-time academic staff not on the faculty list
- number of undergraduate majors and graduate students in the department
- number of distinct courses offered by the department or program
- number of senior projects and master's theses submitted

The author, William H. Walters, created vertical columns for each of the measures; each value was expressed as a percentage of the total of the column, summing to 100.00 percent. The data were then exported into a statistical application program with factor analysis capabilities (e.g., SPSS). Running the factor analysis sums the rows, resulting in a demand column and calculation that sums to 100.00. This column is a row-by-row variable representing each department's share of the total institutional demand (demand = 100.00) for library resources.[16]

## SUPPLEMENTING THE MIS

Because of the ubiquity of access, some libraries are turning to Web-based applications to supplement MISs. They might use a Wiki to input, revise, and access information. For example, SCONUL (Society of National, College and University Libraries) used Wiki software to enable members and others active in library performance measurement to submit, share, and discuss approaches (each with a definition), tools, techniques, and local experience through case studies, papers, reports, or links. There is the editorial control necessary to maintain the site and to ensure that the form and content are suitable to the membership.[17]

Social bookmarking systems may be a new source of usage-based metrics. Social bookmarking is a method for Internet users to store, organize, search, and manage bookmarks of links to Web pages. The bookmarks, informally organized using metadata tags, can remain private or be shared publicly with others. Bookmarks tagged for a specific Web site can be counted. Nature Publishing Group's Connotea (http://www.connotea.org/) and Springer's CiteULike (http://www.citeulike.org/) are two examples of social bookmarking systems for scholarly references.

Citation managers, such as ProQuest's RefWorks and EndNotes from Thomson ISI ResearchSoft (http://www.thomsonreuters.com/products_services/scientific/ResearchSoft), may also yield usage measures. Counting the number of times an article is held by a citation manager may quantitatively indicate the source's popularity and/or relevance.

## CONCLUSION

There are a few issues concerning management information systems. Variations of the definition of a metric, the means of its data collection, and the authority of the data may hinder reliable application because there is a lack of standardization. An example is online usage data of information resources from licensed third-party databases as output metrics. To resolve some of these problems, COUNTER

(Counting Online Usage of NeTworked Electronic Resources, http://www.projectcounter.org/) is an international initiative working with libraries, publishers, and other information vendors to set standards that guide the recording and reporting of online usage statistics in a reliable and compatible way by managing and refining an accepted set of term definitions, data processing rules, and reporting formats concerning the online usage of electronic resources including databases, journals, and books. COUNTER's consistency for compiling and reporting electronic usage information enables libraries to compare usage statistics from different publishers and vendors, while also deriving useful metrics (e.g., cost-per-use) to support purchasing and other collection development decisions.[18]

Academic libraries could locally develop the MIS applications to gather, organize, and store the data as well as manipulate and present the data for presentation and reporting. However, designing a MIS can takes years, requiring human resources and financial commitments to do it properly. Therefore, it is worthwhile to use off-the-shelf applications when available and to seek existing data and information to populate the system. Internally developing a library MIS may be neither viable nor cost efficient.

Another issue concerns the management of a MIS itself. To be successful, senior library management must instill in the organizational culture the belief that the MIS is important and helps to improve processes and to make decisions. It is recommended that a person in the library be designated as the MIS administrator. Only one person should have the authority to make changes to the original or master documents in use. Otherwise, it becomes difficult to keep track of which is the current version.[19]

The ideal MIS:

- is inexpensive to create, update, and maintain
- is manageable without requiring numerous technicians for day-to-day support
- has the capability to gather inputs from a variety of devices (e.g., barcode scanner, OCR [optical character recognition], and keypad), from other software applications, and from sources of institutional data
- updates the data instantaneously when a file is saved or when the application closes
- can be used on a multiplicity of devices
- stores data centrally but enables remote access
- enables automatic backups
- can refresh the data without loss when they are migrated to new formats
- is scalable (can add modules and expand the amount of data stored)
- is securable to protect privacy and the data

With all of the metrics identified in this book that libraries may want to adopt and provide their stakeholders, perhaps accompanied by trend data, a MIS is a necessity and not a luxury.

## NOTES

1. Issues concerning MISs include data consistency based on definitions, policies, standards, and practices; accuracy; usefulness of the measures, especially to stakeholders; the

ability to integrate other data and other formats; the ability to centrally manage the data but to make them accessible and reusable to everyone needing them; and security (including protecting privacy). See J. A. Vayghan, S. M. Garfinkle, C. Walenta, D. C. Healy, and Z. Valentin, "The Internal Information Transformation of IBM," *IBM Systems Journal* 46, no. 4 (2007): 669–83, available at http://www.research.ibm.com/journal/sj/464/ vayghaut.html (accessed November 21, 2008). For background information, see Peter Brophy, *Management Information and Decision Support Systems in Libraries* (Brookfield, VT: Gower, 1986); Peter Hernon and Charles R. McClure, *Microcomputers for Library Decision Making: Issues, Trends, and Applications* (Norwood, NJ: Ablex, 1986).

2. Nancy A. Van House, "Output Measures in Libraries," *Library Trends* 38, no. 2 (Fall 1989), 268.

3. Joseph R. Matthews, *Scorecard for Results: A Guide for Developing a Library Balanced Scorecard* (Westport, CT: Libraries Unlimited, 2008), 102.

4. Sara Laughlin and Ray W. Wilson, *The Quality Library: A Guide to Staff-driven Improvement, Better Efficiency, and Happier Customers* (Chicago: American Library Association, 2008), 22, 68.

5. Ibid., 71.

6. Ibid., 76.

7. Matthews, *Scorecard for Results,* 70–1.

8. Laughlin and Wilson, *The Quality Library,* 116–17.

9. Utah State University, Merrill-Cazier Library, "Merrill-Cazier Library Performance Dashboard-January 2006" (Logan, UT: Utah State University). Available at http:// ranger2.lib.usu.edu/main/portrait/DashBoard05.pdf (accessed December 12, 2008.

10. Minnesota State Colleges and Universities System, Board of Trustees, "Accountability Dashboard." Available at http://accountability.mnscu.edu/workspace/passthrough/ hyperion_passthrough_opener.html?url=/workspace/browse/withnav_get/Accountability%20 Framework/Accountability%20Dashboard (accessed December 12, 2008)

11. Thomas J. Hennen, Jr., "Hennen's American Public Library Ratings" (October 8, 2008). Available at http://www.haplr-index.com/ (accessed December 7, 2008).

12. See, for instance, Donald S. Elliott, Glen E. Holt, Sterling W. Hayden, and Leslie E. Holt, *Measuring Your Library's Value: How to Do a Cost-benefit Analysis for Your Public Library* (Chicago: American Library Association, 2007).

13. Wonsik Shim, "Applying DEA Technique to Library Evaluation in Academic Research Libraries (Academic Libraries).(Data Envelopment Analysis)," *Library Trends* 51, no. 3 (Winter 2003), 312.

14. Stancheva Nevena and Vyara Angelova, "Measuring the Efficiency of University Libraries Using Data Envelopment Analysis," *Proceedings from INFORUM 2004* (May 25–27, 2004). Available at http://www.inforum.cz/archiv/inforum2004/english/prispevek.php-prispevek=93.htm (accessed December 8, 2008).

15. Donald W. King, Peter B. Boyce, Carol H. Montgomery, and Carol Tenopir, "Library Economic Metrics: Examples of the Comparison of Electronic and Print Journal Collections and Collection Services—Academic Libraries," *Library Trends* 51, no. 3 (Winter 2003), 397.

16. William H. Walters, "A Fund Allocation Formula Based on Demand, Cost, and Supply," *The Library Quarterly* 78, no. 3 (2008), 305–09.

17. J. Stephen Town, "VAMP gets WIKI'd," *SCONUL Focus* 40 (Spring 2007), 103. Available at http://www.sconul.ac.uk/publications/newsletter/40/33.pdf (accessed on November 23, 2008).

18. COUNTER (Counting Online Usage of Networked Electronic Resources), "About COUNTER." Available at http://www.projectcounter.org/about.html (accessed January 29, 2009).

19. Laughlin and Wilson, *The Quality Library,* 117.

# 11

---

# UTILIZING METRICS:
# INTERPRETATION, SYNTHESIS,
# AND PRESENTATION

Many recent publications on the topic of measurement in libraries begin with an observation that libraries are faced with growing pressures to demonstrate performance accountability and to advocate, persuasively, for sustaining or incrementing support. There are changes in the ways that librarians tell the story of their libraries, and they acknowledge that the traditional anecdotal accounts of demand and value for libraries are shifting to the use of hard evidence. Such evidence involves the use of metrics that convey insights into resources, performance of operations, and perceptions. Not until the data gathered are interpreted within a context, however, do they constitute evidence useful for decision making and advocacy.

This chapter reviews three important stages in the utilization of metrics: interpretation, synthesis, and presentation. Each of these stages is influenced, to varying degrees, by several common factors. Fundamental to the utilization of a metric is the purpose to which it is designed or selected for application. Purpose can be identified in terms of questions for which data are sought. The need to have a clear understanding of why metrics are employed in a particular setting should not be underestimated. The purpose drives what metrics will be interpreted, effective ways to synthesize them, and strategic approaches to present them.

Similarly, selection is a common factor in all stages of using metrics. The choice of metrics is important to make in order to interpret, bring together, and ultimately present the case for decision making or the promotion of effective programs and services. In reviewing each stage of utilizing metrics, the audience or recipient must also be considered. This factor is particularly important in designing the presentation of an analysis of metrics. Such factors as the extent to which the audience is knowledgeable about the metrics and techniques to interpret them, as well as the audience's degree of interest in learning about the details of data collection, influence the successful preparation of results and help evaluators decide on whether they rely on written or oral forms, textual or graphic descriptions, in-person delivery of conclusions, or interactive engagement with information sources. To repeat, these three factors—purpose, selection, and audience—are both individual and codependent in their influence on the processes of utilizing metrics, through stages of interpretation, synthesis, and presentation.

## INTERPRETATION

This book addresses the managerial purposes for which metrics are used, including, for example, measuring inputs related to outputs (for the purpose of allocating resources), evaluating operations (for efficiencies), understanding customer behavior (for projecting a new service or revising an ongoing one), or gauging perceptions of value among donors (for developing fund-raising strategies).

Although an appropriate metric offers information about any of these purposes, managers must be careful how they interpret the results so that they can draw accurate and relevant conclusions. Most metrics are associated with a data-gathering method that has established protocols and that enable managers to understand the limitations and applicability of the data obtained. Regardless of the specifics of how to interpret the data collected, common principles govern the ethical use of the data. Striving for accuracy (motivated by honesty) is an obvious principle, but one that inadvertently may be compromised in the haste of making a decision, completing a report, or seeking empathetic support. Each year, many academic and public libraries, for example, are required to report key input and performance metrics relating to resources expended on acquisitions or levels of services. It is not uncommon to hear of reports based on estimates created from assumptions based on past experiences. For instance, because this year is no different than the last one, except for inflation, across all categories of expenditures, a percent increase is added and a new figure seemingly reflecting growth is reported. Metrics based on sampling and not on total counts might limit what interpretations can be made, that is if the sampling involves nonprobability sampling, which does not involve random selection.

### Preparing to Understand Metrics

Measurement, a specialized form of description, assigns numbers to differing characteristics of a variable. It provides a means for quantifying variables and making comparisons among them. The data collected through the use of metrics might involve measurement and the use of scales that are categorical (nominal or ordinal) or quantitative measurement (interval or ratio). All four of the scales classify objects, whereas only the nominal scale does not involve ranking objects.

Nominal scale measurement, the simplest of the four, identifies or differentiates groups of objects without placing them in numerical order. Such measurement names, but does not order, groups or objects. Examples include gender, the types of resources libraries provide (e.g., books, journals, government publications, and maps), and the purpose for visiting a library. Ordinal measures differentiate and rank objects, from lowest to highest (or vice versa), according to some characteristic. These measures indicate whether a group or object falls into certain categories and the numerical order of the categories. Although the order of the category shows the relative position of something, that order does not indicate the extent of the difference between the positions.

Interval measurement scales quantify the difference between categories, and those categories have equal distances from each other. The range between the highest and lowest scores is divided into a number of equal units, like degrees on a thermometer. Thus, evaluators can see how far apart each measure is and where a measure falls along the low, middle, or high ends of the scale.

Ratio scales are interval scales with an absolute zero point. With such scales, we can compute the ratio between two measures. Examples of ratio scales might include the actual dollar amount of library budgets and the actual age of survey respondents.

## Interpreting Input and Output Metrics

Libraries have long traditions of counting what they have (resources) and what they have done (production or service activities). Input and output metrics are reported as number, and thus most librarians feel confident in interpreting them as factual reflections of resources and activities. Any manager, however, should question why and how a metric has been measured before assuming it is useful in a particular application. For example, in recent years, the Association of Research Libraries has changed the metric for size of collection, previously basing it on a physical volume count and more recently adding counts of electronic resources acquired. For the purpose of comparing the extent of information resources acquired among its membership, this is a valuable metric. However, if a manager is interested in comparing shelving needs among peer institutions, then the growth rate presented by this traditional input metric no longer applies. The interpretation of the metric must begin with how it is constructed and why it is used. Another precaution in interchanging applications of metrics is to consider what elements are selected to define the metric. A common service output is the number of reference questions answered each year. If defined to include responses to all queries posed at a desk or through a designated Web box or e-mail address, then, although a possible indicator of traffic, the metric does not reflect the nature of reference demand or level of staffing required to provide the service. The basis for making decisions about resource allocations or the continuation of consulting services should not rely solely on such simple traffic measures.

Recently, automated systems are allowing the creation of data farms that capture information about the use of e-journals and databases, gate counts, photocopier and printer use, image collection use, and more. The data are then mined or presented in the form of specific metrics that assess library performance, indicate resource use, and are useful for improving services. The University of Pennsylvania Library, for instance, maintains the Penn Library Data Farm, which is a repository of quantitative information developed to aid the measurement and assessment of library resource use and organizational performance. In its design, this repository is multipurpose; it provides space to assemble, process, integrate, analyze, and disseminate data.[1]

Size of collections, expenditures for added volumes, and circulation of materials have been among the standard metrics used to monitor changes or to compare these activities to peer institutions. In his account of how Phineas Windsor, University of Illinois librarian, communicated with his president nearly a century ago, Kendon Stubbs describes an example of implied assumptions about such input metrics in relation to the need for increased revenues. In 1914, Windsor forwarded a copy of the latest statistics in hopes that the president saw that Illinois had fewer volumes than Oberlin or even the young University of California at Berkeley. The president, however, focused on other metrics and asked why the library only added 29,000 volumes and expended $86,000. Yale University, on the other hand, added

37,000 volumes at an expense of $34,000. The interpretation led to a question of whether Yale University was getting much better bargains or the University of Illinois was purchasing more expensive books.[2] Input metrics (the number of volumes added and dollars spent over the fiscal year) do not offer insights into the buying strategies of reporting libraries. Employing metrics as standards for gathering data must be done in a clearly specified context. The purpose is to avoid making unwarranted interpretations of numbers that involve competing perspectives.

As libraries acquire or license electronic resources, the need to describe their contributions to their community in terms of available resources, the requirement to justify the cost of doing so, or the evidence of return on such investments, call for revisions in traditional input metrics. Oliver Pesch illustrates the variety of uses of e-metrics pertaining to e-resources. For example, elements that capture use may include the number of full-text journals, the number of electronic reference sources, or the number of electronic books. Libraries use these elements when they participate in collection sharing, report on collections by subject or topic grouping, and perform overlap analysis of individual and packaged journals to assist in budget allocation. Such metrics are also useful to publishers and electronic aggregators in their marketing efforts.[3]

Similarly, the use of electronic resources calls for a revision in output metrics. The number of log-ins serves as a gauge of usage, not that different from the traditional number of loans or building gate counts, which comprise core metrics for usage of physical libraries. The purpose for such metrics in the electronic environment is to portray the extent to which a given service is used or the patterns of use by hour of the day, day of week, or month of the year in order to plan hardware needs or maintenance schedules. Managers should be cautious not to misinterpret the data gathered for such output metrics and conclude that a low number of log-ins, for example, indicates a lack of interest or presumed need for a particular resource when, in fact, the data might suggest that customers have difficulty in finding electronic resources or do not understand their use.[4]

The interpretation should also be based on an understanding of the design of the metric. For instance, is the duration of a log-in calculated in terms of a total session with the resource, or does it represent the time between interactions with the search protocols? One cannot assume that the time connected reflects discovery effort or reading time in using a resource, or anything about a customer's success in finding information sought to meet a need.

## Interpreting Outcome Metrics

In higher education, outcomes are typically grouped around students and their learning as well as faculty research. Student outcomes are aggregate statistics on groups and depict percentages that indicate the rates, for example, of student graduation, retention, transfer, course and program completion, license examination pass, enrollment in graduate program, and job placement. Student learning outcomes, as discussed in chapter 8, might examine learning over the duration of a program of study. Similarly, the impact that universities have on research, or the institution's research outcomes, are presented as aggregated counts of publications and associated extent of their being cited, the numbers and amounts of grants received by academic departments, and recognition or prestige measured by numbers of awards, prizes, or mentions in news reports. Such outcomes apply to institutions and are useful for comparing performance across institutions. In fact, however, such statistics are outputs that reflect what the institution has accomplished and are assumed to reflect impact, and they neither reflect what or how much students learned nor what faculty contribute to knowledge.

As Roswitha Poll observes, libraries in Europe tend to develop indirect measures of value such as studying use of collections and services, speed of delivery, accuracy of delivery, costs of products and services, adequacy of processes, and satisfaction rate of those served. An underlying assumption is made that such measures when gauged to be successful are indicators of outcomes, that high use indicates benefits to meeting users' information needs, that quick and reliable delivery of services will increase this benefit, that cost-efficiency processes will release resources to improve services, and that user satisfaction indicates good performance.[5] However, in the United States, such a characterization is outside the scope of outcomes assessment as envisioned by government and accreditation organizations.

Student learning outcomes, for these stakeholders, apply to the course, program, or institutional level, and they reflect what students learned over the school term or duration of their program of study. Such outcomes might relate to learning goals associated with critical and creative thinking, written and oral communication, quantitative or information literacy, and teamwork and problem solving (see Figure 8.2). The learning goals might be linked to a rubric or scoring guide, which describes a set of the criteria (with levels of achievement along explicit dimensions) that characterize the student's program of study over time. It is possible to determine what portion of students fall within each level of achievement. Gauging student learning, however, might be linked to pre- and posttesting over a term or program of study and involve the use of various statistical tests.[6]

### Interpreting Perceptions and Opinions

The difference between perception and reality is not always considered when interpreting metrics about use of a library or its services. Particularly misleading is the use of quantified measures of opinions. For example, a director wants to make an evidence-based decision about the schedule of opening the library, specifically responding to customer demands to extend hours of access. An important metric used to make decisions about the hours of opening has been the number of people using the collections and services per hour. An advisory committee member might suggest that a customer survey be conducted to find out the amount of library use during specific hours. High numbers indicate that customers want the library open later hours, yet staff might complain that nobody was present at the time of closing. People's perception of expected use and observed actual use are different metrics, and they generate different data for making decisions.

Metrics based on opinions might provide valuable information. For example, customer satisfaction, in particular the number suggesting delight with the library or a given service, is typically characterized from survey responses or point-of-use questions about reactions to services. Specifically, a library might periodically survey its customers and ask them to rate on some scale the extent of their satisfaction with the library during a designated period of time. A metric is derived from the responses, and it might consist of the percent of respondents answering in the top quartile of the scale or the item reflecting the highest level of satisfaction (e.g., very satisfied on a 5-, 7-, 9-, or 10-point scale).

## SYNTHESIS

Utilizing metrics for decision making involves an interpretation of the data collected and presenting the data with a purposeful intention. This activity involves synthesizing the collected data, preferably by someone with expertise in data collection, and interpretation of its application to the metrics selected for the decision-making purpose. In other words, making the argument for a decision based on collected data and established metrics requires a systematic synthesis. The Canadian Health Services Research Foundation defines the process for program evaluations:

A synthesis is an evaluation or analysis of research evidence and expert opinion on a specific topic to aid in decision-making or help decision makers in the development of policies. It can help place the results of a single study in context by providing the overall body of research evidence. There are many forms of synthesis, ranging from very formal systematic reviews . . . to informal literature reviews. . . . [S]yntheses [are] aimed at making "best practice" recommendations for a specific area of management or policy development.[7]

Well-established techniques exist to analyze data. They reflect the nature of the data as well as the purpose for their analysis. A rich literature discusses the theoretical basis for these techniques as well as specific guidance in their application. This section outlines some of the basic concepts for those new to data analysis, and it raises awareness of areas to explore or to seek assistance from specialists. First, evaluation research is designed to explain and predict a singular reality through factual data, addressing questions such as what, when, and where. Second, data are categorized as quantitative or qualitative, reflecting two different approaches for data collection. Quantitative data are analyzed using applied mathematics, often inferential statistics that involve hypothesis testing and enable evaluators to draw inferences about a population from a sample of responses. Qualitative data, on the other hand, are analyzed through a variety of ways in which it is possible to construct insights and generate hypotheses.

Qualitative research aims to develop an understanding of behavior and multiple perspectives of constructed realities through data that address such questions as why and how. Qualitative analysis explores conclusions reached through quantitative research, identifies new variables, or tests reactions to survey items, for example, which then are examined through quantitative research.

In evaluations and studies related to library activities, quantitative data might be generated from transaction logs or tallies generated manually or through automated reports, or surveys of randomly selected samples of populations served by the library. Qualitative data are gathered through individual or group interviews, observations, reviews of documents or literature, and surveys that offer open-ended questions and opportunities to express unguided comments. Findings from well-designed and well-executed quantitative research describe conditions and may be generalized to larger populations, whereas results of qualitative research may not be generalized beyond the source of data. Qualitative research may contribute to understanding explanations or identifying continued areas for exploration of issues addressed.

Much of the data analysis reported in library-based studies for managerial decisions use descriptive statistics for quantitative data or content analysis for qualitative data. More advanced quantitative analyses utilizing inferential statistics may be found when generalizations from a sample to a larger population are made. A few reminders about these basic methods of analyses are offered here to highlight key elements about which anyone preparing or reading reports using metrics should be well aware.

## Analyzing Quantitative Data

Descriptive statistics, which convert raw data into indices that summarize or characterize datasets, describe quantitative data and include the following methods: numerical counts or frequencies, percentages, measures of central tendency, and measures of variability. Such statistics commonly appear in the popular literature and are routinely reported in news broadcasts, and yet library managers sometimes have difficulty interpreting what they mean.

Counts or frequencies are indications of how many, for example, how many times something (e.g., loans, reference queries, processing errors, or e-book log-ins) occur, or how many responses fall within specified options (e.g., on-site, office, or dorm locations for accessing library resources, or levels of satisfaction with a service). Sometimes it is sufficient to determine that, for example, the library added 60,000 volumes to its collection this year, or 35 faculty respondents indicated they are "very satisfied" with the library instruction that librarians provided to their classes this semester. In some cases, such counts are used to calculate other metrics, such as a percentage, which indicates a proportion of a whole. The percentage shows relationships between categories of data or summarizes the frequency distribution of grouped data. For example, this year the percentage of the collection budget that the library spent on print materials was 45 percent, on electronic resources was 30 percent, and on audiovisuals was 25 percent.

Calculating the percentage consists of dividing the part (numerator) by the whole (denominator) and multiplying by 100. Although this appears simple and straightforward, there are common types of errors that are made in using the percentage.[8] Lack of clarity over the correct base, or the whole from which the percentage is calculated, may lead to confusion in the interpretation of results. If the base is unspecified in analyzing responses to a survey for example, reporting 75 percent may refer to all respondents, all who answered the question, or all to whom the question applied. Similarly, 70 yes responses to a specific question may be represented as 70 percent of all 100 respondents (i.e., returned questionnaires), or with a very different impression, as 78 percent of the number (90) actually giving an answer to the question. Lack of response may be an indication of no opinion or oversight, or the question may not apply to the respondent. In the analysis of the data, it is important to indicate what constitutes the whole base used in calculating the percentage, as in the example either 100 or 90. Rounding decimals may also leave false impressions of precision of measurements (e.g., over two decimal points) or may dilute the differences between responses (e.g., to deciles, which divide the distribution of raw scores into units of 10%). Another source of error is adding percentages when there is overlap in the categories. For example, respondents may select more than one multiple choice option on a questionnaire, and the researcher calculates the percentage of each option; these percentages may not be added to produce the whole. Another inaccurate use of arithmetic is to average percentages by adding them up in a frequency distribution and dividing by the number of categories used. One must return to the total number responding and the total respondents to obtain an average percentage of responses.

Measures of central tendency are descriptive statistics that identify typical characteristics of the data. Most commonly used measures are the mean, the mode, and the median. The mean, the arithmetic average, is calculated by adding all scores or rankings and dividing by the number of scores or rankings. While commonly used to report the character of a dataset and in calculating quantitative metrics and statistical tests, its disadvantage is that it gives undue value to scores that are very uncharacteristic of the set. The mode indicates the most commonly occurring answer or value and is sometimes used to describe *the typical* response. Unlike the mean, it is not affected by extreme values but is only useful when a large number of values are described. The median is the middle value, or the midpoint when half the values appear above and half below it. The median is used to divide the data into upper and lower groupings. Use of these three measures is dependent on the data and the purpose of the analysis.

Measures of variability indicate how widely the scores or data are dispensed around the central point or central tendency. These descriptive statistics help managers to understand the results and to see, for example, if all respondents or responses are similar to the mean, or if a few respondents differ from the rest. Variance is described by a number of measures, most commonly the range (the difference between the highest and lowest values), variance (measures the amount of dispersion of a value from the mean), and standard deviation (measures the dispersion of scores around the mean), which is the square root of the variance.

In addition to using data to calculate metrics, quantitative analysis also may include creating metrics to impose sequencing or order on the data. Rankings indicate the relation of one value to another or to the total in terms of position in the sequence or ordering. For example, considering two rankings, Library A ranks 5th in its overall expenditures on collections and 10th in its size of staff. Some metrics used to compare organizations or activities may be based on rankings; it is advisable to explain clearly the meaning of metrics when using rankings. The reason is to avoid giving undue importance to minor differences that may separate the standing among items in the order.

The final step in analyzing quantitative data is to examine the characterizations calculated and to identify patterns or relationships that might offer insights into the questions posed by the purpose of the study. Summarizing the data in tables or graphs may help visualize such patterns. Looking at the data in different ways or compared to different elements may stimulate insights. Depending on the data, the use of cross tabulations, which is associated with the chi-square test of independence and which indicates whether there is an interdependent relationship between two variables, might be useful. When presenting the arguments for which data are collected and analyzed, and for which descriptive statistics are relevant, it is critical to have already determined which metrics will support the case that librarians ultimately want to make. Related to this is a determination of which metrics those stakeholders to whom the library reports will accept and value.

## Analyzing Qualitative Data

Qualitative data also appear among metrics used in libraries. Their analyses require different procedures than do quantitative measures. Rather than conveying numbers, they consist of words recording opinions or describing observations. Content analysis is the most commonly used method to make sense of the words and observations, and it may involve either quantitative or qualitative data collection. Qualitative data might be produced from a variety of sources, including responses to open-ended questions and comments on questionnaires, documents, notes and transcriptions of interviews or focus group discussions, correspondence, blogs, Wikis, diaries or journals maintained by staff or users, and notes describing observations. Beyond words, videotaped observations and interviews, as well as photographs, might reflect library use and the information-seeking behavior and preferences of users.[9]

There is no one recommended way to analyze qualitative data, although all approaches depend on the purpose for the analysis (what is asked and the need for the data) and the availability of resources. The process of data collection is not strictly linear or fixed but may involve flow back and forth between steps.

Five basic steps to analyze and interpret textual or narrative data include the following: get to know the data, focus the analysis, categorize information, identify patterns and connections within and between categories, and bring it all together.[10] The first step is to examine the data repeatedly, noting initial impressions. In becoming familiar with the data, the analyst should determine data quality (data reliability and validity) and decide on the level of effort the data support; determine any limitations such as those due to poor recording, biased collection techniques, or other flaws. Next, when starting the analysis, it is important to identify a few key questions for the analysis that reflect the purpose of the evaluation and let these questions guide the review of the text. The analyst might look at how individuals respond to topics, for a given time period or event, or possibly organize the data by case, individual, or group, and then seek to develop the overall picture. The third element of content analysis is to categorize, index, or code the data, not by applying numerical codes as in quantitative analysis, but by identifying themes or patterns and then grouping the text into categories reflecting those relevant to the purpose of the study. This labor-intensive step, crucial to content analysis, involves rereading the text and identifying meaningful categories. During this stage, new categories may emerge and call for rereading the text and organizing it in different ways. Some approaches to this type of analysis start with a list of preset categories that guide what is sought from the data, while other approaches rely on categories emerging from the iterative readings of text. As the data are organized into categories, the next step is to identify patterns and connections within and between the categories and assess the importance of those relevant to the purpose of the analysis. The connections might suggest cause-and-effect relationships or time sequences, from which explanations about behavior may be argued. Development of *theories* of explanation should be critically reviewed by seeking data that support the interpretation, looking for other contributing factors, and questioning what does not fit into the pattern. The final step is to attach meaning and value to the analysis; some consider this step as interpretation of the data. Some suggest starting this step by developing a list of key points found through the categorizing of data. Then, they reflect on what they learned, returning to the purpose of the analysis and the needs of those who will use the data to make decisions. Getting feedback and input from others is a useful way to enhance the analysis and strengthen the reliability of results.

The mechanics of undertaking a narrative analysis can be messy and involve organizing and tracking text. Basically, the work is that of cutting and sorting, and it can be done by hand with pen and paper, or with the assistance of software. Either way, tips to complete the analysis include checking the data for quality; keeping the data together; adding identification numbers to each questionnaire, respondent, group, or site; and transcribing taped interviews, selecting usable sections, and deciding on the amount of effort worth investing in analyzing the text.

Furthermore, making copies of all data and identifying sources of all data are good practices. With small amounts of narrative data, analysis might be done directly on the text; in other instances, analysis, word processing, and spreadsheet programs (e.g., Microsoft Word or Excel) might be helpful. Relational database management programs such as Microsoft Access are used for some analyses. Computer software packages (e.g., Ethnograph, http://www.qualisresearch.com/, and NVIVO, http://www.qsrinternational.com/) have been designed specifically for qualitative data analysis, facilitating the steps of such analysis. Other software such as SAS has been used to manipulate precategorized responses to summarize answers to open-ended questions.[11]

As with quantitative analysis, there are a few sources of errors or misinterpretations to avoid or to be sensitive to when reading reports of analysis of qualitative data. The key is to avoid generalizing the results. The aim of qualitative analysis is not to generalize to a population, but rather to provide understanding and explanation from the respondent's perspective. Use of quotes offers valuable support to the analysis and interpretation of data, but anonymity of those interviewed should always be protected.

## E-metrics

Since the 1990s there has been a growing interest in data about the use of electronic resources generated from transaction logs. One of the challenges that librarians face in making sense of the use of these virtual collections is that they have been dependent on reports on journal usage that come from multiple files produced in different formats by different vendors and aggregators who use differing counts. The development of standards in this area of e-metrics offers some relief. For example, the National Information Standards Organization (NISO), a nonprofit association accredited by the American National Standards Institute, has the library statistics standard Z39.7, which provides a set of definitions and element names. COUNTER (Count Online Usage of Networked Electronic Resources), developed and launched in 2002, is a code of practice for the recording and exchange of online usage statistics.[12] Using the NISO definition elements and providing required reports for journals and databases qualifies a vendor as COUNTER Compliant. The code specifies, for example, report columns and row headings, and it defines file formats to deliver data, ways to process data, and an auditing requirement.[13] In addition to reporting the number of full-text articles requested by month, total searches and sessions by month and database, COUNTER defines reports for successful item requests and turnaways (denials or unsuccessful access) by month, journal, or database; more detailed levels of information could include use by a consortium or an institution.[14] COUNTER reports, received from various vendors and aggregators with whom librarians work for licensed access to electronic journals and databases, are increasingly used in making collection development and budget allocation decisions. Indirectly, these metrics feed into decisions about the physical library, including space allocations for housing physical collections, and about weeding or shelving in remote locations.

Finally, the manuals included in Table 2.1, such as the five-part one from the Association of Research Libraries, cover e-metrics for libraries. This manual defines terms and offers a standardized procedure for quantitative data collection. Older manuals in that table apply to traditional data collection for outputs and performance metrics. The appendices of this book amplify on the metrics presented in various chapters.

# PRESENTATION

Three key factors govern the presentation of metrics for decision making: the target audience, the data to report, and the manner of displaying the results. Consideration of who will receive the gathered and analyzed data involves having knowledge about the audience's level of understanding and background, the amount of data needed for making decisions, and the extent to which the report or appeal is relevant and of interest. The data selected for inclusion in any presentation should address the decisions for which the evaluation has been conducted and the metrics used. Principles for effective communications apply to preparation of any presentation, whether in written or oral form. Results should be presented with clarity and brevity, and with appropriate use of text, charts, and tables. A focus on these three factors is offered here to assist anyone preparing a report that applies metrics to decision making.

## Target Audience

Different audiences are likely to have an interest in the metrics and the data they report about specific aspects of library activities. Although one might not have the resources and time to prepare separate reports for each audience, it is advisable to prepare the primary report for a strategically positioned audience that will either make decisions, be advocates to those who will, or be most affected by the results. These important stakeholders may include governing groups outside the library such as accreditation organizations and their visiting teams, boards of directors, state and federal funding agencies, parents, donors and foundation officers, or internal library administrators or staff. In preparing an effective presentation of metrics, one should be aware of what information, with what level of detail, the target audience seeks and the receptivity of the reader in terms of understanding the metrics, the types of data gathered, and the analyses used.

The report should provide the information needed by the reader to take action, in a format that is easily understood and in sufficient detail to be useful. Regional accreditation organizations for institutions of higher education, for example, focus on accountability defined in terms of student outcomes and student learning outcomes; libraries might demonstrate their contributions to such indicators within the context of the standard criteria or metrics set. Funding organizations and foundations are concerned about the cost of education and might find the number of services used in comparison to grant or state funding to be relevant to understand the fiscal dynamics within an institution. Parents, also attentive to the affordability of their children's education, might be interested in the relation of library services and facilities to tuition expenditures.

As a metric of efficiency, a library director may want to see changes over time in production rates. That director expects to have details about the distribution of workflow and perhaps the staffing levels that influence the design of the metric. On the other hand, a foundation requiring a report of the impact of grant funds may be more interested in the overall outcome of the award, presented through metrics that indicate changes in behavior or attitudes and that draw on testimonial narratives of success or descriptions of barriers overcome.

The importance of the need to understand the readers of the report and particularly their interest in the metrics and data cannot be overstressed: "if stakeholders do not understand findings then they cannot properly plan for or take the appropriate actions to address service issues, for understanding the needs of the library is a necessary component of the strategic planning process."[15]

## Selection of Data to Report

To address the readers' needs during the drafting of the report, it is important to include data that relate to those needs. Asked how much data should be included, an advisor might simply say, enough to make the point and not too much to loose the reader's interest and not too little to waste the reader's time when expecting a substantiated argument.

Information should be sequenced for the target audience. The content of the report typically covers three essential areas. The amount of information for each varies according to the interests of the audience, and the writer of the report should select what works best for the specific situation. First, it is often helpful to give content and indicate what was done, including what data were sought and what metrics were used. In more formal reports, written for a research audience, this summary of work done might include identification of decisions addressed, questions posed, procedures or research design, and methods of data collection and analysis.

Second, the findings can be summarized as bare essentials or embellished to indicate strengths and opportunities for improvement. The findings section explains the results of what was done, the data collected, and the resulting metrics. It should be organized around the purpose and specific questions posed (e.g., what library resources need to be added to meet the needs of distant learning classes, or how well has the library contributed to the campus goal of improving the information literacy skills of students?).

Since any report should have a strategic purpose, it should close with recommendations and evidence to support the views of the author. Tim Bower and Bradford Dennis, for example, have provided a detailed analysis of the LibQUAL+™ survey results for a set of libraries and explored what they perceived to be difficulty in understanding the complexity of the findings. From the survey framework, they developed a single score metric, which offers readers different ways to utilize the data gathered in order to better understand their population's perceptions of the library's service quality.[16] The score puts the reader's perceptions of service quality in the context of levels of expectations. Decision makers who wish to use such evidence in making decisions need to understand this new metric, whereas a funding agency perhaps does not.

Discussions about the presentation of e-metrics address a variety of managerial needs and determine which data to include in reports. John Carlo Bertot and others, for example, suggest four core areas where e-metrics are needed: vendor data, network service data, network resources, and expenditures.[17] Vendor data provide information on commercial sessions, searches, and items examined through use of a database, e-journal, e-book, and other licensed or purchased content. Such data have led to metrics about turnaways, created by exceeding a licensed limit for simultaneous use. Inclusion of such data strengthens discussions about the overall use of the resources. Similarly, network service data are used to extend metrics used in traditional library services into networked environments (e.g., virtual reference transactions conducted through e-mail or instant messaging). If the report describes the use of services, then inclusion of counts of participants or hours of activities in these networked environments should be included.

Input measures about the availability of resources form core metrics describing potential library value, and e-metrics in the area of network resources are important. The number of Web-based resources (e.g., digital collections or licensed access) become important components of the data selected for inclusion in reports. Traditional metrics designed to measure a library's expenditure on collections have been expanded to include data on the costs of electronic materials relating to databases, e-journals, and e-books. Taken together, managers can use appropriately selected data to learn how much their electronic resources cost, how often and by whom they are used, cost per session, and whether the library has adequate capacity to meet user demands. Data presented in the context of metrics for determining the cost-effectiveness and efficiency of specific resources and services assist managers in making decisions about budget allocations and vendor negotiations.[18]

## Data Display

The third important set of issues to consider when preparing a presentation involving metrics is the display and delivery of content. The selection of data creates the content, and the awareness of the target audience clarifies the recipient, but the manner in which the data are delivered is the communication component that links the content to the needs of the target audience. The motivation behind such communication is ultimately for decision makers to have useful information on which to act, and the setting for the communication of metrics is to focus such action on the improved management of library services and resources.

The management situation and organizational culture for making decisions influence the appropriate communication mode for completing the link between content and receiver in a library. Traditionally, management data have been presented either through oral presentations or written reports. These methods of delivery presuppose a communication process that is created in a time frame, providing a snapshot of data at a fixed moment. As participatory and evidence-based management approaches have evolved in libraries, however, there is a growing need for the communication of data for decision making to be as current as possible and available from multiple and often distributed points within the organization or community of stakeholders. Different organizations and different situations call for different methods of communicating metrics and data gathered to interpret them for decision making. In some cases, an annual report, prepared as an attractively illustrated and embellished publication may be the expected method for targeted donors to receive information, for example, about the library's rankings, trends in expenditures, and impact on education or research. For supervisors, however, metrics on the count of new materials processed compared to space available to shelve them, or on the number of students enrolled in a course related to the number of titles placed on reserved circulation, are critical for making routine changes in workflow and staffing assignments.

Work to address critical operations affecting efficiencies and profits in the business sector has produced different ways to present data for weighing multiple perspectives and reaching time-sensitive managerial decisions. Introduced in the early 1990s, the balanced scorecard is one such method that has received some successful application in libraries. The University of Virginia Library, as discussed in previous chapters, makes extensive use of the balanced scorecard and offers a Web site (e.g., http://www.lib.virginia.edu/bsc/) that elaborates on its application.

*Written Reports.* Common to any method of presenting information is the importance of the organization and language used to communicate content. Concise and clear sentences, the proper use of language combined with accurate spellings and verb tense, the avoidance of jargon and undefined acronyms, and the use of an appropriate balance of quantitative data and textual narrative are obvious principles for any communicator to follow. The selection of style, whether formal or casual, and of the use of tables, charts, or narrative accounts should reflect the nature of the data gathered and the target audience's expectations. In some academic settings, for example, descriptive accounts or quotes from key stakeholders will be received better than bulleted data points. In other instances, a short summary of data presented in terms of key metrics and placed in an e-mail attachment might comprise the preferred form of a written report.

Readers with a basic understanding of statistical concepts expect standard elements. In reporting inferential statistics—drawing inferences from a sample about a population—they want to know the magnitude or value of the test, the degrees of freedom, the sample size, the probability level, and the direction of the effect. Likewise, for reporting descriptive statistics, a reader should expect to see measures of variability, assuming the data cover an interval or ratio scale, and enough additional information sufficient to corroborate the analyses made. There is a growing tendency to place colorful charts and graphs in reports, many clearly a product of discovering display options in the Excel software. Tables and figures offer visual ways to summarize a large volume of data. Tables typically provide exact or raw data in a concise manner. Figures are less precise, illustrate interactions among data, and offer a way to compare datasets. Most style manuals offer detailed discussions on how to prepare data and present them for effective communications.

The outline of a research publication offers a loose framework for organizing written reports about results of an evaluation or data-gathering procedure to supply metric-based data and findings. Such a report provides readers with a combination of information and answers the following questions:

- Why was the report prepared? For what reasons were the data sought?
- What else is known about the issue? Does the literature or benchmarking with peer or best-in-class organizations contribute to addressing the purpose?
- Specifically, what was explored? What metrics are used to evaluate the program performance, service efficiencies, or the achievement of goals?
- How were data gathered?
- What was found?
- What does it mean? What more do we know about the library or its users in light of the purpose for which the data were sought?
- What recommendations, if any and if appropriate, are made by those preparing the report?

The formats for written reports may range from short written updates presented daily on a card, e-mail text or attachments, charts on the Web, or glossy publications. The length of presentation and timing of delivery should also be planned in recognition of the receiver's need for detail and schedule of decision making.

Examples of well written reports that use the presentation of metrics to support developed themes and arguments are found among library annual reports. One example is the annual report of the Library at the University of Massachusetts, Amherst. Concise, Web-accessible, and produced in color, it offers a number of easy to read graphs that highlight its learning commons.[19] Another, longer example, which utilizes e-metrics to illustrate the library's value, is the annual report template developed by the Information Use Management Policy Institute, Florida State University, for its E-Metrics Instructional System.[20] The recommended combination of narrative text, graphs, tables, and charts present data related to metrics for advocacy and accountability.

*Oral Presentations.* The layout of the venue for this means of communication has an impact on the atmosphere and thus how well the information is received. Experience recommends having one person present the results, but others (e.g., members of a team preparing the report or experts available to interpret the implications of findings on services, budget, or operations) can be present. These individuals might be seated in a U-shape or at small-group tables. The aim of avoiding the impression of us versus them or one person being a messenger of news about the library may not work in all organizations. Ultimately, the oral presentation enables senior leaders or influential stakeholders to see the organization from the perspective of the evaluation team or staff member assigned to gather data, who in turn present the multiple perspectives of clients, supervisors, fiscal controllers, and whoever else influences the drafting of the report. By adding nonverbal cues and audio inflections, a comfortable and inviting physical atmosphere, and including various individuals who will contribute to a conversation, oral presentations in some organizations may help decision makers experience and understand the data and the metrics better. They might possibly draw the same conclusions.

Similar to a written report, such oral presentations review how the evaluation was conducted and aid in understanding and accepting the findings. That review should also include strategic directions, for example, to process improvements, evaluate the team's recommendations, or provide rewards or recognition of employee performance in achieving goals soon to be reached. The audience should be reminded of the criteria, or metrics, used for evaluation, with highlights of their strengths and opportunities for program and service improvement. The session might start with key introductions and then a summary of the session's agenda, the objectives for data collection, and what was done. The presenter should then move fairly quickly to the findings. Finally, there should be ample opportunity for discussion.

*Balanced Scorecard Displays.* Progressively, methods to utilize data in management decision making have focused on using metrics as milestones in project management and as criteria to evaluate progress in continuous improvement initiatives. Milestones in project management measure the achievement of goals, typically striving for efficiencies. Criteria for continuous improvement add the customer perspective to the metrics used. The balanced scorecard recognizes that an organization's strategic directions evolve from more perspectives than cost efficiencies and the customer. The balanced scorecard visually presents information that influences leaders in making managerial decisions, with the aim to improve performance. Devised by Robert S. Kaplan and David P. Norton from research with companies at the "leading edge of performance measurement," the balanced scorecard is a set of measures that gives top managers a fast but comprehensive view of the business. . . [It] includes financial measures that tell the results of actions already taken. And it complements the financial measures with operational measures on customer satisfaction, internal processes, and the organization's innovation and improvement activities—operational measures that are the drivers of future financial performance.[21]

In its truest form, the balanced scorecard links performance information to the organization's strategic directions. It includes explicit information about perspectives (the high-level strategic areas), objectives, measures (the metrics or they are sometimes referred to as the key performance indicators [KPIs]), and stoplight indicators, which are symbols that offer a quick view of each metric's performance.[22]

The balanced scorecard presentation includes four strategic perspectives:

1. the customer (How do customers see us?)
2. internal (What must we excel at?)
3. innovation and learning (Can we continue to improve and create value?)
4. financial (How do we look to shareholders?)

These four perspectives were developed from exploration of success in the private sector, and although many government and nonprofit organizations have adapted them, the developers of the scorecard methodology have evolved their recommendations to suggest that these particular four perspectives might not be most appropriate for all organizations. As they later note, the four perspectives "should be considered a template, not a straitjacket."[23] Chapters 3 and 10, as well as Joseph Matthews in *Scorecard for Results,* describe these perspectives and discuss the development of a balanced scorecard that is applicable to libraries.[24]

As more libraries embrace service quality and customer service, their strategic perspectives might place the customer perspective more central to the depiction of their scorecard. "Libraries do not strive for maximum gain but for best service," and thus when adapting the balanced scorecard model, they place the customer rather than the financial perspective foremost.[25]

Within a decade after its inception, the balanced scorecard was used to improve presentation of data for decision making in libraries, It was first documented to be adopted in three of the largest libraries in Germany beginning in 1999, and then in 2001, was introduced at the University of Virginia (UVa) Library, where it has been maintained since (see Figure 11.1).[26] The Germans chose metrics for the customer perspective that support the goals of reaching the population served and of satisfying their information needs through services offered. For example, these include market penetration (percentage of population actually using the library), user satisfaction rate, opening hours compared to demand, and availability (number of immediate loans compared to all loans including those resulting from interlibrary loan and recalls). These early adapting libraries also devised indicators for the other perspectives presented in the balanced scorecard: for the financial perspective, metrics include total costs of the library per member of the population, total costs of the library per case of use, and percentage of staff costs per library service; for the internal processes perspective, metrics include average media processing time; and, for the innovation perspective, metrics include library budget as percentage of university's budget, number of formal training hours per staff member, and number of sick days taken per staff member.[27]

| The Balanced Scorecard (BSC) | Components of the Scorecard |
|---|---|
| Is a representation of the organization's shared vision | Measurements of performance indicators, based on library objectives |
| Clarifies and communicates this vision to mobilize and focus the organization | Reflecting the organization's mission and strategies |
| Provides a quick, but comprehensive, picture of the organization's health and success | Evaluating current performance and potential for the future |

**The scorecard measures are *balanced* into four areas.**

| User Perspective | Finance Perspective |
|---|---|
| How can we fulfill user expectations? | How can we secure and use resources in an effective way? |
| Customer ratings in our periodic surveys | Cost per use of purchased materials |
| Use of materials | Revenue from state and private sources |
| Turnaround time for patron requests | Library expenditures as a proportion of university expenditures |

| Internal Process Perspective | Learning/Growth Perspective |
|---|---|
| How should we organize internal processes to meet user needs and expectations? | How can we secure the future capability of our services? |
| Throughput times for making materials available | Staff training outcomes |
| Satisfaction ratings from internal surveys | Measure of job satisfaction and salary competitiveness |
| Quality of physical infrastructure | Progress in staff diversity |
| | Indicators of growth in our digital environment |

Figure 11.1   Balanced Scorecard (University of Virginia Library)*

*Source: University of Virginia Library, "Overview about the Balanced Scorecard" (Charlottesville, VA: University of Virginia Library, 2008). Available at http://www2.lib.virginia.edu/bsc/overview.html (accessed December 26, 2008).

The UVa library has devised four to eight metrics for each perspective, and managers there, following best practices among business users of the balanced scorecard, have identified multiple targets for each metric, one that indicates complete success and a second one that suggests partial success in achieving the metric. For example, the library established a metric for expenditures for circulating monographs as a proportion of all monographic expenditures. The targets for full and partial success are described as follows:

- Full achievement target: monographs that circulate within the first two years should account for at least 60 percent of the monographic budget.
- Partial achievement target: the circulated items should account for at least 50 percent of the monographic budget.[28]

Seventeen university libraries in Germany agreed to use a set of 10 core metrics, derived from their work with the balanced scorecard to develop a focused view of a library's performance and to facilitate benchmarking between those libraries with similar mission and structure. When embarking on this project, they expected that having such comparable data for quantity, quality, and costs of the library would be valuable when presenting their services to their universities, funders, and the general public.[29]

## Dashboard Displays

Kaplan and Norton suggest an image of the balanced scorecard as analogous to an airplane pilot's dashboard, where information for a variety of sources, all timely, are available at a glance for making decisions to fly the aircraft.[30] Elazar C. Harel and Toby D. Sitko offer a different analogy.

Would you drive a car without looking at the dashboard? The simple gauges on the instrument panel display what you need to know to operate the car safely and effectively: how fast you are driving, when the engine is working too hard, and how much fuel is left, for example. You cannot drive a car safely without a dashboard. The same can be said for managing a university. Regrettably, many managers currently operate without such an instrument panel, making decisions based on old data or no data at all. Many decisions require current information: Do we need to open another section of English 101? Do we have enough grant funds to take advantage of specially priced equipment? Are there anomalies in our enrollment data that need immediate attention?[31]

Furthermore,

Graphical dashboards turn voluminous business data into something easy to comprehend. A quick glance at the dashboard shows data in intuitive formats, such as charts and other gauges. Dashboards allow you to focus on business priorities by filtering out irrelevant information. Dashboards that provide drill-down capability allow tailored views of reports and data at the level of detail that an individual finds most helpful.[32]

Dashboards have developed as more than a metaphor for presentation. Organizations use them to communicate complex and extensive information about performance. In contrast to the prescriptive and formal character of balanced scorecards, dashboards are designed to be more open to interpretation. They present a series of graphs, charts, and various visual indicators, leaving to the viewer to select what is of interest, whether linked to strategic directions or not. Typically, the objective statements that appear in balanced scorecards as the link to strategic directions do not appear in dashboards.[33]

Harel and Sitko compare different gauges and indicators between a car and university. For example, for the fuel gauge in a car, the indicator is "Can you continue to drive?" In a university, the equivalent gauge is the resource gauge, and the indicator is "Do you have enough resources (money, faculty, staff members) to do your work?" They offer other comparisons: speedometer to threat dial, battery to input graph, tachometer to institutional pulse chart, temperature to opportunity gauge, oil pressure to environmental scan, mileage to trend statistics, and warning lights. They do not, however, indicate where the needle in a gauge should appear for a healthy organization, and they offer more gauges than a typical car would have. Still, their analogy is interesting and provocative.

With simple dashboards becoming more relevant and conveying metrics and ordinal data in the form of a car's dashboard, pic chart, line graph, bar chart, simple tables, and so forth, it is easy to see insights into the four perspectives without having to read narrative text.[34] More precisely, dashboard indicators might cover teaching/learning, scholarship/research, service/outreach, workplace satisfaction, and financial.[35] As an alternative, the system of Minnesota state colleges and universities has created an accountability dashboard for the board of trustees, policymakers, and other stakeholders that display key metrics that apply to all 32 institutions. The board and system institutions use the data to improve their services to students and to citizens of the state. The gauges, such as those found in a car, are used to display the status of achieving goals and objectives, or of a static metric within a range (see Figure 11.2).[36] Results are shown for the system as a whole, for the four-year universities, for the two-year colleges, and for each institution. Given these developments, two key questions become "Will a dashboard enhance library decision making?" and "How might the library relate its activities to the dashboard indicators that colleges and universities compile?"

Figure 11.3 is an example of the presentation from the dashboard of the Merrill-Cazier Library, Utah State University.[37] Finally, Texas Tech University has created an assessment dashboard that highlights "academic excellence," "access and diversity," "engagement" (gate count), and "technology" (number of public workstations and the percentage of computer uptime). The dashboard presents numbers in terms of "progress," defined as "toward target," "minimal change," "away from target," and "target reached." For each metric, the library is actually working "toward target" or experiencing "minimal change" (see Figure 11.4). A symbol reflects the change from the previous year.[38] What makes this dashboard most interesting is that it is linked to strategic planning for the university's colleges and academic and support areas and then to their individual dashboards. Another link is to "state accountability measures" and another set of dashboards.[39]

## Strategy Map and Report Card

From its introduction in 1992, the balanced scorecard provides a comprehensive framework to communicate an organization's strategy, in terms of a set of strategic objectives and performance metrics. The strategy map, developed by Kaplan and Norton, provides a visual framework that logically integrates the objectives across the four perspectives of the balanced scorecard.[40] The scorecard presentation is in the form of a quadrant grid, with objectives and metrics organized by each

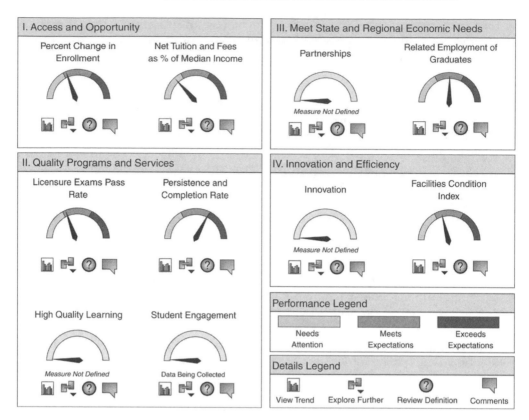

Figure 11.2    The Dashboard for the Minnesota State Colleges and Universities System*

* Minnesota State Colleges and Universities System, Board of Trustees. "Accountability Dashboard."
Available at http://accountability.mnscu.edu/workspace/passthrough/hyperion_passthrough_opener.
html?url=/workspace/browse/withnav_get/Accountability%20Framework/Accountability%20Dashboard
(accessed December 12, 2008).

perspective, and it is used for communicating the measurement of the organization's performance. The strategic map, by comparison, illustrates the cause-and-effect relationship among and across the objectives and perspectives outlined in the scorecard. The map, together with the performance measurement presentation of the balanced scorecard, comprise what their designers characterize as a "measurement technology for managing in a knowledge-based economy."[41]

Paul R. Niven, in his discussion of the application of the balanced scorecard in government and nonprofit organizations, characterizes the benefit of the accompanying strategy map as providing "an early warning system for the organization's strategy, signaling trouble when indicators suggest a problem with any element of the plan that has been designed to elevate the organization to prosperity."[42] He offers an example of a strategy map using a fictitious city library as the organization and reminding managers that no two maps look the same since each should translate the unique strategy of the organization it represents.[43] The cause-and-effect arrangement of the ovals graphically relate the objectives and specific drivers within each of the four perspectives from the balanced scorecard to highlight the organization's strategy to achieve the outcomes that characterize its mission.

Although the balanced scorecard and strategy map are recognized as useful in organizing and communicating organization-wide metrics, some organizations view them as too complex to use in managing service organizations. The report card takes this approach further by simplifying the presentation of data. As described by an information technology (IT) organization, "rather than grouping the metrics by type of data, we look at our services in light of the customers' view of our performance."[44] In this IT setting, for example, the four quadrants of the balanced scorecard, with the specific metrics used for each perspective, are complicated. Furthermore, the quadrants consider categories of data that emphasize how the scorecard measures rather than what it measures. For example, the categories include the following:

- effectiveness (the customer's view of the organization)
- efficiency (the business view of the organization)
- human resources (the worker's view)
- visibility (management's need for more insight into the organization)[45]

The report card developed for this service organization exclusively reports on effectiveness, looking at itself through its customer's perspective, and includes such metrics as delivery of service (availability, speed, and accuracy), usage, and customer satisfaction in its grading rubric.

The use of the report card to regularly check progress, overall performance, as well as communicate the resulting *health* of an organization to stakeholders, managers, and customers, is based on the educational practice of using this tool in grade school to highlight students' strengths and weaknesses and to identify areas for improvement. The grading rubric for each area combines multiple metrics and sources of data. Grades are not prescriptive (scores do not identify what caused poor performance) but are excellent diagnostic devices. Pulled together, the overall report card reflects the *health* of the student or organization and, with frequent feedback, highlights problem areas as a way to foster improvement.

Examples of the use of the report card can also be found in libraries. Although sometimes used to solicit customer feedback, the report card also appears as a summary format for presenting metrics about a library's success from multiple perspectives. The report card for the London public library in Canada, for example, focuses on the customer perspective and reflects overall customer satisfaction as well as the number of in-person visits, Web-site visits, borrowed items, reference transactions, computer use in the library, electronic database use, holds placed, new registrations, programs, and program attendance. For each bar chart covering a four-year period, the metrics card indicates the target and action taken. The Orange County Library System is another example of a public library using a report card to "gauge how well OCLS enlightens the community by providing opportunities for self-education, lifelong learning and self-improvement." (see www.ocls.info/About/Promo/documents/Report_Card.pdf). The Samaritan Medical Center Library offers another good illustration of the report card approach to communicate its story to the public.[46] As a presentation tool for information linked to metrics, however, a report card's selection of *graded* elements should reflect the purposefully selected indicators for which data are sought to make decisions.

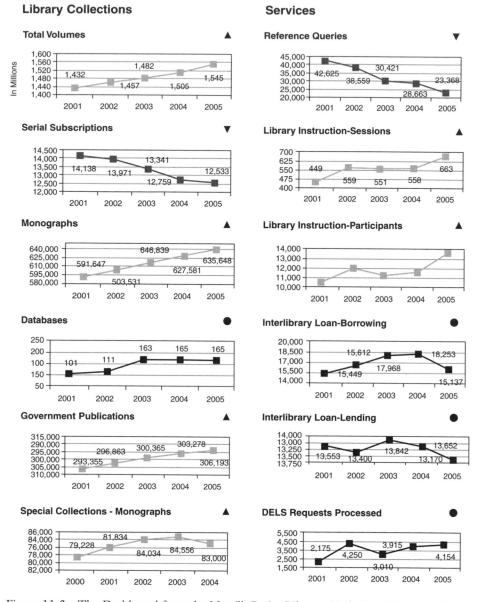

Figure 11.3    The Dashboard from the Merrill-Cazier Library, Utah State University*

# CONCLUSION

Many businesses are engaged in management-based accountability and evidence-based decision making. A number of stakeholders expect higher education to do the same. Accreditation organizations and government expect higher education to demonstrate how institutions meet their mission and improve the quality of the educational experience. Libraries are not exempt from having similar demands placed on them and, in essence, demonstrating value for money (or that the library budget

## Usage

**Gate Count** ▼

| | 2001 | 2002 | 2003 | 2004 | 2005 |
|---|---|---|---|---|---|

938,251 943,851 908,198 927,105 707,650

**Circulation** ▼

191,768 209,559 191,062 198,337 147,549

2001 2002 2003 2004 2005

**Electronic Reserves** ▲

261,603 270,117 154,709 194,305 187,088

2001 2002 2003 2004 2005

## Finance

**Total Expenditure** ▲

*In Millions*

6,874 6,965 6,305 6,815 5,408

2001 2002 2003 2004 2005

**Serials Expenditure** ▲

*In Millions*

2,158 2,079 2,333 2,412 2,269

2001 2002 2003 2004 2005

**Monograph Expenditures** ▲

*In Millions*

585,433 623,617 592,681 515,598 579,065

2001 2002 2003 2004 2005

| TREND | |
|---|---|
| ▲ higher | Light gray = better |
| ▼ lower | gray = worse |
| ● no-change | black = neutral |

Figure 11.3    *(Continued)*

*Reprinted with permission Utah State University, Merrill-Cazier Library, "Merrrill-Cazier Library Performance Dashboard-January 2006" (Logan, UT: Utah State University). Available at http://ranger2.lib.usu.edu/main/portrait/DashBoard05.pdf (accessed December 12, 2008).

reflects the library's mission and that of the broader institution). Metrics play an important role in accountability and providing evidence useful for continuous quality improvement, especially when the focus is on inputs, outputs, and student outcomes. Student learning outcomes, however, are not so easily depicted by simple metrics.

As the chapter indicates, libraries should not merely be engaged in the collecting of metrics that deal with quantitative measurement; qualitative data have a role as well. Librarians should pay attention to how they analyze, interpret, and present the results. As Martha Kyrillidou and Sarah Giersch note in their discussion of e-metrics, appropriate data "must be easy to collect, . . . must be comparable to traditional service indicators[,] . . . must be easily understood for those who fund libraries[,] and, preferably, [must be] compared to those collected in other libraries."[47]

Furthermore, it is important to show how the library contributes to the metrics that institutions gather and report to various stakeholders. If the institution, for instance, provides its stakeholders with a series of dashboards, how can the library add to the set of metrics and reflect its contribution? In part, there may be a need for a qualitative aspect to a set of metrics; however, that story must be short and simply told.

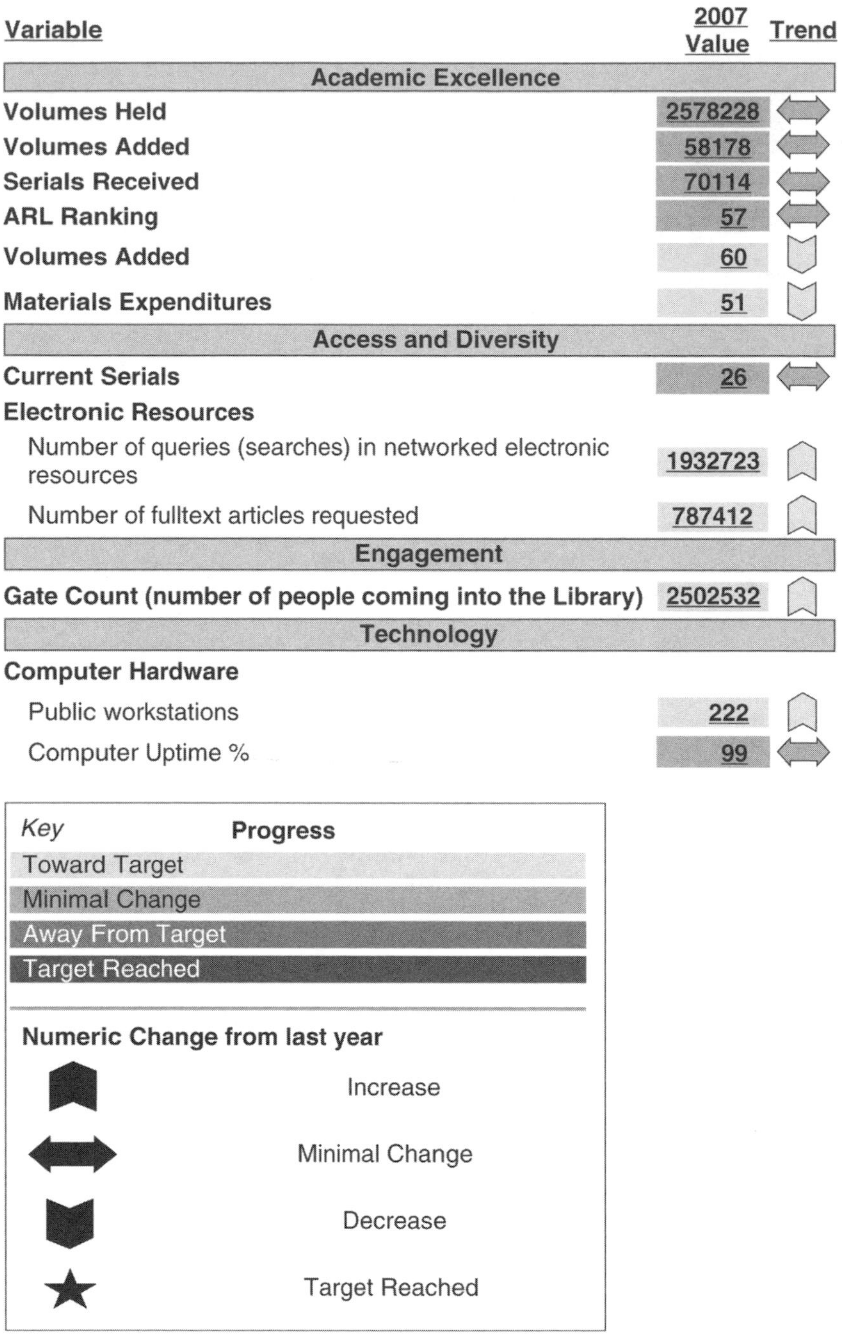

| Variable | 2007 Value | Trend |
|---|---|---|
| **Academic Excellence** | | |
| **Volumes Held** | 2578228 | ⇔ |
| **Volumes Added** | 58178 | ⇔ |
| **Serials Received** | 70114 | ⇔ |
| **ARL Ranking** | 57 | ⇔ |
| **Volumes Added** | 60 | ⬇ |
| **Materials Expenditures** | 51 | ⬇ |
| **Access and Diversity** | | |
| **Current Serials** | 26 | ⇔ |
| **Electronic Resources** | | |
| Number of queries (searches) in networked electronic resources | 1932723 | ⬆ |
| Number of fulltext articles requested | 787412 | ⬆ |
| **Engagement** | | |
| **Gate Count (number of people coming into the Library)** | 2502532 | ⬆ |
| **Technology** | | |
| **Computer Hardware** | | |
| Public workstations | 222 | ⬆ |
| Computer Uptime % | 99 | ⇔ |

| Key | Progress |
|---|---|
| Toward Target | |
| Minimal Change | |
| Away From Target | |
| Target Reached | |

**Numeric Change from last year**

⬆ Increase

⬌ Minimal Change

⬇ Decrease

★ Target Reached

Figure 11.4   The Dashboard from Texas Tech University Libraries*

Texas Tech University Libraries will have the resources necessary to offer uncompromising service; be a research library of international stature; magnify the reputation of the university; be a key component in the intellectual life of the University.

*Texas Tech University, Library, "Assessment Dashboards" (Lubbock: Texas Tech University). Available at http://www.irs.ttu.edu/dashboardareas/Dashboard.aspx?collid=35&year=2007&deptid=0 (accessed December 12, 2008).

Although the following questions are outside the scope of this book, nonetheless, they are important to ask as managerial leaders look to the future and the continued successful management of libraries:

• How do librarians prepare for a future in which library management is driven by data?
• What skills do librarians and library staff require to participate in such management efforts?
• What questions remain to be researched to provide new insights for library leaders to understand how to direct the library as an organization that relies on evidence?

Currently, these questions are approached from the context of e-metrics and preparation of staff to use them.[48] But the success of a 21st-century library goes far beyond its functioning in the digital world, and thus these are important issues to address for utilizing the numerous metrics created to describe the complexities of its operations and the multiple perspectives of its stakeholders. The requirements for engaging with metrics, including the demands for relevant interpretation, accurate synthesis, and effective presentation, focus managerial attention on improving the library's services and ultimately its value. The basis for crafting the stories of library value may shift between its resources, its productivity, and its impact—and among its rich dimensions in all these metric settings, whether electronic or paper collections, reader assistance or material processing, student learning, or research discoveries. As the chapter indicates, the complexities of utilizing metrics may be simplified when at least three factors are kept in mind. The *purpose* for engaging with metrics (improvement as the fundamental reason) drives the *selection* of evidence from the array of gathered data and ultimately shapes the response to needs, expectations, and requirements of different *audiences*. With this framework, library managers and staff may be reassured that they understand the benefits of using metrics and that they are confident in developing their own skills to master the powerful components of interpreting, synthesizing, and presenting the metrics for advocating improvement and soliciting the necessary support to achieve it.

## NOTES

1. University of Pennsylvania Libraries, "Data Farm." Available at http://metrics.library.upenn.edu/prototype/about/index.html (accessed November 11, 2008).

2. Kendon Stubbs, "Apples and Oranges and ARL Statistics," *The Journal of Academic Librarianship* 14, no. 4 (September 1988), 231.

3. Oliver Pesch, "Usage Statistics: Taking E-metrics to the Next Level," *The Serials Librarian* 46, no. 1/2 (2004): 144.

4. Ibid., 145.

5. Roswitha Poll, "Performance, Processes, and Costs: Managing Service Quality with the Balanced Scorecard," *Library Trends* 49, no. 4 (Spring 2001): 710.

6. See, for instance, Sudip Bhattacharjee and Lewis Shaw, "Enhancing Skills through Technology: A Project for Advanced Accounting Students," in *An Action Plan for Outcomes Assessment in Your Library,* edited by Peter Hernon and Robert E. Dugan (Chicago: American Library Association, 2002), 171–82.

7. Canadian Health Services Research Foundation, "Glossary of Knowledge Exchange Terms as Used by the Foundation." Available at http://www.chsrf.ca/keys/glossary_e.php (accessed October 24, 2008).

8. See Ellen Taylor-Powell, "Analyzing Quantitative Data" (Madison, WI: University of Wisconsin-Extension, Cooperative Extension Program Development & Evaluation, 2003). Available at http://learningstore.uwex.edu/pdf/G3658-6.pdf (accessed October 22, 2008).

9. See Nancy Fried Foster, and Susan Gibbons (ed.), *Studying Students: The Undergraduate Research Project at the University of Rochester* (Chicago: American Library Association, Association of College and Research Libraries, 2007). Available at http://www.ala.org/ala/mgrps/divs/acrl/acrlpubs/downloadables/Foster-Gibbons_cmpd.pdf (accessed September 23, 2008); http://docushare.lib.rochester.edu/docushare/dsweb/GetRendition/Document-27276/html (accessed August 17, 2003).

10. Ellen Taylor-Powell, and Marcus Renner, "Analyzing Qualitative Data" (Madison, WI: University of Wisconsin-Extension, Cooperative Extension Program Development & Evaluation, 2003). Available at http://learningstore.uwex.edu/pdf/G3658-12.pdf (accessed October 22, 2008).

11. For more detailed guidance on conducting data analysis, see Taylor-Powell and Renner, "Analyzing Qualitative Data"; Richard A. Krueger, *Focus Groups: A Practical Guide for Applied Research* (Newbury Park, CA: Sage Publications, 1998); Matthew B. Miles, and Michael Huberman, *Qualitative Data Analysis: An Expanded Sourcebook*, 2nd ed. (Thousand Oaks, CA: Sage Publications, 1994); Michael Quinn Patton, *Qualitative Evaluation and Research Methods*, 2nd ed. (Newbury Park, CA: Sage Publication, 1990).

12. Count Online Usage of Networked Electronic Resources, "Codes of Practice." Available at http://www.projectcounter.org/code_practice.html (accessed November 11, 2008).

13. Pesch, "Usage Statistics," 151.

14. Ibid., 154.

15. Tim Bower and Bradford Dennis, "How to Get More from Your Quantitative LibQUAL+™ Dataset: Making Results Practical," *Performance Measurement and Metrics* 8, no. 2 (2007): 111.

16. Ibid.

17. John Carlo Bertot, Charles R. McClure, Denise M. Davis, and Joe Ryan, "Capture Usage with E-Metrics," *Library Journal* 129, no. 8 (May 1, 2004): 30–2.

18. Ibid., 31–2.

19. University of Massachusetts, Amherst, Libraries, *Annual Report 2006* (Amherst: University of Massachusetts, 2006). Available at http://scholarworks.umass.edu/cgi/viewcontent.cgi?article=1000&context=libraries_reports (accessed November 18, 2008).

20. John Bertot, "E-metrics Information" (Tallahassee, FL: Florida State University, School of Information Studies, Information Use Management Policy Institute). Available at http://www.ii.fsu.edu/EMIS/contact.cfm (accessed November 27, 2008). This link connects to *Modules: Large Urban Public Library Electronic Resources and Services Annual Report*.

21. Robert S. Kaplan, and David P. Norton, "The Balanced Scorecard—Measures That Drive Performance," *The Harvard Business Review* 70, no. 1 (January–February, 1992), 71.

22. Ibid., 71–72. See also Active Strategy, "Balanced Scorecard Basics: Create Structure: Balanced Scorecard vs. Dashboards." Available at http://www.activestrategy.com/strategy_execution/scorecards_vs_dashboards.aspx (accessed November 15, 2008).

23. Robert S. Kaplan, and David P. Norton, *The Balanced Scorecard: Translating Strategy into Action* (Boston, MA: Harvard Business School Press, 1996), 34.

24. Joseph R. Matthews, *Scorecard for Results: A Guide for Developing a Library Balanced Scorecard* (Westport, CT: Libraries Unlimited, 2008). For a detailed summary of the background and elements of the balanced scorecard, see also 12 Manage: The Executive Fast Track, "Balanced Scorecard." Available at http://www.12manage.com/methods_balancedscorecard.html (accessed November 3, 2008).

25. Poll, "Performance, Processes, and Costs," 713.

26. Ibid. See also James Self, "From Values to Metrics: Implementation of the Balanced Scorecard at a University Library," *Performance Measurement and Metrics* 4, no. 2 (2003): 57–63.

27. Poll, "Performance, Processes, and Costs," 714–15.

28. These targets are adapted from Self, "From Values to Metrics."
Over 100 software companies have designed commercially developed software to organize and report results of data gathering for each metric identified as important to decision making through the balanced scorecard development process. As advised by the Balanced Scorecard Institute, "automation adds structure and discipline to implementing the balanced scorecard system, helps transform disparate incorporate data into information and knowledge, and helps communicate performance information. In short, automation helps people make better decisions because it offers quick access to actual performance data" (Balanced Scorecard Institute, "The Balanced Scorecard & Technology." Available at http://www.balancedscorecard.org/BSCResources/BalancedScorecardSoftware/tabid/61/Default.aspx [accessed November 3, 2008]).

29. See Poll, "Performance, Processes and Costs," 717. She lists the 10 core metrics that include inputs (e.g., library costs per capita), services offered (e.g., opening hours per week), and usage (e.g., user satisfaction rate).

30. Kaplan and Norton, "The Balanced Scorecard—Measures That Drive Performance."

31. Elazar C. Harel and Toby D. Sitko, "Digital Dashboards: Driving Higher Education Decisions," EDUCAUSE (Center for Applied Research) *Research Bulletin,* 19 (2003): 2. Available at http://net.educause.edu/ir/library/pdf/ERB0319.pdf (accessed November 13, 2008).

32. Ibid.

33. See Active Strategy, "Balanced Scorecard Basics."

34. An example of the dashboard display of information offered through use of one software package can be downloaded at iDashboards. Available at http://examples.idashboards.com/idashboards/?guestuser=wpsc1 (accessed November 3, 2008).

35. Brent D. Ruben, "Toward a Balanced Scorecard for Higher Education: Rethinking the College and University Excellence Indicators Framework," The Hunter Group White Paper Series (October, 1999), 4–5. Available at http://oqi.wisc.edu/resourcelibrary/uploads/resources/Balanced%20Scorecard%20in%20Higher%20Education.pdf (accessed November 13, 2008).

36. Minnesota State University, Mankato, "News: Minnesota State Colleges, Universities System Launched an Online Accountability Dashboard to Track Performance." Available at http://www.mnsu.edu/news/read/?id=1213796988&paper=topstories (accessed on July 6, 2008).

37. Utah State University, Merrill-Cazier Library, "Merrill-Cazier Library Performance Dashboard-January 2006" (Logan, UT: Utah State University). Available at http://ranger2.lib.usu.edu/main/portrait/DashBoard05.pdf (accessed December 12, 2008).

38. Texas Tech University, Library, "Assessment Dashboards" (Lubbock, TX: Texas Tech University). Available at http://www.irs.ttu.edu/dashboardareas/Dashboard.aspx?collid=35&year=2007&deptid=0 (accessed December 12, 2008).

39. Texas Tech University, "Assessment Dashboards" (Lubbock, TX: Texas Tech University), available at http://www.irs.ttu.edu/dashboardareas/index.aspx (accessed December 12, 2008); Texas Tech University, "State Accountability Measures" (Lubbock, TX: Texas Tech University), available at http://www.irim.ttu.edu/dashboard/ (accessed December 12, 2008).

40. Robert S. Kaplan and David P. Norton, *The Strategy-focused Organization: How Balanced Scorecard Companies Thrive in the New Business Environment* (Boston: Harvard Business School Press, 2001).

41. Ibid., 11.

42. Paul R. Niven, *Balanced Scorecard Step-by-step for Government and Nonprofit Agencies,* 2nd ed. (Hoboken, NJ: John Wiley and Sons, 2008), 154.

43. Ibid., 154–55.

44. Martin Klubeck and Michael Langthorne, "Applying a Metrics Report Card," *Educause Quarterly* 31, no.2 (April–June 2008), 77. Available at http://connect.educause.edu/Library/ED (accessed November 26, 2008).

45. Ibid., 77.

46. London Public Library, "Balanced Score Card Metrics." Available at http://www.londonpubliclibrary.ca/files/u3/aboutmylibrary/boardreports2008/june2008/WC2008 bsc1stquarter.pdf (accessed November 22, 2008). Orange County Library System, "Library Report Card." Available at http://www.ocls.info/About/Promo/documents/Report_Card.pdf (accessed November 24, 2008). Samaritan Medical Center Library, "Library 2004–2005 Report Card: 2004 and 2005 at a Glance" (Watertown, NY: Samaritan Medical Center Library). Available at http://library.samaritanhealth.com/library/Newsletter/2005%20Report%20Card.pdf (accessed November 25, 2008).

47. Martha Kyrillidou and Sarah Giersch, "Qualitative Analysis of Association of Research Libraries' E-metrics Participant Feedback about the Evolution of Measures for Networked Electronic Resources," *The Library Quarterly* 74, no. 4 (2004): 429.

48. Bertot, McClure, Davis, and Ryan, "Capture Usage with E-Metrics," 30. They have developed an e-metrics instructional system with funding from the Institute of Museum and Library Services, as "a web-based interactive instructional system to help librarians understand selected e-metrics, how to collect them, and how to use them for decision-making and communication."

# 12

---•◦•---

# THE JOY OF METRICS

Few library or information professionals would link joy to metrics. And, yet those who engage in conceptualizing, interpreting, defining, sharing, and utilizing metrics experience joy from doing so. This book's authors, though not expecting to make metrics fanatics out of its readers, aimed in these dozen chapters to share some of their enthusiasm for metrics and their conviction that metrics are powerful tools for those who manage information-centric organizations and who provide leadership toward transforming the central role of information resources in society. In this concluding chapter, five characteristics of joy serve as headings for reviewing key themes presented in earlier chapters: the grounding of purpose, the satisfaction of improvement and knowledge of excellence, the importance of sharing, the reward of impact, and the challenges of engagement. These characteristics have been expressed in various ways. Selected quotes found through a simple Google™ scan of the Web inspire the association of joy with the work of thinking about measurements in library settings and identifying metrics to evaluate expectations of stakeholders, performance of activities, and progress in reaching goals for quality improvement.

## GROUNDING OF PURPOSE

*Real joy comes not from ease or riches or from the praise of men, but from doing something worthwhile*

—Sir Wilfred Grenfell
English missionary and physician (1865–1940)

*I define joy as a sustained sense of well-being and internal peace—a connection to what matters.*

—Oprah Winfrey
U.S. actress and television talk show host (1954–)

Metrics are designed to be purposeful measurements. They are meaningless and worthless when they are perceived only to be counts taken because the library needs to report something to someone during some periodic intervals. The purposes for identifying metrics are many, as have been discussed. Most cited reasons include accountability, advocacy, and improvement.

It is well established that managers of organizations are expected, if not required, to be accountable for the resources they steward and to the stakeholders they serve. As financial pressures increase to allocate limited resources effectively, and as highly visible business people are exposed in the media for their self-serving behaviors, the call for accountability among managers also becomes a social and moral demand. Metrics provide a framework of specified and often (but not always) quantifiable goals by which managers can gather data to justify decisions and record their associated resource investments, activities, and outcomes. When metrics are utilized well, the resulting transparency serves as a check on an organization and in turn as either a protection for the honest manager or an avenue toward exposure for the misled leader.

Another strong motivator for a manager to engage with metrics is the need for advocacy. As pointed out in earlier chapters, libraries exist within political organizations. Directors must be entrepreneurial and competitive for resources and support. Their major challenges to do so stem from the inherent contradiction of setting and values. The library traditionally has been viewed, at least in democracies, as an important common good for society. Library collections and access to information resources have grown through pooled resources with the intention that they are available for shared use, but to meet personalized needs of individuals. Yet, the support for a library must be weighed against, for example in the civic sector, other social services such as public safety, health, or child services that are also valued as very important and require major funding to operate. The life of the mind and the exchange of knowledge central to libraries are often viewed as secondary to the safety and physical well-being of citizens. Therefore, publicly funded libraries are called to make creative alliances in order to argue for their contributions to the society's highest priorities and to produce evidence that they indeed deliver such support. Metrics in such settings may be direct measures of focused outputs, or outcomes expressed through collected testimonies of those who benefit from the existence of the library and its mission. They may also be indirect measures through comparisons, as, for example, are witnessed in academic settings where rankings of the library across specific metrics are associated with research and potential for learning; these are important for a university or college in turn to advocate for greater support from administrators and donors who are seeking prestige and evidence of intellectual achievements.

A third major function that metrics offer is in the library's commitment to continuous improvement, whether in its efficiency of workflows and production, or in perceived service quality among its customers. Performance metrics are emerging that assist managers in developing evidence to monitor progress in streamlining procedures and initiatives to lower costs and reduce time to deliver services such as cataloged records of holdings, document delivery, or answers to reference queries. In turn, metrics that are used to meet goals of improvement are the foundation for strategies to change the operations and sometimes even the role and impact of the library. Metrics based on perceptions of service quality are also important for making decisions toward improvement—whether of those receiving the service, those providing it, or those who pay for it. Changing library practices is not easy. Both staff close to the procedures and workflows, and stake-holders watching for the improvements are engaged when they can witness the change and are motivated to continue in the effort especially when they can see progress. Metrics again offer a framework by which such illustrative evidence can be purposefully gathered and shared within an impassioned presentation. As for other purposes, such metrics may be designed for direct measures of such factors as costs, staff time, or output, or for indirect measures of performance elements gathered through benchmarking.

Whatever the reason or the perspective for which they are developed, metrics are grounded in purpose. Clarification of purpose, coupled with articulation of specific factors to be examined, are the first and perhaps most important steps in identifying metrics appropriate for use in libraries. Achieving this clarity is not always straight-forward and may require the library manager to examine intentions, environmental influences, and strategies. This process is pursued through the application of ana-lytical skills, experiential insights, and professional values. The metrics that follow provide a way to gather data that can account for achievement toward the purpose and advocate for its continued pursuit. Successful results are rewarding not only to reaffirm the manager's leadership role but also to reinforce the practitioner's professional identity. These, in turn, are sources of joy.

## SATISFACTION OF IMPROVEMENT AND KNOWLEDGE OF EXCELLENCE

*The secret of joy in work is contained in one word—excellence.*
*To know how to do something well is to enjoy it.*

—Pearl S. Buck
U.S. writer, humanitarian, and women's rights activist (1892–1973)

Excellence in organizations has been a topic of evolving interest among both practitioners and researchers seeking to understand what contributes to successful businesses. By the late 20th century, this exploration moved across manufacturing as well as service organizations and became a topic of interest among librarians too. Excellence became closely associated with concepts of quality. In discussion of defining quality, Benjamin Schneider and Susan S. White characterize the technical approach and the user-based approach.[1] The technical approach takes the objective and absolute perspective and uses statistical controls to minimize or correct error in production. The user-based subjective approach places attention on continu-ous improvement efforts to respond to service quality gaps in customer expecta-tions for excellence and their perceptions of service delivery. The quest for quality, however defined, has led many to examine how organizations can become high achievers and ways to engage its employees in that ambition toward excellence. In their discussion of excellent companies, Thomas J. Peters and Robert H. Water-man, Jr., note,

By offering meaning as well as money, they give their employees a mission as well as a sense of feeling great. Every man becomes a pioneer, an experimenter, a leader. The institution provides guiding belief and creates a sense of excitement, a sense of being a part of the best, a sense of producing something of quality that is generally valued. And in this way it draws out the best.[2]

A common wisdom has evolved among managers of high-achieving organizations that "employees care about doing their best and continually strive to improve. Personal accountability for job execution and recognition for excellent performance contribute to this climate of achievement."[3]

To create such a work "environment in which people can blossom, develop self-esteem, and otherwise be excited participants in the business and society as a whole"[4] becomes a challenge for managers. The quality movement has produced a number of suggested ways to meet this challenge, but common to them is a continuous cycle of improvement that involves measurement of performance, initiatives to make improvements, and further monitoring to gauge successful change and to share that achievement with employees as reward and motivation to continue improvement efforts. The assessment stages require structured examination of an organization's activities, employee performance, and customer perceptions.

Specific methods to approach designing measurements and the appropriate metrics for excellence in libraries have been presented in earlier chapters. The multiple perspectives on library metrics presented point to the complexity of the nature of library activities. The nature of work in libraries includes both activities closely aligned to production with well-advanced standards (e.g., cataloging) and to service enactments with a mix of guiding procedures and expected judgment on the part of service staff (e.g., reference). Although not clearly mutually exclusive, these suggest a technical approach and a user-centered approach to the measurements needed to monitor these activities. Staff involved in gathering data as well as those receiving the results may be partial to thinking about their processes as what Joseph M. Hall and M. Eric Johnson describe as either art or science, and associated metrics to obtain feedback to be customer focused or process focused. At one extreme of their matrix are standardized procedures that aim to minimize variations in output; catalog records and locating books on shelves illustrate this technical, process-focused approach in the library setting. At the other end of their matrix is the artistic processes that "leverage variability . . . to create variations of products or services that customers value"; tailored reference consultations or instructional sessions illustrate this user-centered approach.[5]

An understanding of the nature of the processes being evaluated and the types of metrics used to do so may be helpful information to employees in appreciating their contributions to the excellence of the library. Clerical staff who take pride in performance of standard routines and librarians or discipline-based specialists who identify with applying their expertise to their work may easily be confused if the inappropriate metrics are used to define excellence. However, when there is alignment of metrics with defining approaches to quality, the resulting evidence reinforces the library's excellence and motivation for striving for continuous improvement. Employees' pride in the evidence of the library's quality achievement and pride in their own contributions to that achievement are powerful sources of joy.

## IMPORTANCE OF SHARING

*To get the full value of a joy you must have somebody to divide it with.*

—Mark Twain
U.S. humorist, novelist, and short-story author (1835–1910)

Metrics are seldom identified or used in isolation. They are vehicles by which managers can capture information about the library's inputs, outputs, and impact for purposes that involve other people. As discussed throughout the book, metrics are used for accountability to stakeholders such as governance boards, tuition-paying parents, or state legislators; for advocacy with donors, alumni, or others who offer important political and financial support; and for continuous improvement efforts that closely engage employees, as well as faculty, students, and other customers of library services.

Chapter 11 discussed the important stages involved to utilize metrics. Interpretation, synthesis, and presentation of metrics convert gathered data into insights about resources, performance, and perceptions and interpret them within a context useful for decision making and advocacy. These stages rely on the purpose, selection, and audience surrounding the metrics. Awareness and understanding of the audience are key factors in placing metrics into the management of a library, and particularly in preparing successful presentations of evidence. Aside from any residual enjoyment managers have in their personal and social contacts working with employees and external stakeholders, they experience a similar joy in the core benefit of sharing what they learn about their library and its position in serving its constituents.

## REWARD OF IMPACT

*There is no greater joy nor greater reward than to make a fundamental difference in someone's life.*
—Sister Mary Rose McGeady
Catholic nun, administrator, and advocate of children services (1928–)

The draw to devote energy to librarianship is not expressed by pride in the amount of resources held by a library or the number of books cataloged or questions answered each year. Rather, for some there is a calling to be a librarian or related information professional, with its devotion, its passion, and its rewards. What elevates activities beyond the routines of work are the results of the effort and the conviction among those who practice that it is a noble good for society and for individuals. The impact that those working in libraries have is diverse and includes, for example, the identification of knowledge needed to solve life-threatening illnesses, the preservation of cultural heritage for people to understand their ancestors, guidance to people so that they become self-sufficient in finding information that benefits the quality of their lives, or helping an individual to learn to read. Some librarians resist the idea that outcomes can be measured and that there is a need to do so, given their assumption that the *good* is recognized and appreciated by all.

The long-standing metrics that libraries have used to present what they are and what they do have been inputs and outputs. These might be institutionally descriptive, but they are not inspiring for those attracted to libraries. They are inadequate for tracking what difference libraries make. Alternatively, as discussed in detail in earlier chapters, outcome metrics are being identified for the impact that libraries have on individuals and society. Such metrics become useful to articulate the importance of library resources and the value of its services. They become critical to planning in strategic, and not only operational, ways. Outcome metrics can closely align the library to its institution through contributions to a shared mission and to collaborative ambitions for success with stakeholders. The immense and sustaining satisfaction that comes with exerting the energy of working in and about libraries is surpassed by the fulfillment experienced in changing the lives of others in positive ways. Outcome metrics are the powerful vocabulary that presents the impact of libraries and the benefits that they offer to those they serve. In telling the story, such metrics become a source of joy for those devoted to achieving such benefits.

## CHALLENGES OF ENGAGEMENT

*Winning is important to me, but what brings me real joy is the experience of being fully engaged in whatever I'm doing.*

—Phil Jackson
Professional basketball player and coach (1945–)

*Things won are done; joy's soul lies in the doing.*

—William Shakespeare
English dramatist and poet (1564–1616)
*Troilus and Cressida*, Act 1, Scene 2

Although the rewards of impact recorded by metrics may be a strong driving force by which librarians are drawn to the profession, it may not be enough to engage practitioners in pursuing metrics, specifically through the discipline of applied research—the articulation of purpose; the formation of clear questions of inquiry; the identity of data gathering methods; and the interpretation, synthesis, and presentation of results. Numerous reasons have been identified as to why there is not a strong attraction to such pursuit among library and information professionals. Some suggest that the preparation of practitioners lacks adequate attention to development of research understanding and skills. Students preparing to enter the profession have *statistical anxiety,* lack role models to motivate use of research results in practice, and do not perceive relevance of research findings to managerial decision making. Those already in the profession are not often exposed to research, and what they see they find to be irrelevant, too time consuming to produce to be useful, and presented in language that is hard to understand. And yet, there is another characteristic of joy that some find applies as well to working with metrics, and that is the joy of full engagement or *the doing.* Rather than repeat the criticisms of why most information professionals are ill equipped to engage more deeply with the development and use of metrics, the remainder of this chapter suggests ways to reverse that shortfall. Two strategies are examined. One is to encourage an environment of learning, and the other is to visualize what there is to learn.

Encouraging an environment of learning is core to Peter Senge's concept of *learning organizations,* which is described in his 1990 book *The Fifth Discipline* as,

organizations where people continually expand their capacity to create the results they truly desire, where new and expansive patterns of thinking are nurtured, where collective aspiration is set free, and where people are continually learning to see the whole together.[6]

Building on this influential construct for organizational development, Amos Lakos and Shelley Phipps developed the concept of *culture of assessment* applied to libraries. They developed workshops that stress the importance of continuous learning, with support both from the organization and peers of employees to learn new skills.[7] They were influenced by an earlier article written by Carla Stoffle, Robert Renaud, and Jerilyn Veldof in which the authors emphasized the need to make decisions based on data and stressed the importance of staff undertaking the needed assessment work.[8]

The prescription for a successful organization to change toward creating a culture of assessment includes investment in development of new skills among staff, designing systems to focus on the customer, enabling shared learning, measuring results, and using information for decision making.[9] To accomplish change, organizations need to involve all of the staff and to create a culture that places value on monitoring the extent to which change is proceeding in the way the organization favors. This means that evidence is gathered for accountability and service improvement. Developing that culture depends on a learning organization, one that learns how to learn. "Developing a culture of assessment is about learning how to learn."[10] It requires the commitment of senior leadership particularly in support of strategic planning processes. Rewards are also important to changing an organization culture. Yale University Library, for example, created a Service Quality Improvement Award, which provides low-key but publicly celebrated praise through a focused reception at which time the university librarian details the contributions of 10 or so annual winners. One of several criteria for these awards includes "developing new, or improving existing, procedures that resulted in significant improvement in productivity or work methods that have positive outcomes for library readers."[11] Among the best nominations for these awards are ones with some reference to metrics that measure, if not the outcomes, at least the effort. Over the few years of presenting the awards, a greater awareness of staff involvement and contribution to improvement has spread through the library. As Lakos and Phipps reflect on the challenges of engaging staff and creating a culture of assessment, they note,

The new competence, experience, and learning agility that are part of the creation of a culture of assessment lead to new confidence and enhanced expertise. This new expertise leads to more effective and measurable outcomes for customers and stakeholders, which in turn heighten the potential for survival and relevancy in a competitive information service environment.[12]

Another approach to foster staff learning and engaging in the use of metrics for improvement is to create teams to conduct evaluation or assessment efforts and to support others in doing so. For example, the University of Washington Library has successfully taken this approach for several years,[13] as has the University of Iowa Library where a User Needs Assessment Group published findings of their research to assess the needs for library services among faculty, students, and staff.[14]

Developing valid measurements of library inputs, outputs, processes, and outcomes is not easy, and most library employees are not only unskilled in doing so but also have little appreciation of some of the basic principles of assessment, validation, research design, selection of appropriate methodologies, or execution of data gathering. In short, they are neither familiar with the diversity of metrics nor the context for using them when considered from any of a multitude of perspectives. Frequently, when planning to embark on an assessment effort, staff turn immediately to designing a data gathering tool before clarifying the purpose for undertaking the task, articulating the questions to address, or strategizing the best research design and methodology to use. Bringing together well-intentioned or enthusiastic staff eager to pursue metrics without the appropriate knowledge of what they are and how to use them will not result in useful data.

A magic lesson has not been found that instills this knowledge among students or practitioners, but different approaches to teaching about metrics through research methods or evaluation can be found. For example, the authors have evolved an assignment for doctoral students in the Simmons College Ph.D. program for Managerial Leadership for Library and Information Professions (see the chapter appendix). It invites students to identify examples of metrics (inputs, outputs, customer-related, and outcomes) from four stakeholders' perspectives (e.g., the library customer, the library staff, the parent organization, society in general), and then to consider how the metric may be used to gather data and in planning or decision making. Consistently, this is a challenging exercise for students, all of whom are successful mid-career library managers, who take the course in their first year. The assignment generates discussions and reviews of the rich potential that metrics can have in planning improvement and advocating the library's value in different settings. Though it is a stretch to say that students enjoy this assignment, it does provide delayed joy for their coaches when they see them evolve a mind-set that seeks metrics for practical managerial applications. The satisfaction comes from the engagement, overcoming the barriers posed by initial ignorance about metrics, bridging the gap of irrelevance to practice, and the shared insights that follow from use.

## CONCLUSION

*Joy: cleans to a brilliant shine. Juice up your . . . routine and invigorate your senses.*

—Proctor and Gamble
Multinational manufacturing company (1837–)

This book is about looking at metrics from different perspectives. Beginning with the reasons for bothering with metrics in the first place, through raising awareness of who cares, selecting which metrics matter, and framing how to communicate their applicability, the multitude of choices is what faces library and information managers. The authors intended to shake up the way readers think about metrics. They offer an "advanced technique and deeper view" of the topic, similar to what readers expect of another, earlier and more popular book about joy.[15] The results, if the intentions have been successfully met, alter routines and possibly even brilliantly shed light on an area of management that is not frequently invigorating. Four questions haunt the conclusions of any book, and this one is no exception:

1. Why bother?
2. Who cares?
3. What matters?
4. How to communicate?

### Why Bother?

The purpose for metrics, repeatedly stressed through the book's chapters, drives many of the choices a library manager has about utilizing measurements. High among the reasons for turning to metrics are accountability and advocacy, followed closely by comparing, continuous improvement, and transparency. Managers, especially in today's politicized organizations, need the evidence to be accountable for the resources entrusted to their care and for the results they achieve through using them. They look for grounding to advocate for the values, the potential impact that libraries have, and thus to appeal to continue to support them. Corresponding arguments are strengthened by quantified metrics used in comparing libraries or institutions hosting them with other ones that are viewed as successful. Internal use of metrics is central to a library's continuous improvement efforts, where measures fuel the cycle with repeated review and feedback or processes. Respected metrics, used wisely by managers, also reinforce commitment to transparency in the review and assessment processes.

## Who Cares?

Stakeholders by definition care about a library, its resources and operations. They each carry their own agenda and reasons for being interested in the library. The library manager, in turn, has a reason to care about stakeholder interests. It is the intersection of these perspectives—that of a stakeholder and the library manager—which gives context to any metric designed for library application.

## What Matters?

To use metrics effectively, the basic steps of a research process should be followed. What needs to be measured must be clearly identified. Understanding whose perspective is relevant and important is mandatory before designing a set of metrics that matter. Knowledge and skills in terms of how to collect data are closely linked but not most important to having useful data. To complete the cycle and maintain or change a culture of assessment, managers must reach proper interpretation and presentation of data. In short, metrics matter to minimize the gaps in knowledge about what is relevant and what is monitored.

## How to Communicate?

Information about metrics and the resulting data collected through their use should be among the messages library managers communicate every chance they get. It should be the content of training for local staff and professionals beyond a specific library. Publishing and distributing standards that define metrics and guide their design offer another way to communicate the importance and usefulness they offer library managers. One of the most forceful ways to communicate the power and the joy of metrics is through engagement—with staff through meetings, among staff through shared team assignments, and with clients in marketing how the library can meet their needs. In the end, the impact of metrics, driven by whatever perspective is addressed, is the brilliant shine that results from purposeful and systematic gathering and sharing of data to measure achievement, improvement, efficiency, or value of the library with someone who cares.

# NOTES

1. Benjamin Schneider and Susan S. White, *Service Quality: Research Perspectives* (Thousand Oaks, CA: Sage Publications, 2004), 10.

2. Thomas J. Peters and Robert H. Waterman, Jr., *In Search of Excellence: Lessons from America's Best-Run Companies* (New York: Warner Books, 1982), 323.

3. Leonard L. Berry, *On Great Service: A Framework for Action* (New York: Free Press, 1995), 242.

4. Peters and Waterman, *In Search of Excellence,* 86.

5. Joseph M. Hall and M. Eric Johnson, "When Should a Process Be Art, Not Science?" *Harvard Business Review* 87, no. 3 (March 2009): 58–65.

6. Mark K. Smith, "Peter Senge and the Learning Organization," *The Encyclopedia of Informal Education* (2001). Available at http://www.infed.org/thinkers/senge.htm (accessed February 22, 2009).

7. Amos Lakos and Shelley Phipps, "Creating a Culture of Assessment: A Catalyst for Organizational Change," *portal: Libraries and the Academy* 4, no. 3 (2004): 345–61.

8. Carla J. Stoffle, Robert Renaud, and Jerilyn R. Veldof, "Choosing Our Futures," *College & Research Libraries* 57, no. 3 (May 1996): 213–25.

9. Lakos and Phipps, "Creating a Culture of Assessment," 351.

10. Ibid., 359.

11. Yale University Library, "Service Quality Improvement Awards Program." Available at http://www.library.yale.edu/Administration/SQIC/sqiawards1.html (accessed February 23, 2009).

12. Lakos and Phipps, "Creating a Culture of Assessment," 359.

13. University of Washington Library, "Assessment Group." Available at http://www.lib.washington.edu/assessment/Group.html (accessed February 2, 2009).

14. Carlette Washington-Hoagland and Leo Clougherty, "Faculty and Staff Use of Academic Library Resources and Services: A University of Iowa Libraries' Perspective," *portal: Libraries and the Academy* 2, no. 4 (2002): 627–46.

15. Susan Donaldson James, "'Joy of Sex' Reinvented for Today's Lovers," ABC News (September 18, 2008). Available at http://abcnews.go.com/Health/Story?id=5826372&page=1 (accessed February 20, 2009).

# APPENDIX: METRICS ANALYSIS

Analyze metrics that represent inputs, outputs, and outcomes that cover the following perspectives: the library customer, the library, the library's parent institution/organization, and one outside stakeholder. Conduct the review for a single given service, and post two examples of each metric (input, output, and outcome) for each perspective (library, customer, parent institution/organization, and stakeholder)—for a total of 24 metrics.

For each perspective, collectively address the following points:

- Lay out the metric as a ratio or percentage.
- Explain why it is imperative that the metric be adopted.
- How might these metrics be gathered: offer a strategy for data collection that addresses either probability sampling or nonprobability sampling—spell it out.
- How might the set of metrics be used for planning and decision making?
- Would the organizational culture need changing to collect these metrics on a regular basis? If the culture needs changing, how can this be accomplished?
- Do any of these metrics have a "best practices" application? Discuss.

**Table 12.1**
**Metrics by Perspective (A Summary)**

|  | Input | Output | Outcome or Impact |
|---|---|---|---|
| Library |  |  |  |
| Customer |  |  |  |
| Parent Organization |  |  |  |
| Other Stakeholder (select ONE) |  |  |  |

# ABOUT THE APPENDICES

These appendices comprise an organized listing of many of the metrics identified in this text as well as ones that we (and others) have found useful over the years. These appendices are not, nor are they intended to be, an exhaustive summary of metrics for academic libraries. They include examples of metrics available and applied by libraries to support accountability efforts, demonstrate value to the institution, make decisions, discover the status of operations and services, measure progress towards meeting identified standards and benchmarks, and make comparisons to other libraries.

Appendix A    Inputs: Library Perspective (reported as numbers)

Appendix B    Inputs: Library Perspective (reported as ratios/percentages)

Appendix C    Outputs: Library Perspective (reported as numbers)

Appendix D    Outputs: Library Perspective (reported as ratios/percentages)

Appendix E    Selected Examples of Process Metrics. Process metrics reflect the transformation of inputs into outputs.

Appendix F    Selected Examples of Trend Metrics. Such metrics reveal trends when collected, organized, and reviewed over a span of time.

Appendix G    Examples of Qualitative Metrics. Some qualitative metrics cannot be represented by a measurable quantity (e.g., an input or output metric).

Appendix H    Customer Perspective. Quantitative and qualitative metrics address internal and external customers.

Appendix I    Institutional Perspective

Table I-1 Librarians Should Be Aware of These Institutional Metrics and Their Implications Concerning the Library

Table I-2: Measures of, or from, the Library about Value to the Institution

Appendix J    Stakeholder Perspectives (Examples).

Table J-1: Stakeholders Directly/Indirectly Benefiting from the Library

Table J-1a: Library Infrastructure and Capacity

# Appendix A

---

## INPUTS: LIBRARY PERSPECTIVE (REPORTED AS NUMBERS)

| Categories | Metrics |
|---|---|
| **Expenditures** | Total expenditures<br>• From all sources (e.g., tuition, research grants, special projects, gifts and endowments, fees, and fines)<br>• From student contributions only (e.g., tuition)<br>Total information resources (library materials) expenditures<br>• One-time purchases<br>  + Monographs, print<br>  + Electronic books (e-books)<br>  + Microfilm/fiche backfiles<br>  + Serial backfiles<br>  + Electronic backfiles<br>  + AV materials<br>    − video<br>    − audio<br>  + Reference<br>    − print<br>    − electronic<br>  + Reserves<br>    − print<br>    − electronic (e-reserves)<br>• Current serials subscriptions (continuations)<br>  + Print<br>  + Electronic<br>    − full-text journal subscriptions<br>    − individual titles not in full text<br>    − reference sources<br>    − database subscriptions accounted for by subscriptions through consortia<br>  + Database fees<br>  + Microfilm continuations |

| Categories | Metrics |
|---|---|
| | • Maps<br>• Software<br>• Computer files<br>• Other information resources<br>  + Document delivery<br>  + Interlibrary loan<br>  + Preservation of materials otherwise lost<br>• Digital materials created or converted by the library and made available electronically<br>Other operating expenditures<br>• Bibliographic utilities, consortia, and networks<br>• Computer hardware<br>• Computer software<br>• Contract binding<br>• Furniture<br>• Memberships<br>• Supplies<br>• Other equipment<br>Total salaries and wages<br>• All staff<br>  + Full time<br>  + Part time<br>    − student assistants<br>• Professional (master's degree in librarianship or equivalent)<br>• Other professional (required education in related fields)<br>• Support (technical and clerical)<br>• Student assistants<br>• Fringe benefits |
| Collections | Volumes added in fiscal year<br>• Monographic volumes<br>  + Print<br>  + Electronic (e-books)<br>• Serial backfiles (bound volumes)<br>• Other paper materials<br>  + Government documents<br>• Microforms<br>• AV materials<br>  + Audio<br>  + Visual<br>Titles added in fiscal year<br>• Monographic volumes<br>  + Print<br>  + Electronic (e-books)<br>• Serial backfiles (bound volumes)<br>• Other paper materials<br>  + Government documents<br>• Microforms<br>• Computer files<br>• AV materials<br>  + Audio<br>  + Visual |

| Categories | Metrics |
|---|---|
| | Current serial titles added in fiscal year<br>• Journals<br>  + Print<br>  + Electronic<br>• Microforms<br>Serial titles canceled during fiscal year<br>• Journals<br>  + Print<br>  + Electronic<br>• Microforms<br>Electronic reference sources and aggregate services added during fiscal year<br>• Citation indexes and abstracts<br>• Full-text article databases<br>• Full-text reference sources<br>• Dissertation and conference proceedings' databases<br>• Databases that the library mounts locally<br>Volumes held, sum<br>• Volumes added past fiscal year<br>• Volumes withdrawn past fiscal year<br>• Volumes added minus those withdrawn = Volumes added net<br>• Total in collection<br>Volumes held, details<br>• Monographic volumes<br>  + Print<br>  + Electronic (e-books)<br>• Serial backfiles (bound volumes)<br>• Other paper materials<br>  + Government documents<br>• Microforms<br>• AV materials<br>  + Audio<br>  + Visual<br>Current serials subscriptions held<br>• Journals<br>  + Print<br>  + Electronic<br>    – full-text journals<br>• Microforms<br>Electronic reference sources and aggregate services held<br>• Citation indexes and abstracts<br>• Full-text article databases<br>• Full-text reference sources<br>• Dissertation and conference proceedings' databases<br>• Databases that the library mounts locally<br>Titles held<br>• Print<br>• Electronic<br>• Total in collection |

| Categories | Metrics |
|---|---|
|  | Titles held, detail<br>• Monographic volumes<br>  + Print<br>  + Electronic (e-books)<br>• Serial backfiles (bound volumes)<br>• Government documents<br>  + Print<br>  + Electronic<br>• Other paper materials<br>• Microforms<br>• AV materials<br>  + Audio<br>  + Visual<br>Other types of information sources held (volumes)<br>• Reference collection<br>  + Electronic reference sources<br>  + Print reference sources<br>• Maps<br>• Computer files<br>• Software<br>• Still images (items)<br>  + Stored electronically<br>• Manuscripts/archives (linear feet)<br>• Digital materials created or converted by the library and made available electronically<br>• CD-ROM/DVD<br>• Web-based resources<br>  + Digital collections<br>  + Licensed access<br>• Otherwise stored (e.g., servers)<br>Reserves<br>• Items placed per academic term<br>  + Print<br>  + AV<br>  + Digital<br>Archives and Manuscripts<br>• In linear feet<br>• Number of archival and manuscript finding aids available<br>Off-site storage<br>• Number of collection-based resources shelved in organized and accessible off-site storage<br>Bibliographic records<br>• Included in the library's electronic catalog<br>• Documents not accessible through the library's catalog<br>Resource contracts supporting collections and collection development<br>• Number of formal contracts with third party information resource providers/vendors (excluding library consortia) |
| **Communities Served** | Students<br>• Undergraduates (FTE)<br>  + Newly enrolled |

| Categories | Metrics |
|---|---|
|  | • Graduate students (FTE)<br>  + Newly enrolled<br>• Total student FTE<br>  + Total head count<br>• Total credit hours<br>Faculty<br>• Full time (FTE)<br>• Part time (FTE) |
| **Facilities (physical)** | Total square feet<br>• In public areas<br>• In staff areas<br>Shelving (in linear feet)<br>Discrete user seats (total)<br>• At equipment<br>• At nonequipment<br>• At tables (nonequipment)<br>• At individual carrels<br>• In group study rooms<br>• In reading areas<br>Number of user-available electrical jacks<br>Number of user-available electrical receptacles |
| **Information/ Learning Commons** | Café sales<br>Amount expended<br>Hours open<br>Collections available<br>Cost of staff<br>Breakdown of staff (by constituency group, e.g., IT and library)<br>IT support |
| **Interlibrary Loan/ Document Delivery** | Requests<br>• Number of requests from students, faculty, and staff to borrow from other libraries<br>• Number of request received to loan from other libraries |
| **Library Staff (with or without faculty status)** | Expressed in terms of FTE<br>• Total staff<br>• Professional (master's degree in librarianship or equivalent)<br>• Other professional (required education in related fields)<br>• Support staff (technical and clerical)<br>• Student assistants<br>Library budget spent on<br>• Professional development<br>• Research grants to staff<br>Time spent on<br>• Research<br>• Service<br>Number of staff participating on<br>• Library committees<br>• Nonlibrary committees at any hierarchical level (e.g., school, program) |

| Categories | Metrics |
|---|---|
| **Services** | Hours open<br>  • Per week during academic term<br>  • Per week during nonacademic sessions<br>Number of staffed service points<br>Library's Web site<br>  • Number of links<br>  • Number of pages<br>Library-created research (help) guides<br>Passes available for loan<br>  • Museum<br>  • Other<br>Suggestions and comments from users<br>  • Number received via all means (e.g., suggestion box, e-mail) |
| **Technology** | Technology equipment available for loan<br>  • Laptops<br>  • Audiovisual<br>  • Playback units<br>  • Other<br>Public computer workstations<br>  • Research workstations<br>  • OPAC workstations<br>  • User productivity workstations<br>    + Desk<br>    + Laptops<br>  • Workstations with accessibility software available<br>Workstations in library used for instruction<br>Library printers for users<br>Photocopiers |
| **Partnerships** | Internal<br>  • Formal institutional relationships (based upon agreements)<br>External memberships (e.g., has formal governance)<br>  • Library consortia<br>  • Community organizations |

# Appendix B

## INPUTS: LIBRARY PERSPECTIVE (REPORTED AS RATIOS/ PERCENTAGES)*

| Categories | Metrics |
|---|---|
| **Expenditures: Summary** | Percent of total library budget expended from all sources (e.g., tuition, research grants, special projects, gifts and endowments, fees, and fines)<br>• From student contributions only (e.g., tuition)<br>Percent of total library budget expended<br>• For all information resources (library materials) (one time and continuations)<br>• For all staff and student assistants (including fringe benefits)<br>• For all other operating expenditures<br>Total library expenditures per<br>• Student FTE<br>• Faculty FTE |
| **Expenditures: Information Resources/ Materials** | Information resources (library materials) expended per<br>• Student FTE<br>• Undergraduate student FTE<br>• Graduate student FTE<br>• Faculty FTE<br>One-time information resources (library materials) expenditures<br>• As a percentage of all information resources (library materials) by type of resource<br>  + Monographs, print<br>  + Electronic books (e-books)<br>  + Microfilm/fiche backfiles<br>  + Serial backfiles<br>  + Electronic backfiles<br>  + AV materials<br>    – video<br>    – audio<br>  + Reference<br>    – print<br>    – electronic |

| Categories | Metrics |
|---|---|
|  | + Reserves<br>    − print<br>    − electronic (e-reserves)<br>• Average cost of information resources (library materials) by type of resource added in fiscal year<br>    + Monographs, print<br>    + Electronic books (e-books)<br>    + Microfilm/fiche backfiles<br>    + Serial backfiles<br>    + Electronic backfiles<br>    + AV materials<br>        − video<br>        − audio<br>    + Reference<br>        − print<br>        − electronic<br>    + Reserves<br>        − print<br>        − electronic (e-reserves)<br>• Per student FTE<br>• Per faculty FTE |
| **Expenditures: Monographs** | Ratio of monographs purchased in<br>• Print<br>• Electronic<br>Ratio of monographs purchased per<br>• Student FTE<br>• Faculty FTE |
| **Expenditures: Serials** | Serials expenditures as a percent of<br>• All information resources (library materials) expenditures<br>• Total library expenditures<br>Serials expenditure per<br>• Student FTE<br>• Faculty FTE<br>Current serials subscriptions (continuations)<br>• As a percentage of current serials subscriptions (continuations) by type of resource<br>    + Print<br>    + Electronic<br>        − full-text journal subscriptions<br>        − individual titles not in full text<br>        − reference sources<br>    + Database fees<br>    + Microfilm continuations<br>Cost (serials)<br>• Average cost per subscription<br>• Average cost per subscription added in fiscal year<br>• Average cost per access (average cost of each access event to full-text article)<br>  = subscription price divided by number of articles accessed<br>• Average cost per article<br>  = subscription price of journal divided by number of articles contained in the journal<br>• Cost-adjusted usage |

| Categories | Metrics |
|---|---|
| | Divide the number of full-text accesses of an article (number of time an HTML file is viewed or a PDF file is downloaded) by the number of available articles<br>• Cost-based usage benchmarks<br>  Price of desired resources divided by the cost per access of peer product in collection[1] |
| **Expenditures: Databases** | Average cost per database added in fiscal year<br>Electronic databases as a percent of<br>• All information resources (library materials) expenditures<br>• Serials<br>Percentage of database subscriptions accounted for by subscriptions through consortia<br>Electronic databases per<br>• Student FTE<br>• Faculty FTE<br>Electronic resource cost per<br>• Item<br>• Session<br>• Download<br>• Title |
| **Expenditures: Other Information Sources** | Other information sources<br>• As a percentage of all information resources (library materials) by type of resource<br>  + Maps<br>  + Software<br>  + Computer files<br>  + Document delivery<br>  + Interlibrary loan<br>  + Preservation of materials otherwise lost<br>  + Digital materials created or converted by the library and made available electronically<br>• Average cost of information resources (library materials) by type of resource added in fiscal year<br>  + Maps<br>  + Software<br>  + Computer files<br>  + Document delivery<br>  + Interlibrary loan<br>  + Preservation of materials otherwise lost<br>  + Digital materials created or converted by the library and made available electronically<br>Other information sources per<br>• Student FTE<br>• Faculty FTE |
| **Expenditures: Other Operating Expenditures** | Other operating expenditures<br>• As a percentage of all other operating expenditures by type of resource<br>  + Bibliographic utilities, consortia, and networks<br>  + Computer hardware<br>  + Computer software<br>  + Contract binding<br>  + Furniture |

| Categories | Metrics |
|---|---|
| | + Memberships<br>+ Supplies<br>+ Other equipment<br>Other operating expenditures per<br>• Student FTE<br>• Faculty FTE<br>Unit cost<br>• Processing a monograph<br>• Processing a serial |
| **Expenditures: Staffing** | Expended as a percentage of total staffing by type of staff<br>• Professional (master's degree in librarianship or equivalent)<br>• Other professional (required education in related fields)<br>• Support (technical and clerical)<br>• Student assistants<br>• Full-time staff<br>• Part-time staff<br>• By library function (e.g., reference, technical services)<br>Staffing expenditures per<br>• Student FTE<br>• Faculty FTE<br>Library administrative cost per library employee |
| **Expenditures: Technology** | Cost per page printed on library printers |
| **Collections: Volumes** | Total collection<br>• Held by various collections (e.g., general circulating, reserves, special, image, sound)<br>Volumes<br>• Held to total student FTE (could subdivide by undergraduate and graduate)<br>• Held to faculty FTE<br>• Added per year to total student FTE (could subdivide by undergraduate and graduate)<br>• Added per year to total faculty FTE<br>Number of volumes by discipline<br>• By classification number<br>Collection age<br>• By copyright date<br>  – by discipline or classification number<br>Ratio of items on reserve to<br>• Student FTE (# of reserves for each student FTE)<br>• Faculty FTE (# of reserves for each faculty FTE)<br>Percentage of recommended or required readings on course syllabi material held<br>• In circulating collection<br>• In reserve collection |
| **Collections: Serials** | Total serials collection<br>• Equals total print journal tiles + total e-journal title<br>• Total serials collection available in electronic format<br>• Portion of journal collection available in electronic format<br>Ratio of currently subscribed serial titles per<br>• Student FTE<br>• Faculty FTE |

| Categories | Metrics |
|---|---|
| **Collections: Reference** | Reference<br>• Ratio of total reference collection to all collections |
| **Collections: Electronic** | Portion of collection available electronically (compared to print version and total collection)<br>• Monographs (e-books)<br>• Journals<br>• Reference collection<br>Reference<br>• Ratio of total reference collection devoted to digital reference sources |
| **Collections: Other** | Percentage of federal depository items selected<br>Percentage of materials in all collections accessible through the library's catalog |
| **Facilities (physical)** | Public square feet in library space per<br>• Student FTE<br>• Faculty FTE<br>Per public library seat (1 chair for X number of that population)<br>• Student FTE<br>• Faculty FTE<br>Ratio of library seating to<br>• Student FTE<br>• Faculty FTE<br>Ratio of occupied shelving to empty shelf space (in linear feet)<br>Percentage of library facilities meeting accessibility standards |
| **Interlibrary Loan/ Document Delivery** | Cost (e.g., staff, supplies, postage) per interlibrary loan for each<br>• Request from students, faculty, and staff to borrow from other libraries<br>• Request received to loan from other libraries |
| **Library Staff (with or without faculty status)** | FTE library staff (including student assistants) to<br>• Student FTE<br>• Per 1,000 students<br>• Faculty FTE<br>FTE library staff to<br>• Professional (master's degree in librarianship or equivalent) staff FTE<br>• Other professional (required education in related fields) staff FTE<br>• Support (technical and clerical) staff FTE<br>• Student assistants FTE<br>• Professional staff FTE to support (technical and clerical) staff FTE<br>FTE library staff to student FTE<br>• Professional (master's degree in librarianship or equivalent) staff FTE<br>• Other professional (required education in related fields) staff FTE<br>• Support (technical and clerical) staff FTE<br>• Student assistants FTE<br>FTE library staff to faculty FTE<br>• Professional (master's degree in librarianship or equivalent) staff FTE |

| Categories | Metrics |
|---|---|
|  | • Other professional (required education in related fields) staff FTE<br>• Support (technical and clerical) staff FTE<br>• Student assistants FTE<br>FTE library public services staff to<br>• Student FTE<br>• Faculty FTE |
| Technology | Public computer workstations to<br>• Student FTE<br>• Faculty FTE<br>Workstations in library used for instruction to Student FTE<br>Percentage of public workstations with accessibility software available |

* Note: Many of the ratios involving student and faculty FTE could be combined into one ratio: ratio of $X$ to combined student and faculty FTE.

## NOTE

1. See Karla Hahn and Lila Faulkner, "Evaluative Usage–Based Metrics for the Selection of E–Journals," *College & Research Libraries* 63, no. 3 (May 2002), 221; Joanna Duy and Liwen Vaughan, "Can Electronic Journal Usage Data Replace Citation Data as a Measure of Journal Use? An Empirical Examination," *The Journal of Academic Librarianship 32*, no. 5 (September 2006): 512–17.

# Appendix C

## OUTPUTS: LIBRARY PERSPECTIVE (REPORTED AS NUMBERS)

| Categories | Metrics |
|---|---|
| **Collections Use** | Circulation transactions (excluding reserves)<br>• Initial transactions<br>• Renewals<br>• Separate out by format (e.g., video, CD)<br>• Separate out books purchased that fiscal year<br>• Separate out by user status (e.g., undergraduate students, faculty, graduate students, institutional staff)<br>• Holds placed by users on items in circulation<br>Reserve transactions<br>• Initial transaction<br>• Renewals<br>• By type of information source<br>  + Print<br>  + AV<br>  + Electronic<br>Electronic database use<br>• Number of databases<br>• Logins (sessions) to electronic databases<br>  + From on-campus<br>  + From off-campus<br>  + Electronic turnaways<br>• Proxy server logins to databases<br>  + From on-campus<br>  + From off-campus<br>  + Electronic turnaways<br>• Searches<br>  + Abstracts examined<br>  + Full-text documents examined<br>  + E-books<br>  + Electronic turnaways<br>  + Successful |

| Categories | Metrics |
|---|---|
| | • Items examined<br>• Downloads<br>   + Number of documents<br>   + By database<br>     − abstracts<br>     − full text/images<br>   + E-books<br>   + Electronic turnaways<br>In-library use of material<br>• Books<br>• Journals<br>• Other<br>Digital materials created or converted by the library and made available electronically |
| Services | Weekly public service hours<br>• Per typical full-service week<br>Staff public work hours per typical full-service week<br>• Number of total hours (overlapping) of staffed circulation service<br>• Number of nonoverlapping hours of staffed reference service<br>• Number of total hours (overlapping) of staffed reference service<br>Reference transactions<br>• Number of reference questions asked<br>   + Face-to-face<br>   + Mail (physical)<br>   + Telephone<br>   + Electronic<br>     − chat<br>     − e-mail<br>     − text messaging<br>• Number of reference questions answered<br>   + Face-to-face<br>   + Mail (physical)<br>   + Telephone<br>   + Electronic<br>     − chat<br>     − e-mail<br>     − text messaging<br>• Number of reference questions answered correctly<br>Research consultations conducted<br>• Number of hours<br>Library's Web site<br>• Site visits<br>   + Month of year<br>   + Day of week<br>   + Time of day<br>   + Unique visitors<br>• Use of library's Web-based forms<br>• Number of pages viewed<br>OPAC searches conducted<br>• Author<br>• Keyword<br>• Subject |

| Categories | Metrics |
|---|---|
| | • Title<br>Programs and presentations (excluding library instruction)<br>• Sponsored by the library<br>• Attendance<br>Library-created research (help) guides viewed/downloaded<br>RSS<br>• Subscriptions to the library's blog |
| Facilities/<br>Space Use | Library visitors (in-person)<br>• Library visits/gate counts<br>+ hour of the day<br>+ day of week<br>+ month of year<br>Length of time spent in library<br>Use of group study rooms<br>• Total<br>• By discipline<br>• Undergraduate<br>• Graduate |
| Information/<br>Learning<br>Commons | Use of information/learning commons<br>• Gate count<br>+ Month of year<br>+ Day of week<br>+ Time of day<br>• By discipline<br>• Services used<br>+ Writing tutor<br>+ Reference service<br>+ IT support<br>+ Etc. |
| Instruction<br>Sessions and<br>Presentations | Library instruction sessions<br>• Given per academic term<br>• Number of participants<br>Presentations to groups (e.g., orientations, library tours)<br>• Given per academic term<br>• Number of participants<br>• Electronic presentations<br>+ Given per academic term<br>+ Participants |
| Interlibrary<br>Loan/<br>Document<br>Delivery | Intercampus requests<br>• Total filled<br>+ Electronically-delivered<br>• Total unfilled<br>Intercampus transactions<br>• Loaned to others<br>+ Returnable<br>+ Nonreturnable<br>• Borrowed from others<br>+ Returnable<br>+ Nonreturnable<br>Intracampus requests<br>• Total filled<br>+ Electronically-delivered<br>• Total unfilled |

| Categories | Metrics |
|---|---|
| | Commercial documents delivered<br>Unit cost<br>  • Borrowing<br>  • Lending |
| **Library Staff (with or without faculty status)** | Types of publications[1]<br>  • Articles (peer-reviewed journals)<br>  • Articles (non-peer-reviewed journals)<br>  • Conference papers (in proceedings)<br>  • Books<br>  • Poster sessions (peer selected)<br>Speeches given<br>  • Internationally<br>  • Nationally<br>  • Regionally<br>  • State<br>  • Local<br>Service<br>  • Number of staff who served on internal library committees<br>  • Number of staff who served on committees external to the library<br>Staff attendance at<br>  • Workshops<br>  • Conferences<br>  • Other professional development sessions<br>Staff training<br>  • Total number of hours received<br>    + Technology training<br>Staff turnover<br>  • Number joining the staff<br>  • Number which left the staff |
| **Technology** | Microform reader/printers<br>  • Number of times used<br>  • Number of pages printed<br>Workstations<br>  • Number of times fixed workstations used<br>  • Number of times laptops loaned for use<br>Printing<br>  • Number of pages printed in the library by users<br>Computer connection time<br>  • User<br>Photocopiers<br>  • Number of pages printed |
| **Uptime** | Availability, in hours per year<br>  • Access to the library's integrated library system<br>  • Access to the library's Web-base subscription/leased databases via the library/institutional servers (as opposed to vendor servers) |

## NOTE

1. For other possibilities, see Michael F. Middaugh, *Understanding Faculty Productivity: Standards and Benchmarks for Colleges and Universities* (San Francisco, CA: Jossey-Bass, 2001), 87.

# Appendix D

## OUTPUTS: LIBRARY PERSPECTIVE (REPORTED AS RATIOS/ PERCENTAGES)*

| Categories | Metrics |
|---|---|
| **Collections Use** | Volumes circulated to total volumes available (turnover)<br>Number of times each book circulated (average transactions per item)<br>  &bull; Total number of circulations within a subject area divided by total number of holdings in that subject area<br>Circulation transactions (excluding reserve) to<br>  &bull; Student FTE (number of circulations for each student FTE)<br>  &bull; Faculty FTE (number of circulations for each faculty FTE)<br>Circulation transactions<br>  &bull; Total by month<br>  &bull; Total by calendar/academic/fiscal year<br>  &bull; Average per hour open<br>  &bull; Average per day<br>  &bull; Average per month<br>Reserve transactions<br>  &bull; Use of reserve collection by student FTE<br>  &bull; Ratio of reserve collection used in electronic formats<br>Total information resources (library materials) use<br>  &bull; Equals total circulation + total in-house use of materials + total full-text electronic resources viewed or downloaded<br>  &bull; Ratio of total information resources (library materials) used in electronic form<br>  &bull; In-library information resources use as a ratio of total circulation<br>Book use<br>  &bull; Ratio of new books purchased in a FY and how often they are used (book use rate)<br>Electronic full-text articles use<br>  &bull; Average by hour<br>  &bull; Average by day<br>  &bull; Average by month |

| Categories | Metrics |
|---|---|
|  | Electronic database use averages by hour, day, and month<br>• Number of databases<br>• Logins (sessions) to electronic databases<br>  + From on-campus<br>  + From off-campus<br>  + Electronic turnaways<br>  + Student FTE<br>  + Faculty FTE<br>• Proxy server logins to databases<br>  + From on-campus<br>  + From off-campus<br>  + Electronic turnaways<br>  + Student FTE<br>  + Faculty FTE<br>• Searches<br>  + Abstracts examined<br>  + Full-text documents examined<br>  + E-books<br>  + Electronic turnaways<br>• Items examined<br>• Downloads<br>  + Number of documents<br>  + By database<br>    − abstracts<br>    − full text/images<br>  + E-books<br>  + Electronic turnaways |
| **Services** | Reference questions asked by<br>• Student FTE<br>• Faculty FTE<br>Reference activity<br>• Equals total in-person transactions + total telephone transactions + total virtual transactions<br>• Percentage of electronic reference transactions to total reference transactions<br>  + Student FTE<br>  + Faculty FTE<br>• Percentage of reference questions answered correctly<br>Library Web site visits<br>• Average by hour<br>• Average by day<br>• Average by month<br>Library Web site visits to<br>• Student FTE<br>• Faculty FTE<br>OPAC searches conducted<br>• Average by hour<br>• Average by day<br>• Average by month<br>• Search success rate by subject |
| **Facilities/<br>Space Use** | Library visits per<br>• Student FTE<br>• Faculty FTE |

| Categories | Metrics |
|---|---|
|  | • Communities served (combined)<br>• Average per hour open<br>Total library visits<br>• Equals total gate count + total virtual visits<br>• Percentage of virtual library visits to all library visits<br>Identification of busiest<br>• Hour of the day<br>• Day of the week<br>• Week of the month<br>• Month (academic term or year) |
| **Information/ Learning Commons** | Use of information/learning commons<br>• Average use<br>  + Hourly<br>  ⊦ Weekly<br>• Student FTE<br>  + Ratio of undergraduate vs. graduate |
| **Instruction Sessions and Presentations** | Number of students attending library instructional sessions to<br>• Student FTE<br>• Faculty FTE |
| **Interlibrary Loan/ Document Delivery** | Requests compared to the number of holdings in the specific subject area<br>ILL requests to<br>• Student FTE<br>• Faculty FTE<br>Fill rate (requests filled)<br>• As borrower<br>• As lender<br>Intercampus requests to intercampus requests<br>• Filled<br>• Unfilled |
| **Library Faculty (with or without faculty status)** | Cost (library research grants or other money given)<br>• Per article<br>• Conference paper<br>• Poster session<br>• Other<br>Staff training<br>• Formal training hours per staff<br>  + Technology training<br>Library employee turnover rate (number of staff divided by the number of staff who left, then multiplied by 100) |
| **Technology** | Printing<br>• Number of pages printed per FTE student |
| **Uptime** | Ratio of availability, in hours per year<br>• Access to the library's integrated library system<br>• Access to the library's Web-base subscription/leased databases via the library/institutional servers (as opposed to vendor servers) |

*Note: Many of the ratios involving student and faculty FTE could be combined into a ratio: ratio of $X$ to combined student and faculty FTE.

# Appendix E

## SELECTED EXAMPLES
## OF PROCESS METRICS

Process metrics are the transformation of inputs into outputs.

| Categories | Metrics |
|---|---|
| **Time (elapsed time, wait time, cycle time, response time)**[1] | In general<br>• Total time per identified activity<br>Information Resources<br>• Length of time for new resource order placement and receipt of resource<br>• Length of time a book is in the processing area after its arrival before it is shelved for user access<br>• Length of time to shelve a returned book<br>• Length of time it takes to retrieve a book from remote storage<br>Customer<br>• Average customer wait time (e.g., at reference and circulation desks; wait time for a reserve before filled)<br>• Number of rings before phone is answered<br>Reference<br>• Average time to answer a reference question<br>Interlibrary Loan<br>• Turnaround time (length of time) to fill an interlibrary loan request<br>• Turnaround time (length of time) to fill an intercampus loan request<br>Repairs<br>• Length of time it takes to execute a repair from filing a report to completion (e.g., replace a burned-out light bulb; fix a printer or photocopy machine)<br>Computer Time<br>• Number of seconds or computer cycles to transact a checkout in the circulation module<br>• Downtime (e.g., in minutes, hours) of the integrated library system<br>Decisions<br>• Average time (in hours or days) for decisions to be made |

| Categories | Metrics |
|---|---|
| **Cost or Cost Savings**[1] | In general<br>• Total cost per identified activity<br>Hours Open<br>• Average cost per hour open<br>Information Resources<br>• Cost to acquire and make available a book in print versus electronic format<br>• Cost of staff to circulate a book to a user<br>Reference<br>• Cost of staff to answer a reference question |
| **Quality (accuracy; error rate)**[1] | In general<br>• Accuracy of the activity undertaken<br>Information Resources<br>• Accuracy of book processing, such as correctly matching the applied item bar code to the item record<br>• Placement accuracy of items shelved<br>Reference<br>• Accuracy rate of providing the correct answer to a question |
| **Customer Satisfaction (complaints, suggestions, compliments)**[1] | In general<br>• Handling of customer feedback<br>Volume<br>• Number of complaints, suggestions, and compliments received and reviewed<br>• Percentage of complaints, suggestions, and compliments to number of customers |
| **Quantity (productivity, throughput, capacity)**[1] | Shelving<br>• Total of linear feet<br>• Amount of empty shelving in linear feet<br>Seating<br>• Total number of seats available for users<br>• Breakdown by type of seating available (e.g., at tables; lounge chairs)<br>Technology<br>• Number of possible simultaneous wireless network connections<br>• Wait time to use a computer<br>Overdues<br>• Number of overdue notices sent<br>• Number of items returned as a result of overdue notice<br>Staff<br>• Number of training hours<br>• Turnover rate<br>• Absentee rate |

# NOTE

1. Sara Laughlin and Ray W. Wilson, *The Quality Library: A Guide to Staff-Driven Improvement, Better Efficiency, and Happier Customers* (Chicago: American Library Association, 2008), 71, 127–31.

# Appendix F

## SELECTED EXAMPLES
## OF TREND METRICS

Trend lines compile data from past years. Trend data are most often used for internal analysis, gauging progress toward meeting internal benchmarks, and comparative purposes with other libraries. They are also used as an input into decision making. Data used should have identical definitions and applied consistent methods when gathering and compiling.

| Categories | Metrics |
|---|---|
| **Expenditures** | Total library expenditures<br>• Per student FTE<br>• Per faculty FTE<br>Percent of total library budget expended<br>• For all information resources (library materials) (one time and continuations)<br>• For all staff and student assistants (including fringe benefits)<br>• For all other operating expenditures<br>Library expenditures per student FTE<br>• For all information resources (library materials) (one time and continuations)<br>• For all staff and student assistants (including fringe benefits)<br>• For all other operating expenditures<br>Information resources (library materials) expended per student FTE<br>• Monographs and electronic books<br>• Serials<br>• Electronic databases |
| **Collections** | Ratio of print volumes held<br>• Per student FTE<br>• Per faculty FTE<br>Ratio of print volumes added each fiscal year<br>• Per student FTE<br>• Per faculty FTE |

| Categories | Metrics |
|---|---|
| | Ratio of current serials titles<br>• Per student FTE<br>• Per faculty FTE<br>Growth of collection resources<br>• Print volumes<br>• Electronic books (e-books)<br>• E-journals<br>• Print serials<br>• Videos |
| **Usage** | Circulation transactions<br>• By time periods (day, month, year)<br>• Per student FTE<br>• Per faculty FTE<br>• By borrowers status<br>  + Undergraduate student FTE<br>  + Graduate student FTE<br>  + Faculty FTE<br>Reserve transactions<br>• By time periods (day, month, year)<br>• Per student FTE<br>Audiovisual circulation transactions |
| **Facilities/Space Use** | Library visits<br>• Number of entrances into library (gate count)<br>Library hours open during a typical week<br>Public square feet in library space per<br>• Per student FTE<br>• Per faculty FTE<br>Per public library seat (1 chair for $X$ number of that population)<br>• Per student FTE<br>• Per faculty FTE |
| **Services** | Reference transactions<br>• Reference questions asked per student FTE<br>• Reference questions answered per student FTE<br>Interlibrary loans<br>• Borrowed<br>• Loaned |
| **Instruction Sessions and Presentations** | Library instruction sessions<br>• Number conducted<br>• Total number of students participating<br>• Average number of students per instruction session<br>Number of students attending library instructional sessions to<br>• Student FTE<br>Ratio of student FTE to library instruction workstations |
| **Library Staff (with or without faculty status)** | Library staff FTE (including student assistants) to<br>• Student FTE<br>• Per 1,000 students<br>• Faculty FTE<br>Student FTE to Professional (master's degree in librarianship or equivalent) staff FTE |

| Categories | Metrics |
|---|---|
| **Technology** | Ratio of student FTE to public workstations |
| **Other** | Growth of library endowments |
| **Satisfaction** | Satisfaction indexes<br>  • Customer<br>  • Staff<br>Complaints, comments, and compliments<br>  • Customer<br>  • Staff<br>Suggestions<br>  • Customer<br>  • Staff |

# Appendix G

## EXAMPLES OF QUALITATIVE METRICS

Qualitative metrics cannot be represented by a measurable quantity (e.g., an input or output metric), and, in a library environment, they are inherently dependent on an individual's interactions. The metrics therefore yield perceptions and opinions based on the individual's expectations and experiences.

Wording concerning a measure may well alter it from a quantifiable output to a qualitative metric. For example, "the percentage of reference questions answered correctly" is an output, it is measurable in that the answer can be right or wrong ("60% of questions answered were correct"). However, by altering the phrase to "the percentage of reference questions answered successfully" or "the percentage of reference questions answered satisfactorily," a perception (an opinion) surfaces in place of a number. What would be *successful* or *satisfactory* to one individual may be different for another individual with differing expectations and experiences. To be answered successfully, the questioner may have expected a photograph in addition to a paragraph. To another questioner, the paragraph may have sufficed, but it did not fully answer the question asked. The percentage of reference questions answered successfully or satisfactorily is a qualitative metric.

Other examples of qualitative measures:

- Impacts and outcomes. An outcome is a beneficial change from program participants that include changes in their skills, knowledge, behavior, attitudes, and status or life conditions. What is the impact/outcome of library services, resources and instruction
  - on an individual?
  - on the broader community?
- The study environment of the facility
  - Are appropriate seating and user space available for the varieties of ways students need to be able to work?
  - Is space appropriately allocated for use including group and instructional use, study, research, and use of information technologies?
  - Is technology adequate and up-to-date to meet user needs? Is there adequate access to the technology?

- Usefulness and quality of the collection
  - Are the size and depth of the collection adequate to support student and faculty course and program needs?
- Quantitative metrics can become qualitative when the definition of the metric and the manner for which the data are collected or generated is questionable
  - total number of logins (what is the definition of a login and how are the data gathered?)
  - total number of page hits (what is the definition of a hit and how are the data gathered?)

# Appendix H

## CUSTOMER PERSPECTIVE

**Internal Customers**

*Quantitative Metrics*

- Processing requests
  - Speed in doing so
  - Accuracy in doing so
    Promptness in response
- Employee Culture Index
  - Rating of
    + Job satisfaction
    + Recognition for job performance
    + Satisfaction with salary
    + Work environment
    + Communication with other employees in the organization
- Helpfulness
  - Was the issue or problem resolved or was valuable progress made in its resolution?
- Responsiveness
  - Was the request for assistance received and answered promptly?
- Respectfulness
  - Were sincere interest and cooperation shown?
- Technical competency[1]
  - Knowledge of subject matter (related to one's work)
  - Ability to perform the work assigned effectively
- Personal service provided[2]
  - Ability to carry out the work assigned
  - Commitment to providing high quality customer service

- SERVQUAL Dimensions[3]
  - Reliability
    + The skill to perform the promised service dependably and accurately
  - Responsiveness
    + The willingness to help customers and provide prompt service
  - Assurance
    + Knowledge and courtesy of employees and their ability to inspire trust and confidence
  - Empathy
    + Caring, individualized attention to customers
  - Tangibles
    + Physical facilities, equipment, and appearance of personnel

Since previous research has probed the perceptions of internal customers on the service-quality dimensions associated with SERVQUAL (SQ), similar dimensions for LibQUAL+™ (affect of service, library as place, and information control) or e-SQ,[4] or for that matter on other statements (e.g., "When I use the university's computer network, I can log on easily/quickly," "Employees who deal with users in a caring fashion," or "Employees who understand the needs of their users"). Such statements might form the basis for probing the perceptions of internal customers.

- Listening skills

Librarians might want to measure listening skills.[5]

*Qualitative Metrics*

Any of the above metrics could contain a qualitative aspect, namely, asking employees to comment on their ratings.

**External Customers**

*Quantitative Metrics*

  Input

Expenditure (value for tuition dollars)
  - Amount spent
    + Café (associated with library)
    + At vending machines (in library)

  Output

- Any of the statements selected from Table 5.1 could be converted into a metric, one that need not rely on indirect evidence—the use of a survey. For instance, if the staff develop a policy stating that no public workstation will be down longer than one hour, without it being reported and substitute equipment in place, they might test that policy by conducting a walk-through, noting any problems, and documenting time how long it takes for replacement equipment that works to be in place.
- Regarding Table 5.3, questions such as willingness to use the library or a service again are quantifiable as to whether they would recommend the library or a service to others and how many others have received a recommendation. For questions asking for a rating of

collections and services on a scale (e.g., 1 [poor] to 10 [excellent]), the staff might compile a mean score. The same applies to a question such as "Please indicate whether we fall short of, exactly meet, or exceed your expectations:"

| FALL SHORT OF EXPECTATIONS | | EXACTLY MEET EXPECTATIONS | | | EXCEED EXPECTATIONS | |
|---|---|---|---|---|---|---|
| -3 | -2 | -1 | 0 | +1 | +2 | +3 |

- Facilities used
  - Frequency of use of
    + Group study rooms
    + Academic support services available the physical space in the library (e.g., writing tutors and IT support)
    + Seating
    + Computers
- Fundraising
  - Use of the funds to support customer services
- Satisfaction
  - Expressed as willingness to return (use again)
    + Per visit
    + Some measurement over time
    + By service
    + Overall library use
  - Those expressing satisfaction in relation to the total number of respondents
    + Per visit
    + Some measurement over time
    + By service
    + Overall library use
    + Willingness to recommend service/library to another customer
  - Those expressing "very satisfied" in relation to the total number of respondents expressing any degree of satisfaction ("customer delight")
    + Per visit
    + Some measurement over time
    + By service
    + Overall library use
    + Willingness to recommend service/library to another customer
  - Viewed in terms of:
    + *Affordability* (reserves—purchase of textbooks and their placement on reserve, lending laptops, information/learning commons)
    + *Accessibility* (proxy server [input, however] and results gained [output])
    + *Availability* (no complaints beyond the library and satisfaction with service provided)
  - Receipt and resolution of complaints
    + Decline in the number
    + Those complaining once do not do so again

+ Those complaining become *delighted* customers

• Turning to service quality, because the library selects the statements to probe and those statements do not involve open-ended responses; quantitative metrics could emerge whenever customers select a number on a scale (1 to 5, 1 to 7, or 1 to 10).

*Qualitative Metrics*

Output

• Lost customers. By using nonprobability sampling (e.g., snowball sampling), student workers and perhaps others will be asked to identify anyone who comprises a lost customer (see Figure 5.1) and such individuals will be contacted to participate in a focus group interview. The final point covered in that interview will be a request for the names of other lost customers who might participate in a similar interview. The number of lost customers, as a metric, is general but indicative of the library's effort to expand those it serves. Questions asked in the focus group interview center around why they are lost and what the library can do to regain them. Several months later, the participants might be invited back and probed about any subsequent library use.

• Never-gained customers. Depending on the population, it is possible to conduct a census, poll the entire population, or use probability or nonprobability sampling to select a sample. Obviously, incoming freshmen comprise one population as do new faculty and students transferring to the institution.

• Some of the questions in Table 5.3 are open-ended and give customers an opportunity to express their thoughts and feelings. Two such questions are "What are we doing that you particularly like?" and "What are we doing that you particularly dislike?"

In summary, qualitative metrics add an important dimension and should not be ignored. Still, as with much social science research, any findings are suggestive rather than conclusive.

## NOTES

1. See G. Ronald Gilbert, "Measuring Internal Customer Satisfaction," *Managing Service Quality* 10, no. 3 (2000): 178–86. He notes that individuals rate themselves higher than do those for whom they are intended to serve.

2. Ibid.

3. For an overview see Steve Farner, Fred Luthans, and Steven M. Sommer, "An Empirical Assessment of Internal Customers," *Managing Service Quality* 11, no. 5 (2001): 350–58.

4. For an introduction to e-SQ see Peter Hernon and Philip Calvert, "E-service Quality in Libraries: Exploring Its Features and Dimensions," *Library & Information Science Research* 27, no. 3 (2005): 377–404.

5. See C. David Shepherd, Stephen B. Castleberry, and Rick E. Ridnour, "Linking Effective Listening with Salesperson Performance: An Exploratory Investigation," *Journal of Business & Industrial Marketing* 12, no. 5 (1997): 315–22; Shinya Kubota, Norio Mishima, and Shoji Nagata, "A Study of the Effects of Active Listening on Listening Attitudes of Middle Managers," *Journal of Occupational Health* 46 (2004): 60–67.

# Appendix I

# INSTITUTIONAL PERSPECTIVE

**Table I-1: Librarians Should Be Aware of These Institutional Metrics and Their Implications Concerning the Library**

| Categories | Metrics |
|---|---|
| **Institution** | In general<br>&bull; Academic reputation<br>&bull; Tuition and fees<br>&bull; Average net price to attend<br>&bull; Average number of students in a class<br>University expenditures<br>Endowments<br>&bull; Size of the endowment<br>Accreditation(s)<br>&bull; Specific accreditations held |
| **Admissions** | Admission process<br>&bull; Number of students formally applying<br>&bull; Acceptance rate for those formally applying<br>&bull; Number of students formally accepted enrolling (admissions yield rate)<br>Students transferring into institution<br>Enrolling student performance<br>&bull; Average on SAT/ACT<br>&bull; Average high school GPA<br>&bull; Number of National Merit Scholars<br>&bull; Number of students with advanced standing |
| **Student Demographics** | Student body<br>&bull; Total number of students enrolled<br>  + Student FTE<br>  + Headcount<br>  + Total credit hours<br>&bull; Diversity of the student body |

| Categories | Metrics |
|---|---|
|  | Enrollment<br>  • Number of students by college/program/department<br>    + Student FTE<br>    + Headcount<br>  • Number of students by major<br>    + Student FTE<br>    + Headcount<br>  • Number of students enrolled in courses<br>    + Number of students enrolled in distance education<br>      courses<br>Financial aid<br>  • Number of applications for financial aid submitted<br>  • Number of applications for financial aid approved<br>  • Average amount of financial aid award<br>  • Total amount of financial aid distributed |
| Academics | Faculty<br>  • Faculty academic credentials<br>  • Student to faculty ratio<br>  • Number of full-time faculty<br>    + By college/program/department<br>  • Number of part-time faculty<br>    + By college/program/department<br>  • Number of adjuncts<br>    + By college/program/department<br>  • Aggregate count of publications<br>  • Number of awards, prizes, or mentions in news reports<br>  • Grants<br>    + Number and amount of grants received by departments<br>Courses<br>  • Number of students enrolled in specific courses<br>    + Number of students enrolled in distance education<br>      courses<br>  • Number of senior projects, theses, and dissertations<br>    underway<br>Retention<br>  • Rate from fall to following spring semester<br>  • Rate from spring to following fall semester<br>  • Persistence from academic year to academic year<br>Graduation<br>  • Number of degrees awarded<br>  • Rate—persistence in years |
| Post Graduation | Post Graduate Testing<br>  • Student performance on graduate and professional school<br>    admissions tests<br>  • Student performance on licensure examinations<br>Career/Employment<br>  • Percentage of students with jobs after graduation in their<br>    chosen field<br>Continuing education<br>  • Enrolled in postgraduate programs<br>Debt<br>  • Average debt related to educational expenses incurred |

| Categories | Metrics |
|---|---|
| **Information from Applied Instruments** | Instruments used by the institution, and the findings. Examples of instruments include:<br>• CSEQ – College Student Experiences Questionnaire<br>• NSSE – National Survey of Student Engagement<br>• CAAP – Collegiate Assessment of Academic Proficiency<br>• MAPP – Measure of Academic Proficiency and Progress<br>• CLA – Collegiate Learning Assessment |

**Table I-2: Measures of, or from, the Library of Value to the Institution.**

| Categories | Metrics |
|---|---|
| **Accountability** | Reporting<br>• Evaluation and assessment measures<br>• Transparency in annual reporting<br>• Using tools such as the balanced scorecard or the report card<br>Library contribution to recruiting students<br>• Number of tours of the library<br>Library contribution to retaining students<br>• Measured student satisfaction with library resources and services including:<br>  + *Affordability* (e.g., reserves—number of textbooks acquired and placed on reserve, lending laptops, information/learning commons)<br>  + *Accessibility* (e.g., number of proxy server logins to use databases from off-campus)<br>  + *Availability* (e.g., no complaints beyond the library and satisfaction with service provided)<br>Library contribution to graduation rate<br>• Measured student satisfaction with library resources and services<br>• Measured student engagement concerning the library (National Student Engagement Survey [NSSE])<br>Accreditations<br>• Number held<br>• Focus on the library role in meeting accreditation standards |
| **Affordability** | Cost of operating the library<br>• Per hour, day, week, month<br>Value for tuition dollars (e.g., how library contributes to the question of affordability)<br>• Documented and estimated savings to students (e.g., number of items used from the reserve collection; number of pages printed at no or reduced cost)<br>Fundraising<br>• Amount of money raised<br>  + How much is used to support student needs<br>  + How much is used to support faculty classroom and research needs<br>Library consortia<br>• Number of memberships in library consortia for resource sharing (such as walk in interlibrary loan), etc.<br>• Number of shared resource licensing agreements for information content realizing an economy of scale which saves funds<br>Tools and instruments applied:<br>• Cost-benefit analysis<br>• Value in use<br>• Data Envelopment Analysis<br>• Factor analysis |

| Categories | Metrics |
|---|---|
| **Infrastructure** | Collections<br>• Size of the collection<br>  + By format<br>  + Net gain/loss last fiscal year by format |
| | • Number of unique holdings (e.g., special collections)<br>• the Conspectus strengths of the collections<br>• Collection age (based upon copyright dates) report<br>  + By subject<br>Staff<br>• Number of staff in FTE<br>  + Professional staff in FTE<br>  + Support staff in FTE<br>Technology<br>• Number of available computer workstations for users<br>• Number of instruction workstations for teaching<br>Facilities<br>• Square feet<br>• Number of user seats<br>• Types of learning spaces (e.g., group study rooms) |
| **Support to Faculty** | Teaching<br>• Percentage of course-required texts available in the library<br>  + In the general collection<br>  + In the reserve collection<br>• Number of course-based persistent URLs to library resources (e.g., articles, e-books, help guides) embedded in electronic syllabi<br>• Quality of information resources referenced by students in submitted papers and projects<br>Research<br>• Number of interlibrary loans filled<br>• Number of times library staff provided assistance to locate needed research resources<br>• Usage of library resources in research projects<br>  + Citations to resources in library collections<br>• Acknowledgment of library contribution to the final product (e.g., book or scholarly article)<br>Service<br>• Library fulfillment of requests from service committee members |
| **Academic Support Services** | Partnerships<br>• Campus relations/services (internal)<br>  + Number of library staff serving as members of committees<br>• Library organizations and consortia (external)<br>  + Productivity (e.g., shared cataloging)<br>  + Resource sharing |
| **Student Learning** | Library instruction/support<br>• Number of librarian-led program/discipline- or course-based instruction sessions |

| Categories | Metrics |
|---|---|
| | + Number of program/discipline- or course-based instruction sessions in which a librarian provides a supporting role to the faculty member<br>• Measured student learning outcomes from<br>  + Locally developed pre/post testing<br>  + Application of standardized testing (e.g., *iSkills*)<br>• Number of library created and maintained subject/topic guides to resources (help guides)<br>  + Number of subject/topic guides created by the library to support a specific course<br>• Number of students formally mentored by library staff<br>Partnering with faculty<br>• Number of student portfolios inclusive of library participation<br>This category cannot always be reduced to a metric unless there is a number (and percent) for rubric categories (e.g., "novice" and "proficient"); SAILS and ETS produce quantitative results on a pre-test and posttest basis |
| **Availability and Accessibility** | In general<br>• Hours open per week<br>• Off-campus availability of electronic resources<br>Continued library use<br>• Extent to which customers are repeat users |
| **Community Good Will** | In general<br>• Availability of the library collection to be used onsite by community members<br>  + Number of community members visiting the library<br>  + Number of community-accessible items within internal digital projects<br>• Number of programs offered that the community may attend<br>  + number of community members attending programs<br>• Availability of the online catalog to the general public for browsing<br>• Number of interlibrary loans filled for the general public<br>• Number of annual community organizational contacts concerning library services<br>Economic impact analysis<br>• Direct benefit (e.g., library salaries; purchase from local vendors)<br>• Indirect benefits (e.g., economic multipliers in the geopolitical area based upon the presence of library expenditures)<br>Alumni<br>• Number of uses of library resources and services by alumni |

# Appendix J

## STAKEHOLDER PERSPECTIVES (EXAMPLES)

**Table J-1: Stakeholders Directly/Indirectly Benefiting from the Library**

**Table J-1a: Library Infrastructure and Capacity**

| Parents and Students | Employers | Alumnae and Larger Community |
|---|---|---|
| General<br>• Hours open per week<br>• Off-campus availability of electronic resources<br>Collections<br>• Size of the collection<br>• the Conspectus strengths of the collections<br>Staff<br>• Number of staff in FTE<br>Technology<br>• Number of available computer workstations for users<br>Facilities<br>• Square feet<br>• Number of user seats<br>• Types of learning spaces (e.g., group study rooms) | | General<br>• Number of uses of library resources and services by alumni<br>• Hours open per week<br>• Off-campus availability of electronic resources<br>• Availability of the library collection to be used onsite by community members<br>  + Number of community members visiting the library<br>  + Number of community accessible items within internal digital projects<br>• Number of programs offered that the community may attend<br>  + Number of community members attending programs<br>• Availability of the online catalog to the general public for browsing<br>• Number of interlibrary loans filled for the general public<br>• Number of annual community organizational contacts concerning library services |

**Table J-1b: Library Contribution to Outcomes**

| Parents and Students | Employers | Alumnae and Larger Community |
|---|---|---|
| Library instruction/ support for learning<br>• Measured student learning outcomes from<br>  + Locally developed pre/post testing<br>  + Application of standardized testing (e.g., *iSkills*)<br>• Number of library created and maintained subject/topic guides to resources (help guides)<br>  + Number of subject/ topic guides created by the library to support a specific course<br>• Number of students formally mentored by library staff<br>This category cannot always be reduced to a metric unless there is a number (and percent) for rubric categories (e.g., "novice" and "proficient").<br><br>Ongoing education (post-graduation; lifelong learning)<br><br>Career placement via E-portfolio development<br>• Aiding in their production resulting in the use of the portfolio in applying for a job upon graduation or hiring of individuals based on the quality of the portfolio<br>• Skills, abilities, and values as demonstrated in the portfolio<br>• Number of student portfolios inclusive of library participation | Library instruction/ support for learning<br>• Measured student learning outcomes from<br>  + Locally developed pre/post testing<br>• Number of students formally mentored by library staff<br>This category cannot always be reduced to a metric unless there is a number (and percent) for rubric categories (e.g., "novice" and "proficient").<br><br>Ongoing education (postgraduation; lifelong learning)<br><br>Career placement via e-portfolio development<br>• Aiding in their production resulting in the use of the portfolio in applying for a job upon graduation or hiring of individuals based on the quality of the portfolio<br>• Skills, abilities, and values as demonstrated in the portfolio | Career placement<br><br>Accreditation<br>• Number held<br>• Type of accreditation<br><br>Ongoing education (post-graduation; lifelong learning)<br><br>Economic impact analysis<br>• Direct benefit (e.g., library salaries; purchase from local vendors)<br>• Indirect benefits (e.g., economic multipliers in the geopolitical area based on the presence of library expenditures) |

**Table J-1c: Library Contribution to Satisfaction**

| Parents and Students | Employers | Alumnae and Larger Community |
|---|---|---|
| Library contribution to student retention:<br>• Affordability: documented and estimated savings to students (examples)<br>  + Reserves<br>    − purchase of textbooks and their placement on reserve<br>    − number of items used from the reserve collection<br>  + Number of pages printed at no or reduced cost<br>  + Laptops loaned<br>  + Use of information/ learning commons<br>  + Number of memberships in library consortia for resource sharing (such as walk in interlibrary loan)<br>  + Number of shared resource licensing agreements for information content realizing an economy of scale which saves funds<br>• Accessibility (example)<br>  + Use of proxy server<br>• Availability (example)<br>  + No complaints beyond the library and satisfaction with service provided<br><br>Library contribution to graduation rate:<br>• Measured student satisfaction with library resources and services<br>• Measured student engagement concerning the library (National Student Engagement Survey [NSSE]) | | Library contribution to graduation rate:<br>• Measured student engagement concerning the library (National Student Engagement Survey [NSSE]) |

**Table J-2: Stakeholders with Oversight Interest in the Library**

|  | Government Officials and Agencies | Accrediting Organizations* |
|---|---|---|
| **Accountability** | Reporting <ul><li>Application of evaluation and assessment practices and measures</li></ul> | Reporting <ul><li>Reporting annually</li><li>Application of evaluation and assessment practices and measures</li></ul> |
| **Library Infrastructure and Capacity** |  | General <ul><li>Hours open per week</li><li>Off-campus availability of electronic resources</li></ul> Collections <ul><li>Size of the collection</li><li>the Conspectus strengths of the collections</li></ul> Staff <ul><li>Number of staff in FTE</li></ul> Technology <ul><li>Number of available computer workstations for users</li></ul> Facilities <ul><li>Square feet</li><li>Number of user seats</li><li>Types of learning spaces (e.g., group study rooms)</li></ul> |
| **Outcomes** | Accreditation <ul><li>Number held</li><li>Type of accreditation</li></ul> Library instruction/support for learning <ul><li>Measured student learning outcomes from<br>+ Locally developed pre/post testing<br>+ Application of standardized testing (e.g., *iSkills*)</li></ul> This category cannot always be reduced to a metric unless there is a number (and percent) for rubric categories (e.g., "novice" and "proficient"). Career placement via e-portfolio development <ul><li>Skills, abilities, and values as demonstrated in the portfolio</li><li>Number of student portfolios inclusive of library participation</li></ul> | Library instruction/support for learning <ul><li>Number of librarian-led program/discipline- or course-based instruction sessions<br>+ Number of program and discipline- or course-based instruction sessions in which a librarian provides a supporting role to the faculty member</li><li>Measured student learning outcomes from<br>+ Locally developed pre/post testing<br>+ Application of standardized testing (e.g., *iSkills*)</li><li>Number of library created and maintained subject/topic guides to resources (help guides)<br>+ Number of subject/topic guides created by the library to support a specific course</li></ul> |

|  | Government Officials and Agencies | Accrediting Organizations* |
|---|---|---|
|  | Ongoing education (postgraduation; lifelong learning)<br><br>Library contribution to graduation rate:<br>• Measured student engagement concerning the library (National Student Engagement Survey [NSSE]) | This category cannot always be reduced to a metric unless there is a number (and percent) for rubric categories (e.g., "novice" and "proficient").<br>E-portfolio development<br>• Skills, abilities, and values as demonstrated in the portfolio<br>• Number of student portfolios inclusive of library participation<br>Ongoing education (postgraduation; lifelong learning) |
| **Satisfaction** | Library contribution to student retention:<br>• Affordability: documented and estimated savings to students<br>  + Reserves<br>    – purchase of textbooks and their placement on reserve<br>  + Number of memberships in library consortia for resource sharing (such as walk in interlibrary loan)<br>  + Number of shared resource licensing agreements for information content realizing an economy of scale, which saves funds | Library contribution to student retention:<br>• Affordability: documented and estimated savings to students (examples)<br>  + Reserves<br>    – purchase of textbooks and their placement on reserve<br>    – number of items used from the reserve collection<br>  + Number of pages printed at no or reduced cost<br>  + Laptops loaned<br>  + Use of information/ learning commons<br>  + Number of memberships in library consortia for resource sharing (such as walk in interlibrary loan)<br>  + Number of shared resource licensing agreements for information content realizing an economy of scale, which saves funds<br>• Accessibility (example)<br>  + Use of proxy server<br>• Availability (example)<br>  + No complaints beyond the library and satisfaction with service provided |

|  | Government Officials and Agencies | Accrediting Organizations* |
|---|---|---|
|  |  | Library contribution to graduation rate:<br>• Measured student satisfaction with library resources and services<br>• Measured student engagement concerning the library (National Student Engagement Survey [NSSE]) |
| Academic Support and Partnerships |  | Partnering with faculty: e-portfolio development<br>• Aiding in their production resulting in the use of the portfolio in applying for a job upon graduation or hiring of individuals based on the quality of the portfolio<br>Campus relations/services (internal)<br>• Number of library staff serving as members of committees<br>Library organizations and consortia (external)<br>• Productivity (e.g., shared cataloging)<br>• Resource sharing |

*The list of relevant metrics varies according to the standards set by the accreditation organization.

# Appendix K

## SELECTED METRICS USED BY LIBRARIES FOR BENCHMARKING AND BEST PRACTICES

For the inputs listed in the table, an output could be constructed. That output would examine the input in terms of cost-benefit or cost-effectiveness.

| Categories | Metric |
|---|---|
| **Expenditures: General** | Total library expenditures<br>  • Per student FTE<br>  • Per faculty FTE<br>Percent of total library budget expended<br>  • For all information resources (library materials) (one time and continuations)<br>  • For all staff and student assistants (including fringe benefits)<br>  • For all other operating expenditures<br>Percent of total library budget expended from all sources (e.g., tuition, research grants, special projects, gifts and endowments, fees and fines)<br>  • From student contributions only (e.g., tuition) |
| **Expenditures: Collections** | Information resources (library materials)<br>  • Per student FTE<br>  • Per faculty FTE<br>  • Percent expended on electronic resources<br>Selected information resources (library materials) expended as a percentage on<br>  • Books<br>    + Electronic books (e-books)<br>  • Subscriptions<br>    + To print and electronic versions of scholarly journals<br>    + To print and electronic periodicals (not scholarly)<br>  • Audiovisual materials<br>  • Microforms |
| **Expenditures: Staff** | Salaries and wages<br>  • Per student FTE<br>  • Per faculty FTE |

| Categories | Metric |
|---|---|
| | Salaries and wages<br>  &bull; Professional (master's degree in librarianship or equivalent)<br>  &bull; Other professional (required education in related fields)<br>  &bull; Support staff (technical and clerical)<br>  &bull; Student assistants<br>Minimum beginning professional salary<br>Staff development<br>Continuing education<br>Workshops<br>Training |
| **Collections** | Book volumes held<br>  &bull; Per student FTE<br>  &bull; Per faculty FTE<br>Book volumes added<br>  &bull; Per student FTE<br>  &bull; Per faculty FTE<br>Current serial titles<br>  &bull; Paper<br>  &bull; Electronic<br>Percentage of information resources (library materials) by type<br>  &bull; Print books<br>  &bull; Electronic books (e-books)<br>  &bull; Print serials<br>  &bull; Electronic serials<br>  &bull; Microforms<br>  &bull; Audiovisual<br>  &bull; Streaming content |
| **Collections Use** | Circulation transactions<br>  &bull; Per student FTE<br>  &bull; Per faculty FTE<br>Reserve transactions<br>  &bull; Paper<br>  &bull; Electronic |
| **Communities Served** | Enrollment FTE<br>  &bull; Undergraduates<br>  &bull; Graduate<br>  &bull; Combined<br>Faculty FTE |
| **Facilities/ Space Use** | Library visits (gate count)<br>Number of hours open per week<br>Ratio of<br>  &bull; Usable square feet library space to student FTE<br>  &bull; Usable square feet library space to faculty FTE<br>  &bull; Library seating to student FTE<br>  &bull; Library seating to faculty FTE<br>Archival and manuscripts<br>  &bull; Number of linear feet of shelving |
| **Services** | Reference<br>  &bull; Number of questions asked<br>  &bull; Number of questions answered |

| Categories | Metric |
|---|---|
|  | • Ratio of reference questions asked in a typical week to student FTE<br>Instruction programs<br>• Ratio of number of students attending instruction programs to students FTE<br>Library-created finding aids<br>• Research<br>• Special collections |
| **Interlibrary Loan/Document Delivery** | Total<br>• Interlibrary loans borrowed (received)<br>• Interlibrary loan lent (provided)<br>Ratio of interlibrary loan<br>• Requests to borrow by student FTE<br>• Requests to borrow by faculty FTE<br>• Lending to borrowing<br>Interlibrary loan borrowing<br>• Turnaround time<br>• Fill rate<br>• Unit cost<br>Interlibrary loan lending<br>• Turnaround time<br>• Fill rate<br>• Unit cost |
| **Library Staff (with or without faculty status)** | Expressed in terms of FTE<br>• Total staff<br>• Professional (master's degree in librarianship or equivalent)<br>• Other professional (required education in related fields)<br>• Support staff (technical and clerical)<br>• Student assistants<br>Library FTE<br>• Ratio of FTE library staff to student FTE<br>• Ratio of FTE library staff to faculty FTE<br>• Professional librarian FTE as a percentage of library FTE<br>• Other professional as a percentage of library FTE<br>• Support staff FTE as a percentage of library FTE<br>• Student assistants FTE as a percentage of library FTE<br>Library staff FTE per organizational function<br>• Public services<br>• Collection development and management<br>• Information processing (cataloging and other technical services)<br>• Information technology and digital development<br>• Administration<br>Total library staff FTE per 1,000 enrolled students FTE<br>Librarian and other professionals FTE per 1,000 enrolled students FTE |
| **Technology** | Number of workstations maintained by the library<br>• For use by library users<br>• For use by library staff<br>• For use in library instruction<br>Ratio of<br>• Public computer workstations to student FTE |

| Categories | Metric |
|---|---|
| | Number of hours spent related to interruption of access to subscription databases<br>  • Identification for reason for interruption<br>    + Database provider<br>    + Change of URL<br>    + Institutional network malfunctions<br>    + External to the institutional network malfunctions<br>Percentage of uptime of<br>  • Integrated library system<br>  • Library's home page |

# Appendix L

## MARKETING AND PUBLIC RELATIONS

| Categories | Metrics |
|---|---|
| **Evaluate the Effectiveness and Impact of Marketing Activities to Gain Customers and the Use of Libraries** | In general<br>• Selected indicators, such as salary expenditure as a percentage of total expenditure<br>• Selected use metrics (building use and number of reference transactions)<br>• Customer satisfaction survey<br>• Client feedback from suggestion boxes<br>Services<br>• Adequacy of support for library users<br>  + Information desk surveys<br>• Ease of access and use of electronic library services<br>  + Web usability survey<br>  + Transaction log analysis<br>• Impact on user<br>  + Information literacy evaluation<br>Information resources<br>• Collection adequacy, shelving adequacy, catalog error rate, and library skills of user<br>  + Materials availability survey<br>  + Transaction log analysis<br>• Turnaround time and fill rate<br>  + Intercampus loans and document delivery<br>  + Reshelving survey<br>  + New book order placement and receipt<br>• Electronic database usage statistics<br>  + Transaction log analysis<br>Facilities<br>• Adequacy of library space<br>  + Study seating usage survey<br>  + Computer workstation usage |

| Categories | Metrics |
|---|---|
| | • Adequacy of access to the building<br>  + Opening hours survey<br>Efficiency<br>• Monograph and serial processing<br>  + Unit cost<br>• Turnaround time<br>  + Intercampus loans and document delivery<br>  + Reshelving survey<br>  + New book order placement and receipt[1] |
| **Promote the Library (gain customers)** | Target customers to use library resources and services<br>Outreach activities<br>• Electronic newsletters |
| **Gather Information to Help Understand Customers** | Customer segmentation<br>• Customer characteristics<br>  + Age<br>  + Location<br>  + Frequency of use<br>  + Day and/or time of use<br>  + Ability or willingness to pay<br>  + Job function or status<br>  + Subject interest<br>  + Desired information delivery mechanism<br>  + Specific needs and problems<br>  + Factors critical to the customer's success[2]<br>• Customer satisfaction with services<br>  + Satisfaction surveys<br>• Customer expectations (service quality)<br>  + Surveys<br>• Customer use habits and behaviors<br>  + Percentage of registered library users within a community<br>  + Number of document loans<br>  + Documents use rate<br>  + Percent of titles requested in the collection<br>  + Average search time for direct access documents<br>  + Search success by catalogue subject<br>  + Transaction log analysis[3] |

# NOTES

1. Helen King, "Evaluating Library Services—Best Practice Initiatives in Australian University Libraries," in *Management, Marketing, and Promotion of Library Services Based on Statistics, Analyses, and Evaluation*, edited by Trine Kolderup Flaten (IFLA Publication 120/121) (Munich: Germany: K. G. Saur, 2006), 297–98.

2. Keith Hart, Putting Marketing Ideas into Action (London: Library Association Publishing, 1999), 26.

3. Ksibi Ahmed, "Statistical Indicators on Reading and Literacy for the 'Information Society' versus ITU's 'Technicist' Indices," in *Management, Marketing, and Promotion of Library Services Based on Statistics, Analyses, and Evaluation*, edited by Trine Kolderup Flaten (IFLA Publication 120/121) (Munich: Germany: K. G. Saur, 2006), 349.

# Appendix M

## SELECTED METRICS FROM LIBRARY REPORTS[1]

| Categories | Metrics |
|---|---|
| **Expenditures: General** | Total library expenditures<br>• FTE student<br>  + Per full-time student FTE<br>  + Per full-time graduate student FTE<br>  + To faculty FTE<br>• FTE faculty<br>Total information resources (library materials)<br>• As a percentage of total library expenditures<br>• FTE student<br>• FTE faculty<br>Total library staff salaries and wages expenditures<br>• As a percentage of total library expenditures<br>• FTE student<br>• FTE faculty<br>Total other operating expenditures<br>• As a percentage of total library expenditures<br>• FTE student<br>• FTE faculty |
| **Expenditures: Collection** | Monographs<br>• As a percentage of total information resources (library materials)<br>Current serials<br>• As a percentage of total information resources (library materials)<br>• Print<br>• Electronic<br>• Microform<br>Microform units<br>Government documents / publications<br>Computer files |

| Categories | Metrics |
|---|---|
| | Electronic resources<br>• One-time electronic resource purchases (e.g., e-books)<br>• Ongoing electronic resource purchases<br>• As a percentage of total information resources (library materials)<br>Archives and manuscripts<br>Cartographic materials<br>Graphic materials<br>Audio materials<br>Film and video<br>Digital collection (locally created)<br>• Cost of personnel<br>• Equipment, software, and/or contract services<br>Other library materials<br>Miscellaneous materials<br>Commercial delivery of documents |
| **Expenditures: Long-Term Changes in Collections** | For the above total library expenditures and total library materials, provide the percent change on vertical axis and years on horizontal axis (span of about 10–12 years) and then chart<br>• Serial unit costs (per title)<br>• Serial expenditures<br>• Monograph unit cost<br>• Monograph expenditures<br>• Percent change in number of serial subscriptions<br>• Percent change in number of monograph purchase<br>• Total salaries<br>• Other operating expenses |
| **Expenditures: Staffing** | Salaries and wages<br>• Total staff<br>• Professional (master's degree in librarianship or equivalent) staff<br>• Other professional (required education in related fields) staff<br>• Support staff (technical and clerical) staff<br>• Student assistants<br>Minimum beginning professional salary |
| **Expenditures: Other Operating** | Contract binding<br>Preservation<br>Bibliographic utilities/networks/consortia<br>• Library<br>• External<br>Computer hardware and software<br>Document delivery and interlibrary loan |
| **Collections** | Number of<br>• Total volumes held<br>  + Electronic books (e.g., e-reference)<br>  + Per student FTE<br>  + Per faculty FTE<br>  + Per combined student and faculty FTE<br>• Volumes added last fiscal year (gross)<br>  + Per student FTE<br>  + Per faculty FTE<br>  + Per combined student and faculty FTE |

| Categories | Metrics |
|---|---|
|  | • Volumes added last fiscal year (net)<br>  + Per student FTE<br>  + Per faculty FTE<br>  + Per combined student and faculty FTE<br>• Monographs purchased (volumes)<br>  + Electronic titles (e-books)<br>• Current serials purchased<br>  + Print<br>  + Electronic<br>• Current serials not purchased<br>  + Print<br>  + Electronic<br>• Total current serials received<br>• Serials patrons have access to<br>• Serial titles (replaces serial subscriptions)<br>  + Print<br>  + Electronic<br>  + Microform<br>• Electronic databases<br>  + Number of databases<br>  + Number of log-ins<br>  + Number of searches<br>  + Number of full-text article requests<br>• Digital collection (locally created)<br>  + Number of items<br>  + Number of times accessed<br>  + Number of queries<br>• Microform units<br>• Government publications<br>• Computer files<br>• Archives and manuscripts<br>  + Linear feet<br>• Cartographic materials<br>• Graphic materials<br>• Audio materials<br>• Film and video<br>• Bibliographic records in catalog |
| **Communities Served** | Student FTE<br>• Undergraduates<br>  + Full time<br>  + Part time<br>• Graduate<br>  + Full time<br>  + Part time<br>• Combined<br>Faculty FTE<br>• Full time<br>• Part time<br>• Combined<br>Ph.D.'s<br>• Awarded<br>• Number of Ph.D. fields |

| Categories | Metrics |
|---|---|
| **Facilities (physical)** | Number of<br>• Linear feet of shelving<br>• Total discrete user seats (do not overlap)<br>  + At equipment<br>  + At nonequipment<br>  + At tables (nonequipment)<br>  + At individual carrels<br>  + In group study rooms<br>  + In reading rooms |
| **Library Staff (with or without faculty status)** | Total staff FTE (including student assistants)<br>• Professional (master's degree in librarianship or equivalent) FTE<br>  + As a percentage of total staff FTE<br>• Other professional (required education in related fields) FTE<br>  + As a percentage of total staff FTE<br>• Support staff (technical and clerical) FTE<br>  + As a percentage of total staff FTE<br>• Student assistants FTE<br>Ratio of professional staff to support staff (exclude student assistants)<br>Total library staff FTE (including student assistants)<br>• Per student FTE<br>• Per faculty FTE<br>• Per combined<br>Total library staff per 1,000 student FTE<br>Librarians and other professional staff per 1,000 student FTE |
| **Services** | Number of<br>• Library visitors<br>• Web site visits<br>• Hours open per week<br>  + Public service hours in average week<br>• Number of staffed service points<br>• Reference transactions<br>  + In a typical week<br>  + Asked (annual)<br>    − per student FTE<br>    − per faculty FTE<br>  + Answered (annual)<br>    − per student FTE<br>    − per faculty FTE<br>  + Virtual reference transactions<br>• Library-conducted instruction sessions<br>  + Number of students attending<br>• Library presentations to groups (noninstruction)<br>  + Participants in groups presentations<br>• Circulation transactions<br>  + Initial<br>  + Student FTE<br>  + Faculty FTE<br>  + Other<br>• Reserve transactions<br>  + Paper<br>  + Electronic |

| Categories | Metrics |
|------------|---------|
|            | + Laptops loaned<br>+ Student FTE<br>• Interlibrary loans<br>  + Loaned (materials provided)<br>    – per student FTE<br>    – per faculty FTE<br>  + Borrowed (materials received)<br>    – per student FTE<br>    – per faculty FTE<br>  + Ratio of items loaned to items borrowed<br>• Online catalog<br>  + Number of visits<br>• Library Web site<br>  + Number of visits |
| **Technology** | Workstations for users<br>Printers for users |

## NOTE

1. Sources used to compile this appendix include: American Library Association, Association of College and Research Libraries, *2007 Statistical Summaries,* available at http://www.ala.org/ala/mgrps/divs/acrl/publications/trends/2007/index.cfm (accessed January 21, 2009); Association of Research Libraries, *ARL Statistics 2006–07,* available at http://www.arl.org/bm--doc/arlstat07.pdf (accessed January 21, 2009); National Center for Education Statistics, "Library Statistics Program: Compare Academic Libraries. Choose Comparison Group by Variable," available at http://nces.ed.gov/surveys/libraries/compare/index.asp?LibraryType=Academic (accessed on January 21, 2009).

# Appendix N

## SOME METRICS RELATED TO SCHOLARLY COMMUNICATIONS

*Scholarly communications* is a broad term that refers to how faculty (and presumably other specialists) seek, value, use, and exchange scholarly and research literatures. It also encompasses how they interact—communicate—with each another (their peer networks) and the process they use to share the results of their research. Complicating matters, scholarly communications includes ways to expand access to scholarly literatures, the changing landscape of the publishing industry (including libraries and universities as publishers), the usage of journals and one's work, the economics of publishing, and journal impact and prestige, and the preservation of research and scholarship for future use. It also addresses the engagement of faculty and others in generating new knowledge and the recognition of their work—individually and collectively. A facet of this last component is a productivity index, which is a composite of the extent to which one creates publications (however the output is defined). Produced on a regular basis, that index measures per capita scholarly accomplishment and might be used to compare productivity across institutions or departments. The index might also cover teaching loads, class enrollment, course levels (e.g., undergraduate or graduate), and so forth.

### Some Terms

| | |
|---|---|
| Impact factor | Ratio between citations and recent citable items published. It is calculated by dividing the number of current year citations to the source items published in that journal during the previous two years. |
| Eigenfactor | "The Eigenfactor™ score of a journal is an estimate of the percentage of time that library users spend with that journal." See Eigenfactor. org, http://www.eigenfactor.org/methods.htm. |
| H-factor | Also known as the H-index, it reflects research productivity. More precisely, it quantifies an individual's productivity and impact. The index is based on the set of the scholar's most cited papers and the number of citations that they have received in the publications of other. |
| Use | Vendors such as Thomson Reuters™ report usage data through the *Journal Citation Reports*.* This database draws on institutional COUNTER-compliant journal usage reports from publishers and vendors. |

* The *Journal Citation Reports* includes features such as a five-year impact factor and journal self-citations (an analysis of journal self-citations).

## Selected Sources

Adkins, Denise, and John Budd, "Scholarly Productivity of U.S. LIS Faculty," *Library & Information Science Research* 28, no. 3 (2006): 374–89.

American Library Association, Association of College and Research Libraries, "Scholarly Communication Toolkit" [Web site]. Available at http://www.acrl.ala.org/scholcomm/accessed (January 29, 2009).

Association of Research Libraries, "Scholarly Communication" [Web site]. Available at http://www.arl.org/sc/index.shtml (accessed January 29, 2009).

Bergstrom, Ted, and Preston McAfee. Journal Cost-effectiveness 2006-8 BETA. Available at http://www.hss.caltech.edu/~mcafee/Journal/ (accessed January 27, 2009).

Bolton, Johan, Marko A. Rodriguez, and Herbert Van de Sompel, "MESUR: Usage-based Metrics of Scholarly Impact." Available at http://mesur.lanl.gov/JCDL07poster_bollen.pdf (accessed January 28, 2009).

Henry, Geneva, "On-line Publishing in the 21st Century: Challenges and Opportunities," *D-Lib Magazine* 9, no. 10 (October 2003). Available at http://www.dlib.org/dlib/october03/henry/10henry.html (accessed January 28, 2009).

Los Alamos National Laboratory, Research Library, The MESUR Project. Available at http://www.mesur.org/schemas/2007-01/mesur/ (accessed January 27, 2009).

Middaugh, Michael F., *Understanding Faculty Productivity: Standards and Benchmarks for Colleges and Universities* (San Francisco: Jossey-Bass, 2001).

## Scholarly Communications

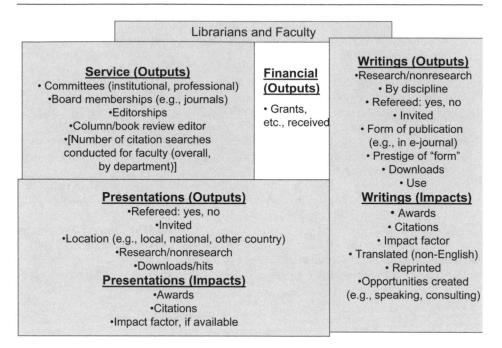

Librarians and Faculty

**Service (Outputs)**
• Committees (institutional, professional)
•Board memberships (e.g., journals)
•Editorships
•Column/book review editor
•[Number of citation searches
conducted for faculty (overall,
by department)]

**Financial (Outputs)**
• Grants,
etc., received

**Writings (Outputs)**
•Research/nonresearch
• By discipline
• Refereed: yes, no
• Invited
• Form of publication
(e.g., in e-journal)
• Prestige of "form"
• Downloads
• Use

**Writings (Impacts)**
• Awards
• Citations
• Impact factor
• Translated (non-English)
• Reprinted
•Opportunities created
(e.g., speaking, consulting)

**Presentations (Outputs)**
•Refereed: yes, no
•Invited
•Location (e.g., local, national, other country)
•Research/nonresearch
•Downloads/hits

**Presentations (Impacts)**
•Awards
•Citations
•Impact factor, if available

# Appendix O

## COUNTER (COUNTING ONLINE USAGE OF NETWORKED ELECTRONIC RESOURCES) CODE OF PRACTICE, RELEASE 3 (AUGUST 2008)[1]

## REQUIRED USAGE REPORTS FROM PUBLISHERS AND INTERMEDIARIES TO BE COUNTER COMPLIANT

| Usage Reports | Usage Data Reported |
|---|---|
| **Journal Report 1** | Number of successful full-text article requests by month and journal<br>• full journal name<br>• publisher<br>• platform<br>• print ISSN<br>• online ISSN |
| **Journal Report 1a (if applicable to the publisher or intermediary)** | Number of successful full-text article requests from an archive by month and journal<br>• full journal name<br>• publisher<br>• platform<br>• print ISSN<br>• online ISSN |
| **Journal Report 2** | Turnaways by month and journal<br>• full journal name<br>• publisher<br>• platform<br>• print ISSN<br>• online ISSN |
| **Journal Report 5** | Number of successful full-text article requests by year and journal<br>• full journal name<br>• publisher<br>• platform<br>• print ISSN<br>• online ISSN |
| **Database Report 1** | Total searches and sessions by month and journal<br>• database name<br>• publisher |

| | |
|---|---|
| | • platform<br>• total searches run<br>• searches-federated and automated<br>• total sessions<br>• sessions-federated and automated |
| **Database Report 2** | Turnaways by month and journal<br>• database name<br>• publisher<br>• platform<br>• database turnaways |
| **Database Report 3** | Total searches and sessions by month and journal<br>• name of the service<br>• platform<br>• total searches run<br>• searches-federated and automated<br>• total sessions<br>• sessions-federated and automated |
| **Consortium Report 1** | Number of successful full-text journal article or book chapter requests by month<br>• institution<br>• item name (can be a book or journal)<br>• print or online ISSN or ISBN<br>• publisher<br>• platform<br>• request and metric type<br>  + full-text HTML<br>  + full-text PDF |
| **Consortium Report 2** | Total searches by month and database<br>• institution<br>• database name<br>• publisher<br>• platform<br>• total searches run<br>• searches-federated and automated<br>• total sessions<br>• sessions-federated and automated |

# NOTE

1. COUNTER (Counting Online Usage of Networked Electronic Resources), COUNTER Codes of Practice, "The COUNTER Code of Practice, Journals and Databases, Release 3." August 2008. Available at http://www.projectcounter.org/r3/Release3D9.pdf (accessed on January 28, 2009).

# BIBLIOGRAPHY

## ARTICLES

Adkins, Denise, and John Budd. "Scholarly Productivity of U.S. LIS Faculty," *Library & Information Science Research* 28, no. 3 (2006): 374–89.

Al-Turki, Umar, and Salih Duffuaa. "Performance Measures for Academic Departments," *International Journal of Educational Management* 17, no. 7 (2003): 330–38.

Attewell, Paul, and David E. Lavin. "Point of View: Distorted Statistics on Graduation Rates," *The Chronicle of Higher Education* LIII, no. 44 (July 6, 2007): B16.

Basken, Paul. "Boeing to Rank Colleges by Measuring Graduates' Job Success," *The Chronicle of Higher Education* LV, no. 4 (September 19, 2008): A1, A16.

Bennett, Douglas C. "Assessing Quality in Higher Education," *Liberal Education* 87, no. 2 (2001): 40–45.

Bertot, John Carlo. "Libraries and Networked Information Services: Issues and Consideration in Measurement," *Performance Measurement and Metrics* 5, no. 1 (2004): 11–19.

Bertot, John Carlo, and Charles R. McClure. "Outcomes Assessment in the Networked Environment: Research Questions, Issues, Considerations, and Moving Forward," *Library Trends* 51, no. 4 (Spring 2003): 590–625.

Bertot, John Carlo, Charles R. McClure, Denise M. Davis, and Joe Ryan. "Capture Usage with E-Metrics," *Library Journal* 129, no. 8 (May 1, 2004): 30–32.

Birdsall, Douglas G. "The Micropolitics of Budgeting in Universities: Lessons for Library Administrators," *The Journal of Academic Librarianship* 21, no. 6 (November 1995): 427–37.

Blecic, Deborah D., Joan B. Fiscella, and Stephen E. Wiberley, Jr. "Measurement of Use of Electronic Resources: Advances in Use of Statistics and Innovations in Resource Functionality," *College & Research Libraries* 68, no.1 (January 2007): 26–44.

Booth, Andrew. "Counting What Counts: Performance Measurement and Evidence-based Practice," *Performance Measurement and Metrics* 7, no. 2 (2006): 63–74.

Bower, Tim, and Bradford Dennis. "How to Get More from Your Quantitative LibQUAL+™ Dataset: Making Results Practical," *Performance Measurement and Metrics* 8, no. 2 (2007): 110–26.

Breidenbaugh, Andrew. "Budget Planning and Performance Measures for Virtual Reference Services," *The Reference Librarian* 46, no. 95 (2006): 113–24.

Breneman, David. "Elite Colleges Must Stop Spurning Critiques of Higher Education," *The Chronicle of Higher Education* (February 15, 2008): A40.

Brophy, Peter. "Telling the Story: Qualitative Approaches to Measuring the Performance of Emerging Library Services," *Performance Measurement and Metrics* 9, no. 1 (2008): 7–17.

Burell, Jennifer. "Performance Measures: Some New South Wales Experience," *APLIS* 3, no. 2 (June 1990): 81–91.

Cabrera, Alberto F., Amaury Nora, and Maria B. Castaneda. "College Persistence: Structural Equations Modeling Test of an Integrated Model of Student Retention," *Journal of Higher Education* 64, no. 2 (March–April 1993): 123–39.

Callan, Patrick, and John Immerwahr. "What Colleges Must Do to Keep the Public's Good Will," *The Chronicle of Higher Education* LIV, no. 18 (January 11, 2008): A 56.

Calvert, Philip, and Rowena Cullen. "Further Dimensions of Public Library Effectiveness II: The Second Stage of the New Zealand Study," *Library & Information Science Research* 16 (Spring 1994): 87–104.

Calvert, Philip, and Rowena Cullen. "The New Zealand Public Libraries Effectiveness Study and the New Zealand University Libraries Effectiveness Study," *Australian Academic & Research Libraries* 26 (June 1995): 97–106.

Calvert, Philip, and Rowena Cullen. "Performance Measurement in New Zealand Public Libraries: A Research Project," *APLIS* 5, no. 1 (March 1992): 3–13.

Campbell, Jerry D. "Changing a Cultural Icon: The Academic Library as a Virtual Destination," *EDUCAUSE Review* 41, no. 1 (January/February 2006): 16–31.

Carey, Kevin. "'Measuring up': The Right Report at the Right Time," *The Chronicle of Higher Education* (December 5, 2008): A88.

Conyers, Angela. "Building on Sand? Using Statistical Measures to Assess the Impact of Electronic Services," *Performance Measurement and Metrics* 7, no. 1 (2006): 37–44.

Cullen, Rowena, and Philip Calvert. "New Zealand University Libraries Effectiveness Project: Dimensions and Concepts of Organizational Effectiveness," *Library & Information Science Research* 18 (Spring 1996): 99–119.

Dole, Wanda V., Anne Liebst, and Jitka M. Hurych. "Using Performance Measurement for Decision Making in Mid-sized Academic Libraries," *Performance Measurement and Metrics* 7, no. 3 (2006): 173–84.

Dugan, Robert E., and Peter Hernon. "Outcomes Assessment: Not Synonymous with Inputs and Outputs," *Journal of Academic Librarianship* 28, no. 6 (November 2002): 376–80.

Dyer, Esther, and Daniel O'Connor. "The Library Quotient: Evaluating School Media Centres," *Information and Library Manager* 2, no. 3 (December 1982): 82–88.

Ellis-Newman, Jennifer. "Activity-based Costing in User Services of an Academic Library," *Library Trends* 51, no. 3 (Winter 2003): 333–48.

Farner, Steve, Fred Luthans, and Steven M. Sommer. "An Empirical Assessment of Internal Customers," *Managing Service Quality* 11, no. 5 (2001): 350–58.

Field, Kelly. "Congress's Cost Cure May Have Side Effects," *The Chronicle of Higher Education* (February 8, 2008): A1, A15–16.

Gilbert, G. Ronald "Measuring Internal Customer Satisfaction," *Managing Service Quality* 10, no. 3 (2000): 178–86.

Given, Lisa M., and Gloria J. Leckie. "Sweeping the Library: Mapping the Social Activity Space of the Public Library," *Library & Information Science Research* 25 (2003): 365–85.

Goodall, Deborah L. "Performance Measurement: A Historical Perspective," *Journal of Librarianship* 20, no. 2 (April 1988): 128–44.

Hahn, Karla, and Lila Faulkner. "Evaluative Usage-Based Metrics for the Selection of E–Journals," *College & Research Libraries* 63, no. 3 (May 2002): 215–27.

Hall, Joseph M., and M. Eric Johnson. "When Should a Process Be Art, Not Science?" *Harvard Business Review* 87, no. 3 (March 2009), 58–65.

Hallmark, Elizabeth Kennedy, Laura Schwartz, and Loriene Roy. "Developing a Long-range and Outreach Plan for Your Academic Library: The Need for a Marketing Outreach Plan," *College & Research Libraries News* 68, no. 2 (February 2007): 92–95.

Harer, John B., and Bryan R. Cole. "The Importance of the Stakeholder in Performance Measurement: Critical Processes and Performance Measures for Assessing and Improving Academic Library Services and Programs," *College & Research Libraries* 66, no. 2 (March 2005): 149–70.

Hennen, Thomas J., Jr. "Hennen's American Public Library Ratings 2008," *American Libraries* 39, no. 9 (October 2008): 56–61.

Hennen, Thomas J., Jr. "Public Library Ratings Corrected," *American Libraries* 39, no. 10 (November 2008): 54–55.

Hernon, Peter, and Philip Calvert. "E-service Quality in Libraries: Exploring Its Features and Dimensions," *Library & Information Science Research* 27, no. 3 (2005): 377–404.

Hernon, Peter, and Danuta A. Nitecki. "Service Quality: A Concept Not Fully Explored," *Library Trends* 49, no. 4 (Spring 2001): 687–708.

Hiller, Steve. "Measure by Measure: Assessing the Viability of the Physical Library," *The Bottom Line* 17, no. 4 (2004): 126–31.

Hiller, Steve, Martha Kyrillidou, and Jim Self. "When the Evidence Is Not Enough: Organizational Factors That Influence Effective and Successful Library Assessment," *Performance Measurement and Metrics* 9, no. 3 (2008): 223–30.

Hitchingham, Eileen E., and Donald Kenney. "Extracting Meaningful Measures of User Satisfaction from LibQUAL+™ for the University Libraries at Virginia Tech," *Performance Measurement and Metrics* 3, no. 2 (2002): 48–58.

Jackson, Norman. "Benchmarking in UK HE: An Overview," *Quality Assurance in Education,* vol. 9, no. 4 (2001): 218–35.

Jordan, Elizabeth. "LibStats: An Open Source Online Tool for Collecting and Reporting Statistics in an Academic Library," *Performance Measurement and Metrics* 9, no. 1 (2008): 18–25.

Kaplan, Robert S. "Strategic Performance Measurement in Nonprofit Organizations," *Nonprofit Management and Leadership* 11, no. 3 (Spring 2001): 353–70.

Kaplan, Robert S., and David P. Norton. "The Balanced Scorecard—Measures That Drive Performance," *The Harvard Business Review* 70, no. 1 (January–February, 1992): 71–79.

Kaufman, Paula T. "The Library as Strategic Investment: Results of the Illinois Return on Investment Study," *LIBER Quarterly: The Journal of European Research Libraries* 18, no. 3–4 (2008): 424–36.

Kendrick, Curtis L. "Performance Measures of Shelving Accuracy," *The Journal of Academic Librarianship* 17, no. 1 (1991): 16–18.

King, Donald W., Peter B. Boyce, Carol H. Montgomery, and Carol Tenopir. "Library Economic Metrics: Examples of the Comparison of Electronic and Print Journal Collections and Collection Services—Academic Libraries," *Library Trends* 51, no. 3 (Winter 2003): 376–405.

Klubeck, Martin, and Michael Langthorne. "Applying a Metrics Report Card," *Educause Quarterly* 31, no. 2 (2008): 75–77.

Kramer, Lloyd A., and Martha B. Kramer. "The College Library and the Drop-out," *College & Research Libraries* 29, no. 4 (July 1968): 310–12.

Kubota, Shinya, Norio Mishima, and Shoji Nagata. "A Study of the Effects of Active Listening on Listening Attitudes of Middle Managers," *Journal of Occupational Health* 46 (2004): 60–67.

Kuh, George D., and Robert M. Gonyea. "The Role of the Academic Library in Promoting Student Engagement Learning," *College & Research Libraries* 64, no. 4 (July 2003): 256–82.

Kyrillidou, Martha. "An Overview of Performance Measures in Higher Education and Libraries," *Journal of Library Administration* 35, no. 4 (2001): 7–18.

Kyrillidou, Martha, and Sarah Giersch. "Qualitative Analysis of Association of Research Libraries' E-metrics Participant Feedback about the Evolution of Measures for Networked Electronic Resources," *The Library Quarterly* 74, no. 4 (2004): 423–40.

Lakos, Amos, and Shelley Phipps. "Creating a Culture of Assessment: A Catalyst for Organizational Change," *portal: Libraries and the Academy* 4, no. 3 (2004): 345–61.

Lawrence, Stephen R., Lynn S. Connaway, and Keith H. Brigham. "Life Cycle Costs of Library Collections: Creation of Effective Performance and Cost Metrics for Library Resources," *College & Research Libraries* 62, no. 6 (November 2001): 541–53.

Lewin, Tamar. "Higher Education May Soon Be Unaffordable for Most Americans, Report Says," *New York Times* (December 3, 2008): A17.

Lewis, David W. "A Strategy for Academic Libraries in the First Quarter of the 21st Century," *College & Research Libraries* 68, no. 5 (September 2007): 418–34.

Lindauer, Bonnie Gratch. "Comparing the Regional Accreditation Standards: Outcomes Assessment and Other Trends," *The Journal of Academic Librarianship* 28, no. 1/2 (January–March, 2002): 14–25.

Lindauer, Bonnie Gratch. "Defining and Measuring the Library's Impact on Campuswide Outcomes," *College & Research Libraries* 59, no. 6 (November 1998): 546–70.

Ludwig, Logan, and Susan Starr. "Library as Place: Results of a Delphi Study," *Journal of the Medical Library Association* 93, no. 3 (2005): 315–24.

Mallinbckrodt, Brent, and William E. Sedlacek. "Student Retention and the Use of Campus Facilities by Race," *NASPA Journal* 24, no. 3 (Winter 1987): 28–32.

McNeil, Beth, and Joan Giesecke. "Using LibQUAL+™ to Improve Services to Library Constituents: A Preliminary Report on the University of Nebraska-Lincoln Experience," *Performance Measurement and Metrics* 3, no. 2 (2002): 96–99.

Mezick, Elizabeth M. "Return on Investment: Libraries and Student Retention," *The Journal of Academic Librarianship* 33, no. 5 (2007): 561–66.

Nitecki, Danuta A., and Peter Hernon. "Measuring Service Quality at Yale University's Libraries," *The Journal of Academic Librarianship* 26, no. 3 (July 2000): 259–73.

Nitecki, Danuta A., and Peter Hernon. "Service Quality: A Concept Not Fully Explored," *Library Trends* 49, no. 4 (Spring 2001): 687–708.

Parasuraman, A. "Assessing Improving Service Performance for Maximum Impact: Insights from a Two-decade-long Research Journey," *Performance Measurement and Metrics* 5, no. 2 (2004): 45–52.

Pesch, Oliver. "Usage Statistics: Taking E-metrics to the Next Level," *The Serials Librarian* 46, no. 1/2 (2004): 143–54.

Poll, Roswitha. "Benchmarking with Quality Indicators: National Projects," *Performance Measurement and Metrics* 8, no. 1 (2007): 41–53.

Poll, Roswitha. "The Cat's Py[a]jamas? Performance Indicators for National Libraries," *Performance Measurement and Metrics* 9, no. 2 (2008): 110–17.

Poll, Roswitha. "Performance, Processes, and Costs: Managing Service Quality with the Balanced Scorecard," *Library Trends* 49, no. 4 (Spring 2001): 709–17.

Poll, Roswitha. "Standardized Measures in the Changing Information Environment," *Performance Measurement and Metrics* 7, no. 3 (2006): 127–41.

Powell, Ronald R. "Evaluation Research: An Overview," *Library Trends* 55, no. 1 (2006): 102–20.

Powell, Ronald R. "The Relationship of Library User Studies to Performance Measures: A Review of the Literature," *Occasional Papers* No. 181 (Urbana-Champaign: University of Illinois, Graduate School of Library and Information Science, 1988): 1–41.

Powell, Ronald R., Lynda M. Baker, and Joseph J. Mika. "Library and Information Science Practitioners and Research," *Library & Information Science Research* 24, no. 1 (2002): 49–72.

Pritchard, Sarah M. "Library Benchmarking: Old Wine in New Bottles?" *The Journal of Academic Librarianship* 21, no. 6 (1996): 491–95.

Reichmann, Gerhard. "Measuring University Library Efficiency Using Data Envelopment Analysis," *Libri: International Journal of Libraries and Information Services* 54, no. 2 (2004): 136–46.

Reifsnyder, Betty, and Charles R. McClure. "Performance Measures for Corporate Information Centers," *Special Libraries* 75, no. 3 (1984): 193–204.

Roszkowski, Michael J., John S. Baky, and David B. Jones. "So Which Score on the LibQUAL+™ Tells Me If Library Users Are Satisfied?" *Library & Information Science Research* 27, no. 4 (2005): 424–39.

Schachter, Debbie. "Performance Measures for Information Centers," *Information Outlook* 9, no. 8 (August 2005): 8–9.

Schmitz, Constance C. "Assessing the Validity of Higher Education Indicators," *Journal of Higher Education* 64, no. 5 (1993): 503–21.

Self, James. "From Values to Metrics: Implementation of the Balanced Scorecard at a University Library," *Performance Measurement and Metrics* 4, no. 2 (2003): 57–63.

Self, James. "Metrics and Management: Applying the Results of the Balanced Scorecard," *Performance Measurement and Metrics* 5, no. 3 (2004): 101–5.

Shachaf, Pnina, Shannon M. Oltmann, and Sarah M. Horowitz. "Service Equity in Virtual Reference," *Journal of the American Society for Information Science and Technology* 59, no. 4 (2008): 535–50.

Shepherd, C. David, Stephen B. Castleberry, and Rick E. Ridnour. "Linking Effective Listening with Salesperson Performance: An Exploratory Investigation," *Journal of Business & Industrial Marketing* 12, no. 5 (1997): 315–22.

Shepherd, Peter T. "COUNTER: Usage Statistics for Performance Measurement," *Performance Measurement and Metrics* 7, no. 3 (2006): 142–52.

Shepherd, Peter T., and Denise M. Davis." Electronic Metrics, Performance Measures, and Statistics for Publishers and Libraries: Building Common Ground and Standards," *portal: Libraries and the Academy* 2, no. 4 (October 2002): 659–63.

Shi, Xi, and Sarah Levy. "A Theory-guided Approach to Library Services Assessment," *College & Research Libraries* 66, no. 3 (May 2005): 266–77.

Shill, Harold B., and Shawn Tonner. "Does the Building Still Matter? Usage Patterns in New, Expanded, and Renovated Libraries, 1995–2002," *College & Research Libraries* 65, no. 2 (2004): 123–50.

Shim, Wonsik. "Applying DEA Technique to Library Evaluation in Academic Research Libraries (Academic Libraries) (Data Envelopment Analysis)," *Library Trends* 51, no. 3 (Winter 2003): 312–33.

Smith, Ian. "Benchmarking Human Resource Development: An Emerging Area of Practice," *Library Management* 27, no. 6/7 (2006): 401–10.

Stein, Joan. "Measuring the Performance of ILL and Document Supply, 1986 to 1998," *Performance Measurement and Metrics* 2, no. 1 (2001): 11–72

Stevens, Christy R., and Patricia J. Campbell. "Collaborating to Connect Global Citizenship, Information Literacy, and Lifelong Learning in the Global Studies Classroom," *Reference Services Review* 34, no. 4 (2006): 536–56.

Stoffle, Carla J., Robert Renaud, and Jerilyn R. Veldof. "Choosing Our Futures," *College & Research Libraries* 57, no. 3 (May 1996): 213–25.

Stubbs, Kendon. "Apples and Oranges and ARL Statistics," *The Journal of Academic Librarianship* 14, no. 4 (September 1988): 231–35.

Thornton, Steve. "Two Years of Impact Assessment," *Performance Measurement and Metrics* 1, no. 3 (2000): 147–56.

Town, Stephen. "E-measures: A Comprehensive Waste of Time?" *VINE* 34, no. 4 (2004): 190–95.

Valiris, George, and Panagiotis Chytas. "Making Decisions Using the Balanced Scorecard and the Simple Multi-attribute Rating Technique," *Performance Measurement and Metrics* 6, no. 3 (2006): 159–71.

Van House, Nancy A. "Output Measures in Libraries," *Library Trends* 38, no. 2 (Fall 1989): 269–79.

Vitaliano, Donald F. "Assessing Public Library Efficiency Using Data Envelopment Analysis," *Annual of Public and Cooperative Economics* 69, no. 1 (1998): 107–22.

Walters, William H. "A Fund Allocation Formula Based on Demand, Cost, and Supply," *The Library Quarterly* 78, no. 3 (2008): 303–14.

Washington-Hoagland, Carlette and Leo Clougherty. "Faculty and Staff Use of Academic Library Resources and Services: A University of Iowa Libraries' Perspective," *portal: Libraries and the Academy* 2, no. 4 (2002): 627–46.

Wasley, Paula. "Faculty-productivity Index Offers Surprises," *The Chronicle of Higher Education* (November 16, 2007): A10, A12.

Weeks, S. F., D. Puckett, and R. Daron. "Developing Peer Groups for the Oregon University System: From Politics to Analysis (and Back)," *Research in Higher Education* 41, no. 1 (February 2000): 1–20.

Weiner, Sharon. "The Contribution of the Library to the Reputation of a University," *The Journal of Academic Librarianship* 35, no. 1 (2009): 3–13.

Weiner, Sharon. "Library Quality and Impact: Is There a Relationship between New Measures and Traditional Measures?" *The Journal of Academic Librarianship* 31, no. 5 (2005): 432–37.

Whitmere, Ethelene. "Development of Critical Thinking Skills: An Analysis of Academic Library Experiences and Other Measures," *College & Research Libraries* 59, no. 3 (May 1998): 266–73.

# BOOKS

Association of Research Libraries, Office of Leadership and Management. *Marketing and Public Relations Activities in ARL Libraries.* Washington, DC: Association of Research Libraries, 1999.

Berry, Leonard L. *On Great Service: A Framework for Action.* New York: Free Press, 1995.

Bradburn, Frances B. *Output Measures for School Media Center Programs.* Englewood, CO: Libraries Unlimited, 1999.

Brophy, Peter. *Management Information and Decision Support Systems in Libraries.* Brookfield, VT: Gower, 1986.

Coopers & Lybrand, *Valuing the Economic Costs and Benefits of Libraries.* Wellington, New Zealand: New Zealand Library & Information Association, 1996.

*Corporate Library Benchmarks,* 2009 ed. New York: Primary Research Group, 2009.

Covey, Denise Troll. *Usage and Usability Assessment: Library Practices and Concerns.* Washington, DC: Digital Library Federation and Council on Library and Information Resources, 2002.

Davis, Nicholas. *Applying Theoretical Perspectives to the Balanced Scorecard.* Wagga Wagga, NSW (Australia): Faculty of Commerce, Charles Sturt University, 2006.

de Sáez, Eileen Elliott. *Marketing Concepts for Libraries and Information Services,* 2nd ed. London: Facet Publishing, 2002.

Dwyer, Carol A., Catherine M. Millett, and David G. Payne. *A Culture of Evidence: Post-secondary Assessment and Learning Outcomes.* Princeton, NJ: Educational Testing Service, June 2006.

Elliott, Donald S., Glen E. Holt, Sterling W. Hayden, and Leslie E. Holt. *Measuring Your Library's Value: How to Do a Cost-benefit Analysis for Your Public Library.* Chicago: American Library Association, 2007.

Hart, Keith. *Putting Marketing Ideas into Action.* London: Library Association Publishing, 1999.

Hayes, Bob E. Measuring *Customer Satisfaction and Loyalty: Survey Design, Use, and Statistical Analysis Methods.* Milwaukee, WI: ASQ Quality Press, 2008.

Hernon, Peter, and Ellen Altman. *Assessing Service Quality: Satisfying the Expectations of Library Customers.* Chicago: American Library Association, 1998.

Hernon, Peter, and Philip Calvert. *Improving the Quality of Library Services for Students with Disabilities*. Westport, CT: Libraries Unlimited, 2006.

Hernon, Peter, and Robert E. Dugan. *An Action Plan for Outcomes Assessment in Your Library*. Chicago: American Library Association, 2002.

Hernon, Peter, and Robert E. Dugan. *Outcomes Assessment in Higher Education: Views and Perspectives*. Westport, CT: Libraries Unlimited, 2004.

Hernon, Peter, Robert E. Dugan, and Candy Schwartz. *Revisiting Outcomes Assessment in Higher Education*. Westport, CT: Libraries Unlimited, 2006.

Hernon, Peter, and Charles R. McClure. *Microcomputers for Library Decision Making: Issues, Trends, and Applications*. Norwood, NJ: Ablex, 1986.

Hernon, Peter, and John R. Whitman. *Delivering Satisfaction and Service Quality: A Customer-based Approach for Libraries*. Chicago: American Library Association, 2001.

Kaplan, Robert S., and David P. Norton. *The Balanced Scorecard: Translating Strategy into Action*. Boston, MA: Harvard Business School Press, 1996.

Kaplan, Robert S., and David P. Norton. *The Strategy-focused Organization: How Balanced Scorecard Companies Thrive in the New Business Environment* Boston: Harvard Business School Press, 2001.

Kelly, Maurie Caitlin, and Andrea Kross. *Making the Grade: Academic Libraries and Student Success*. Chicago: Association of College and Research Libraries, 2002.

Kotler, Philip. *Marketing for Nonprofit Organizations*. Englewood Cliffs, NJ: Prentice-Hall, 1975.

Krueger, Richard A. *Focus Groups: A Practical Guide for Applied Research*. Newbury Park, CA: Sage Publications, 1998.

Laughlin, Sara, and Ray W. Wilson. *The Quality Library: A Guide to Staff-driven Improvement, Better Efficiency, and Happier Customers*. Chicago: American Library Association.

Maki, Peggy L. *Assessing for Learning: Building a Sustainable Commitment across the Institution*. Sterling, VA: Stylus Publishing, 2004.

Matthews, Joseph R. *The Evaluation and Measurement of Library Services*. Westport, CT: Libraries Unlimited, 2007.

Matthews, Joseph R. *Measuring for Results: The Dimensions of Public Library Effectiveness*. Westport, CT: Libraries Unlimited, 2004.

Matthews, Joseph R. *Scorecard for Results: A Guide for Developing a Library Balanced Scorecard*. Westport, CT: Libraries Unlimited, 2008.

McClure, Charles R., and Paul T. Jaeger. *Public Libraries and Internet Service Roles: Measuring and Maximizing Internet Services*. Chicago: American Library Association, 2009.

Middaugh, Michael F. *Understanding Faculty Productivity: Standards and Benchmarks for Colleges and Universities*. San Francisco: Jossey-Bass, 2001.

Miles, Matthew B., and Michael Huberman. *Qualitative Data Analysis: An Expanded Sourcebook*, 2nd ed. Thousand Oaks, CA: Sage Publications, 1994.

Niven, Paul R. *Balanced Scorecard Step-by-step for Government and Nonprofit Agencies*, 2nd ed. Hoboken, NJ: John Wiley and Sons, 2008.

Patton, Michael Quinn. *Qualitative Evaluation and Research Methods*, 2nd ed. Newbury Park, CA: Sage Publication, 1990.

Peters, Thomas J., and Robert H. Waterman, Jr. *In Search of Excellence: Lessons from America's Best-Run Companies*. New York: Warner Books, 1982.

Putruzzelli, Barbara Whitney (ed.). *Real-Life Marketing and Promotion Strategies in College Libraries: Connecting with Campus and Community*. Binghamton, NY: The Haworth Information Press, 2005.

Rossi, Peter H., Howard E. Freeman, and Sonia R. Wright. *Evaluation: A Systematic Approach*. Beverly Hills, CA: Sage Publications, 1979

Rossi, Peter H., Mark W. Lipsey, and Howard E. Freeman. *Evaluation: A Systematic Approach*. Beverly Hills, CA: Sage Publications, 2003.

Rubin, Rhea Joyce. *Demonstrating Results: Using Outcome Measurement in Your Library*. Chicago: American Library Association, 2006.

Schneider, Benjamin, and Susan S. White. *Service Quality: Research Perspectives*. Thousand Oaks, CA: Sage Publications, 2004.

Smith, G. Stevenson. *Managerial Accounting for Libraries and Other Not-for-Profit Organizations,* 2nd ed. Chicago: American Library Association, 2002.

Suskie, Linda. *Assessing Student Learning Outcomes: A Common Sense Guide*. Bolton, MA: Anker Publishing, 2004.

Vavra, Terry G. *Improving Your Measurement of Customer Satisfaction: A Guide to Creating, Conducting, Analyzing, and Reporting Customer Satisfaction Measurement Programs*. Milwaukee, WI: ASQ Quality Press, 1997.

Weingand, Darlene E. *Marketing/Planning Library and Information Services,* 2nd ed. Englewood, CO: Libraries Unlimited, 1999.

Woodward, Jeannette. *Creating the Customer-driven Academic Library*. Chicago: American Library Association, 2009.

Zeithaml, Valarie A., A. Parasuraman, and Leonard L. Berry. *Delivering Quality Service: Balancing Customer Perceptions and Expectations*. Toronto: The Free Press, 1990.

# BOOK CHAPTERS

Ahmed, Ksibi. "Statistical Indicators on Reading and Literacy for the 'Information Society' versus ITU's "Technicist' Indices," in *Management, Marketing, and Promotion of Library Services Based on Statistics, Analyses, and Evaluation*, edited by Trine Kolderup Flaten (IFLA Publication 120/121). Munich: Germany: K.G. Saur, 2006.

Arahova, Antonia, and Sarantos Kapidakis. "Promoting Library Services, Designing Marketing Strategies, Evaluating Our Past and Our Present, Feeling More Optimistic about Our Libraries' Future," in *Management, Marketing, and Promotion of Library Services Based on Statistics, Analyses and Evaluation*, edited by Trine Kolderup Flaten (IFLA Publication 120/121). Munich: Germany: K.G. Saur, 2006.

Bhattacharjee, Sudip, and Lewis Shaw. "Enhancing Skills through Technology: A Project for Advanced Accounting Students," in *An Action Plan for Outcomes Assessment in Your Library,* edited by Peter Hernon and Robert E. Dugan. Chicago: American Library Association, 2002.

Bloomberg, Sandra, and Melanie McDonald. "Assessment: A Case Study in Synergy," in *Outcomes Assessment in Higher Education: Views and Perspectives,* edited by Peter Hernon and Robert E. Dugan. Westport, CT: Libraries Unlimited, 2004.

Borden, Victor M. H., and Gary R. Pike. "Sharing Responsibility for Student Learning," in *Assessing and Accounting for Student Learning: Beyond the Spellings Commission,* edited by Victor M. H. Borden and Gary R. Pike, New Directions for Institutional Research [Series]; Assessment Supplement. San Francisco, CA: Jossey-Bass, 2007.

Carcedo, Elena Roseras. "Management and Marketing in the Library and Coumentation Centre of Artium Basque Centre-Museum of Contemporary Art," in *Management, Marketing, and Promotion of Library Services Based on Statistics, Analyses, and Evaluation,* edited by Trine Kolderup Flaten (IFLA Publication 120/121). Munich: Germany: K.G. Saur, 2006.

Crawford, John. "The Use of Electronic Information Services and Information Literacy: A Glasgow Caledonian University Study," in *Management, Marketing, and Promotion of Library Services Based on Statistics, Analyses, and Evaluation,* edited by Trine Kolderup Flaten (IFLA Publication 120/121). Munich: Germany: K. G. Saur, 2006.

Daniel, Evelyn H. "Performance Measures for School Librarians: Complexities and Potential," in *Advances in Librarianship* 6, edited by M. J. Voigt and M. H. Harris. New York: Academic Press, 1976.

Keller, Christine M., and John M. Hammang. "The Voluntary System of Accountability for Accountability and Institutional Assessment," in *Assessing and Accounting for Student Learning: Beyond the Spellings Commission*, edited by Victor M. H. Borden and Gary R. Pike, New Directions for Institutional Research [Series]; Assessment Supplement. San Francisco, CA: Jossey-Bass, 2007.

King, Helen. "Evaluating Library Services—Best Practice Initiatives in Australian University Libraries," in *Management, Marketing, and Promotion of Library Services Based on Statistics, Analyses, and Evaluation,* edited by Trine Kolderup Flaten (IFLA Publication 120/121). Munich: Germany: K. G. Saur, 2006.

McKnight, Sue. "Customers Value Research," in *Management, Marketing, and Promotion of Library Services Based on Statistics, Analyses, and Evaluation,* edited by Trine Kolderup Flaten (IFLA Publication 120/121). Munich: Germany: K. G. Saur, 2006.

Nitecki, Danuta A., and William Rando. "Evolving an Assessment of the Impact on Pedagogy, Learning and Library Support of Teaching with Digital Images," in *Outcomes Assessment in Higher Education Views and Perspectives,* edited by Peter Hernon and Robert E. Dugan. Westport, CT: Libraries Unlimited, 2004.

Ryan, Joe, Charles R. McClure, and John Carlo Bertot. "Choosing Measures to Evaluate Networked Information Resources and Services: Selected Issues." in *Evaluating Networked Information Services,* edited by Charles R. McClure and John Carlo Bertot. Medford, NJ: American Society for Information Science and Technology, 2001.

Song, Yoo-Seong. "Marketing Library Services: A Case Study at University of Illinois at Urbana-Champaign USA," in *Management, Marketing, and Promotion of Library Services Based on Statistics, Analyses, and Evaluation,* edited by Trine Kolderup Flaten (IFLA Publication 120/121). Munich: Germany: K. G. Saur, 2006.

Vercruyssen, Bart. "The Library as a Part of Cultural Behavior. Summary of a Large Scale Survey to Identify User Trends and Reading Behavior in Flanders Libraries," in *Management, Marketing, and Promotion of Library Services Based on Statistics, Analyses, and Evaluation,* edited by Trine Kolderup Flaten (IFLA Publication 120/121). Munich: Germany: K. G. Saur, 2006.

Wolff, Ralph A. "Using the Accreditation Process to Transform the Mission of the Library," in "Information Technology and the Remaking of the University Library," edited by Beverly P. Lynch, *New Directions for Higher Education* [Jossey-Bass Publishers] 90 (Summer 1993).

## DISSERTATIONS AND THESES

Causey, Enid R. *Impact of Assessment of Institutional Effectiveness on Academic Libraries in South Carolina,* Ph.D. diss. Columbia, SC: University of South Carolina, 1992, AAT 9239025. Available from *Dissertations & Theses: Full Text* (accessed February 2, 2008).

Cook, C. Colleen *A. Mixed-methods Approach to the Identification and Measurement of Academic Library Service Quality Constructs: LibQUAL+™,* Ph.D. diss. College Station, TX: Texas A&M University, 2001. Available from *Dissertations & Theses: Full Text,* AAT 3020024 (accessed August 7, 2007).

Evans, John E. *Cost Analysis of Public Services in Academic Libraries,* Ed.D. Memphis, TN: Memphis State University, 1989, AAT 9004345. Available from *Dissertations & Theses: Full Text* (accessed February 2, 2008).

Harer, John B. *Performance Measures of Quality for Academic Libraries Implementing Continuous Quality Improvement Programs: A Delphi Study,* Ph.D. diss. College Station, TX: Texas A&M University, 2001, AAT 30117718. Available from *Dissertations & Theses: Full Text* (accessed February 23, 2008).

Hayek, John C. "A Student-centered Approach for Identifying High-performing Colleges and Universities" Ph.D. diss. Bloomington, IN: Indiana University, 2001, AAT 3024295. Available from *Dissertations & Theses: Full Text* (accessed February 2, 2008).

Higgins, Susan E. *A Study of the Effectiveness of Public Library Service to Young Adults,* Ph.D. diss. Tallahassee, FL: The Florida State University, 1992, AAT 9306058. Available from *Dissertations & Theses: Full Text* (accessed February 2, 2008).

Lund, Patricia A. *An Investigation of the Use of Performance Measures in Public Libraries: An Application of the Locke Goal Setting Theory,* Ph.D. diss. Madison, WI: The University of Wisconsin, 1990, AAT 9030802. Available from *Dissertations & Theses: Full Text* (accessed February 2, 2008).

## GOVERNMENT PUBLICATIONS

*The Baldrige National Quality Program: Education Criteria for Performance Excellence.* Gaithersburg, MD: National Institute of Standards and Technology, 2007.

McClure, Charles R., John Carlo Bertot, and John C. Beachboard. *Internet Costs and Cost Models for Public Libraries: Final Report.* Washington, DC: National Commission on Libraries and Information Science; GPO, 1995.

Minnesota Office of the Legislative Auditor. *Program Evaluation Division. State Agency Use of Customer Satisfaction Surveys.* St. Paul, MN: Office of the Legislative Auditor, 1995.

## REPORTS

Carnegie Mellon University, Center for Economic Development. *Carnegie Library of Pittsburgh: Community Impact and Benefits.* Pittsburgh, PA: Carnegie Mellon University, 2006.

Friends of the San Francisco Public Library. *Providing for Knowledge, Growth, and Prosperity: A Benefit Study of the San Francisco Public Library.* San Francisco, CA: Friends of the San Francisco Public Library, 2007.

Indiana Business Research Center. *The Economic Impact of Libraries in Indiana.* Indianapolis, IN: Indiana State Library, 2007.

McClure, Charles R., Bruce T. Fraser, Timothy W. Nelson, and Jane B. Robbins. *Economic Benefits and Impacts from Public Libraries in the State of Florida.* Tallahassee, FL: Florida State University, School of Information Studies, Information Use Management and Policy Institute, 2000 (revised January 2001).

## WEB RESOURCES

Abels, Eileen G., Keith W. Cogdill, and Lisl Zach. "Identifying and Communicating the Contributions of Library and Information Services in Hospitals and Academic Health Science Centers," *JMA* [*Journal of the Medical Library Association*] 92, no. 1 (January 2004). Available at http://www.pubmedcentral.nih.gov/articlerender.fcgi?artid=314102 (accessed February 1, 2008).

Abram, Stephen. "The Value of Libraries: Impact, Normative Data, & Influencing Funders" (May 5, 2005). Available at http://www.imakenews.com/sirsi/e_article000396335.cfm?x=b4TcM1g,b2rpmkgK,w. (accessed August 18, 2008).

Active Strategy, "Balanced Scorecard Basics: Create Structure: Balanced Scorecard vs. Dashboards." Available at http://www.activestrategy.com/strategy_execution/score cards_vs_dashboards.aspx (accessed November 15, 2008).

Adams Six Sigma. "Customer Satisfaction and Customer Loyalty Are the Best Predictors of Customer Retention." Available at http://www.adamssixsigma.com/Newsletters/customers_results.htm (accessed September 18, 2007).

Allen, Jo. *Assessing the Work of Higher Education: Institutional Effectiveness and Student Learning.* Philadelphia, PA: Middle States Commission on Higher Education, April 2008. Available at http://www.msche.org/documents/PRR_08-Presentation—Allen.ppt (accessed October 2, 2008).

American Library Association, Association of College and Research Libraries. "Academic Library Statistics." Chicago: Association of College and Research Libraries. Available at http://www.ala.org/ala/acrl/acrlpubs/acadlibrarystats/academiclibrary.cfm (accessed July 8, 2008, September 30, 2008, November 4, 2008).

American Library Association, Association of College and Research Libraries. *Academic and Research Libraries Campaign Research* (Chicago, American Library Association, 2009). Available at http://www.ala.org/ala/issuesadvocacy/advocacy/public awareness/campaign@yourlibrary/academicresearch/academicresearchlibraries.cfm (accessed May 12, 2009).

American Library Association, Association of College and Research Libraries. *Academic Library Trends and Statistics.* Chicago, American Library Association, 2007. Available at http://staging.ala.org/ala/mgrps/divs/acrl/acrlpubs/nonserialtitles/06trendsstats. cfm (accessed February 13, 2009).

American Library Association, Association of College and Research Libraries. *The Campaign for America's Libraries @your library TM: Toolkit for Academic and Research Libraries.* Chicago: Association of College and Research Libraries, 2007. Available at http://www.ala.org/@yourlibrary (accessed June 20, 2008).

American Library Association, Association of College and Research Libraries. *Guidelines for Distance Learning Library Services.* Available at http://www.ala.org/ala/acrl/ acrlstandards/guidelinesdistancelearning.cfm (accessed October 27, 2007).

American Library Association, Association of College and Research Libraries. *Information Literacy Competency Standards for Higher Education.* Chicago: American Library Association, 2000. Available at http://www.ala.org/ala/acrl/acrlstandards/information literacycompetency.cfm (accessed October 30, 2007).

American Library Association, Association of College and Research Libraries. *Information Literacy Standards for Anthropology and Sociology Students.* Chicago: American Library Association, 2008. Available at http://www.ala.org/ala/acrl/acrlstandards/ anthro_soc_standards.cfm (accessed April 4, 2008).

American Library Association, Association of College and Research Libraries. *Information Literacy Standards for Science and Engineering/Technology.* Chicago: American Library Association, 2006. Available at http://www.ala.org/ala/acrl/acrlstandards/ infolitscitech.cfm (accessed October 14, 2007).

American Library Association, Association of College and Research Libraries. *Objectives for Information Literacy Instruction: A Model Statement for Academic Librarians.* Chicago: American Library Association, 2001. Available at http://www.ala.org/ala/ acrl/acrlstandards/objectivesinformation.cfm (accessed October 14, 2007).

American Library Association, Association of College & Research Libraries. *Political Science Research Competency Guidelines Students* (Chicago: American Library Association, 2008). Available at http://www.ala.org/ala/mgrps/divs/acrl/standards/PoliSci Guide.pdf (accessed January 21, 2009).

American Library Association, Association of College and Research Libraries, *Publications: 2007 Statistical Summaries.* Available at http://acrl.telusys.net/trendstat/2007/ index.html (accessed February 13, 2009).

American Library Association, Association of College and Research Libraries, "Scholarly Communication Toolkit" [Web site]. Available at http://www.acrl.ala.org/scholcomm/ accessed (January 29, 2009).

American Library Association, Association of College and Research Libraries. *Standards for Libraries in Higher Education.* Chicago: American Library Association, 2004. Available at http://www.ala.org/ala/acrl/acrlstandards/standardslibraries.cfm (accessed October 27, 2007).

American Library Association, Association of College and Research Libraries, ACRL's Task Force on Academic Library Outcomes Assessment. *Task Force on Academic Library Outcomes Assessment Report* (Chicago, IL: American Library Association, 1998). Available at http://www.ala.org/ala/acrl/acrlpubs/whitepapers/taskforce academic.cfm (accessed September 22, 2008).

American Library Association, Association of College and Research Libraries, Research Committee. "Environmental Scan 2007." Chicago: Association of College and Research Libraries, 2007. Available at http://www.ala.org/ala/acrl/acrlpubs/white papers/Environmental_Scan_2.pdf (accessed July 10, 2008); http://www.ala.org/

ala/mgrps/divs/acrl/acrlpubs/whitepapers/Environmental_Scan_2.pdf (accessed October 12, 2008).

American Library Association, Association of College and Research Libraries. *2007 Statistical Summaries*. Available at http://www.ala.org/ala/mgrps/divs/acrl/publications/trends/2007/index.cfm (accessed January 21, 2009).

American Library Association, Office for Research and Statistics, "Statistics about Libraries," (Chicago, American Library Association, 2009). Available at http://www.ala.org/ala/aboutala/offices/ors/statsaboutlib/statisticsabout.cfm (accessed May 12, 2009).

American Library Association, Science & Technology Section, STS Assessment Committee. [Homepage]. Available at http://www.ala.org/ala/mgrps/divs/acrl/about/sections/sts/committees/assessment/assesscommlist.cfm (accessed February 14, 2008).

Americans for Libraries Council. *Worth Their Weight: An Assessment of the Evolving Field of Library Valuation*. New York: Americans for Libraries Council, 2007. Available at http://www.actforlibraries.org/pdf/WorthTheirWeight.pdf (accessed October 8, 2008).

Anderson, Heidi Milia. "Preparing Effective Presentations: Perspectives for Pharmacy Educators." Available at http://www.mc.uky.edu/pharmacy/facstaff/files/Preparing%20Effective%20Presentations.pdf (accessed May 27, 2008).

"Asian Library Statistics," *Access* 61 (June 2007). Available at http://www.aardvarknet.info/access/number61/monthnews.cfm?monthnews=05 (accessed February 14, 2009).

Association of Research Libraries. "ARL Index." Washington, DC: Association of Research Libraries, 2007. Available at http://www.arl.org/stats/index/ (accessed October 15, 2007).

Association of Research Libraries. *ARL Statistics 2006–07*. Available at http://www.arl.org/bm~doc/arlstat07.pdf (accessed January 21, 2009).

Association of Research Libraries. *ClimateQUAL TM- Organizational Climate and Diversity Assessment*. Washington, DC: Association of Research Libraries. Available at http://www.lib.umd.edu/ocda/ (accessed January 4, 2009).

Association of Research Libraries. "Issues in Research Libraries Measurement," *ARL: A Bimonthly Report,* no. 197. Washington, DC: Association of Research Libraries, 1998. Available at http://www.arl.org/resources/pubs/br/br197.shtml.

Association of Research Libraries. *MINES for Libraries ™: Measuring the Impact of Networked Electronic Services and the Ontario Council of University Libraries' Scholars Portal,* Final Report (Washington, DC: Association of Research Libraries, 2005), 6–8. Available at http://www.libqual.org/documents/admin/FINAL%20REPORT_Jan26mk.pdf (accessed September 10, 2008).

Association of Research Libraries. "Press Releases: ARL Statistics 2006–07." Available at http://www.arl.org/news/pr/arl-statistics-18dec08.shtml (accessed December 22, 2008).

Association of Research Libraries, "Scholarly Communication" [Web site]. Available at http://www.arl.org/sc/index.shtml (accessed January 29, 2009).

Association of Research Libraries. "Statistics & Measurement." Washington, DC: Association of Research Libraries. Available at http://www.arl.org/stats/annualsurveys/arlstats/index.shtml (accessed July 8, 2008, September 30, 2008).

Association of Research Libraries. "Statistics and Measures: Annual Surveys, ARL Statistics." Washington, DC: Association of Research Libraries. Available at http://www.arl.org/stats/annualsurveys/arlstats/index.shtml (accessed November 4, 2008).

Association of Research Libraries. "Welcome to LibQUAL+™." Washington, DC: Association of Research Libraries. Available at http://www.libqual.org/ (accessed July 8, 2008).

Atlanta Regional Council for Higher Education. *Atlanta Higher Ed Adds Spending, Jobs, Talent to Georgia and Atlanta Economies*. Atlanta, GA: Atlanta Regional Council for Higher Education, 2006. Available at http://www.atlantahighered.org/ Portals/12/ArcheImages/Reports/Docs/ARCHEeconimpactrelease.pdf (accessed October 8, 2008).

Atlanta Regional Council for Higher Education. *The Atlanta Region: National Leader in Higher Education.* Atlanta, GA: Atlanta Regional Council for Higher Education. Available at http://www.atlantahighered.org/default.aspx?tabid=627&Report=5& xmid=557 (accessed October 8, 2008).

Atlanta Regional Council for Higher Education. *Study: Atlanta a National Leader in Higher Education Growth Region Ranks in Top 10 Across All Measures.* Atlanta, GA: Atlanta Regional Council for Higher Education, 2008. Available at http://archednn.web transit.com/Newsroom/FeatureStoryDetail/tabid/604/xmid/632/Default.aspx (accessed October 8, 2008).

Balanced Scorecard Institute. "The Balanced Scorecard & Technology." Available at http://www.balancedscorecard.org/BSCResources/BalancedScorecardSoftware/tabid/61/ Default.aspx (accessed November 3, 2008).

Balanced Scorecard Institute. "What Is the Balanced Scorecard?" Available at http://www. balancedscorecard.org/BSCResources/AbouttheBalancedScorecard/tabid/55/De fault.aspx (accessed September 28, 2008).

Basken, Paul. "Accreditors Honor College—and Hope to Send a Message about Themselves," *The Chronicle of Higher Education* (February 1, 2008). Available at http:// chronicle.com/weekly/v54/i21/21a01801.htm (accessed July 28, 2008).

Basken, Paul. "Boeing to Rank Colleges by Measuring Graduates' Job Success," *The Chronicle of Higher Education* (September 19, 2008). Available at http://chronicle.com/ weekly/v55/i04/04a00102.htm (accessed October 13, 2008).

Bell, Steven. "What's Our Contribution to Retention," ACRLog [Association of College & Research Libraries]. Available at http://acrlblog.org/2006/10/02/whats-our-contribution-to-retention/ (accessed October 24, 2007).

Bergstrom, Ted, and Preston McAfee. Journal Cost-effectiveness 2006–8 BETA. Available at http://www.hss.caltech.edu/~mcafee/Journal/ (accessed January 27, 2009).

Bertot, John. "E-metrics Information." Tallahassee, FL: Florida State University, School of Information Studies, Information Use Management Policy Institute. Available at http://www.ii.fsu.edu/EMIS/contact.cfm (accessed November 27, 2008); http:// www.ii.fsu.edu/emis/resources.cfm?display=subject&subject_key=49 (accessed November 27, 2008).

Blixrud, Julia C. "Assessing Library Performance: New Measures, Methods, and Models." Libraries and Education in the Networked Information Environment: 24th International Association of Technological University Libraries (IATUL) Conference, June 2–5, 2003, Middle Eastern Technical University, Düsseldorf, Germany. Available at http://www.iatul.org/doclibrary/public/Conf_Proceedings/2003/ BLIXRUD_fulltext.pdf (accessed October 16, 2008).

Blumensyyk, Goldie. "The $375-Billion Question: Why Does College Cost So Much?" *The Chronicle of Higher Education* (June 5, 2008). Available at http://chronicle.com/ weekly/v55/i06/06a00101.htm (accessed October 8, 2008).

Bolton, Johan, Marko A. Rodriguez, and Herbert Van de Sompel. "MESUR: Usage-based Metrics of Scholarly Impact." Available at http://mesur.lanl.gov/JCDL07poster_ bollen.pdf (accessed January 28, 2009).

Brophy, Peter, Zoe Clarke, Monica Brinkley, Sebastian Mundt, and Roswita Poll. "EQUINOX, Performance Indicators for Electronic Library Services," (November 2000). Available at http://equinox.dcu.ie/reports/pilist.html (accessed February 13, 2009).

Business Resource Center. "Want to Deliver 'Outrageous Service'? Then You Must Keep Turnover Low." Available at http://www.mandtbank.com/smallbusiness/brc_ management_outrageous.cfm (accessed September 18, 2007).

Butler, Linda, and Ian McAllister. "Metrics or Peer Review? Evaluating the 2001 UK Research Assessment Exercise in Political Science." Canberra, Australia: Australian

National University, 2007. Available at http://repp.anu.edu.au/papers/2007_uk researchassess.pdf (accessed October 23, 2007).

Cain, David, and Gary L. Reynolds. "The Impact of Facilities on Recruitment and Retention of Students," *Facilities Manager* (March/April 2006): 54–59. Available at http://www.appa.org/files/FMArticles/fm030406_f7_impact.pdf (accessed October 24, 2007).

California State University, Long Beach. "Measuring Quality and Satisfaction." Available at http://www.csulb.edu/library/WASC/Q1_CSS_Report.pdf (accessed August 7, 2007).

Canadian Health Services Research Foundation. "Glossary of Knowledge Exchange Terms as Used by the Foundation." Available at http://www.chsrf.ca/keys/glossary_e.php (accessed October 24, 2008).

CAVAL. "Linking Leading Libraries." Available at http://www.caval.edu.au/home.html (accessed August 29, 2008.

CAVAL. Web site, http://www.caval.edu.au/ (accessed February 14, 2009).

"Changing Roles of Academic and Research Libraries." Roundtable on Technology and Change in Academic Libraries, convened by the Association of College and Research Libraries on November 2–3, 2006, in Chicago. Available at http://www.ala.org/ala/acrl/acrlissues/future/changingroles.cfm (accessed March 25, 2008).

Chelmsford Public Library. "Information Calculator." Chelmsford, MA: Chelmsford Public Library. Available at http://www.chelmsfordlibrary.org/library_info/calculator_custom.html (accessed November 9, 2008).

Chelmsford Public Library. "Library Information: The Value of Your Library." Chelmsford, MA: Chelmsford Public Library. Available at http://www.chelmsfordlibrary.org/library_info/calculator.html (accessed November 9, 2008).

Collegiate Learning Assessment. Available at http://www.cae.org/conent/pro_collegiate.htm (accessed July 8, 2008).

Council of Australian University Librarians. homepage. Available at http://www.caul.edu.au/ (accessed October 10, 2008).

Council of Australian University Librarians. "Performance Indicators." Canberra, ACT: Council of Australian University Librarians, 2007. Available at http://www.caul.edu.au/best-practice/PerfInd.html (accessed October 5, 2007).

Council for Higher Education Accreditation. "Student Learning Outcomes Workshop," *The CHEA Chronicle* 5, no. 2 (2002). Available at http://www.chea.org/Chronicle/vol5/no2/Chron-vol5-no2.pdf (accessed October 24, 2007).

Council on Library and Information Resources. *Library as Place: Rethinking Roles, Rethinking Space,* CLIR Report 129. Washington, DC: Council on Library and Information Resources, 2005. Available at http://www.clir.org/pubs/reports/pub129/contents.html (accessed October 24, 2007).

Count Online Usage of Networked Electronic Resources. "Codes of Practice." Available at http://www.projectcounter.org/code_practice.html (accessed November 11, 2008.

COUNTER (Counting Online Usage of Networked Electronic Resources). "About COUNTER." Available at http://www.projectcounter.org/about.html (accessed January 29, 2009).

COUNTER. Web site, http://www.projectcounter.org/ (accessed January 10, 2009).

COUNTER, COUNTER Codes of Practice, "The COUNTER Code of Practice, Journals and Databases, Release 3." August 2008. Available at http://www.projectcounter.org/r3/Release3D9.pdf (accessed on January 28, 2009).

COUNTER. Release 3 of the COUNTER Code of Practice for Journals and Databases (August 2008), "Introduction to the Release." Available at http://www.projectcounter.org/r3/r3_intro.pdf (accessed January 2, 2009).

Cullen, Rowena. "Measure for Measure: A Post Modern Critique of Performance Measurement in Libraries and Information Services," ERIC ED 434 664 (ERIC Full Text, http://www.eric.ed.gov/ERICWebPortal/custom/portlets/recordDetails/

detailmini.jsp?_nfpb=true&_&ERICExtSearch_SearchValue_0=ED434664&ERIC
ExtSearch_SearchType_0=eric_accno&accno=ED434664) (accessed October 5, 2007).

Deiss, Kathryn J. "ARL New Measures: Organizational Capacity White Paper." Washington, DC: Association of Research Libraries, April 21, 1999. Available at http://www,arl.org/bm~doc/capacity.pdf (accessed October 8, 2008).

DePaul University, Office for Teaching, Learning, and Assessment., "Assessment Resources: Rubrics." Chicago: DePaul University, 2007. Available at http://condor.depaul.edu/~tla/html/assessment_resources.html#rubrics (accessed October 30, 2007).

Dickenson, Don. *How Academic Libraries Help Faculty Teach and Students Learn: The Colorado Academic Library Impact Study.* Denver: Colorado State Library, Library Research Service, 2006. Available at http://www.lrs.org/documents/academic/ALIS_final.pdf (accessed October 18, 2008).

Educational Testing Service. "ETS iSkills Assessment: Overview." Washington, DC: Educational Testing Service. Available at http://www.ets.org/iskills/ (accessed July 8, 2008).

Educational Testing Service. "iSkills™—Information and Communication Technology Literacy Test." Washington, DC: Educational Testing Service. Available at http://www.ets.org/portal/site/ets/menuitem.435c0b5cc7bd0ae7015d9510c3921509/?vgnextoid=b8a246f1674f4010VgnVCM10000022f95190RCRD (accessed August 8, 2007).

Educause Learning Initiative. "Learning Space Design Survey" (2008). Available at https://spreadsheets.google.com/viewform?key=pkvhukUVEX0B8Q5Qk-l3UYQ&hl=en (accessed October 28, 2008).

Eggers, Michele. "The 'Holy Grail'" of Marketing Metrics," *Chief Marketer.* Available at http://chiefmarketer.com/crm_loop/roi/holy_grail_metrics (accessed June 20, 2008).

8th Northumbria International Conference on Performance Measurement in Libraries and Information Services. Available at http://www.northumbria.ac.uk/sd/academic/ceis/re/isrc/conf/prn8/?view=Standard (accessed February 15, 2009).

Emerald. *Performance Measurement and Metrics* [Information Page]. Available at http://info.emeraldinsight.com/products/journals/journals.htm?id=pmm (accessed February 15, 2009).

E-metrics Instructional System. Available at http://www.ii.fsu.edu/emis/index.cfm.

EQUINOX. [Homepage]. Available at http://equinox.dcu.ie/index.html (accessed February 13, 2009).

EQUINOX. "Library Performance Measurement and Quality Management System: Performance Indicators for Electronic Library Services" (2000). Available at http://equinox.dcu.ie/reports/pilist.html (accessed October 3, 2007).

Executive Fast Track. "Balanced Scorecard." Available at http://www.12manage.com/methods_balancedscorecard.html (accessed November 9, 2008).

Foley, Christopher R. "Mission Statements: A Definition, an Assessment, a Call for Action." Available at http://www.uvm.edu/~vtconn/v16/foley.html (accessed September 8, 2008).

Foster, Nancy Fried, and Susan Gibbons (Ed). *Studying Students: The Undergraduate Research Project at the University of Rochester* (Chicago: American Library Association, Association of College and Research Libraries, 2007). Available at http://www.ala.org/ala/mgrps/divs/acrl/acrlpubs/downloadables/Foster-Gibbons_cmpd.pdf (accessed September 23, 2008); http://docushare.lib.rochester.edu/docushare/dsweb/GetRendition/Document-27276/html (accessed August 17, 2003).

Frederick, Peter. "The Power of Student Stories: Connections that Enhance Learning," *Essays on Teaching Excellence: Toward the Best in the Academy* 16, no. 2 (2004/2005). Available at http://www.colorado.edu/ftep/research/protected_memos/power stude.html (accessed October 27, 2007).

George Mason University Libraries. "Go for the Gold." Fairfax, VA: George Mason University Libraries. Available at https://www.lib.jmu.edu/gold/secure.aspx (accessed July 8, 2008).

Gratch-Lindauer, Bonnie. "Information Literacy-Related Student Behaviors: Results from the NSSE Items," *College & Research Libraries News* 68, no. 7 (July/August 2007). Available at http://www.ala.org/ala/acrl/acrlpubs/crlnews/backissues2007/july august07/infolitstudent.cfm (accessed September 28, 2008).

Hamrick, Florence A., John H. Schuh, and Mack C. Shelley II. "Predicting Higher Education Graduation Rates from Institutional Characteristics and Resource Allocation," *Education Policy Analysis Archives,* 12, no. 19 (May 4, 2004). Available at http://epaa.asu.edu/epaa/v12n19/ (accessed October 27, 2007).

Harel, Elazar C., and Toby D. Sitko. "Digital Dashboards: Driving Higher Education Decisions," EDUCAUSE (Center for Applied Research) *Research Bulletin,* 19 (2003). Available at http://net.educause.edu/ir/library/pdf/ERB0319.pdf (accessed November 13, 2008).

Hatleberg, J. *Summary: Assessment of Library Day Learning Outcomes.* College Park, MD: University of Maryland Libraries, 2007. Available at http://www.lib.umd.edu/UES/engl101/onlineassessment0607.pdf (accessed November 19, 2008).

Hennen, Thomas J., Jr. "Hennen's American Public Library Ratings." Available at http://www.haplr-index.com/backtobasics.html (accessed August 7, 2007); http://www.haplr-index.com/ (accessed December 7, 2008).

Henry, Geneva. "On-line Publishing in the 21st Century: Challenges and Opportunities," *D-Lib Magazine* 9, no. 10 (October 2003). Available at http://www.dlib.org/dlib/october03/henry/10henry.html (accessed January 28, 2009).

Hiller, Steve, and Cathie Jilovsky. "Measuring Value: A Comparison of Performance Quality Measures and Outcomes Identified by Australian and North American Libraries," at the conference on Evolution of Evidence: Global Perspectives on Linking Research with Practice. Available at http://conferences.alia.org.au/ebl2005/Hiller.pdf (accessed August 29, 2008).

Hulme, Claire. "Using Cost Effectiveness Analysis: A Beginners Guide," *Evidenced Based Library and Information Practice* 1, no. 4 (2006): 17–29. Available at http://ejournals.library.ualberta.ca/index.php/EBLIP (accessed December 12, 2008).

iDashboards. Available at http://examples.idashboards.com/idashboards/?guestuser=wpsc1 (accessed November 3, 2008).

iDashboards. "Turn Your Data into Insight" (product advertisement). Available at http://www.idashboards.com/?gclid=CJ_Dsfv2vZQCFQRJFQodSB2VUQ (accessed July 13, 2008).

Immerwahr, John, and Jean Johnson. *Squeeze Play: How Parents and the Public Look at Higher Education Today.* New York: Public Agenda for the National Center for Public Policy and Higher Education, 2007. Available at http://www.highereducation.org/reports/squeeze_play/squeeze_play.pdf (accessed October 8, 2008).

Indiana University East, Division of Education. "Appendix D: Capstone Portfolio Rubric." Bloomington, IN: Indiana University East, 2006. Available at http://webdev.iue.edu/departments/doe/appendix_d1_07.pdf (accessed October 30, 2007).

"Information Valuation," *LibraryConnect Newsletter,* 6, no. 1 (January 2008). Available at http://libraryconnect.elsevier.com/lcn/0601/lcn0601.pdf (accessed May 14, 2008).

Insync Surveys. Homepage. Flinders Lane, Australia. Available at http://www.insyncsurveys.com.au/ (accessed January 8, 2009). "External Customer Surveys." Available at http://www.insyncsurveys.com.au/Info/?content=ExternalCustomerResearch (accessed January 8, 2009).

International Archive of Education Data. [Web site]. Available at http://webapp.icpsr.umich.edu/cocoon/IAED/SERIES/00030.xml (accessed February 13, 2009).

International Coalition of Library Consortia. Available at http://www.library.yale.edu/consortia (accessed February 18, 2009).

International Coalition of Library Consortia. "Revised Guidelines for Statistical Measures of Usage of Web-based Information Resources" (revised in 2001 and 2006). Available at http://www.library.yale.edu/consortia/webstats06.htm (accessed December 23 2008).

International Federation of Library Associations. [Google™ search of Web site.] Available at http://www.google.com/custom?q=performance+measures+guidelines&safe=strict& sa=Google+Search&cof=GALT%3A%23CC0000%3BS%3Ahttp%3A%2F%2Fwww.ifla. org%3BVLC%3A%23666633%3BAH%3Aleft%3BBGC%3AWhite%3BLH%3A106%3B LC%3A%23990000%3BL%3Ahttp%3A%2F%2Fwww.ifla.org%2Fimages%2Fiflas.gif%3 BALC%3A%23666699%3BLW%3A96%3BT%3A%23007B00%3BGIMP%3ARed%3B AWFID%3A4e7b40884c7332ee%3B&domains=ifla.org&sitesearch=ifla.org (accessed October 6, 2007).

International Federation of Library Associations. *Global Library Statistics 1990-2000: Draft* (September 2003). Available at http://www.ifla.org/III/wsis/wsis-stats4pub_v.pdf (accessed February 13, 2009).

International Organization for Standardization, http://www.iso.org/iso/home.htm (accessed February 18, 2009).

James, Susan Donaldson. "'Joy of Sex' Reinvented for Today's Lovers," ABC News (September 18, 2008). Available at http://abcnews.go.com/Health/Story?id=5826372& page=1 (accessed February 20, 2009).

Jaschik, Scott. "Accountability System Launch," *Insider Higher Ed* (November 12, 2007). Available at http://www.insidehighered.com/news/2007/11/12/nasulgc (accessed October 13, 2008).

Jaschik, Scott. "Mixed Grades for Grads and Assessment," *Inside Higher Ed* (January 23, 2008).Availableathttp://www.insidehighered.com/news/2008/01/23/employers (assessed October 8, 2008).

Jaschik, Scott. "Refusing to Rank Inside Higher Ed," *Inside Higher Education* (August 17, 2007). Available at http://www.insidehighered.com/news/2007/08/17/usnews (accessed June 28, 2008).

Jun, Minjoon. "'Consumer Perception of E-service Quality' from Internet Purchaser and Non-purchaser Perspectives," *Journal of Business Strategies*. Available at http://find articles.com/p/articles/mi_hb3254/is_200203/ai_n7952947 (accessed February 22, 2008).

Kansas State University, Office of the Provost and Senior Vice President. "A Vision for the Future of Kansas State University, 2000–2005." Manhattan, KS: Kansas State University, 2006. Available at http://www.k-state.edu/provost/planning/strategy/vision99. htm (accessed October 27, 2007).

Kaske, Neal. "Choosing the Best Tools for Evaluating Your Library," Library Assessment Conference, 2006. Available at http://www.nclis.gov/statsurv/presentations/ ChoosingtheBestToolsforYourEvaluation8-28-6.pdf (accessed January 31, 2008).

Kaufman, Paula, and Scott Walter. *The Library as Strategic Investment: Results of the University of Illinois "Return on Investment" Study*. Available at http://hdl.handle. net/2142/8768 (accessed August 9, 2008).

Kerns, Charles D. "Serving Each Other on the Inside: Proven Methods for Improving Internal Customer Service." Available at http://gbr.pepperdine.edu/002/inside.html (accessed September 18, 2007).

Klubeck, Martin, and Michael Langthorne. "Applying a Metrics Report Card," *Educause Quarterly* 31, no.2 (April–June 2008): 75–77. Available at http://connect.educause. edu/Library/ED (accessed November 26, 2008).

Kyrillidou, Martha. "From Input and Output Measures to Quality and Outcome Measures, or, from the User in the Life of the Library to the Library in the Life of the User." Available at http://www.arl.org/bm~doc/jal01.pdf (accessed January 31, 2008).

Larson, Ronald L. "The DLib Test Suite and Metrics Working Group: Harvesting the Experience from the Digital Library Initiative." Available at http://www.dlib.org/

metrics/public/papers/The_Dlib_Test_Suite_and_Metrics.pdf (accessed December 15, 2008).

Lederman, Doug. "Calling out Colleges on Student Learning," *Inside Higher Ed* (January 31, 2008). Available at http://www.insidehighered.com/news/2008/01/31/aacu (accessed October 13, 2008).

Lederman, Doug. "Let the Assessment PR Wars Begin," *Insider Higher Ed* (August, 18, 2008). Available at http://www.insidehighered.com/news/2008/08/18/cla (accessed October 8, 2008).

Lederman, Doug. "Warning from a Friend," *Inside Higher Ed* (January 31, 2008). Available at http://www.insidehighered.com/news/2008/01/31/lamar (accessed October 13, 2008).

LibQUAL+™. Available at http://www.libqual.org/About/Information/index.cfm (accessed August 6, 2006).

Library Assessment Conference. *Building Effective, Sustainable, Practical Assessment* (Seattle, WA, August 2008). Available at http://www.libraryassessment.org/ (accessed February 15, 2009).

London Public Library. "Balanced Score Card Metrics." Available at http://www.london publiclibrary.ca/files/u3/aboutmylibrary/boardreports2008/june2008/WC2008bsc1stquarter.pdf (accessed November 22, 2008).

Los Alamos National Laboratory, Research Library. "The *MESUR* Project." Available at http://www.mesur.org/schemas/2007-01/mesur/ (accessed January 27, 2009).

Luther, Judy. "University Investment in the Library: What's the Return? A Case Study at the University of Illinois at Urbana-Champaign," *LibraryConnect* (San Diego, CA: Elsevier, 2008). Available at http://libraryconnect.elsevier.com/whitepapers/0108/lcwp (accessed May 14, 2008).

"Marketing Metrics: Where to Get Them? Which Ones Work?" *Advertising & Marketing Review*, 3–9. Available at http://www.ad-mkt-review.com/publics_html/docs/fs059.html (accessed July 13, 2008).

McClure, Charles R., R. David Lankes, Melissa Gross, and Beverly Choltco-Devlin. *Statistics, Measures and Quality Standards for Assessing Digital Reference Library Services: Guidelines and Procedures*. Available at http://quartz.syr.edu/quality/Quality.pdf (accessed July 26, 2008).

McGregor, Felicity. "Performance Measures, Benchmarking, and Value." Available at http://conferences.alia.org.au/alia2000/proceedings/felicity.mcgregor.html;http://ro.uow.edu.au/cgi/viewcontent.cgi?article=1028&context=asdpapers (accessed October 4, 2007).

McKeon, Howard P. (Buck). "Real Progress (Finally) on College Affordability," *Inside Higher Education* (February 7, 2008). Available at http://www.insidehighered.com/views/2008/02/07/mckeon (accessed on June 28, 2008).

"Measuring Library Value: Interview with Carole Moore, Chief Librarian, University of Toronto, ON, Canada," *Library Connect* [Elsevier newsletter]. Available at http://libraryconnect.elsevier.com/lcn/0103/lcn010302.html (accessed June 20, 2008).

Mid-America Regional Council, Government Training Institute. "Serving the 'Invisible' Internal Customers: Explore Sunken Treasure." Available at http://www.marc.org/gti/Customer_Service_Skills/cs-invisiblecustomers.htm (accessed September 18, 2007).

MINES for Libraries™ (under the umbrella of StatsQUAL™). Available at http://www.digiqual.org/mines/index.cfm (accessed May 12, 2009).

Minnesota State Colleges and Universities, Office of the Chancellor Research and Planning. *Overview Accountability Dashboard*. Available at http://www.mnscu.edu/board/accountability/index.html (accessed July 7, 2008).

Minnesota State Colleges and Universities System, Board of Trustees. "Accountability Dashboard." Available at http://accountability.mnscu.edu/workspace/passthrough/hyperion_passthrough_opener.html?url=/workspace/browse/withnav_get/Accountability%20Framework/Accountability%20Dashboard (accessed December 12, 2008).

Minnesota State University, Mankato. "News: Minnesota State Colleges, Universities System Launched an Online Accountability Dashboard to Track Performance." Available at http://www.mnsu.edu/news/read/?id=1213796988&paper=topstories (accessed on July 6, 2008).

Molyneux, Robert E. *The Gerould Statistics 1907/08–1961/62* (Washington, DC: Association of Research Libraries, 1998). Available at http://www.arl.org/news/pr/arl-statistics-18dec08.shtml (accessed December 22, 2008); Chapter 1, "Introduction;" available at http://fisher.lib.virginia.edu/libsites/gerould/ (accessed January 7, 2009).

The National Center for Public Policy and Higher Education. *Measuring Up 2008: The National Report Card on Higher Education.* San Jose, CA: The National Center for Public Policy and Higher Education, 2008. Available at http://measuringup2008.highereducation.org/print/NCPPHEMUNationalRpt.pdf (accessed December 15, 2008).

National Information Standards Organization. *ANSI/NISO Z39.7-2004: Information Services and Use: Metrics & Statistics for Libraries and Information Providers—Data Dictionary.* Baltimore, MD: National Information Standards Organization. Available at http://www.niso.org/dictionary/emetrics_elements/ (accessed December 23, 2008).

National Information Standards Organization. *ANSI/NISO Z39.7-2004: Information Services and Use: Metrics & Statistics for Libraries and Information Providers—Data Dictionary.* Baltimore, MD: National Information Standards Organization. Forward available at http://www.niso.org/dictionary/foreword/ (accessed December 23, 2008).

National Leadership Council for Liberal Education & America's Promise. *College Learning for the New Global Century.* Washington, DC: Association of American Colleges and Universities, 2007. Available at http://www.aacu.org/leap/documents/Global Century_final.pdf (accessed January 2, 2009).

National Survey of Student Engagement. Available at http://nsse.iub.edu/index.cfm (accessed August 6, 2007).

National Survey of Student Engagement. "About NSEE." Available at http://nsse.iub.edu/html/quick_facts.cfm (accessed on July 13, 2008).

National Survey of Student Engagement. "Benchmarks of Effective Educational Practice." Available at http://nsse.iub.edu/pdf/nsse_benchmarks.pdf (accessed July 6, 2008).

National Survey of Student Engagement. "Our Origins and Potential." Available at http://nsse.iub.edu/html/origins.cfm (accessed September 15, 27, 2008).

National Survey of Student Engagement. "What Is BCSSE?" Bloomington, IN: Indiana University, 2007. Available at http://bcsse.iub.edu/about.cfm (accessed October 24, 2007).

Nevena, Stancheva, and Vyara Angelova. "Measuring the Efficiency of University Libraries Using Data Envelopment Analysis," *Proceedings from INFORUM 2004* (May 25–27, 2004). Available at http://www.inforum.cz/archiv/inforum2004/english/prispevek.php-prispevek=93.htm (accessed August 23, 2008; December 8, 2008).

"New Jersey State Library's Knowledge Initiative Wins National Award." Trenton, NJ: New Jersey State Library, October 10, 2007. Available at http://www.njstatelib.org/News/news_item.php?item_id=817 (accessed October 18, 2008).

Nordstrom Careers. "Our Culture." Available at http://www.recruitingsite.com/csbsites/nordstrom/company/culture/index.asp (accessed September 18, 2007).

North Carolina State University, University Planning & Analysis. *Internet Resources for Higher Education Outcomes Assessment.* Raleigh, NC: North Carolina State University, 2007. Available at http://www2.acs.ncsu.edu/UPA/assmt/resource.htm (accessed October 6, 2007).

North Central Regional Library. "Washington State Balanced Scorecard." Wenatchee, WA: North Central Regional Library. Available at http://www.ncrl.org/resources/pdf/scorecard.pdf (accessed November 15, 2008).

Olshen, Toni. "Outcome Assessment Tools for the Library of the Future: MINES at OCUL." Washington, DC: Association of Research Libraries, April 7, 2005. Available at http://www.libqual.org (accessed January 2, 2009).

Orange County Library System, "Library Report Card." Available at http://www.ocls.info/About/Promo/documents/Report_Card.pdf (accessed November 24, 2008).

Partnership among South Carolina Academic Libraries. "Letter to Senator Hugh K. Leatherman Sr. of South Carolina." Columbia, SC: Partnership among South Carolina Academic Libraries, 2008. Available at http://pascalsc.org/component/option,com_docman/task,doc_download/gid,390/ (accessed November 8, 2008).

Partnership among South Carolina Academic Libraries. "PASCAL's Funding Crisis." Columbia, SC: Partnership among South Carolina Academic Libraries, 2008. Available at http://pascalsc.org/content/view/173/1/ (accessed November 17, 2008).

Partnership among South Carolina Academic Libraries. "PASCAL Testimonials." Columbia, SC: Partnership among South Carolina Academic Libraries. Available at http://pascalsc.org/content/view/170/1/ (accessed November 17, 2008).

Payne, Jim. "Marketing Metrics—More Than Just ROI," *S-Market Strategies* (January 2008). Available at http://www.adhub.com/columns/jimpayne03.html (accessed May 11, 2008).

Peter D. Hart Research Associates Inc. *How Should Colleges Assess and Improve Student Learning? Employers' Views on the Accountability Challenge.* Washington, DC: The Association of American Colleges and Universities, 2008. Available at http://www.aacu.org/leap/documents/2008_Business_Leader_Poll.pdf (accessed November 7, 2008).

Proctor and Gamble. "Joy Product Web site." Available at http://www.pg.com/product_card/prod_card_main_joy.shtml (accessed February 21, 2009).

Project SAILS. "About Project SAILS." Kent, OH: Kent State University. Available at https://www.projectsails.org/sails/aboutSAILS.php (accessed July 8, 2008).

Project SAILS. "Overview." Available at https://www.projectsails.org/sails/overview.php?page=aboutSAILS (accessed October 1, 2008).

"Ranking America's Leading Universities on Their Success in Integrating African Americans," *The Journal of Blacks in Higher Education* (2002). Available at http://www.jbhe.com/features/36_leading_universities.html (accessed October 30, 2007).

Ray, Kathlin L. "The Postmodern Library in an Age of Assessment," ACRL Tenth National Conference, March 15–18. Denver, CO: Association of College and Research Libraries, 2002, 250–54. Available at http://www.ala.org/ala/mgrps/divs/acrl/events/pdf/kray.pdf (accessed February 18, 2009).

Regulations.gov. Available at http:www/regulations.gov. See also http://www.regulations.gov/fdmspublic/component/main (accessed October 3, 2007).

Research and Markets. *The Survey of Academic Libraries,* 2006–07 ed. Dublin, Ireland: Research and Markets. Available at http://www.researchandmarkets.com/reportinfo.asp?report_id=444575 (accessed January 11, 2009).

Research and Markets. *The Survey of Library Database Licensing Practices.* Dublin, Ireland: Research and Markets, December 2007. Available at http://www.researchandmarkets.com/reportinfo.asp?report_id=586437&t=d&cat_id=(accessed November 2, 2008).

Research Assessment Exercise. "RAE2008" (2008). Available at http://www.rae.ac.uk/ (accessed March 4, 2008).

Roy, Joe. *Marketing Metrics Made Simple.* Available at http://www.marketing.metrics.made.simple.com/marketing-meterics-list.html (accessed July 13, 2008).

Ruben, Brent D. "Toward a Balanced Scorecard for Higher Education: Rethinking the College and University Excellence Indicators Framework," The Hunter Group White Paper Series (October, 1999), 4–5. Available at http://oqi.wisc.edu/resourcelibrary/uploads/resources/Balanced%20Scorecard%20in%20Higher%20Education.pdf (accessed November 13, 2008).

Samaritan Medical Center Library. "Library 2004–2005 Report Card: 2004 and 2005 at a Glance." Watertown, NY: Samaritan Medical Center Library. Available at http://

library.samaritanhealth.com/library/Newsletter/2005%20Report%20Card.pdf (accessed November 25, 2008).

Saw, Grace. "Reading Rodski: User Surveys Revisited." Queensland, Australia: University of Queensland, n.d. Available at http://www.library.uq.edu.au/papers/reading_rodski.pdf (accessed July 26, 2008).

SCONUL (Society of College, National and University Libraries). "The Performance Portal." Available at http://vamp.diglib.shrivenham.cranfield.ac.uk/ (accessed August 29, 2008); SCONUL, The Performance Portal Web site, http://vamp.diglib.shrivenham.cranfield.ac.uk/ (accessed February 14, 2009).

SCONUL. Statistical Questionnaire Web site, http://vamp.diglib.shrivenham.cranfield.ac.uk/statistics/sconul-statistical-questionnaire (accessed February 14, 2009).

Self, Jim. "Using Data to Make Choices: The Balanced Scorecard at the University of Virginia Library." *Association of Research Libraries Bimonthly Report*, 230/231 (October–December, 2003). Available at http://www.arl.org/newsltr/230/balscorecard.html (accessed October 29, 2008).

Simmel, Leslie L., and Colleen D. Anderson. "Why Services Matter: Building Your Value Story & Business Case." Presentation delivered at NERCOMP 2007 Annual Conference, Worcester, MA, March 21, 2007. Available at http://net.educause.edu/ir/library/pdf/NCP07062.pdf (accessed October 12, 2008).

Smith, Mark K. "Peter Senge and the Learning Organization," *The Encyclopedia of Informal Education* (2001). Available at http://www.infed.org/thinkers/senge.htm (accessed February 22, 2009).

Stylus Publishing, LLC (Sterling, VA). Available at http://styluspub.com/Books/Features.aspx (accessed October 12, 2008).

Suffolk University, Mildred F. Sawyer Library. "Calculations" (Boston: Suffolk University, 2007). Available at http://www.suffolk.edu/files/SawLib/ay2008-9-value.pdf (accessed January 7, 2009).

Suffolk University, Mildred F. Sawyer Library. "FAQ: How Can I Get My Tuition Money's Worth from the Library?" Boston: Suffolk University. Available at http://www.suffolk.edu/sawlib/faq.htm#anchor13273 (accessed January 7, 2009).

Suffolk University, Mildred F. Sawyer Library. "FAQ: What Does the Sawyer Library Do With All of My Tuition Money? Boston: Suffolk University. Available at http://www.suffolk.edu/sawlib/faq.htm (accessed November 14, 2008).

Taylor-Powell, Ellen. "Analyzing Quantitative Data." Madison, WI: University of Wisconsin-Extension, Cooperative Extension Program Development & Evaluation, 2003. Available at http://learningstore.uwex.edu/pdf/G3658-6.pdf (accessed October 22, 2008).

Taylor-Powell, Ellen, and Marcus Renner. "Analyzing Qualitative Data" Madison, WI: University of Wisconsin-Extension, Cooperative Extension Program Development & Evaluation, 2003. Available at http://learningstore.uwex.edu/pdf/G3658-12.pdf (accessed October 22, 2008).

Tenopir, Carol, and Donald W. King. "Designing Electronic Journals with 30 Years of Lessons from Print," *Journal of Electronic Publishing* 4, no. 2 (December 1998). Available at http://quod.lib.umich.edu/cgi/t/text/text-idx?c=jep;view=text;rgn=main;idno=3336451.0004.202 (accessed February 15, 2009).

Texas State Library and Archives Commission. "Outcomes Measures." Austin, TX: Texas State Library and Archives Commission. Available at http://www.tsl.state.tx.us/outcomes/ (accessed October 3, 2007).

Texas State Library and Archives Commission, Texas Academic Library Statistics. "2005 Academic Library Statistics." Austin, TX: Texas State Library and Archives Commission. Available at http://www.tsl.state.tx.us/ld/pubs/als/2005/find.html (accessed July 8, 2008).

Texas Tech University. "Assessment Dashboards." Lubbock, TX: Texas Tech University. Available at http://www.irs.ttu.edu/dashboardareas/index.aspx (accessed December 12, 2008).

Texas Tech University. "State Accountability Measures." Lubbock, TX: Texas Tech University. Available at http://www.irim.ttu.edu/dashboard/ (accessed December 12, 2008).

Texas Tech University, Library. "Assessment Dashboards." Lubbock, TX: Texas Tech University. Available at http://www.irs.ttu.edu/dashboardareas/Dashboard.aspx?collid=35&year=2007&deptid=0 (accessed December 12, 2008).

Town, Stephen. "Academic Library Performance, Quality and Evaluation in the UK and Europe." Available at http://www.libqual.org/documents/admin/StephenGreece Paper.doc (accessed October 12, 2007).

Town, J. Stephen. "VAMP gets WIKI'd," *SCONUL Focus* 40 (Spring 2007): 101–4. Available at http://www.sconul.ac.uk/publications/newsletter/40/33.pdf (accessed on November 23, 2008).

12 Manage: The Executive Fast Track. "Balanced Scorecard." Available at http://www.12manage.com/methods_balancedscorecard.html (accessed November 3, 2008).

UCAN: University and College Accountability Network. "Commonly Asked Questions about U-CAN." Available at http://ucan-network.org/commonly-asked-questions-about-u-can-2 (accessed October 13, 2008; November 13, 2008).

University of Albany. "Institutional and Student Learning Assessment." Available at https://wiki.albany.edu/display/middlestates/Institutional+and+Student+Learning+Assessment- (accessed October 3, 2008).

University of California. *University of California Accountability Framework: Draft for Discussion*. Oakland, CA: University of California, September 21, 2008. Available at http://www.ucop.edu/ucal/accountability/documents/accountabilityframework_draft.pdf (accessed November 21, 2008).

University of Colorado at Boulder. "LibQUAL+™ 2006 Survey." Available at http://ucbli braries.colorado.edu/internal/assessment/libqual/2006results.pdf (accessed September 20, 2007).

University of Colorado at Boulder. "2006 Summary." Available at http://ucblibraries. colorado.edu/libqual/2006.htm (accessed September 20, 2007).

University of Illinois at Urbana-Champaign, Library Diversity Committee. Available at http://www.library.uiuc.edu/ugl/diversity/committee.html (accessed February 20, 2009).

University of Massachusetts, Amherst, Libraries. *Annual Report 2006*. Amherst: University of Massachusetts, 2006. Available at http://scholarworks.umass.edu/cgi/viewcon tent.cgi?article=1000&context=libraries_reports (accessed November 18, 2008).

University of Memphis. "LibQUAL+™." Available at http://exlibris.memphis.edu/about/reports/libqual/usr_dim.html (accessed September 19, 2007).

University of Pennsylvania Libraries. "Data Farm." Available at http://metrics.library. upenn.edu/prototype/about/index.html (accessed November 11, 2008).

University of Texas System, Office of Strategic Management. "Accountability." Austin, TX: University of Texas System. Available at http://www.utsystem.edu/osm/account ability/homepage.htm (accessed October 23, 2007).

University of Virginia Library. "Balanced Scorecard at UVa Library." Charlottesville VA: University of Virginia Library, 2007. Available at http://www.lib.virginia.edu/bsc/ (accessed October 1, 11, 2007; November 11, 2008).

University of Virginia Library. "Overview about the Balanced Scorecard." Charlottesville, VA: University of Virginia Library, 2008. Available at http://www2.lib.virginia. edu/bsc/overview.html (accessed December 26, 2008).

University of Washington Library, "Assessment Group." Available at http://www.lib. washington.edu/assessment/Group.html (accessed February 2, 2009).

U.S. Department of Defense. "Best Practices & Benchmarking." Available at http://www. defenselink.mil/comptroller/icenter/learn/bestprac.htm (accessed August 7, 2007).

U.S. Department of Education, National Center for Education Statistics. "About IPEDS." Available at http://nces.ed.gov/IPEDS/about/ (accessed July 8, 2008).

U.S. Department of Education, National Center for Education Statistics. "Choose Comparison Group." Washington, DC: Department of Education. Available at http://nces.ed.gov/surveys/libraries/compare/PeerVariable.asp (accessed October 18, 2008).

U.S. Department of Education, National Center for Education Statistics. *College Navigator*. Washington, DC: Department of Education. Available at http://nces.ed.gov/collegenavigator/ (accessed October 14, 2008; July 8, 2008).

U.S. Department of Education. National Center for Education Statistics. "Compare Academic Libraries." Washington, DC: Department of Education. Available at http://nces.ed.gov/surveys/libraries/compare/index.asp?LibraryType=Academic (accessed on November 4, 2008).

U.S. Department of Education, National Center for Education Statistics. "Library Statistics Program: Academic Libraries." Washington, DC: National Center for Education Statistics. Available at http://nces.ed.gov/surveys/libraries/Academic.asp (accessed July 8, 2008; October 18, 2008).

U.S. Department of Education, National Center for Education Statistics. "Library Statistics Program: Compare Academic Libraries." Washington, DC: National Center for Education. Available at http://nces.ed.gov/surveys/libraries/compare/index.asp?LibraryType=Academic (accessed July 8, 2008).

U.S. Department of Education, National Center for Education Statistics. "Library Statistics Program: Compare Academic Libraries. Choose Comparison Group by Variable." Available at http://nces.ed.gov/surveys/libraries/compare/index.asp?LibraryType=Academic. (accessed on January 21, 2009).

U.S. Department of Education, National Center for Education Statistics. "Welcome to Compare Academic Libraries." Washington, DC: Department of Education. Available at http://nces.ed.gov/surveys/libraries/compare/index.asp?LibraryType=Academic (accessed October 18, 2008).

U.S. General Accounting Office. *Best Practices Methodology: A New Approach for Improving Government Operations*, GAO/NSIAD-95-154. Washington, DC: General Accounting Office, 1995. Available at http://www.gao.gov/archive/1995/ns95154.pdf (accessed August 10, 2007).

U.S. Government Accountability Office. *Electronic Government: Initiatives Sponsored by the Office of Management and Budget Have Made Mixed Progress*, GAO-04-561T. Washington, DC: Government Accountability Office, 2004. Available at http://www.gao.gov (accessed October 3, 2007).

U.S. Government Accountability Office. *Federal Contract Centers: Mechanism for Sharing Metrics and Oversight Practices*, GAO-06-270. Washington, DC: Government Accountability Office, 2006. Available at http://www.gao.gov (accessed October 3, 2007).

U.S. Government Printing Office. "Library Services and Content Management Performance Metrics." Available at http://www.access.gpo.gov/su_docs/fdlp/metrics/index.html (accessed February 1, 2008).

U.S. Institute of Museums and Library Service. "Grant Applications: Outcomes Based Assessment." Washington, DC: Institute of Museums and Library Service, 2008. Available at http://www.imls.gov/applicants/learning.shtm (accessed October 6, 2008).

U.S. Library of Congress. "The ARL E-Metrics Projects: Counting and Evaluating the Use of Electronic Resources." Washington, DC: Library of Congress, 2004. Available at http://www.loc.gov/acq/conser/emetrics.html (accessed October 14, 2007).

U.S. National Partnership for Reinventing Government. *Balancing Measures: Best Practices in Performance Management*. Washington, DC: National Partnership for Reinventing Government, 1999. Available at http://govinfo.library.unt.edu/npr/library/papers/bkgrd/balmeasure.html (accessed October 7, 2007).

Utah State University, Merrill-Cazier Library. "Merrill-Cazier Library Performance Dashboard-January 2006." Logan, UT: Utah State University. Available at http://ranger2.lib.usu.edu/main/portrait/DashBoard05.pdf (accessed December 12, 2008).

Vayghan, J. A., S. M. Garfinkle, C. Walenta, D. C. Healy, and Z. Valentin. "The Internal Information Transformation of IBM," *IBM Systems Journal* 46, no. 4 (2007): 669–83. Available at http://www.research.ibm.com/journal/sj/464/vayghaut. html (accessed November 21, 2008).

Voluntary System of Accountability. "About VSA." Available at http://www.voluntarysystem. org/index.cfm?page=about_vsa (accessed July 6, 2008).

Voluntary System of Accountability. "Welcome to the VSA Online!" Available at http:// www.voluntarysystem.org/index.cfm?page=homepage (accessed July 8, 2008).

Wilson, Anne, and Leeanne Pitman. *Best Practice Handbook for Australian University Libraries*. Canberra Department of Education, Training and Youth Affairs, Evaluations and Investigations Programme, Higher Education Division, 2000. Available at http://www.dest.gov.au/archive/highered/eippubs/eip00_10/00_10.pdf (accessed August 10, 2007).

Wilson, Anne, Isabella Trahn, Leanne Pitman, and Gaynor Austen. "Best Practice in Australian University Libraries: Lessons from a National Project," a paper presented at the 3rd Northumbria Conference on Performance Measurement in Libraries and Information Services (1999). Available at http://info.library.unsw.edu.au/libadmin/ conf/bestprac.html (accessed August 10, 2007).

Yale University Library. "Service Quality Improvement Awards Program." Available at http://www.library.yale.edu/Administration/SQIC/sqiawards1.html (accessed February 23, 2009).

Ying, Zhong, and Johanna Alexander. "Academic Success: How Library Services Make a Difference." Bakersfield, CA: California State University, Bakersfield. Available at http://www.eshow2000.com/acrl/2007/handouts/735_CPZhong_ Ying_093852_031607050311.pps (accessed November 4, 2008).

Young, Peter R. "Electronic Services and Library Performance Measurement: A Definitional Challenge," a keynote presentation at the Fourth Northumbria International Conference on Performance Measurement in Libraries and Information Services: "Meaningful Measures for Emerging Realities," Pittsburgh, PA, August 13, 2001. Available at http://www.niso.org/committees/ay/Young_Northumbria_presentation_2001. pdf (accessed October 5, 2007).

## UNPUBLISHED MATERIAL

Webster, Duane E. "Scenarios for Contemplating Research Library Futures," reconceived in July, 2007, for use in the UCLA Senior Fellows Program.

# INDEX

# ABOUT THE AUTHORS

**ROBERT E. DUGAN** became the Director of the Mildred F. Sawyer Library at Suffolk University (8 Ashburton Place, Boston, MA 02108; rdugan@suffolk.edu) in 1998. During his career he has dealt with library services and issues at the local, state, and federal levels, and has worked in public, state, and academic libraries. His writings cover outcomes assessment, planning, policy implications, and the application of information technologies, financial management, and the federal depository library program. His current interest concerns issues of institutional and organizational accountability, focusing on identifying and considering measures applied by higher education and academic libraries and their presentation to, and usage by, their various stakeholders.

**PETER HERNON** is a professor at Simmons College (Graduate School of Library and Information Science, 300 The Fenway, Boston, MA 02115-5898; peter.hernon@simmons.edu), where he teaches courses on government information policy and resources, evaluation of information services, research methods, leadership, and academic librarianship. He received his Ph.D. from Indiana University and has taught at Simmons College, the University of Arizona, and Victoria University of Wellington (New Zealand). Besides his various activities in New Zealand, he has delivered keynote addresses in eight other countries: Canada, England, France, Finland, Greece, Portugal, Spain, and South Africa.

Hernon is the principle faculty member for the Simmons Ph.D. program, Managerial Leadership in the Information Professions. He is the recipient of the two grants from the Institute of Museum and Library Services, which helps to fund the program.

Hernon is the co-editor of *Library & Information Science Research,* founding editor of *Government Information Quarterly,* and past editor of *The Journal of Academic Librarianship.* He is the author of 283 publications, 47 of which are books. Among these are *Improving the Quality of Library Services for Students with Disabilities* (2006), *Comparative Perspectives on E-government* (2006), *Revisiting*

*Outcomes Assessment in Higher Education* (2006), *Outcomes Assessment in Higher Education* (2004), and *Assessing Service Quality* (1998), which received the Highsmith award for outstanding contribution to the literature of library and information science in 1999. He is the 2008 recipient of the Association of College and Research Libraries' (ACRL) award for Academic/Research Librarian of the Year.

**DANUTA A. NITECKI** has been an Associate University Librarian at the Yale University Library (P.O. Box 208240, New Haven, CT 06520-8240, danuta.nitecki@yale.edu) since 1996, being responsible for its public services programs. She has been a manager or administrator in academic research libraries since 1972, working at the University of Tennessee, University of Illinois, and University of Maryland before coming to Yale. On occasion, she has taught research methods and evaluation online for professional development, and in classrooms at the master's and Ph.D. levels in the United States and abroad. She is also a professor of practice in the Ph.D. program, Managerial Leadership in the Information Professions, at Simmons College.

Nitecki has presented papers nationally and internationally and has authored more than 65 publications, covering topics related to service quality, document delivery, impact of digital images on teaching and learning, and application of technologies to public services. She has co-edited several collections, including *Library Off-Site Shelving: Guide for High Density Facilities* (2001) and *Advances in Librarianship* (2004–2008). Her current interests include assessment of public services, the challenges of preparing librarians to engage in research-driven management, and collaborations in support of teaching and learning. She received her Ph.D. from the University of Maryland, College Park, and holds master's degrees from Drexel University (library and information science) and the University of Tennessee (communications).